The Passage of Power

STUDIES IN POLITICAL SUCCESSION

STUDIES IN ANTHROPOLOGY

Under the Consulting Editorship of E. A. Hammel,
UNIVERSITY OF CALIFORNIA, BERKELEY

Andrei Simić, THE PEASANT URBANITES: A Study of Rural-Urban Mobility in Serbia

John U. Ogbu, THE NEXT GENERATION: An Ethnography of Education in an Urban Neighborhood

Bennett Dyke and Jean Walters MacCluer (Eds.), COMPUTER SIMULATION IN HUMAN POPULATION STUDIES

Robbins Burling, THE PASSAGE OF POWER: Studies in Political Succession

in preparation

Piotr Sztompka, SYSTEM AND FUNCTION: Toward a Theory of Society

THE PASSAGE OF POWER

STUDIES IN POLITICAL SUCCESSION

Robbins Burling

Department of Anthropology
University of Michigan
Ann Arbor, Michigan

ACADEMIC PRESS   New York and London

A Subsidiary of Harcourt Brace Jovanovich, Publishers

ACADEMIC PRESS, INC.
111 Fifth Avenue, New York, New York 10003

United Kingdom Edition published by
ACADEMIC PRESS, INC. (LONDON) LTD.
24/28 Oval Road, London NW1

Library of Congress Cataloging in Publication Data

Burling, Robbins.
    The passage of power.

    (Studies in anthropology)
    Includes bibliographical references.
    1.   Kings and rulers—Succession.   2.   Government,
Primitive.   3.   Power (Social sciences)   I.   Title.
JF285.B87   301.5'92   73-5319
ISBN 0-12-785085-6

TO SIBYL

Contents

Chapter 1 **Introduction**

Chapter 2 **Our Tribal Heritage**

Chapter 3   The Marathas of India

Chapter 4   China of the Manchus

Chapter 5   The Decline of Heredity

Chapter 6   Latin America

Chapter 7   Eastern Europe and the Soviet Union

Chapter 8   Conclusions: Both Theoretical and Applied

Appendix I   Inheritance of Bemba Titles

Appendix II   The Maratha Rulers

Preface

My interest in succession grew first from two concerns: On the one hand, succession techniques seemed to offer a tractable ethnographic problem, one that could be subjected to sensible cross-cultural comparisons; on the other, succession was also a serious matter in our own society. I wondered whether ethnographic data could have any bearing on our practical political lives.

Ethnographically I was impressed by the many problems posed by the need to transfer power from one chief or tribal leader to his successor. There appeared to be only a few basic patterns by which power could be transferred, and, however varied these might be in detail, it seemed to me that a revealing typology of succession practices might emerge rather quickly from a cross-cultural study. I began to examine cases, hoping to construct such a typology, but it soon became apparent that my initial question—What are the mechanisms by which a new man can be chosen to fill the top position of power in his society?—could not be dealt with in isolation. I was forced to consider power from many angles, and I was led into many facets of political organization that I had first supposed to have little relation to succession. What has emerged, therefore, is a cross-cultural study of an unexpectedly wide segment of the political process.

From the beginning, however, I hoped to do more than offer a parade of ethnographic curiosities. I wanted my examples to illuminate a problem that our society shares with all others, for it is obvious that we are far from achieving an ideal method of choosing our own leaders. I wanted to ask not only how leaders *can* be chosen, but also to ask how we *should* choose our leaders. It was this second question that made it seem worthwhile to assemble my ethnographic and historical examples in the first place. Thus, while most of this book deals, in proper anthropological fashion, with societies that are remote in time and space from our own, I turn at the end to the implications that a cross-cultural study of succession holds for us in the United States.

Among my conclusions was the observation that, with the passing of the years and generations, all systems of succession change. In the American case I noted my concern with the "seemingly inexorable growth of the presidency" and I asked how long this growth could continue "before a president will finally be able to use his massive power to subvert the very system that put him into office." I raised this question in what was intended to be the final draft of my manuscript. This was completed in February 1973, just a few weeks before the Watergate affair exploded onto the front pages of our newspapers. Suddenly, subversion from the top and the possibility of radical changes in our own succession system looked like far more immediate threats than I had imagined them to be.

This book is not about Watergate, but it is about power and it is about the techniques by which men reach for power—matters that the Watergate revelations have thrown into sudden sharp relief for Americans. As this book goes to press it is impossible to know where, if anywhere, Watergate will lead us, but I would like to believe that it might help us to find a way of reversing the centralizing trend with which we have lived for so long, and I would like to imagine that the examples described in this book might offer one kind of perspective upon some very old problems: How should we choose our leaders? How can we keep them subject to the control of the people?

Acknowledgments

This book could never even have been started without both personal and institutional help. Institutional help came first from the Ford Foundation's International Studies Grant to the University of Michigan which, by freeing me from daily chores of university life, provided two wonderfully productive terms in the winters of 1968 and 1969 when I first began intensive work. I was then given time to finish the manuscript during a sabbatical year in 1971–1972 that was helped out by a fellowship from the Simon Guggenheim Foundation. To these modern patrons of the letters and sciences, I, like so many of my academic contemporaries, will be forever indebted.

It is presumptuous to write a book on so vast a subject as I have attempted here, but it would have gone far beyond presumption and reached outright frivolity to have not leaned heavily upon the advice of friends and colleagues. In every area I touch upon there are others who know far more than I, and at every stage I have relied upon their help, their criticism, and their suggestions. In particular, I am indebted to many men and women who are scattered among several departments at the University of Michigan.

Some have advised me about books and articles I should read; some have read drafts of chapters; some have engaged me in argument and tried to save me from my many misconceptions. I owe deep thanks to Charles O. Hucker of the Department of Far Eastern Studies, to Rhoads W. Murphey of Geography, to David D. Bien, Albert Feuerwerker, Michael Pearson, and Thomas R. Trautmann of History, and to Norma J. Diamond, Conrad P. Kottak, Gloria A. Marshall, Nan Pendrell, William D. Schorger, Eric R. Wolf, and Aram A. Yengoyan of Anthropology. Bernard S. Cohn of the University of Chicago and Ralph W. Nicholas of Michigan State University advised me on sources and read drafts of my Maratha chapter and Ruben E. Reina of the University of Pennsylvania did the same for my section on Latin America. These men and women saved me from countless blunders. Where blunders persist, it is because I have not been sufficiently wise to follow the counsel of my scholarly friends.

CHAPTER 1

Introduction

SUCCESSION

This book begins with a straightforward question: What are the mechanisms by which a new man can be chosen to assume the chief position of power within his society? From many points of view, this question is an important one, and we have only to look about us to realize how far from solved are the problems of the acquisition and transfer of high power. In most of Latin America, in the newly independent nations of Asia and Africa, and in the Communist world, the death of a president, a prime minister, or a party secretary still brings a period of uncertainty, a period of maneuver, and sometimes a period of violence. Orderly successions are still the exception. Why?

This question first impressed itself upon me more in my role as a citizen than in my role as an anthropologist. Like many of my American contemporaries, I had been disturbed at the many obvious flaws in the way we go about selecting our own leaders. I wondered whether other nations had found secrets by which to transfer power that had escaped us. I was also puzzled about the best role for my country when dealing with changes in government elsewhere. Should we automatically recognize the successful leader of a coup d'etat? Or should we insist, ethnocentrically, upon recognizing only the results of elections? These were questions of obvious importance, and it seemed to me that anthropology might play a role in offering answers. Anthropologists would seem as well equipped as anyone to survey a diverse array of succession systems, both past and present, and to consider the strengths and weaknesses of each.

I began such a survey, but it soon became apparent that succession to high office could not possibly be examined without simultaneously considering many other aspects of politics. The transfer of power is entangled in a nest of other problems. Varying historical circumstances and varying cultural settings encourage different techniques of choosing top leaders, and varying succession practices in their turn have different but always profound impact upon many aspects of society. Periods of succession, for instance, have always been times when central authority has loosened. The departure of one ruler may leave the potential successors with no way to settle their rivalry except by resort to force, and the ensuing violence may even bring the complete collapse of a political system. Throughout recorded history the failure to achieve smooth transitions of power has repeatedly brought havoc to government, and the need to transfer power has been an important force in fostering the rise of new political patterns.

Men have experimented with a hundred techniques for filling their top offices, but none has ever been consistently successful in avoiding violence, in selecting able men, or in satisfying the needs or wishes of the people. By asking how men are chosen for top power, we quickly become involved in some of the most important questions of politics. An examination of succession practices turns out to offer a strategic point of departure from which to approach these many concerns.

In view of the importance of succession, it is surprising how little recent attention it has been given, but the techniques for acquiring top power were not always ignored. Indeed, there was a time when the pursuit of power lay at the core of historical scholarship. History was then the study of kings and their counselors, of statesmen and politicians, the study of how power was won and how it was lost. Ultimately however, economic and cultural history were discovered, and high politics came rightly to be seen as but one limited facet of the human story. Politics hardly deserved the exclusive attention it once had.

Nevertheless, the techniques for gaining power and the patterns by which power is transferred should not be forgotten simply because other matters have come into style, and when we return to these questions today, we can study them in a far wider range of cases than would have been possible only a generation or two ago. As historical and ethnographic knowledge have expanded, we have accumulated voluminous case histories of a thousand succession struggles. It is profitable, once again, to return to these simple but basic questions: How have men of different societies and different eras sought top political power? What are the alternatives that a reading of human history can suggest? What are the implications of various succession techniques for political unity, stability, and justice? It is to old-fashioned questions such as these that the following pages are addressed.

My general approach should seem familiar to anthropologists, for I follow tradition in offering a series of case studies and in trying to show the ways in which these cases are similar and the ways in which they differ. Like many other anthropologists, I have sought a compromise between the depth of a single case and the breadth of a large sample. I have selected my cases deliberately to be as diverse as possible, but I have repeatedly asked the same question of each society, and I have tried to extract as many generalizations as possible from my comparative data. This much should sound reasonable to anthropologists. At least it strikes me as fairly describing one kind of activity in which we have traditonally been engaged. I have attempted to do for succession what others have done when comparing family organization or subsistence techniques.

As I went deeper into my subject, however, I found myself questioning some widespread anthropological assumptions, and my final work reflects this questioning as much as it reflects the more secure traditions of comparative anthropology. Unless the reader understands the ways in which my assumptions have come to depart from those more traditional in anthropology, he may find himself disoriented. In the remainder of this introduction, therefore, I set forth a few of my own assumptions and I try to suggest where these diverge from the dominant traditions of my discipline.

THE SELECTION OF CASES

First of all, I depart from tradition in my choice of cases. I begin, to be sure, with tribes—traditional anthropological ground. I hope these will provide the breadth of perspective that should be the hallmark of anthropology. To cover the full range of the human experience, however, I need to move to precisely these societies that anthropologists have usually ignored. I need, in particular, to examine societies where records were kept so that events that span long periods of time are known. We know far too little about how our tribes have changed over the course of generations for them to serve as adequate examples, and the subject of political succession really becomes interesting only after leaving anthropological tradition behind. India and China can provide examples of two sharply contrasting kinds of hereditary systems, and both can be seen changing and developing through a very long span of time.

The chapter on tribes, together with those on India and on China, consider a diverse sample of hereditary systems. I hope these will provide a valuable background for understanding the other kinds of succession systems that have replaced heredity in the modern world. These modern succession systems, I feel, fall into three main types and I devote a chapter to each. First, there are republican regimes, and their emergence can only be studied in Europe. Second, there is the modern kind of political instability that suffers periodic military intervention and that seems to be so characteristic of much of today's third world. Latin America is surely the most suitable region from which to draw examples of this kind of political system. Finally, we have the challenge of Communist political theory and practice, and I conclude with a look at Eastern Europe and the Soviet Union. I ask whether the succession practices of other times and other areas can throw any light upon the workings of Communist politics. No examples could be more foreign to anthropology than European, Latin American, or Communist government, but I believe we stand to be enriched by embracing these exotic realms. I have come to regard the boundary between history and anthropolgy, and indeed the boundaries between all of the social sciences, as entirely artificial. It is problems that are important and since the most interesting problems straddle the traditional fields, the boundaries cannot be too quickly forgotten.

STRUCTURE AND CHANGE

My nontraditional selection of cases will be immediately apparent to any anthropologist who inspects the table of contents, but some other departures from tradition may be slightly less obvious. Among these may be my approach to culture change.

When anthropologists have considered change, they have most often taken their examples either from the always fragmentary archaeological record, or from the limited period when one of the forms of western civilization has seemed to be engulfing and destroying all other societies. This has, I believe, distorted the anthropological view of change. We have known only about the long-term changes that we could witness in the archaeological record—primarily the slow but cumulative accretion of technological skills—or about change that is induced by culture contact. Evolution, diffusion, and acculturation have too often summed up what we know about change, and our limited perspectives have led us to exaggerate the technological and material base as the driving force behind most change.

Short-term changes, changes that arise out of the very nature of society itself, have too often been ignored. Indeed, the nature of ethnological field work has made such changes difficult for us to see. The typical ethnologist can spend no more than a year or two among his people. Even if written records exist, he will have neither the training nor the temperament to use them, and the "functional" biases of anthropology are strong enough to encourage field workers to be skeptical of oral history, except as it serves as a symbolic reflection of their people's culture. Seeing his society only in a cross section of time, the field worker is led to emphasize the coherence, pattern, and regularity in his data. Internal contradictions, which might in the long run led to change, simply interfere with the orderly picture that he hopes to construct.

Of course anthropology has its countertraditions, not only the much ridiculed view of culture as a collection of shreds and patches, but also more sophisticated views that look for the genesis of conflict, the points of weakness where a society is vulnerable to outside influence, or even the resolution of contradictions. But these ideas seem to me to have been subordinated rather unfairly to the dominant structural–functional tradition that tells us always and everywhere to look for order.

The questions I ask in this book and the cases I examine encourage a different perspective from that of structural coherence or functional integration. Succession to a society's top office is not likely to occur more than once in several years and often it occurs only once in a generation. In the months or years that he spends in the field, no anthropologist can observe the examples that would allow generalizations about such an infrequent event. We need to watch a society through decades and centuries. As soon as one takes this long view, it becomes obvious that social systems never remain stable. In particular, the techniques by which leaders reach the top seem always to change, and these changes can by no means always be explained by the influence of other societies. It is more profitable, I feel, to see the changes as arising through a kind of internal dynamism. Problems internal to the society itself encourage men to innovate, and their innovations result in new problems and then still more changes. I do not mean to imply that there is anything new in this point of view. The dialectical viewpoint which sees change resulting from internal contradictions is an old strand in the Western intellectual tradition; but more than most anthropologists, I am quite directly concerned with the internal factors that put a social system into a slightly unstable equilibrium.

I would like the cases I describe in this book to go part way toward changing the balance of anthropological attitudes toward change, but I do not want to deny a considerable degree of orderliness and regularity in culture, or to suggest that its parts are not interdependent. Indeed, if they were not in some degree interdependent, there would be no sense in which we could talk about an internal contradiction. It is only when we have partial regularity that the irregularities make any difference. Only then can there be points of strain that encourage change. The ethnological field is not the ideal place to study these internal contradictions nor to check on the changes that follow. If anthropologists are ever to have any understanding of the dynamic nature of society, they will have to expand their vision to include examples that span the generations.

TECHNOLOGY, IDEOLOGY, AND SOCIETY

Students of culture have sometimes found it convenient to distinguish three interrelated facets of their subject: the technological foundation, the social organization of the people, and their ideology. There have been many different conceptions of how these three facets are interrelated, but, often, social organization has been seen as reacting to, or dependent upon, either technology or ideology. The study of ecology has helped us to understand how social organization rests upon a material base and how social relationships can be molded by technological requirements. From the other direction, the study of values has helped us to understand that all men hold fundamental principles or assumptions about the world and about society and that these principles shape behavior and give patterning to social organization. I do not want to minimize the influence of either the material base or of men's ideological postulates upon social organization, but in this book I will be seeking to understand one aspect of social organization in its own terms and will be referring only marginally to either technology or ideology.

About technology, I will have little to say, but I do not want to pretend that technology has no important bearing upon succession. I think it likely, for instance, that the decline in hereditary succession in the last two centuries, which I discuss in Chapter 5, has been quite directly dependent upon technological changes. Increasingly complex technology came to require such complex patterns of social organization that heredity could no longer be trusted to designate men with sufficient ability to give leadership. Nevertheless, I would hazard the suggestion that, within a fairly broad range, the aspects of social organization that interest me in this book are relatively independent of technology. At the risk of some oversimplification, my special attitude toward change and technology might be summed up by saying that while many anthropologists are materialists without being dialectical, I am, for purposes of this book, dialectical without being a materialist.

Ideology, in the abstract sense of the values or basic postulates that differ from society to society and that lead men in varying societies to come to different decisions, will play no more important a part in my analysis than technology. Indeed, it seems to me that succession techniques are, to a considerable degree, independent of such abstract ideology. Nevertheless, all people do have some explicit principles or rules by which they feel that succession should be arranged, and perhaps these principles serve as something of a link between concrete daily social behavior and our more abstract and barely conscious values or postulates. I will have a good deal to say about such principles in this book, but even these principles will be seen more as the *result* of pragmatic decisions in concrete situations than as the *cause* of such decisions. I even find it a useful fiction to look upon power struggles as if the strugglers act entirely without principle. They can be seen as ready to do anything that will increase their power. This point of view provides some protection against a too facile dismissal of some acts as simply traditional or simply "cultural." I would rather seek an explanation for a man's behavior in his attempt at rational calculation of the benefits to him than in the heavy, and to me somewhat mystical, hand of tradition or culture.

Nevertheless, explicit principles do bear upon the struggle for power in two crucial ways. First, no man, however unscrupulous or unprincipled he may be, can ignore the principles and expectations of those around him. He will never be taken seriously if he cannot meet their minimal standards. For us, as observers, it often makes little difference whether an actor in a power struggle *really* believes in the principles or whether he conforms to them out of pure expediency. A man sometimes gives every appearance of principled behavior until he finally works himself into such a strong position that he can defy those very principles. We may then suspect that he had never really held his principles very closely, but such hindsight does not help us much in understanding his earlier behavior. Thus, rules of succession, in the form of the general expectations of other men, constitute an important factor in all the behavior I consider here, but the extent to which men act in the conviction that the rules are good or just, and the extent to which they act with mere expediency, may make little difference and, in the final analysis, may be unknowable.

Ideology does bear upon social organization in one other way. Men in power have an imperative need to clothe their actions with legitimacy. However irregular a man's rise may be, he must construct some justification for his position once it is won. I am often tempted to see the ideological principles a man then proclaims as more or less deliberately constructed doctrines designed to rationalize the existing state of affairs. Ideological principles then begin to look more like the result of social relationships than their cause. Nevertheless, people may come to take this ideology seriously, and when they do, it can set conditions that become binding upon those who follow. In this way, men who gain power by one set of techniques sometimes promote their ideological principles so successfully that they define new conditions for the next succession. Men can, in a sense, become trapped by their own ideology, and if they are not trapped themselves, their children often are. This is one of the forces that pushes a social system away from its original patterns. It is one way in which cumulative changes are brought about.

THE SUCCESSION OF LEADING MEN
AND THE SEQUENCE OF LEADING CLASSES

There is an old and complex problem of the relationship between the individual and his culture, and we can see the relationship from two opposing vantage points. We can look upon an individual as the product of his group's culture, but we can also see culture as the result of individual decisions and individual behavior. In the same way, we can look upon social change in two ways. It can be seen as the product of impersonal forces, forces that are given direction, perhaps, by technical and economic pressures; but alternatively, it can be seen as resulting from the individual innovations of individual actors.

Neither of these views has a unique claim to the truth, but I feel that much of recent social science has gone rather far in the direction of playing down the role of the individual. We have focused our attention upon the cultural, social, and technological forces that impinge upon the individual, and in so doing, we have minimized the contribution of any single individual in effecting change. Individuals tend more often to be seen as caught up in social movements than as guiding them. Leaders are seen as shaped by their movements rather than giving them shape. The doctrine of the great man is hardly stylish in anthropology.

I am concerned, however, with power relationships among small groups of leading men, and I am persuaded that the patterning of these relationships has far-reaching implications for the directions of change in the society over which they preside. I do not mean to imply that we must imagine social change to be merely the result of decisions by great men of genius who are free to act in defiance of their culture, but I do mean to argue that our view of change need not be limited to the more or less Marxian stance that focuses upon impersonal social and economic forces. I am searching, in other words, for a middle ground between a simplistic great-man view of history and an opposite but equally simplistic impersonal view of history. Certainly individuals can act only within the constraints imposed by their culture, and to that extent the great-man view of history can be misleading. At the same time individuals, particularly those who hold positions of great power within their society, can make decisions with wide-ranging ramifications upon the social and economic system, and any view of history that loses sight of the individual actors becomes equally misleading.

An example of the difference between my view and what I take to have been the dominant view in recent social science is the difference between looking at individuals and looking at social classes. Some would argue that the succession of individuals to power is unimportant so long as the same social class retains its dominant position. For Marxists, the sequence of ruling classes has always seemed a far more fruitful topic for investigation than the succession of ruling individuals. I would never deny the legitimacy of investigating the sequence of ruling classes, but I must insist also upon the legitimacy of balancing this view by investigations that take small groups of men and their decisions as the primary topic of investigation. I would maintain, in fact, that the techniques by which individuals are selected for office have profound consequences back upon the social class system. The reader will badly misunderstand my purpose unless he recognizes that my interests lie with the patterns of power among small groups of leading men. I am concerned only incidentally with the dynamics of social class.

CULTURAL RELATIVISM

I was taught that one of my discipline's notable contributions to the modern understanding of man was the doctrine of cultural relativism. I was told, and I was eager to believe, that human customs were not to be judged by any simple and ethnocentric American or Western standard, but only in the context of a people's total way of life. If Swazi "buy" their wives with a bride price of cattle, we must understand that this demonstrates the high value of women and helps to solidify the marriage. If Eskimos abandon their infirm elders, we must see their actions in the light of the starkly limited resources of their barren land.

Like our view of change, our opinions about cultural relativism have been influenced by the conditions of ethnological field work. A field anthropologist is almost forced to suspend judgement temporarily, otherwise he may never learn enough about his people to grasp the full context in which their customary behavior must be understood. But, having once suspended judgment, it is remarkably easy to leave it suspended, to conclude that all human customs are equally defensible, to argue that no culture can be judged as in any way better than another.

In examining a topic such as succession, therefore, the anthropological instinct is to presume that no technique by which a leader can be chosen has any final superiority over its alternatives. Rather, we tend to assume that different techniques will be appropriate in different societies. The belief system of a people and all the intricacies of their social practices would have to be understood before we could show why their particular succession system is so uniquely suitable for their situation. Little in the tradition of modern anthropology would encourage the suggestion that any pattern of succession is better than any other. In struggling against the ethnocentrism of our fellow citizens, however, we have often tried to balance their biases by emphasizing the special virtues of other societies and by pointing up the failings of our own. Eager to counter the vulgar assumption of cultural superiority held by all to many of our countrymen, we have been willing to give other cultures every benefit of our doubts. Ordinarily, we have reserved our severest judgements for our own society.

In writing this book I have wanted to remain true to my anthropological training and I have wanted to look at our own techniques of determining succession with at least as critical an eye as I use for other techniques. I try to point out, therefore, the difficulties of our type of succession system, and I suggest some reasons it has so often failed to live up to its promise. With appropriate anthropological objectivity, I have wanted to see electoral succession as simply one more imperfect solution to an eternal human problem.

In the end, however, I find myself reacting against the ethos of my discipline and against the strain of cultural self-criticism that I see in so many of my colleagues. I have gained no admiration for the unending rebellions, revolutions, fratricides, and tyrannies that have been a part of most political systems and which have so often accompanied or resulted from succession battles. Instead, I have emerged rather pleasantly surprised by my own renewed faith in our electoral processes. I would like, therefore, to keep my cultural relativism under sufficient control to let me cherish our electoral heritage and to try to profit from an understanding of what has made it possible. I would like the cases considered in this book to contribute to that understanding.

APPLICATIONS

When pressed to justify their trade, anthropologists have usually been willing to argue that the more we can learn about a wide variety of human societies, the more intelligently we will be able to make decisions concerning our own. By learning how others live, we may learn to live better ourselves. Perhaps we can find a people who avoid our problems. If adolescence causes difficulties for Americans, let's find a tribe where it causes no problem and find out why. If we murder each other in wars, let's find a peaceful tribe and learn its secrets.

It is in this tradition that I have directed my attention to what I take to be a real and serious problem that faces mankind in the final third of the 20th century: How should we choose our leaders? This is what drew me to my subject, and it is my hope that anthropological data and anthropological perspectives can have a bearing upon this urgent question. From time to time, anthropologists have dealt with topics that might seem to bear upon it. We have gathered data on the way in which chiefs gain power, on the mechanisms of hereditary office, and on the rise of political factions, but we have not put this knowledge into a form that touches directly upon our own society. As the problem presents itself in a practical way to the American citizen, it is with such matters as when the United States should recognize a new government that has just come to power by a coup d'etat or whether the electoral college should be reformed. These questions seem far removed from the study of humble chiefs in humble tribes. Is there any way they could be connected?

It is my conviction that they are connected, though I will need this entire book to justify my belief. Clearly, it is unreasonable to expect any direct and immediate application of knowledge gained from tribal studies to high political decisions, and it is also, I am convinced, unreasonable to expect any entirely satisfactory solution to such an old question as how to designate a leader. The attitude I take in this book, in fact, is that some problems are inherently insoluble. For some problems there may be only an array of second-rate solutions and we should not get trapped into looking for the ideal one. This does not mean that every solution is equally bad. We can still consider the alternatives. We can still ask which of these imperfect solutions entail the fewest problems or the least serious problems, and we can try to decide which evils we are willing to live with in return for avoiding other evils.

In talking of "bad" solutions and "ideal" solutions, I am using terms in a way that is hardly conventional in anthropology, but I do so deliberately and I mean to imply an attitude toward the possibility of coping with problems in our own society. By saying that each solution entails problems, I imply that I have some idea of what problems are. I imply that I have values and goals toward which I am willing to work, and that I believe the kinds of solutions we choose will affect our ability to approach these goals. Such statements may be jarring to some anthropologists, but I think it takes a rather exaggerated sense of cultural relativism to accept a solution that entails widespread warfare and human slaughter to resolve a succession struggle as equivalent to an alternative solution that resolves the matter peacefully. I would go a good deal further. I prefer solutions that offer individual men the freedom to regulate their own lives, to live in a society with a degree of predictable organization, and to participate in the decisions that will affect their destiny. It is my conviction that the techniques by which men designate their leaders have profound implications for our ability to meet all these ideals.

In one sense, cultural relativism and the hope that anthropological knowledge could have practical applications contradict one another. If cultural relativism dissuades us from making judgments about others, we will have difficulty making recommendations that will affect their lives. Of course, so long as we confine our criticism to our own society, we are left free to admire and to learn from others, even while hoping to leave them respectfully alone. But I have already mentioned my admiration for one aspect of my own culture, and at the same time I have come to deplore the alternatives I find elsewhere. Since I am quite unwilling to abandon the hope that ethnological (or historical) knowledge can help us make sensible decisions about practical problems, I find myself forced into the rather unstylish position of asking not only how we can learn from others, but how we can help others to learn from us.

I will, therefore, conclude this study by making a few observations about the state of succession systems in the world today and about the role that Americans and the United States government have played in promoting and discouraging various patterns of succession. I think these conclusions are made plausible by the cases I examine, but I will try not to pretend that they have been, or ever could be, "proved" by the kind of discussion found in this book. Nevertheless, if political anthropology is to have any bearing upon our practical political lives, then the political anthropologist had better be willing to climb out on a limb and offer a few judgments and opinons. In the end, I see no better way to form an opinion than to examine cases, and I even feel that the primary reason for examining cases is to help us reach informed judgments.

Most of this book consists of a series of case studies. These are tied together with occasional comparative statements and concluded with a theoretical summary. I hope that a serious comparative examination of the techniques by which men have achieved power in the widest possible variety of societies will give us some idea of the benefits and evils of the alternatives that lie before us, and that this knowledge can help us to make sensible decisions within our own society. It was with this rather presumptuous hope that this book was undertaken.

CHAPTER 2

Our Tribal Heritage

[handwritten annotations: "The only primitive world here is the world of 'white-te' better known as human rubbish"]

INTRODUCTION

The ~~primitive~~ world, fragmented into hundreds of separate tribes and independent kingdoms, constitutes man's most diverse field of social experimentation. Each tribe or each community has had to work out its own solutions to our human problems, and their political experiments have covered the gamut from tiny migratory bands to powerful centralized kingdoms. Understanding this diversity is anthropology's challenge and its justification.

For a student of succession, unfortunately, the tribes of the anthropologist have one serious drawback: Most of them lack a long tradition of writing. Without written records, our historical knowledge of these people is usually thin, and only rarely do we know how their social organization has

13

changed in the course of past generations or centuries. Since succession practices have a strong tendency to change through time, this means we lack, for most tribes, one important dimension that we would need for a full understanding of succession.

Nevertheless, in a few areas, such as Africa and the Pacific, independent political systems survived long enough to receive the careful scrutiny of skillful anthropological observers, and even where historical knowledge is limited, we can, by examining the practices of a number of different tribes at the time of their early contact with Europeans, gain some idea of the range of possibilities available to people who lacked industrial technology and the types of communication and record keeping that come with writing. We can even start at a level so primitive that we may come to doubt whether societies need to face a succession problem at all.

DIFFUSE LEADERSHIP: THE SIUAI

To those not stung by high ambitions, the reasons for others so relentlessly pursuing power must sometimes be mysterious, but that such men exist can scarcely be questioned. We can try to place ourselves in the position of such a man and ask what he should do. How should he proceed if he wants to rise to a powerful position? A man with a club, a spear, or a gun may temporarily get his way, but if he is not to be murdered in his sleep, he needs more subtle methods.

His first requirement is for men who will assist him and guard him, so the first problem is always to find supporters and to secure their loyalty. To do this he will have to act in ways that others understand and respect, and so he will have to take into account the traditional forms of social relationships that he finds around him. Every aspirant to power must build his position upon the preexisting social forms—upon the expectations of the men over whom he would rule—and this is as true in a tribal society that lacks the trappings of modern technology as it is in the modern nation state. The study of power, therefore, immediately involves us in the study of society. Power is embedded in social organization and it cannot be understood apart from the matrix within which it is set.

Power at its simplest, arises from the human willingness to acknowledge another's leadership. When a man stands out as a hunter, a fighter, or an orator, others may come to admire, then to assist, and finally to obey him. The power of such a leader rests unambiguously upon the willingness of others to be led, and such power can erode rapidly if confidence is lost. Nevertheless, even such a simple acknowledgment of leadership can allow cooperation among considerable numbers of men. Complex social arrangements grow up that guide men's efforts as they compete for leadership and strive for the recognition of others. We can consider an example.

Among the Siuai, a tribe of Bougainville Island in the Solomon Islands in the South Pacific, a man who aspired to leadership had to start by building his economic resources.[1] His first step would be to acquire several wives. He needed wives to work in his gardens and to cultivate a surplus of taro, and he needed taro to feed his herd of pigs. The pigs were served at feasts, and by giving feasts a man could collect followers. Only one who was generous with feasts could build up a reputation as a "big man" and only such a man could mobilize supporters. A man who was sufficiently skilled at organization and sufficiently inspired as a leader could recruit hundreds of men who would work for him in building and transporting a slit gong, or in building a men's clubhouse. Once built, a clubhouse would stand as testimony to the greatness of the organizer. Simply by gathering there, men acknowledged his leadership. Feasts could be held at the clubhouse, and when the slit gongs were sounded it brought further renown to the big man.

As a leader grew in stature, he would have to enlist the help of an ever wider circle of followers. They would raise his pigs and help in the preparation of his feasts, and as long as they could bask in the reflected glory of their leader, they would be willing to contribute their own labor to the common effort. Such a leader could also, if he wished, influence all the affairs of his neighborhood. Others would accept his arbitration of disputes and he could turn his scorn and the scorn of his followers against those who did not cooperate. Such a big man could use his position to help keep the peace within the little realm where his followers lived.

Inevitably, "big men" came to compete with one another, and their rivalry was most characteristically expressed by competitive feasting. Siuai ranked their big men by the relative magnificence of their feasts and each would try to outdo the others, particularly in his serving of pork. The larger a man's following and the more inspired his leadership, the greater would be his feasts, and the greater his renown. Before the British imposed their colonial peace upon Bougainville, the rivalry of big men sometimes led to warfare, and then the big men not only had to try to keep the peace among their own followers, but also to organize aggression and defense against their neighbors. They wielded power both internally within their little domain, and externally when the followers of competing big men faced each other, and, by these means, a degree of coherence was brought to Siuai society. Men could lead their daily lives in relative security. They had

---

[1]Douglas L. Oliver, *A Solomon Island Society* (Cambridge, Massachusetts: Harvard University Press, 1955).

leaders who would guide and defend them, and they had recognized rules by which men competed.

Hundreds, even thousands, of men can be organized and brought into cooperation by a political system like that of the Siuai, but when a Siuai big man died, his office disappeared. His realm, pieced together with the help of his kinsmen, his friends, and his neighbors, would simply dissolve. Others might slowly pick up the fragments, of course. Neighboring big men might attract some of the followers and others might gradually coalesce under new leadership, but no man was able simply to take over an office that another had built up. The political system endured, for new leaders continued to build new centers of power, but no single office had continuity. Loyalty was directed only to a particular man and was never automatically transferred to a successor, and the offices were not even stable during the lifetime of their incumbents, for the followers were always free to desert. When a big man failed to help his followers, when he failed to provide feasts or to defend them in war, or when in competing with his rivals, he demanded too much of his followers, he risked losing their allegiance. They would then drift away and affiliate themselves with other leaders until the big man's power simply evaporated. Of course the idea of the big man's role survived, for new men were always attempting to build up new realms, but old offices also faded away. No particular big man's office could ever outlive the man who had built it.

Big man systems, not identical to the Siuai, of course, but based upon similar principles, have recurred at many times and places. In the absence of any other political order, it may be inevitable that some men will freely offer their personal loyalty to others. So long as they are also free to withdraw their loyalty and so long as loyalty is not automatically transferred to a successor, we cannot really speak of a succession system at all. Only if the realm remains united after its ruler leaves, and only if his office is successfully bestowed upon a new man, has a succession successfully taken place.

Since no single big man's office could be passed onto a successor, the Siuai might be said to have entirely avoided the succession problem. Succession, it seems, is not an inevitable event in every society. Nevertheless, most societies that we know anything about, and all societies of any consequence in the modern world, have more enduring political offices than do the Siuai, and in all such societies successions must regularly occur. The reasons for the predominance of societies with succession surely lie in the competitive advantage that permanent offices confer. No single Siuai man could build on the political accomplishments of his predecessors. Each new man had to start fresh. Where political realms can outlive their founder, they can be built to new levels of size and strength and in the long run, these

societies have unquestionably tended to win out over the less enduring kinds of political systems, such as the one that the Siuai devised.

The heart of the succession problem is how to select one man who will be able to assume the same role and perform the same functions as the old man. How can the followers of the old man be persuaded to transfer their allegiance to the new man? How are common men to be discouraged from withdrawing their loyalty to their former leader? How are former subordinate leaders to be prevented from setting themselves up independently, or from taking their own little band to a new allegiance? How can enduring political bonds be forged?

HEREDITY: THE SWAZI

The device by which many African tribes created enduring political systems was to replace loyalty to an individual with loyalty to an entire royal clan. Among the Siuai, loyalty was given to a man, and when the man died, his political system dissolved; but a clan, unlike an individual, may be immortal, and if loyalties to a clan can be perpetuated, so can political leadership. The mechanisms by which a single large family gained the loyalty of others and so converted itself into a royal clan were varied, but in one way or another, dominant clans repeatedly emerged. Men of the same family could then follow each other in a single office. Hereditary monarchies came to be established. Southern Africa provides examples where we can see how kinship can be used to forge a far more enduring political system than that of the Siuai.

Among the Bantu tribes of southern Africa, the kinsmen upon whom one could most confidently rely were those related through men. Fathers worked with their sons, and brother helped brother. Grown sons often continued to live with their father and their brothers, and so extended families of several brothers, their sons, and even their son's sons were established. This core of related males gave a unity and continuity to an extended family and to the homestead it occupied. The girls born to these families would have to move away when they married, but other girls would move in as wives.

When families grew too large, it sometimes became difficult to keep them united. Brothers might cooperate less willingly after their father's death, and then each might lead his own sons and their families into greater independence, but even when they no longer lived together, kinsmen who were related through males recognized a special bond. Even after several generations, those descended in the male line from a common ancestor recognized their kinship, and symbolized it by a common name. Members of such a "clan," regarded themselves as too closely related to marry. A man automatically belonged to the clan of his father, but the clans were tied to one another by the cross-linking bonds of marriage.

Bantus infiltrated the eastern half of southern Africa in the course of the last several centuries. They displaced earlier hunting bands and brought a fairly simple form of agriculture along with extensive cattle herding. They spread widely, always searching for range for their cattle and new soil for their crops, and their social organization was adjusted to exploitation of this frontier. A Bantu leader might gather a band of his own family and clan members, together with a few relatives by marriage, and lead them to found a new village and exploit new land.

As the population grew, these bands would have to compete for more limited resources. A premium would be placed upon an organization that could induce men to cooperate in defense and aggression. It might be profitable to organize a band that would be strong enough to plunder the neighbor's ever tempting cattle herds. Then, in the face of such danger, others had to organize for defense. Men were ready to accept another's command, offering loyalty and military support and hoping in return at least for protection, but even better for a share in the booty that might come to the strong.

Under these conditions, it is not hard to visualize how one clan could come to be elevated to a position of royalty, and one member of this royal clan to a position of chief or king. Bantus had always bound themselves to efficient and vigorous leaders. The dynamic leader might first attract members of his own clan, but these would bring their wives, and then some of their wives' brothers and their sisters' husbands might also join. An increasing number of followers from other clans might be willing to acknowledge the overlordship of a skillful man. He could pass by gradual stages into a chief of a large domain, and when it became so big that he could no longer rule all of his subjects directly, he would quite naturally call upon members of his own clan for help. These, after all, would be his most reliable supporters and allies. His own position might be made more secure by investing it with a bit of ceremonial grandeur, and the aura of royalty could easily spread to his clansmen.

The centuries preceding the imposition of colonial rule in southeastern Africa were times of chaotic migration and shifting power. People would flock to support any leader who seemed sufficiently strong to guide and protect them. A petty chief might in turn place himself and his followers under the protection of a more august chief, so a hierarchical system grew up in which the king and high chiefs were dependent upon the support of lesser chiefs, each of whom had his own loyal followers. Any tendency toward tyranny was checked by the ability to desert an overlord in a favor of a new man. Bantu subsistence patterns did not bind people irrevocably to one spot, and anyone dissatisfied with his own chief could seek the protection of another. A Bantu chief, like a Siuai big man, had to act with some consideration for his followers, lest he find his support melting away. These sometimes fragile links of loyalty allowed the world of the southern Bantu to be one of kaleidoscopic change. Power built up and collapsed rapidly, as individuals and groups fought, conquered, migrated, rebelled, and split up.

The nucleus of the Swazi nation was formed by tribesmen who, under the leadership of a man known as King Sobhuza, retreated northward from the turbulent conditions brought about in the first part of the 19th century by the Zulu expansion (see Figure 2-1).[2] Sobhuza's followers included many members of his own clan, the Dlamini, but he welcomed men of other clans who sought his protection and who were willing to ally themselves with the Dlamini. The Dlamini became the royal clan of the Swazi and together with their first non-royal adherents, they count as the original Swazi. As they moved northward, they met and incorporated still others. Some submitted and gave tribute to the Swazi leader; some had to be subdued by force. The men of a few groups were exterminated, and their children adopted. In one way and another the numbers of people adhering to the Swazi state grew, and with each expansion, the king became more powerful. In the 1930s, a quarter of a century after their final conquest by the British, about 150,000 people counted themselves as Swazi. These included members of the Dlamini clan, other "original" Swazi, and later adherents who, either voluntarily or by force, had come to accept Dlamini rule.

The Swazi king was ceremonially set apart from his subjects. He possessed the most powerful magic in the kingdom and he was married with an elaborate ritual. The most important Swazi ceremony of the year could not even be carried out without the king, and the songs, dancing, and wide participation of all the people at this ceremony emphasized the kingdom's unity. Internal fights were supposed to be forbidden at this time, but the period that followed was an auspicious moment for war. It was then that the people felt most united and strong. Thus, the unity of the kingdom and the king's unique role within it were closely bound together. The king distributed land to his subjects. He could move them about at will and he even held the power of life and death over them. He led the army, distributed the booty which war might bring, and acted as the final judge in disputes among his subjects. Clearly, the Swazi king had a position very different from the Siuai big man, and when the king died, his throne was expected to survive, not to disappear like the realm of a big man. A successor had to be found.

---

[2]For my discussion of the Swazi in the following pages, I rely, in particular, upon Hilda Kuper's *An African Aristocracy* (London: Oxford University Press, 1947).

Figure 2–1. Tribal states of Swazi, Bemba, Baganda, and Nupe.

Clearly, the Swazi political system grew upon a foundation of kinship. The king was a great chief, and the chief in turn was a great father. Chiefs, and above all the king, headed especially large families that had multitudes of adherents. Many of the symbols of royalty reflected his family base. The king's mother had an important ceremonial role and his brothers were supposed to be his allies. When he died, his family was expected to continue his tradition, and the throne would be passed on to a new member of the family in the same way that property was inherited within all families. In conformity with Bantu traditions, succession to the throne, like inheritance of property, had to be in the male line, but there were always many kinsmen with adequate genealogical qualifications. Among modest families, the property of a man might be divided among his sons; but if a kingdom were to be divided among the sons of a king, it would, in a literal sense, cease to exist and the fragments would become easy prey to their neighbors. The

Swazi succession problem was to define a system of heredity in such a way that a single man from among those qualified by kinship could be selected for the throne.

SUCCESSION STRUGGLES

Claimants to the throne came from among the closest relatives and supporters of the king. In order to understand how the selection was made, we must first know who the claimants were and how they exerted power under the king, for their position after the king's death always reflected their earlier role. A king's first line of supporters was always recruited from his royal relatives, his near and distant kinsmen of the Dlamini clan. In particular, the more closely related princes shared in the glory of the throne, and it was only with their help that the king could hope to establish and maintain his rule over a heterogeneous and turbulent society. Ideally, the men of the royal family were supposed to be loyal and even affectionate to the monarch, but Swazi were well aware of the jealousies that could divide a royal family when only one man could be king. The Swazi felt that the best way to deal with rival clansmen was to let them administer smaller territories within the kingdom. This would give the royal princes what amounted to a stake in the system and at the same time capitalize upon the respect in which their royal blood was held by others. Since the domain of each chief was small—4 to 20 square miles and 100 to 2,000 people—no chief, by himself, had a power base large enough to compete directly with the king. Still, the very aura of royalty that made princes useful as subordinate leaders also gave them a symbol that could make them rivals for the throne itself. A coalition of chiefs could be a real threat.

The kingdom had more than 150 chiefs and almost half came from the Dlamini clan, far more than the proportion of Dlamini within the total population. The other half of the chiefs belonged to "commoner" clans. Some had led their followers into submission to the Swazi and had been allowed to retain their earlier position of leadership. The Swazi king might be happy to reward an old chief in this way so long as his own paramountcy was respected, but the king also had personal motives for welcoming some nonroyal chiefs, for they tended to balance the power of the royals. Since the commoner chiefs could never aspire to the throne themselves, they might have less motive for insubordination.

The king had some power to appoint his chiefs but, like the throne, chieftainships tended to become hereditary, and normally the people expected the son of a chief to follow his father in office. This was one factor that encouraged the Swazi to accept a similar principle for the throne. The king was the biggest chief and he acquired his office in the same way the others did. A king who did not wish to arouse too much antagonism among his subjects was well advised to confirm in office the man with the greatest hereditary claim. On the other hand, the king always had a growing crop of brothers and sons who clamored for their own territories, and the king would want to do his best to satisfy their desires, too. While the kingdom was expanding, some of their demands could be met by assigning them border areas with newly conquered populations, but the king could sometimes appoint a new chief for a long occupied territory as well. When an old chief was unpopular, this might not be difficult, and indeed a replacement might be welcomed. Always, of course, the king's first concern would be to appoint men who would be loyal to himself.

Diplomatic marriages tied the king to the other clans. His harem was recruited from among the commoner clans, and his sisters and daughters were returned as wives for his commoner chieftains. The unity of the state was also encouraged by military regiments that crosscut clan and territorial loyalties, and by councils of advisors, many of whose members were commoners.

It was within this social system that the succession had to be decided, but it is not difficult to see points where rivalry among claimants might be bitter. The doctrine of royalty disqualified men from other clans, but where there were many queens, there would also be many princes, and the families of the various queens might compete bitterly to secure the selection of their own sister's son as king. The Swazi would seem to have needed a few rules to narrow the field, and they did come to recognize certain principles.

In particular, they had a superficially clear rule that the first son (ideally the only son) of the principal wife should succeed. One of the many queens (never the first married) was supposed to have the highest rank, and she should have had the most cattle paid for her in bride price. The king's principal wife was often one of his younger queens. This meant that the most appropriate heir to the throne might be too young to take a personal part in the rivalry for his father's power, and the Swazi tried to minimize rivalry among the princes and among the families of the various queens by having the older co-wives and the older sons agree among themselves to let a younger man succeed and to let a younger co-wife become queen mother.

This apparently clear rule, however, was hedged about with uncertainties, for the Swazi felt it undesirable to designate the heir of the king, or even of a chief, as long as his father lived. The Swazi believed that once the heir was definitely known, the position of the father would be undermined, and the result would be strife among the brothers, among their mothers, and between the father and his sons. Swazi could cite vivid examples of heirs who acted in disgracefully unfilial ways once they became too confident of their own inheritance. They grew disrespectful toward their fathers and arrogant toward their brothers, and at the same time they became targets for the jealousies of all those passed by.

In order to avoid the dangers that were inherent in selecting an heir too soon, the Swazi were usually willing to postpone designating the king's principal wife. Formal recognition of her role usually came only after the old chief had died. Then, however, the ambiguity had to be quickly resolved.

The transition was supposed to be eased by the special role of the first son of the king's first wife. This prince received the special title of "first circumcised" and he was rigidly excluded from the succession. Since he was not himself in competition, he could help fill the gap between the reigns. He was supposed to have been the confidant of his father, as no potential successor and competitor could ever have hoped to be, and later he could become an advisor to his younger half brother. When a successor was young, this older brother's advice and assistance might be quite decisive.

When the king died, the older members of the royal clan, first circumcised and the king's other brothers, his uncles and even his full sisters assembled in council, and tried to agree upon the succession. If they could do so, their decision would be persuasive. In principle, it was the older men who made the decision, but they would choose from among the younger men. Those who made the decision, therefore, had a less direct stake in the choice than the younger men who awaited it. Due regard would be taken of birth order and of the relative ranking of the widows, for the Swazi liked to justify their choice by reference to formal rules, and they criticized the Zulu for allowing the forceful seizure of the throne. Nevertheless, the Swazi were caught in a dilemma since they could not afford to let their rules become *too* explicit for fear that the heir would become known ahead of time. The complexities of Swazi succession practices can be seen as an attempt to solve this dilemma. They seemed to want both clarity and ambiguity at the same time.

Chiefly families sometimes chose successors to the subordinate chiefdoms by a process quite like that of the royal family, but when the kinsmen could not reach a harmonious decision, they might refer the decision to the king. In choosing a new king, of course, there was no higher authority to whom appeal could be directed, and a divided council might lead to civil war. In fact, a threat of violence from one quarter or another hung over almost every royal Swazi succession. Neither the clan council nor the advice of the first circumcised was adequate to insure a peaceful transfer of power.

Succession struggles were inevitable because no king could ever afford to let one man assume an unambiguous role of heir apparent. Every rule and procedure by which the Swazi tried to designate a new king had to be left ambiguous, and the ambiguities were necessary precisely in order to prevent any single unambiguous heir from appearing on the scene. This meant that

once the king died, several potential heirs would always present themselves
or be presented by their various supporters. The ensuing struggles were a
profound source of weakness to the Swazi kingdom, and, on some occasions,
they threatened to destroy it entirely.

SUCCESSION AND DISUNITY

Among the Swazi as among many other people, times of succession were
critical for unity. When men contested the throne, they risked tearing the
kingdom to pieces. The most serious threat to Swazi unity came from the
independent power bases of the chiefs, particularly from those who were
royal princes. Each chief maintained a court that was a miniature of the
capital, complete with a ceremonial mother, counselors, and military regiments. Each had a territory of his own over which to rule. Each chief had
some influence on national politics, either through his participation in an
occasional council, or through his personal and kinship ties with the king,
and he could hope to influence the choice of a successor who would favor
him. Not all interests could be satisfied, however, and the history of other
Bantus, who shared many of the Swazi practices, shows how fragile the
kingdoms were. Dissatisfied or defeated segments of kingdoms led by a
chief or prince would hive off from their fellows, flee when necessary to
safer territory, gather other followers when they could, or join another
promising leader. Fierce succession battles were almost the rule. The Bantu
techniques for maintaining political unity in the face of a king's death were
not really adequate to the task. A strong ruler could keep his chiefs in line
and his people loyal, but when power had to be transferred, individual
leaders might see more advantage to themselves in asserting their own independence than in supporting a king with whom they might be on bad
terms.

Thus among the Swazi, as among the Melanesian Siuai, followers sometimes deserted their leaders, and the period following the death of a king
was a particularly likely time for subordinate chiefs to lead parts of the
former realm into independence. The difference was that the Swazi thought
the kingdom might remain united. The Siuai never imagined that the followers of a big man could stay together after his death. The followers of a
Bantu king might not remain united either, but an aspiring successor could
use the principle of national unity as an inspiration to his followers and as
an excuse to put down his opponents. The problem of how to maintain the
loyalty of their subordinate chiefs was always a difficult one for the Swazi
kings. The question of how to keep the chiefs united in the face of royal
succession was simply the most critical aspect of this more general problem.

The Swazi political system survived without fragmenting from its founding in the early 19th century through a period of independence and into the colonial period. Its time of full independence was not long, however, and had foreign powers not intervened, it is possible that internal cleavages might have led to its fissioning. In the latter part of the 19th century, the Boers and British began to take an interest in Swazi succession struggles and they claimed that in settling the disputes, they had prevented the Swazi from exterminating each other. Perhaps this was only a colonial excuse for intervening, and matters might not have gone so far, but the history of other southern Bantu kingdoms demonstrates just how real were the dangers of fissioning. External pressure to settle in one way or another may have kept the kingdom from fracturing; certainly succession struggles gave the foreign powers an excuse to limit Swazi independence. The kingdom was finally brought under complete British domination in 1910.

ATTEMPTS TO MAINTAIN UNITY—I: THE BEMBA

The potentially destructive consequences of succession struggles imply that any technique for finding a successor must cope with the problem of keeping the realm united. Unless it does stay united, of course, a succession can hardly be said to have been successful. How can unity be maintained?

Let us put ourselves into the position of an African king. Many kings ruled with the assistance of their royal relatives, just as the Swazi did. These were the men who could most easily share the royal aura, and as a man rose to power, his relatives would appear as his most reliable supporters. There came a time, however, when the very qualities that made them useful aids to the king turned them instead into dangerous rivals. What inducement might a king offer to his royal kinsmen in order to secure their loyalty? How might he prevent them from challenging his own position or from quarreling destructively with one another? We can pose this question in the form of a puzzle: How can men organize themselves so as to counteract the tendency toward dissolution that threatens a political system at the time of succession? To pose the question in this way suggests a somewhat artificial but still useful way to consider the problem.

Men sometimes pause to survey their options and they sometimes try to decide what to do about their society. Occasionally they even make conscious and explicit decisions about how best to choose a new leader and how best to preserve unity. Such concerns rarely, if ever, attain an overriding importance, however, for men always have complex and contradictory goals. Many Africans, for instance, had no desire at all to see the unity of their tribe preserved, but worked very hard to destroy it instead. The options available to Africans, moreover, were always limited by their restricted knowledge of societies much different from their own. These considerations give my question its artificiality. Nevertheless, I believe the question can still provide a useful framework for discussion. If, given general African conditions, men want to maintain political unity and achieve a peaceful succession, how might they organize their society? Given such goals, it is entirely reasonable to judge some systems as more successful than others.

One possibility would be to offer subordinate chiefs the hope of rising to higher offices and finally to the throne itself. Men might, in other words, be given the kind of stake in the system that would encourage them to remain loyal, seeing more profit in working themselves upward within the system than in rebelling against it. If men could advance within the established order, their separatist inclinations might be held in check. Africa provides examples of such societies.

Before the colonial period, the Bemba constituted the largest and politically most centralized tribe of what is now northeastern Zambia.[3] With their immediate neighbors, the Bemba shared the tradition of having migrated from the Congo in the late 18th century, and in agriculture, kinship, and language, they remained barely distinguishable from the tribes around them. Their land was well watered, but their soil was poor and the 140,000 Bemba were spread thinly—fewer than four people per square mile. Only with difficulty could unity be imposed upon this scattered population and at the time of colonial conquest, their non-Bemba neighbors lacked any centralized government at all.

In fact, it was only acknowledgment of rule by the *citimukulu*, as the king of the Bemba was called, that really set off the Bemba from their otherwise similar neighbors. The citimukulu's power had grown by conquest, and it was consolidated in the 19th century when Arab traders began to penetrate the area and when the citimukulus managed to gain a monopoly over the firearms that the traders made available.

Like the government of the Swazi, Bemba rule was concentrated in a royal clan that provided most of the chiefs. Every Bemba belonged to a clan and one of these, the "crocodile clan," claimed royalty on the grounds of having been first to arrive in their present location after their migration from the Congo. Not only the title of citimukulu, but also an elaborate hierarchy of lesser titles, each of which gave important economic and political rights to the incumbent, was inherited within the royal crocodile clan.

---

[3]On the Bemba, see the various works listed in the Bibliographic Notes (pp. 296–297), especially those by Audrey I. Richards.

The citimukulu had general jurisdiction over all the Bemba country, but this was in turn divided into smaller territories, each with its own name and with more or less fixed boundaries. One territory belonged specifically to the citimukulu and constituted his home ground, while the others were allotted to the holders of other titles in such a way that each territory fell permanently under the jurisdiction of a particular title. Each territory with its chief formed a more or less self-contained unit, and each had its capital, its court, and its circle of messengers, retainers, and advisors, all of which made it an only slightly reduced replica of the national capital of the citimukulu. From the people of his district, each chief could claim both military service and labor, as well as tribute in kind. In return, the chief granted to headmen the right to collect followers and form villages, and the chief maintained a central granary, performed rituals which ensured the welfare of his people, and kept the sacred relics of his district. Most chiefly titles were held by men, but a few female members of the royal clan were given special women's titles, and like the male titles, they conferred jurisdiction over a number of villages.

Up to this point, Bemba organization appears to be much like that of the Swazi. Both granted jurisdiction over territorial divisions to chiefs of the royal clan and in both tribes, the chiefs presided over secondary capitals. The two tribes differed, however, in the means by which rulership over a territory was acquired. Each Swazi chief was normally attached permanently to a single territory, and each territory was usually inherited within a single family. The king's role in appointing new chiefs was usually limited to cases of disputed succession or the replacement of unpopular leaders. Bemba chiefs, by contrast, were appointed from above and instead of permanent tenure in one district, the chiefs could expect to follow one another upward through a series of higher and higher titles, moving each time to a richer and more important territory. At each step, they would lose one group of subjects but gain another, and at the end of the climb was the throne itself. By the time a man became citimukulu, he had usually ruled by turns several less important territories. The prospect of gaining a richer territory and a more august title must have reduced the separatist tendencies that one man might have had if permanently attached to one territory. It is in the accession to these various titles—ultimately to the highest title of all—that the working out of Bemba principles of succession must be seen.

All titles except that of citimukulu were gained by appointment by a higher chief, but the appointment always had to be made within the constraints of some very complex genealogical rules. These rules limited the high chief's freedom, but since the rules, like the Swazi succession rules, were in some ways ambiguous and even self-contradictory, considerable room was left for maneuver and for adjustments to the realities of personal ability and political interest.

The complexities begin with the fact that the Bemba, unlike the Swazi, derived their clan membership from their mothers. The dogma by which the Bemba justified and explained their descent and clan membership, stated that a man or woman derived his "blood" exclusively from his mother. One's heir and successor should be of one's own "blood," a member of one's clan. The clan would include one's brothers, and one's sister's sons, but never a man's own sons, for these always belonged to the clan of their mother instead. Succession to the various Bemba offices and titles followed this matrilineal rule, for rather than passing from father to son, they passed from brother to brother or, where there were no more brothers, from maternal uncle to sororal nephew.

There might also be cousins to consider, for certain cousins (the daughters of one's mother's sister), would also belong to one's clan, and conflicts could arise between the competing claims of nephews and cousins. Since the ties between Bemba men and their sister's sons were very close, older men were sometimes tempted to maneuver their nephews into office at the expense of more distant cousins, but the cousins could try to claim priority by virtue of their generational seniority. Here was one place where the rules of precedence were not entirely clear and where room was left for political intrigue.

Special rules surrounded the acquisition of the highest title. For one thing, it was widely claimed that the man who held the title of *mwamba,* the second highest title in the kingdom, stood next in line for the citimukuluship. At the same time, it was also felt that the citimukuluship should go to the son of a woman who had held the title of *candamukulu.* Women's titles were inherited by quite different genealogical rules than men's titles, however, and in no conceivable way could these various rules be consistently reconciled, though accidents of genealogy might have brought them into harmony from time to time. The real point is that the various contenders for the throne could call upon somewhat varying rules to justify their own claims, and the succession was by no means as well determined as a mechanical laying out of genealogical rules might first make it appear.

The distribution of the lower titles could be strongly influenced by the citimukulu of the moment, but no higher authority could consistently arbitrate among claimants to the citimukuluship. The decision was influenced, however, by a council of about 30 to 40 officials who had important ritual responsibilities in connection with the monarchy. In particular, the council took charge of an elaborate series of funeral and investiture rituals which were required when a new citimukulu took office. The members of the council occupied their offices by hereditary right, each office being acquired according to the same rules as the major titles. The special ritual prerogatives of each office were largely secret, so it was impossbile for the rituals of investiture to be conducted properly without the cooperation of all the council members, each of whom contributed his own bit of secret knowledge. Though in large measure a ritual body, the council seems to have had considerable influence upon the choice of successor, though the exact manner by which its members exerted their influence is by no means clear from the published reports. Irregularity in succession, and even forceful seizure of the throne occurred rather regularly, and the council seems to have been flexible enough to bow to the inevitable. The council would invest the winner in intrigue or in violence with the dignity of office that only its rituals could confer, but it does seem likely that on some occasions it could encourage a regular succession and help to smooth over a difficult transition. This probably helped to keep the succession to the citimukuluship more regular and less subject to improper deviations than was the case with the subordinate titles.

One factor that prevented complete regularity was the occasional refusal of a man to accept a title for which he qualified. A man could apparently refuse a title without jeopardizing his future right to a still higher title, and this introduced considerable irregularity into the lines of succession. However, it was the machinations of various interested parties in their attempt to influence appointments, and particularly the interest of higher chiefs in securing the appointment of loyal subordinates, that were primarily responsible for keeping the succession from following completely orderly rules. Men who relinquished junior titles when receiving a promotion, for instance, could often influence the choice of their own successor to the junior position.

The most important titles were all held by closely related members of the royal clan. Most qualified men within this group could be accommodated with a title, and all male titles were supposed to pass down according to the same rules. Since a man could hold only a single title at any one time, the death of somebody high up in the hierarchy might result in the promotion of several people below him, each moving into a higher position. The result was a sort of follow-the-leader in which a man would advance steadily toward the top office, and it would seem that the primary requirement for attaining the throne would be to get in line at the bottom and then wait patiently until everyone ahead had died.

The formal genealogical rules and the facts of what actually happened in successive struggles are too tortured to present in detail here, but for the benefit of readers who care to fight their way through them, I give some details in Appendix I. More immediately important is a summary of the results.

With each generation, the royal family had an inexorable tendency to enlarge. Among the Bemba where royal inheritance passed through women rather than through men, it could never expand as explosively as among the Swazi, where every king had dozens of wives and dozens of sons; but even among the Bemba, the family steadily grew. This meant that if the rules of inheritance were followed strictly, each succeeding generation would include a larger number of men among whom the titles would circulate. Many men would die before reaching the highest office, but reigns would still become shorter and shorter, and the kinship ties binding the eligible men to each other would become ever more attenuated. In Bemba history, it soon developed that the claims of closely related nephews to the titles of their uncles began to take precedence over the claims of the ever more distantly related cousins. This meant that various titles came gradually to be lodged in particular branches of the royal family. By the early part of this century, the royal family was drawing apart rather decisively into two branches, each descended from a different sister. Each branch was coming to feel that it had a special claim on one of the two titles that ranked just below that of citimukulu.

A number of lesser titles also came to be attached to one or the other branch of the family, and with the passage of generations they could not help pulling apart, each carrying its own titles with it. Accidents of genealogy might have retarded or hastened this process, but sooner or later it was bound to develop. For a time, the diverging branches of the family might even look upon the division of titles as reasonable and equitable since each branch could then claim certain titles as more or less its own. The highest title of all, that of citimukulu, could never be shared in this way, however, for no branch would be as willing to let it completely escape their control and all would look with special care upon decisions concerning the citimukuluship.

In fact, neither genealogical rules, order of chiefly precedence, nor the ritual council, were capable of preventing the office of citimukulu from being subject to periodic forceful seizure and usurpation. The royal family of the 20th century owes its dominance to a man named Cileshe Cepela who seized the throne from a kinsman several generations ago. When Cileshe Cepela's mentally deficient younger brother was, according to proper genealogical rule, invested with the throne, the situation was so unstable that a nephew who was not even senior in his own generation was able to seize the office. After his nephew's death, the title descended quite regularly several times, but eventually a dispute broke out between the two branches of the family. (See Appendix I for details.) When Citimukulu Ponde died in 1922, no members of his own generation survived. His own nephew claimed the title on the grounds that their branch of the royal family had by then acquired it by permanent right, but a more distantly related cousin asserted a claim on the grounds of belonging to the senior branch of the family. The more distant cousin also claimed precedence by his prior possession of the title of mwamba and by his mother's title of candamukulu, although not all earlier rulers had shared these attributes.

There was really little to choose among the competing claims of the nephew and the cousin and the dispute was finally settled by the British government. Earlier, such a dispute might possibly have been settled by the council of ritual officials, but it seems more likely that the opponents would have resorted to force. By this time, the second and third titles, mwamba and nkulu, were in the firm possession of the different branches of the family, and this gave each branch its own separate power base. The only real resolution to the argument would have been military defeat by one side or the other and a drastic reduction in the power of the losers.

From what is known, it appears that this is approximately what happened at the time of the earlier usurpation by Cileshe Cepela. This man had been one of the senior chiefs, but a collateral kinsman was then citimukulu. The exact relationship of Cileshe Cepela to this earlier citimukulu is no longer remembered, but presumably they were members of different branches of the royal family. They probably possessed titles that had drifted apart into their separate branches. The rebellion of Cileshe Cepela succeeded not only in giving him the throne, but even more important, it resulted in the reconcentration of the other major titles into a single small family group. Having seized supreme power, Cileshe Cepela consolidated it by giving his own kinsmen the important titles. The governing core of the nation was then united.

When the details of Bemba history are examined, it can be shown that in every generation there was some appeal to force in claiming and distributing titles. It seems that Bemba succession rules could not be applied consistently and a resort to force could not be avoided. Allowing men to follow each other through a series of titles may have slowed the kingdom's fragmentation, but it could not halt it entirely.

It is natural to ask to what extent the special characteristics of Bemba succession resulted from their somewhat unusual practice of royal matrilineal descent, but on the whole, it does not seem to have been crucial. In some other society, patrilineal kinsmen might follow each other through a series of titles, just as did the matrilineal kinsmen of the Bemba. In a patrilineal society too, the royal family would enlarge and disputes could arise between the competing claims of sons, brothers, and cousins. Titles could drift apart into separate branches of the family until only a forceful coup could reassemble them. The effects of matrilineal descent do not seem to have been decisive.

The Bemba practice of allowing royal chiefs to rise through a series of higher and higher titles offered a way of counteracting the separatist tendencies of royal chiefs, but it is clear that this technique could do no more than postpone separatist tendencies. If force had not been periodically used to reassemble the titles within a set of closely related kinsmen, then it would be only a matter of time before the titles would drift so far apart, and the title holders would become so weakly bound to one another that the unity of the kingdom would finally be threatened.

If the Bemba technique is insufficient to maintain unity, is there another technique that would be better? Would it be possible to plan a political system that would minimize fissiparous tendencies?

ATTEMPTS TO MAINTAIN UNITY II: THE NUPE

One plausible suggestion would be to insist that the highest title alternate between the major branches of the royal family. If it could alternate in a regular way, then each branch would retain an interest in the throne, and so it might be less inclined either to secede or to risk losing everything in a civil war. Each branch might be willing to accept a period of rule by another if it could be confident of retrieving the title later. The citimukuluship showed some tendency to oscillate between the two major branches of the Bemba royal family, or at least it had less tendency to become fixed in a single branch than did the secondary titles. But the Bemba seem never to have explicitly recognized the transfer of the throne from one branch to the other as a useful device for keeping the family united, and in the absence of a rule, anyone fearing exclusion was tempted to resort to arms. Some other Africans quite deliberately arranged to have the throne circulate from one branch of the family to another, and this seems to have been intended precisely to preserve the unity of the ever expanding royal family.

West Africa was the home of the largest and most complex of the pre-European African kingdoms, and among these, few were more extensive or powerful than the Kingdom of Nupe.[4] The Nupe traditionally traced their kingdom's origins to the 15th century, but the kingdom assumed a new form in the early 19th century when the Nupe area was conquered by the Fulani, a mobile and conquering Muslim people whose influence was felt in a wide band across the northern fringe of Negro Africa. The Fulani conquerors intermarried extensively with the Nupe, and they came to share the Nupe language and most of Nupe culture. Although they began

---

[4]S. F. Nadel, *A Black Byzantium* (London: Oxford University Press, 1942).

as conquering foreigners, they worked themselves into a position not much different from that of the Swazi or Bemba royal clans.

The 300,000 people of central Nigeria who were embraced by the Nupe state were by no means uniform in their cultural traditions. Regional variation, foreign enclaves of craftsmen and traders, and foreign slaves either purchased or captured in the interminable wars made for a cosmopolitan population and the foreign Fulani conquerors constituted only one among many heterogeneous elements. The political system the Fulani conquerors imposed, however, served to give some unity to the kingdom and helped to foster some degree of common sentiment among its varied people.

The man who founded the Fulani dynasty was Mallam Dendo. He first built his power by gathering a rather mixed collection of followers, and he then threw his weight into a factional struggle that divided the heirs of the previous Nupe ruling house. By adroit alliances, he built up his own influence until it surpassed that of the former rulers, but he never took over the symbols of kingship and he advised his sons to rule only in the name of the previous ruling house. Within a few years of his death in 1833, however, his second son, after suppressing one final attempt of the previous house to regain its lost position, assumed the titles of royalty, giving formal recognition to the effective power his father had built up and he had inherited and consolidated.

The first Fulani king of Nupe to rule in his own right, then, was Usman Zaki, the second son of Mallam Dendo (see Figure 2-2), and not even his accession was uncontested. In particular his youngest half brother, Masaba, was ambitious and popular, and he claimed the throne on the grounds that he alone was a real Nupe since his mother, unlike Usman Zaki's mother, was a Nupe. Masaba's mixed descent could symbolize the fusion of the

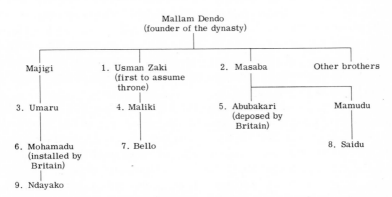

Figure 2–2. Nupe Genealogy. (Reigning monarchs are numbered in order of succession.)

Fulani with the earlier Nupe inhabitants. Masaba gained wide support, including that of the displaced contenders of the previous dynasty, and he led two revolts against his elder half brother, the second one, in 1841, being successful. Usman Zaki was forced to leave the kingdom, and he took Umaru, the son of their eldest brother Majigi, with him.

Nupe history then becomes a tale of constant war against external enemies, internal rebellions by Nupe factions, and fratricidal intrigue among the conquerors. A mercenary general of Masaba rebelled, and this persuaded Usman Zaki and his nephew Umaru to return from exile and to support their kinsman. After a long war, the combined strength of Usman Zaki, Umaru, and Masaba was too much for the rebellious general, and the brothers and their nephew, having been forced into union, were now able to rule with greater harmony.

Comparative peace ensued. Usman Zaki was reinstated on the throne, and the town of Bida at the center of the kingdom was made the capital. It became a cosmopolitan center with enclaves of foreign traders, crafts-men, and slaves, elaborate markets, and the palaces of the kings and nobles. Usman Zaki ruled until his death about 1860 when he was again followed by Masaba, who reigned until 1873. It was then the turn of the nephew, Umaru, who reigned until 1884. By then a number of revolts had been put down, the boundaries of the kingdom were extended by conquest, and the new dynasty was firmly established.

Mallam Dendo had several other sons and grandsons, but it was these three men, Usman Zaki, Masaba, and Umaru who were most successful both in battle and in political affairs, and each of the three founded a royal house. The other sons of Mallam Dendo never gained the throne and they and their descendants lost whatever claim they might initially have had upon it. Instead, the three houses, those founded by two sons and one grandson of Mallam Dendo, came to take turns with the throne, passing it around in strict rotation. Even the nation's capital, Bida, took on a form which symbolized this tripartite division. The city was centrally located in the kingdom and was itself divided into three areas, each with the palace of one of the three royal houses, and each house also controlled its own territory outside of the capital.

It is not clear to what extent this three-way division and the circulating pattern of royal inheritance followed the conscious plan of the three original founders, though the system has something of that appearance. Circu-lating succession was found in a number of other west African kingdoms, and on a much smaller scale, a similar system was used in some Nupe villages, where different branches of the same family might take turns with the headmanship. Of course, the villagers may have copied their rotating headmanship from the practice of the royal family, but, in any event, the royal Nupe system was by no means unique in its region of Africa, and it offered some decisive advantages to the ruling dynasty. Circulation of the throne brought an end to the wars that the brothers had waged against each other, and it probably helped them to monopolize power and to freeze out other members of the royal family.

Umaru died in 1884 and was succeeded first by Maliki, the son of Usman Zaki, and then in 1895 by Abubakari, the son of Masaba. During Abubakari's reign, European power, in the form of the British Niger Company, grew to dominance, and the Nupe capital was captured in 1897. Abubakari was deposed, and the new European government appointed Mohamadu, the son of Umaru in his place. Mohamadu's succession took place with the help of the Niger Company, but it was in line with earlier dynastic practices. In fact, it was a threat to the regular circulation of the throne that allowed the Niger Company to gain its foothold. Abubakari had declined to give Mohamadu the title of heir presumptive, to which he felt entitled, and this led Mohamadu to drag his feet in a battle between the Nupe and the Niger Company troops. Mohamadu thus helped the Niger Company to achieve victory, and the company, in return, rewarded Mohamadu with the throne.

After this time, foreign power was predominant in the Nupe country, and the course of kingship no longer depended primarily upon internal forces. Under British auspices, the three main branches of the royal house continued to take turns on the throne, and while British influence may have made this exchange more regular than it would otherwise have been, the pattern had at least been inaugurated before their time, and we can understand something of the forces that kept the rotation going.

Not only the throne, but many lesser titles as well were rotated among the three royal Nupe houses. As among the Bemba, a lower title would be relinquished when a man assumed a higher one, and it was by working himself upward through the various titles that a man came ever closer to the throne. When men became sick or too feeble with age to exercise the duties of their offices, they would resign their title. The resignation or death of someone high in the hierarchy would result in a general reassignment of offices, and men gradually percolated upward through the hierarchy of titles.

At any particular time, each major royal house was expected to hold one of the three top titles: *etsu, shaba,* and *kpotu.* The etsu was king, the most powerful man in the realm. The title of shaba was ordinarily held by the heir presumptive, the man in the next house who would take over as the new etsu after the last one had died, and this more or less automatic succession helped to avoid a dangerous interregnum. This implied far less ambiguity about the heir presumptive than is found in most political systems, and it is not entirely clear how Nupe kept their heirs from being as dangerous a threat to the throne as other heirs have been. Perhaps the fact that he belonged to an entirely different house removed him, like the leader of an opposition party, from too direct involvement with the ruler; but the rivalry between Abubakari and Mohamadu during the colonial conquest shows that the same kinds of forces acted here as elsewhere and that the designation of an heir could pose problems for the Nupe. The third main title, kpotu, was held by the leading member of the third house, and many other titles were divided among the three major houses.

Appointment to titles, however, depended more upon the exercise of power, and skill at court intrigue, than upon strict genealogical rules. Whichever house was in power was able to build up its own stock of titles, so that in 1936 the house of Masaba which had only recently lost the throne held 17 titles; the house of Umaru which had replaced it had worked its holdings up to 14, while the house of Usman Zaki which had been out of office for the longest time held only 10.

Appointments and promotions were conferred by the king, but he consulted the royal princes and other important men of the state. Appointments were well worth struggling for, since, as among the Bemba, the titles carried rights over territories that were administered as fiefs, and as a man gained ever higher titles, he also gained the income of the more lucrative territories that went with them. Nupe title holders usually maintained their residence at the capital city, and they developed only weak personal ties with their domains. Nevertheless, great wealth could be extracted from these territories, and the title holders had (from their point of view) satisfyingly little in the way of reciprocal responsibilities to their subjects.

Taxes were actually collected by bailiffs and local representatives of the title holders. They kept a small share for themselves and passed the rest on to the title holder, who in turn passed some on to the king. Enough was left to the title holder to support himself and a sizeable retinue. The title holder was responsible to the king for law and order in his domain, and each lord could muster a military force of volunteers, mercenaries, and slaves, both infantry and cavalry.

In conformity with Nupe patrilineal descent, younger brothers and sons had some claim upon the lesser titles of their fathers and older brothers, but genealogy never set sharp limits to the inheritance of titles, and the higher titles had to rotate among the different branches of the royal family. Genealogical rules could not define this rotation in any precise matter. Rather, bribery, intrigue, and royal favoritism all had a part in determining appointments. The levers of power and the channels of influence must have been many and complex. Influence depended in part upon the ability of each individual title holder to build up his own retinue. Powerful and wealthy men could become patrons of lesser men, conferring political support or economic benefits in return for varied sorts of assistance. Men of rank collected henchmen, serfs, and slaves, and these, together with kinsmen and friends, would support their protector and patron. Lesser patrons in their turn would attach themselves to even more powerful royal patrons, until the important men of the kingdom came to be divided along factional lines of patronage and clientship. To build and cling to power, a man would have to act with finesse, using both the economic resources of his territory and his influence at court to gain and hold the loyalty of clients. At the same time, he would have to use the power of his clients to increase his influence at court, always trying to maneuver his way to a higher title and a more lucrative fief.

In this nest of intrigue, the single stabilizing principle was the circulation of the top offices among the three ruling houses. Once set into motion, it is not difficult to see how this rule might be perpetuated. Kingship gave considerable power to the man in office and to his own kinsmen, but no king could risk the complete alienation of the members of the other two main houses. In fact, it is plausible to guess that the two houses which were temporarily out of power would tend to form an alliance against the ruling house. A king would hesitate to act too arrogantly in advancing the power of his own kinsmen lest he invite their united opposition, and the members of his own house would always have to think of their own future status under succeeding reigns. The balance of power implicit in the arrangement seems to have been well understood by the Nupe, and it was well regarded for its ability to inhibit the tendency toward tyranny. A king who did move toward tyranny would evoke a popular reaction in favor of his successor, and this would help to insure that the succession would follow the proper circulating rule. Nevertheless, the system was in precarious balance, and it did not serve to keep an effective long-term peace. The unending rivalry repeatedly erupted into armed battle.

Rivalry among the houses may have been dampened down by circulating the throne, but there was still the danger of rivalry *within* the houses. The kingdom did not retain its independence long enough for this problem to become acute, but each house would eventually have expanded, and sooner or later competing claims within the houses would have been raised. For such disputes, the Nupe system provided no clear resolution.

The Nupe circulating succession had some rather obvious similarities to the alternating succession achieved by party politics in a modern electoral democracy. Both systems grant to other factions a legitimate aspiration to office. In a way quite unusual for hereditary monarchies, the Nupe factions could retain a loyalty to the political system even when out of power, and this loyalty need not have been undermined by its antagonism to the particular faction that happened to be in office. Both among the Nupe and in a party democracy, an alternate group of rulers waits in the wings ready to rule. The availability of this group helps to check the almost inevitable tendency of a ruler to become increasingly autocratic. The faction out of power always serves as a point around which those who are dissatisfied with the present ruler can rally. Both systems require the ruler of the moment to acknowledge, at least in principle, that his own faction may someday be out of power and to soften his actions with this prospect in mind.

The existence of alternative ruling houses went a considerable way toward legitimizing opposition and disagreement, and as in any modern party state, Nupe appointments involved a good deal of haggling and horse trading. But with no device such as elections, to which disagreements could be ultimately appealed, the only final settlement of a serious dispute was a resort to force. In theory, the right to direct force lay with the king, but the leaders of the other two royal houses, and lesser title holders as well, were all able to raise armed contingents. Indeed, the balance of power upon which the Nupe system depended would hardly have been possible had armed power not been widely distributed, but the result was that factional disputes easily grew into armed clashes. The history of Nupe, in the decades before the British arrived to impose their peace, was one of incessant fighting. Direct rebellion against the throne was dangerous, but a wide range of nobles, officials, chiefs, retainers, henchmen, and headmen could throw their weight in one direction or another in the unceasing jockeying for position. Feudal lords attacked the territory of their neighbors. Armies had to use force to extract taxes from feudal domains. Losers were deprived of office and heavily punished. Winners were rewarded with expanded territories. For a few decades the continuity of the kingdom and of its ruling houses were maintained, but the system hardly had long-range staying power, and the Nupe paid a high price in violence for their check upon concentrated tyranny.

The Nupe "solution" to the problem of a quarreling royal family therefore, met with only limited success. As with the Swazi and the Bemba, a time came when quarrels among Nupe royal kinsmen brought violence and bloodshed to the kingdom. It is ironic that kinship, which under some circumstances seems the best of instruments by which to bring unity to a political system, becomes at another time the most destructive and divisive of forces. For one ruler, kinsmen are the most valuable and trustworthy of allies. For another, they become the most dangerous of rivals. There may finally be a time when kinsmen become so dangerous that only one solution will seem possible to the monarch—eliminate them. To kill one's royal half brothers is a heroic cure to the destructive rivalry they pose, but it is a cure to which monarchs in many parts of the world have been driven.

THE TENDENCY TO CHANGE: THE BAGANDA

When Bemba titles drifted apart and when the Nupe throne circulated among more and more distant kinsmen, the political system had to undergo changes. The later chapters of this book will touch upon many examples in which the succession practices of one period gave way to new practices in the next. Cumulative changes have often carried the political system further and further from its origins, and the very difficulty of settling a succession on one occasion has often led men to reorganize their government so that something different will be possible the next time. A good example from Africa is that of the Baganda, a tribe from which we have data that covers an unusually long time span.[5]

The Baganda were the most powerful people in the territory which has become the modern nation of Uganda. Indeed, they gave their name to the new country. In the latter half of the 19th century, the population of the Baganda kingdom may have been as high as three million, but this was reduced by war, famine, and disease, and by the early 20th century when they formed a British protectorate, their population had dropped to about one million. They have a long traditional history of a unified monarchy, and regard their present *kabaka* or king to be the 35th of his line, 24 generations removed from the founder. The earlier history of the kingdom is known only through oral traditions, but except for the earliest period, these traditions are ample and demonstrate an impressive internal consistency. In particular, the patterns of royal succession in the latter part of the dynasty seem quite clear.

Baganda territorial administration differed from that of many other African kingdoms in that the chiefs were not selected from the king's royal kinsmen. Among the Swazi, Bemba, and Nupe, royal territorial chiefs came to pose a serious threat to the unity of a kingdom, so the Baganda motives for excluding royal brothers and cousins from chieftaincies are easily understood. Territorial chiefs sometimes gained office by heredity within nonroyal clans, but the kabakas tended to acquire an increasing power of appointment and dismissal over their chiefs. By their ability to make their own selection, the kabakas were able to inhibit the develop-

---

[5]On the Baganda, I rely particularly upon the work of Martin Southwold. References to books and articles by Southwold and others are given in the Bibliographic Notes (p. 297).

ment of hereditary power in other families, and the Baganda territorial chiefs probably had less independence than those of the other kingdoms.

Scattered across the kingdom's territorial divisions, however, were about 50 patrilineal clans. Each clan included several sub-clans; the sub-clans were composed of small groups of related families, and each clan and each sub-clan had a hereditary head. It was felt best to let these clan headships circulate among a fairly wide group of kinsmen, and, like the Nupe, the Baganda recognized clearly that by circulating these headships, they could keep the various branches of a clan or sub-clan united. To circulate headships was an expression of clan solidarity, and it was the clans and their segments, rather than the territorial divisions, that formed the fundamental political building blocks of the state and that claimed the first loyalties of the people.

Like clan membership, the throne was also inherited in the patrilineal line, from brother to brother, or from father to son, but the royal family was not felt to form the same type of clan as those of the commoners. Each of the other clans had a totem, for instance, but the royalty as a group had none. Instead, each member of the royal family would observe the totem of his mother. This seemed to symbolize some sort of distribution of the members of the royal family among their various maternal clans, and it simultaneously symbolized the lack of unity within the royal family itself. Unlike the commoner clans where unity was emphasized, the Baganda expected members of the royalty to quarrel, and, in particular, they were expected to compete for the throne.

The competition among the king's royal relatives made it quite impossible to trust the princes with territorial administration, but this left them with little to strive for except the throne itself. Thus, the same political developments that allowed the kabaka to appoint and dismiss his commoner territorial administrators and thereby minimize the danger of territorial dismemberment, also made rivalry for the throne even more intense. Instead of forming an alliance whose members helped each other to dominate all other clans, as was ideally the case of the Swazi, Bemba, and Nupe royal clans, the members of the Baganda royal family sought allies among the commoners while competing with each other.

Baganda set some limits to competition for the throne by strictly disqualifying everyone except men whose father or paternal grandfather had already reigned. They also seem not to have allowed the throne to move back to an older generation. Thus, once a man of a junior generation gained the throne, all his uncles and all the other more distant kinsmen of their generation were forever disqualified. These rules served gradually to prune off the more distant members of the royal family, but since the kabakas had many wives and many sons, the number of potential competitors for the throne could still be very large. All the sons and all the younger brothers of the late king were left in competition, and it was among them that succession wars were periodically fought.

The most important of the kabaka's appointed officials held the title of *katikkiro,* sometimes translated as "prime minister." One of the katikkiro's many responsibilities was to help select the successor after the old king had died. The Baganda shared firmly in the widespread opinion that it was dangerous to designate the heir while the king still lived. Once designated, the Baganda expected him to try to seize the throne by violence, and the many occasions on which plausible heirs really did mount rebellions fully justified their fears. In an attempt to forestall rebellion, they delayed the decision until the king's death. The katikkiro was then expected to work for a smooth transfer of power, and since he was always a commoner, he could not compete for the position himself.

Upon the death of a king, the katikkiro would consult the various chiefs and clan heads, and while he was probably free to designate any eligible prince, he would have been rash to go against the wishes of the more powerful men of the kingdom. Thus, a sort of crude electoral process grew up, through which important men could bring their influence to bear upon the choice of the next king. Personal qualifications would affect their preferences. The ages of the candidates and their reputations for cruelty or wisdom might be taken into account. But all other things being equal, a powerful commoner would most like to see the choice fall upon his own sister's son, or at least upon the son of a clan sister. The new king, observing his mother's totem, would then have powerful bonds with her family and her clan. Since each monarch took queens from many clans, the princes always had varied affiliations. This meant that different clan leaders would come naturally to support different princes. With about 50 clans in the kingdom, no single clan could hope to dominate the situation, but clans could try to form alliances to promote a promising candidate. A sufficiently powerful clan coalition might persuade the katikkiro to choose its candidate, but rival coalitions would be likely to form and any coalition that was sufficiently unhappy with the katikkiro's choice might be tempted to help an unsuccessful prince mount a rebellion. During one period of Baganda history, rebellions occurred in virtually every generation.

Succession wars seem to have been most frequent during the middle period of the kingdom. The period began with a disastrous war with the neighboring kingdom of Bunyoro, and it may be that the stringent military requirements of the time encouraged the choice of mature men with good military prospects. On a number of occasions, certainly, mature brothers of the dead king gained the throne in preference to less mature sons. The result was that the sons of former kings grew to maturity during the reigns of their uncles and then faced frustrating delays in realizing their own hopes for the throne. As sons of former monarchs matured, rivalry with the reigning uncle would become intense, and the result was a series of debilitating wars.

The Baganda never attempted circulating success along Nupe lines, for the Baganda felt less need to keep the royal family united. Perhaps the royal family was so secure in its royalty that no such devices were needed to keep it in power. Princes competed for first place instead of agreeing to take turns with it. Since all brothers were equally eligible, anyone not chosen first had every motive for contesting the choice with arms. With no possibility even for becoming a subordinate territorial chief, where else might his ambition find outlet? Such rebels were able to recruit supporters from among disaffected commoner clans, and often they were successful in seizing the throne. The violence inherent in the system led up to a climax in the period preceding the accession of the 27th kabaka, Ssemakookiro, and the history of these conflicts deserves a brief summary.

Mawanda, the man who was to become the 22nd kabaka, quarreled with his predecessor, Kikulwe (see Figure 2-3). These men may have been half brothers although that is not certain. Kikulwe tried by trickery to have Mawanda killed, but Mawanda avoided the trap, collected followers, and mounted a successful rebellion. Mawanda became the 22nd kabaka but he was later overthrown and killed when some younger princes rebelled. Mawanda's nephew, Mwanga, then became the 23rd kabaka. Mwanga reigned for only a few days before being killed in his turn, and his younger full brother, Namugala, was then placed upon the throne. Namu-

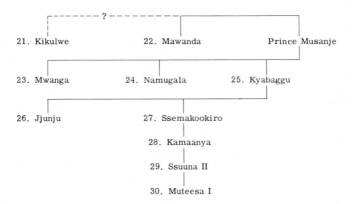

Figure 2–3. Genealogy of the kings of Buganda—middle period. (Reigning monarchs are numbered in order of succession.)

gala soon quarreled with a still younger brother, Kyabaggu, who proceeded to practice sorcery upon the monarch in the hope of removing him and gaining the office himself. Namugala tried to stop Kyabaggu's sorcery, but when he could not do so he abdicated in favor of the younger man, and Kyabaggu became the 25th kabaka.

Kyabaggu was the third in his generation to reign and before he could die peacefully, the men of the next generation grew restless. Kyabaggu was killed in his turn and after another succession war, his son Jjunju defeated his half brothers and emerged victorious as the 26th kabaka. It was probably Jjunju's military strength that also prevented his cousins, the sons of Mwanga and Namugala, from asserting their claims to the throne. Jjunju was the new ruler, but he remained jealous of his younger brother Ssemakookiro and he even had one of Ssemakookiro's wives killed when she refused his advances. Jjunju sent Ssemakookiro into exile, probably hoping that he would perish, but Ssemakookiro raised an army instead and returned to depose his older brother.

Ssemakookiro gained the throne as the 27th kabaka. He came to power after almost unceasing succession struggles and it must have been brutally clear that his remaining kinsmen posed the most serious threat to his own security. He acted decisively to forestall this threat. His soldiers had killed his predecessor Jjunju, and he then had Jjunju's sons and most of his own sons killed. When a rebellion was mounted in the name of his son Kamaanya, he had Kamaanya's mother killed along with her male relatives who had supported their nephew. He imprisoned Kamaanya and tried in various indirect ways to bring about his death, but he stopped short of a straightforward execution, and Kamaanya finally managed to survive. The evidence suggests that kings were strongly restrained from taking the life of the heir apparent, and Kamaanya may well have been regarded as occupying that position. Ssemakookiro did eliminate most of his rivals, however, and he lived to an advanced age—no mean achievement for a Baganda monarch of his day.

Ssemakookiro's successors followed his example and executed most of their potential rivals, particularly their half brothers. Those they did not kill were at least imprisoned. These measures brought an end to rebellion. Ssemakookiro's own son, Kamaanya, did have to battle with a brother after their father's death, but once on the throne he was not again threatened. Stability was gained at the cost of cold-blooded execution. Ssuuna II, the 29th kabaka, and the grandson of Ssemakookiro, is said to have had all but two of his 60 half brothers killed, and large numbers were also killed by other monarchs. These radical measures went far to stabilize the political system of the kingdom, and the Baganda were ruled by a series of remarkably strong and secure kings. So strong and stable was the kingdom that a good deal of its political organization survived into the period of the British protectorate.

In passing judgment upon the Baganda, we have to balance the death of the princes against the deaths that might otherwise have occurred in succession battles; but quite apart from the fate of a king's brothers, the Baganda "solution" to the problem of rebellious royal rivals had at least one serious inherent defect. By drastically reducing the number of men qualified for the throne, the danger arose that on some occasion no fully qualified man at all would be available. Had Kamaanya, the 29th kabaka, died soon after he gained the throne, the only eligible candidates would have been a brother who had stooped to conspiring with their Bunyoro enemies and Kamaanya's own three infant sons. Later, the absence of any suitable mature candidate finally brought a 1-year-old infant to the throne.

When the choice is so limited that children can gain the throne, there is also a chance that incompetent men may succeed. Whatever their faults, succession wars do at least have the virtue that they are usually won by vigorous men. When weak kabakas were placed on the throne, others had to exercise authority in their place, and the office of katikkiro rose to fill the vacuum. The katikkiro had always been entrusted with the responsibility for designating a successor, and this placed the katikkiro in a strong position. When the king was weak or very young, the katikkiro's influence grew. Kings sometimes had to spend years disentangling themselves from the katikkiro they had inherited, and the final step in the practical displacement of the kings by the katikkiros came with the constitution of 1955. The kabaka was then formally designated as a constitutional monarch, while political responsibility was given to the katikkiro. This step was, of course, taken under British rule and with British guidance, but it simply confirmed a tendency that was long inherent in the development of the monarchy.

The Baganda illustrate the difficulty of maintaining a consistent pattern of succession. The methods used in one period seemed to lead inexorably to new methods in the next. Warfare encouraged succession by brothers but this led to usurpation by nephews; repeated usurpation finally persuaded monarchs to kill off their rivals; the killing of rivals brought immature kings to the throne; weak kings allowed power to shift away from the old office and to become concentrated in the office of the katikkiro. Other kingdoms have undergone a comparable progression.

The basic dilemma of the Baganda political system is clear: When able and qualified potential successors are available, they are likely to mount succession wars; once they are eliminated, the office of the king must sooner or later weaken. It is a dilemma that we will find to be true of many other political systems. With the passing of power from the king to the katikkiro, morever, we have the first of many examples in which power shifted not to a new man in an old office, but instead to an entirely separate office.

CYCLES

If succession systems and the political systems within which they are embedded have a tendency to change over the course of generations, the only way to maintain a faith in stability or in long-term political continuity is to suppose that eventually the changing patterns complete a cycle and return to their starting point. In that way the changing system can be seen as maintaining some sort of enduring structure while the particular political patterns of a single era simply represent phases of that enduring cycle.

It has been suggested, for instance, that the Bemba political system was inherently cyclical.[6] Periodic seizures of power followed by reconcentration of titles among a group of close kinsmen have been claimed to be among its necessary features. This would imply a cycle of four or five generations during which time the titles would gradually drift apart to an ever more distantly related set of men until finally the unity of the nation would be threatened. At this point, somebody would have to seize the throne, collect the titles for his close kinsmen, and begin the cycle again. This cycle seems plausible, but our knowledge of earlier Bemba history is, unfortunately, so sketchy that we cannot know how closely the facts fit such a pattern. A cycle of this sort would imply that the formal rules of Bemba succession were incapable of permanent application.

If any continuity of tradition is to be attributed to the Bemba, it is a continuity that can only be seen on a minimum time scale of several generations, the time required to complete a cycle of drifting apart and reconcentration of titles. There are, however, serious difficulties that should make us cautious about taking cycles of this sort too seriously. In the Bemba case, for instance, we ought to wonder whether reunification is the only possible sequel to the drifting apart of titles. Might not titles drift apart so far that the various branches of the royal family would each carry its own political domain into independence? With time, instead of a single branch of the family reimposing unity, it might happen that several branches of the family would lead the kingdom to fragment. Of course, it might happen that a new state would later be constructed from the broken pieces of the old. The centralizing processes that repeatedly led to the formation of African states could again assert themselves as a new kingdom arose. New leaders might weld old fragments into a new system, and here again, we

---

[6]Max Gluckman, "Succession and Civil War Among the Bemba," *Order and Rebellion in Tribal Africa* (London: Cohen and West, 1963).

might visualize a political cycle, but now instead of simply the drifting apart and reconcentration of titles within the same kingdom, we have the possibility of the collapse of one kingdom followed by the rise of another.

The Bemba had neighbors who shared much of their culture, but they did not acknowledge the leadership of the Bemba king and so they were not considered to be Bemba. If one perceives a strictly Bemba cycle in which the royal family alternately expands and contracts, but in which some degree of political centralization is retained, then one may be tempted to credit the Bemba with a fundamentally different structure from their culturally similar, but politically disunified neighbors. On the other hand, if one admits that the centralized Bemba might shatter into decentralized fragments and that their decentralized neighbors might someday coalesce into a more centralized state, and that phases of centralization and decentralization might follow each other in cycles, then the Bemba and their neighbors could seem to represent different phases of the same political cycle. No longer would they seem to have fundamentally different structures at all.

Any view of culture change that can be so easily applied to such different phenomena, and result in such differing interpretations, ought to arouse our suspicions. We can read cycles into phenomena with little difficulty, but whether these cycles represent anything but an exercise in the observer's imagination may be doubted. The question of cycles will arise again in Chapter 4 in which we will face the task of interpreting the rise and fall of Chinese dynasties, and once again we may come to doubt the interpretive utility of the concept.

ALTERNATIVES FOR SUCCESSION

The African tribes whose succession systems have been outlined in this chapter illustrate a number of general points that deserve summary. All four tribes were led by a single top office, but, with the partial exception of the Nupe, one man or one office was never allowed to assume an unambiguous second position. An unambiguous second would have posed too severe a threat to the top man. The absence of a clear second implies the absence of a clear line of succession, and the result was that all the tribes underwent periodic succession struggles. Everywhere, these struggles encouraged rebellion and even fragmentation. Struggling men always needed allies and supporters. These might be found among kinsmen, but reliable allies might be sought elsewhere too, and in some cases complex networks of patronage and clientship grew up that crossed freely over kinship divisions. Complex procedures were developed for selecting the new king and for bridging the interregna, procedures which were often modeled upon those used in that society for selecting lesser leaders. Elaborate rituals might be used to give the procedures sanctity and to legitimize the choice. No procedure and no ritual, however, could consistently avoid violence. Hoping to improve their procedures, men introduced changes into their political rules, but no innovation could solve every problem. Rather, each change led to new problems and these, in turn, led to new changes. In looking at societies in other regions of the world, we will repeatedly see these same forces at work.

In considering Africa, however, we must be struck most of all by the consistent reliance upon heredity. Everywhere, heredity was the main justification for claiming office. Like dozens of other tribes in Africa, and like kingdoms throughout the world, the four tribes considered here were governed by hereditary monarchies. They differed from one another in many ways, but their common reliance upon heredity suggests that heredity has held some very substantial advantages over alternative principles by which office might be transferred.

We can consider the factors that encouraged the similarities among these tribes and also the factors that made them different by proposing a series of concrete alternatives that political systems have to face. In one way or another—rarely, to be sure, by any self-conscious process of decision making—each political system has to choose among these alternatives. Each alternative may bring competing benefits, but one seems often to have a slight competitive advantage. We can consider the several alternatives in turn.

1. One-Man versus Diffuse or Collective Leadership

Succession poses a problem because the departure of a leader leaves a vacuum of power at an important point in the political system. This vacuum might, in principle, be minimized either by having, like the Siuai, no single center of leadership at all, or by having some sort of committee or collective executive which will not be destroyed by the death of a single man.

The diffuse, or Siuai, alternative is found only at the most primitive level of social organization, for in the long run, more centralization of leadership seems to have a competitive advantage. In military competition, the side that can coordinate its campaign most successfully may emerge the victor, and in peace, the group that can settle its internal disputes without fragmenting into eternally feuding segments may survive with the greater strength. Certainly in the long view of history, the trend has been for the diffuse kind of Siuai leadership to give way to political systems where there is a single center of power.

The committee or collective alternative is more characteristic of better developed societies. The Swiss government is led by a committee executive,

and during its periods of collective leadership, the Soviet Union has also
been led by what amounts to a committee. Most men living today, however,
like most who have lived in the past, belong to political systems in which
one man is clearly supreme. It seems that single-man executives have
tended to be successful in competition with other types of leadership. As
several examples in later chapters will demonstrate, triumvirates, collective
leaderships, and committee systems of government are difficult to organize
and often unstable. Both diffuse and committee leadership have tended to
give way to single man leadership, and for this reason most political systems
face periodic successions.

2. Hereditary versus Nonhereditary Succession

Where there is a single dominant office, the question of how to fill that
office must arise. Perhaps the most fundamental alternative lies between
some sort of hereditary designation and a more open competition, and it is
not difficult to identify the forces that encourage heredity. Anyone who
would build or hold power must have help, and kinsmen are often the most
reliable collaborators. The economic interdependence of kinsmen is universal and the inheritance of economic rights is very nearly universal. Where
kinsmen have economic interdependence, it is easy to give them political
interdependence as well. They may assist each other in feuds, and they may
support a kinsman who becomes chief or king. A man who wishes to build a
state finds his kinsmen to be his first and most natural allies, and those close
to a leader during his reign have the best chance to take over his office at his
death.

Kinship and royalty tend to be symbolically related. On the one hand,
the symbolism of royalty is often replete with metaphors of kinship. The
king is a kind of father writ large; his subjects are his children. On the
other hand, the aura of grandeur that grows up around the throne and that
is useful in setting the king apart from common men easily rubs off on his
kinsmen. Like the king, they begin to seem rather grand. When an office
must change hands, it is a kinsman, who already shares in the symbols of
royal authority, who can most easily take the place of the old man.

In Africa, royal authority was often shared by an entire clan. This special
authority was given various historical justifications. The Nupe royal family
claimed to rule by right of conquest. The Bemba royal clan was believed to
be descended from the oldest settlers of the area, and the Dlamini clan of
the Swazi simply claimed dominance by virtue of having won out in competition with all others. Whatever the historical facts, or whatever the
historical myth, the results were much the same. The Bemba, the Swazi, and
in a sense even the Nupe all recognized a royal clan which had precedence
within the kingdom and which was expected to monopolize the right to

occupy the throne. The recognition of one clan as unique simplified the assumption of power by one of its members.

When succession is limited to kinsmen of the previous ruler, the entire society may benefit. If power were open equally to everyone, the resulting free-for-all could be utterly destructive to orderly life. By restricting succession to a relatively small group of kinsmen, some limits to the competition are drawn, and with good luck, the kinsmen may even agree among themselves and manage to avoid a show of arms. It is factors such as these that have led so many of the tribes and nations of the world to accept some sort of hereditary succession.

3. General versus Restricted Inheritance of Rights of Succession

Given centralized leadership and given succession within a kinship group, the next choice must be to determine which kinsman. When kinsmen are counted in all directions, through women as well as through men, through marriage as well as along blood lines, the kinsmen become legion. Perhaps any system of hereditary succession requires priorities, for in the absence of priorities, the unique status of the royal family would soon be diluted by the vast numbers of royal relatives. The scramble for power among the royal kinsmen might then be as destructive as if succession were open to everyone in the society. As a result, no hereditary system gives all kinsmen equal access to office.

4. Patrilineal versus Matrilineal Succession

If the range of qualified royal relatives must be restricted, the simplest solution is surely to define descent unilineally, either along the matrilineal lines of the Bemba where only children of royal women are counted as royal, or along the patrilineal lines of the Swazi, Nupe, and Baganda, where it is the children of royal men who stay royal. An important factor in the choice between patrilineal and matrilineal succession is the nature of the people's preexisting kinship pratcices, but even people who trace their kinship ties and gain clan membership matrilineally, have sometimes let royal offices be inherited along patrilineal lines. The Bemba demonstrate that royal succession rules can be made to follow the same principles as ordinary matrilineal inheritance, but special difficulties do beset matrilineal systems.

For one thing, it is more difficult to state the rules of succession in a clear and unambiguous way when nephews rather than sons are the heirs. A relatively large and ill-defined group of prospective heirs are likely to be available, and it is difficult to define their relative seniority with precision. Who is senior—the eldest nephew or eldest son of the eldest sister? Does the eldest true sister outrank an even older female cousin? Do second cousins have to be taken into account? Do third cousins? Similar problems arise in a patrilineal system when a choice must be made between a senior wife's eldest son and the even older son of a junior wife, but on the whole, such questions are easier to solve in an unambiguous way when there is partilineal descent. Where there is ambiguity, there is a danger of conflict.

A more specific difficulty lies in the structure of a matrilineal group. In all societies, even in a matrilineal one, it is men who have held the major positions of power and who have made the most crucial political decisions. This means that rules of succession cannot be expressed as passing from mother to daughter in a matrilineal society, but must instead be expressed as going from a man to his sister's sons. A man's own sons, of course, will not be his heirs, but he may still develop a special affection for them and he may even look for ways to let his sons have a share of the property or power that rightfully belongs to others. He may, in other words, be tempted to subvert the rules for his own sons' advantage. No system can long survive if it gives those who act within it too strong a motive for defying it. It would seem to be such factors as these that have tended to make patrilineal descent far commoner than matrilineal descent among the world's royal families.

5. Fraternal versus Filial Succession

Within a system of patrilineal descent, there are two main classes of potential claimants to succession: brothers and sons. Both fraternal succession and filial succession have certain advantages. When brothers can succeed, competition among them may be reduced, for the younger brothers can console themselves with the thought that their turn may still come. Moreover, if a king should die as a young man, fraternal succession makes it more likely that an adult will step into power. Children need not come to the throne, and regencies need not be organized. The transfer of power to a brother often involves less disruption to the society than when a much younger man takes over.

Balancing these advantages are serious disadvantages. In the first generation, a brother may be able to succeed without too much difficulty, but a set of brothers must eventually end. Who should then follow? The sons of the eldest brother? The sons of the most recent monarch? Or should the sons of all the brothers take turns? If the sons of the last and perhaps the youngest brother are expected to succeed, then elder brothers will have a rather strong motive for trying, on one pretext or another, to subvert the rule, for they will be able to anticipate its results. Men will be tempted to try to disqualify their younger brothers so that their own sons will be able to succeed instead. On the other hand, if succession is limited to the sons of the eldest brother, then the last brother of a generation will be similarly tempted to subvert the formal rule for the benefit of his own sons. In either case, the formal rule will bring men to power who will have a strong motive for defying that very rule.

If all of the sons of all of the brothers are regarded as qualified, the question of relative seniority among all these cousins must first be solved, but beyond this is the problem of expansion of numbers and the increasing distance of their relationship. Each successive generation is likely to include a larger group of qualified men. They will have progressively shorter average reigns, and as the throne passes among more and more distantly related cousins, they are less likely to be constrained by the sentiments of family loyalty that sometimes check the rivalries of close kinsmen. Sooner or later the strains of the system must prove too great and some of the formerly eligible descendants will have to be sloughed off. No means for accomplishing this is without inherent dangers. There seems to be no way to institutionalize fraternal succession without giving some members of the system both the motives and the means for subverting the rules. The violent seizures of power among the Baganda grow directly out of these dilemmas.

The dangers are not so great if sons are given a firm priority over brothers. In each generation, competition will then be automatically limited by pruning the other brothers and their descendants from eligibility. To limit succession to sons does raise the danger that a king may die with no heirs at all, so it is dangerous to eliminate the brothers completely; but if the priorities can at least be made clear, the problem can be simplified. It would seem to be considerations such as these that have made succession by sons a good deal more common among the world's peoples than succession by brothers.

6. Designated Succession versus Competition among Brothers

The alternatives so far considered serve gradually to narrow the range of qualified candidates. Succession may be simplified by giving priority to a kinsman, to a patrilineal kinsman, and finally to the sons of the previous king. All others can be disqualified more easily than they. Rules of priority can, of course, differentiate among brothers too, and the simplest rules provide for either primogeniture or ultimogeniture. If a rule of primogeniture could be made binding, then competition would be eliminated, but it is impossible to make such a rule completely inflexible since sooner or later it is likely to bring an utterly incompetent man to the throne. For this reason, completely determinant succession systems hardly exist. Various devices are used to narrow competition, but they can never eliminate it completely. Since it is the sons of the previous monarch who are the hardest to eliminate, it is among them that the most severe competition develops.

These many considerations coverage to encourage a single mode of succession. Sons of the previous king are given priority. The eldest may have the highest priority of all, but enough alternatives must be left open to allow a totally unfit man to be bypassed and to provide for the occasions when a monarch dies without issue. Some options must remain open and options encourage competition. It may even be that some element of competition is needed to insure the final selection of a sufficiently vigorous and able candidate.

Not only in Africa but in all of the world's continents and through most of recorded history, filial succession has been favored. Even in northwestern Europe and in southeast Asia where the kinship system of the common people hardly stressed one line of descent over another, royal succession has been traced predominantly in the male line. Because filial succession has been so widespread, it merits special examination. African examples can indicate the diversity possible in succession practices, but for a deeper understanding of the most favored variety, we must turn to parts of the world where fuller historical documentation extends over a period of many generations. The next two chapters consider two dynasties, both patrilineal, both favoring the succession of sons. The Marathas built the last great Hindu kingdom of India, and the Manchus formed the final dynasty of Imperial China. The Marathas and the Manchus show striking parallels, but in their differences as well as in their similarities, they illustrate the many difficulties that beset any hereditary succession system. Indeed, their difficulties are not limited to hereditary systems, for they foreshadow the kinds of difficulties that still face societies today, even after heredity has been abandoned.

CHAPTER 3

The Marathas of India

INTRODUCTION

On June 6, 1671, Shivaji the Maratha had himself enthroned as the Hindu king of his people. Seated on a large square throne beneath the royal umbrella and surrounded by his eight chief ministers, Shivaji was showered with sacred rice and sprinkled with waters carried from the holy rivers of India. Brahman priests from Banaras had been summoned to Shivaji's capital, Raigad, in Maharashtra to conduct the ceremonies, and to give their sanction to his claim to rule as a rightful king. Guests from every part of India had been invited for the coronation. The representatives of foreign states, together with the Brahmans, the nobles, the local magistrates of Shivaji's own realm, and all of their families are said to have numbered 50,000, and all were fed sumptuous meals during months of preparations and festivities. Shivaji's weight in gold—16,000 "pagodas," or about 140 pounds—was distributed as charity to Brahmans. Shivaji assumed the titles Maharaja Chhatrapati, Lord of the Throne, Head of the Kshatriya caste.[1]

Lavish displays of wealth had long been expected of Indian rulers, and more surprising than the mere ostentation of this coronation was the fact that these were Hindu ceremonies, held in a region grown accustomed to Muslim rulers. For almost 500 years before Shivaji's coronation, Muslim power had been growing ever more dominant in the subcontinent. Imposing themselves as rulers over the Hindu majority, invading Muslims and their descendants had filled the major positions of power, and during the century preceding Shivaji's coronation, a Hindu could hardly hope for more than to become a feudal baron under a Muslim overlord, or a general in a Muslim army.

The Muslim rulers themselves had not always been united, but after 1560, under the long and successful reign of the Mughal Emperor Akbar, most of north India was joined into a single empire, ruled at the top by Muslims, but dependent upon an alliance with Hindu chiefs for its strength and stability in the provinces. During the century between Akbar's consolidation of the Mughal empire and the rise of Shivaji, no independent realm of any significance was governed by a Hindu, and the very memory of the time when Hindus had ruled must have been growing weak. yet at the end of that century during the peried when the Mughal empire was nearing its peak, Shivaji was building the Maratha kingdom. Under Hindu rulers, this kingdom would survive for 150 years. Maratha armies would range across most of India. The Marathas would even come to challenge the Mughals themselves, until they finally acted as kingmakers, placing the emperor of their choice upon the Mughal throne. When, after its century and a half of power, it became time for the Maratha kingdom to disintegrate, the British were able to pick up the pieces and incorporate them into their own new Indian empire. But before that happened, a series of monarchs had built the kingdom into the strongest power in the subcontinent, the last major Hindu state of pre-British India.

The Marathas were too strongly influenced by their Muslim contemporaries (and in the end, by Europeans as well) really to deserve being labeled "traditional Hindus," but their rulers tried rather self-consciously to build a Hindu state, partly because they needed a symbol by which to oppose the Muslim rulers they fought against; and Marathas even drew upon ancient Indian tradition to give plausibility and legitimacy to their rule. In their rules of succession at least, the Marathas do not seem to have been greatly

---

[1] A full discussion of the sources upon which I rely for the materials in this chapter can be found in the Bibliographic Notes (pp. 297–299).

different from their much earlier Hindu predecessors, and its recent date and relatively ample documentation make the Maratha kingdom the best example upon which to base an understanding of Hindu succession practices.

The century and a half of Maratha power was an era of incessant intrigue, maneuver, and war. The facts of who intrigued against whom, of how alliances were formed, and of which armies were most successfully organized against which other armies form the essential factual basis from which the principles of succession must be inferred, but a chronological display of these details soon becomes tedious, and then becomes confusing to anyone but a specialist. A chronological skeleton of the various reigns is given in Appendix II, but examples are drawn here from whichever reigns seem best to illustrate the principles by which men schemed and fought. It may be best to begin with an account of the means by which Shivaji first built his kingdom.

SHIVAJI'S RISE

By the middle of the 17th century, European ships had been sailing along the Indian coast for more than a century. Their envoys had visited the courts of Indian princes, and Europeans had established a number of small forts on the coast, but they hardly competed with the Mughal empire or with several lesser Muslim sultanates as serious contenders for power on the land. Like the Europeans, the Muslim rulers looked back to a foreign origin, but long residence in India and adjustment to Indian ways, had given their rule a legitimacy that few Indians or Europeans thought to question. The rulers were Muslims but they came to be tolerant of Hindu practices and indeed, their power could only be consolidated through alliances with local Hindu chiefs.

In the northwestern part of peninsular India (the territory that stretches inland from the present Bombay), the local chiefs were Marathas. They served in the armies not only of the Mughals, then dominant throughout the north, but also in those of some southern sultanates. Shivaji's grandfather served as a petty horseman in the service of the Nizamshahi sultanate, and his father, Shahji, was an army commander who grew powerful enough to set himself up temporarily as an almost independent ruler. Shahji, however, never called himself anything but a regent, and he acted only in the name of a young prince of his sultanate.

Shahji's venture at independence was short-lived. More lasting in its influence was his acquisition of a *jagir* at Poona, southeast of the present Bom-

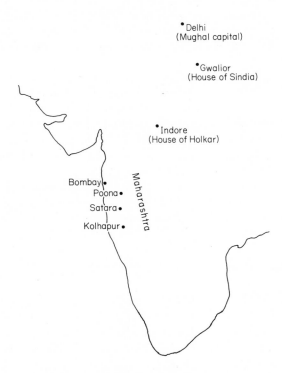

Figure 3–1. India of the Maratha period.

bay (see Figure 3-1). A jagir was a grant of land amounting very nearly to a fief, which a king or sultan could bestow upon a subordinate. The grantee or *jagirdar* was given the right to tax the cultivators who lived in his jagir, and he could use its resources to build up his own military force. In return for his grant, the jagirdar was expected to give financial and military support to his patron king. It was the system of jagirs that ordinarily provided the provincial administration of Indian kingdoms. Jagirs were usually inheritable, and it was Shahji's jagir at Poona that his son Shivaji used as his first base of power. As he matured, Shivaji assumed leadership over the jagir, and he seems to have built it into a well-managed and prosperous petty state.

Shivaji could build upon the reputation of his father and grandfather, both of whom had been respected local officials, but more than any of his successors, Shivaji was a self-made man. With a prosperous home jagir, he began to attract followers, and in the 1640's, at a time when the neighboring states were too weak to resist him effectively, he began to expand his territory. In the next ten years, he built up a compact and vigorous principality, incorporating the services of local Maratha families when he could, crushing them by force when he had to. All contemporary accounts describe him as a man of great personal vigor and political skill, and as a man who could attract and hold the most capable lieutenants. By 1657 Shivaji had become powerful enough to throw his weight into the competition which was then raging between the Mughals and some of the smaller southern sultanates. Although the Mughal empire appeared to be at the height of its power, Shivaji was able to raid widely into Mughal territory, and to enrich his own state with quantities of booty.

After 1657, when Aurangzeb became the Mughal emperor, the traditional alliances between the emperor and the Hindu chiefs tended to weaken. Shivaji could then call upon the defense of Hinduism as an ideological prop for his kingdom. It would be a mistake to simplify the Maratha–Mughal conflict into one of mere Hindu–Muslim rivalry, for both sides regularly employed men of the opposite religion, but the high Maratha officials were always Hindus, just as the high Mughal officials were always Muslims, and it sometimes served Maratha purposes to justify their conquests by the need to protect Hindu shrines and to allow Hindus to worship freely. Shivaji's coronation, replete with Hindu symbolism, was certainly designed to appeal to Hindu sentiments. He formally assumed the Hindu title of *chhatrapati* and he had ancient Indian literature studied so that he could give his high officials Sanskrit titles to replace the Muslim titles they had formerly been content to use.

The major source of Shivaji's strength, however, lay not in his Hindu ideology, but in his military and administrative skill. Maratha traditions are rich with stories of his heroism and he gathered able men to assist him. Since he was building new power, Shivaji, unlike his successors, could insist upon one important administrative principle: He could choose his subordinates for merit rather than for their ancestry. He also rewarded them with cash or valuables rather than with grants of land. Shivaji had built his own power from an inherited estate and he surely recognized the danger that such an independent base of local power might pose to his own rule. When Shivaji annexed the territories of earlier hereditary jagirdars, he ruthlessly imposed his own administrators. Taxes were collected into the central treasury and his military commanders and territorial governors were paid from the treasury rather than rewarded with jagirs. These measures created a body of leaders who were closely bound to Shivaji, and so dependent upon him for their own position that they could not hope to mount a separate claim to power.

GENEALOGICAL PRIORITIES

Shivaji built a new state, but the state survived his death and its leadership passed to other men. Indians never questioned the right of heredity, and they took for granted the right of Shivaji's kinsmen to assume his authority. In fact, the ten principal Maratha rulers—Shivaji and his nine successors—came from two distinct families. The members of the first group were descendants of Shivaji and they assumed his title of chhatrapati, while the members of the second family ruled under the title of *peshwa*. The transfer of ruling power from the chhatrapatis to the peshwas was a complex process which will be described more fully later. Here, two principles require emphasis: the inheritability of the monarchy within each family, and the lack of clarity about which particular kinsmen had priority. The lack of clear priorities meant that disputes broke out after almost every reign, and these disputes could usually be resolved only by armed battle. Inheritability meant that these succession wars were always waged in the name of royal claimants to the throne. To understand these disputes, we first need a clear understanding of those principles of genealogical priority that did exist.

Broadly speaking, the rules by which the royal office, and indeed many subordinate offices, were inherited follow lines made familiar by the African examples given in the previous chapter. Property and office were transferred in the male line. Sons had a greater claim than brothers, elder brothers had precedence over younger brothers, and natural sons had a stronger claim than adopted sons. Except for the exclusive rights of the male line, however, none of these priorities were absolute. Uncles sometimes contested the inheritance of their nephews, younger brothers disputed with older brothers, and adopted sons could dispute the claims of natural sons. In the absence of precise definition of the rules, totally incompetent men would be kept from office, but debilitating succession struggles regularly pitted competing kinsmen and their followers against one another.

Genealogical trees of the two royal families are given in Figure 3-2. The names of the nine men and one woman who successively exercised predominant power within the kingdom are numbered, and an examination of these diagrams will demonstrate the priorities. Only twice did the succession pass to a brother of the late king, once when the ruler died without sons, and once when the only son of the previous ruler was imprisoned by enemies. When sons were available, they could usually claim office at the expense of their uncles. Similarly, older brothers most often gained office at the expense of younger brothers. Sometimes this happened when the younger brother was too young to contest the decision, but at least the direction of preference seems clear. It also seems clear that natural

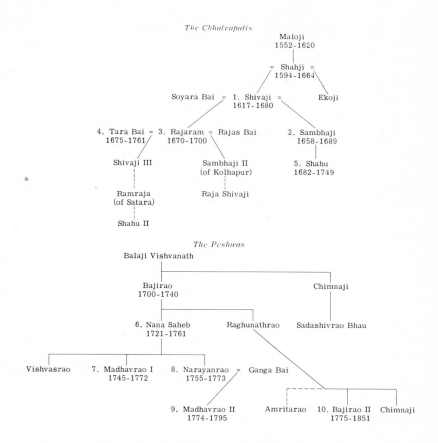

Figure 3–2. Genealogy of the Maratha rulers. (Reigning monarchs are numbered. Adoptive relationships are shown by dashed lines.)

sons had a consistently stronger claim than adopted sons, and no adopted son was able to rise to the monarchy.

None of these priorities was absolute, however. This can be seen both in the fact that in subordinate chiefly families, uncles, younger brothers, and adopted sons sometimes did win out, and also in the fact that, even at the royal level, contests occurred in which these other kinsmen offered themselves for office or were put forward as candidates by supporters. Even when these challenges failed, the mere fact that they were made demonstrates their plausibility in Maratha eyes, and demonstrates that the priorities were hardly firm. Examples of such challenges will be found in Appendix II.

The ability of uncles, younger brothers, and adopted sons to mount serious claims to the throne contrasts sharply with the complete exclusion of both daughters and illegitimate sons. A proper marriage for a Maratha ruler had always to be with a woman of equivalent caste status, and the wedding had to be conducted according to carefully prescribed rituals. A man of high status was not limited to a single marriage, and most Maratha rulers had two or more legitimate wives, but they were also free to maintain secondary consorts. Many of the chhatrapatis and peshwas had "illegitimate," or at least not fully legitimate offspring, by these secondary wives. These children were openly acknowledged by their fathers. They occupied respected positions, and were given sufficient property for their support. These "illegitimate" sons never mounted campaigns to gain their father's position, however, and other men never tried to build up their own power in the name of such a man.

Shahu, the fifth ruler and the last ruling chhatrapati had no legitimate sons. He agonized over the choice of a successor and he searched among his distant collateral kinsmen, even among second and third cousins who had never participated directly in the affairs of the kingdom. He might have adopted such a cousin, and he might have had him accepted as his legitimate successor. But Shahu had two acknowledged sons of his own whose mothers had less than full-wedded status, and he never presumed to suggest that one of these sons might be allowed to succeed. "Illegitimate" sons were completely excluded, as younger sons or adopted sons never were.

Daughters and the husbands and sons of daughters were as severely excluded as "illegitimate" sons. Girls were married at an early age among high caste Marathas, and they became firmly attached to their husband's family. Their children gained their political role from their father, never from their mother, and the claims of kinsmen related in the male line always far outweighed those of kinsmen related through women. This did not rule out a powerful role for women, but when women did rise to political eminence, they did so as wives or mothers within their husband's families, never as sisters or daughters in their fathers' families. Many women schemed to have their own son chosen as ruler.

Surely the most remarkable woman in Maratha history was Tara Bai, the widow of Rajaram, the third chhatrapati. Only 25 years old at the time of Rajaram's death, she must have been both able and strong-willed. She promptly took over the practical direction of Maratha affairs, ruling in the name of her infant son. She personally planned military strategy, appointed generals, and directed campaigns. So successful were her armies that instead of collapsing, as the Mughal Emperor had fondly expected when he heard of Rajaram's death, they now posed an even more serious threat. So powerful was Tara Bai that she deserves to be called the fourth Maratha ruler, though she could rule only in the name of her son.

Many other powerful women emerge from the pages of Maratha history. One illustrious group were the "three Sindia widows." When the great Maratha chief Mahadji Sindia died in 1794, his heir was the adopted Daulatrao, the son of a cousin. Mahadji was survived by three widows, however, and they soon came into conflict with the adopted Dualatrao. The ladies managed to take over and lead a good part of the Sindia military establishment and they waged a substantial, though never decisive, war against Daulatrao. Even without a male heir, they were able to gain the loyalty of their dead husband's junior commanders, to lead military expeditions, and to form alliances in the name of the house of Sindia. For a time, they constituted one of several important military factions within the Maratha state. Clearly women had access to power, but they were excluded from succession. For a daughter to have taken over authority would have been unthinkable, and the most powerful Maratha women all exercised power within their husbands' families, usually in the name of a son.

The basic genealogical rules of royal succession seem clear, but since there was always more than a single plausible candidate (except after Shahu's reign when there were no plausible candidates at all), there was always the possibility of competition, and this competition repeatedly degenerated into violence. In the hope of avoiding violent contention among their heirs, Maratha leaders sometimes tried to settle the succession before their own death but, as always, this carried its own dangers. Maratha crown princes, like those elsewhere, could quarrel with their fathers, and too explicit a designation would build up the power of a son more that the father desired. Later Marathas could always recall a vivid example of such a quarrel, for Shivaji had come into open conflict with his eldest son and heir apparent. Sambhaji, the elder son, quarreled with those who supported his younger brother, and for a time Shivaji placed his son in confinement in order to keep him out of mischief. The bitterness between father and son was so great that Sambhaji even defected temporarily to his father's Mughal enemies. The danger of such quarrels persuaded later Maratha monarchs to avoid giving their sons too much power during their own lifetime. As a result, a succession could rarely take place without a contest. The contests involved many other men and many other offices, and the outcome of these struggles depended upon the patterns of power found at all levels of Maratha society.

INHERITANCE OF SUBORDINATE OFFICES

India was only one of many areas where kinship ties were used as a basis for organizing political power and only one of many areas where hereditary monarchies developed, but nowhere in the world has the principle of heredity been so pervasive, not only at the royal level, but all the way down to the level of the humblest peasant. Even today, many Indian villagers maintain hereditary economic arrangements with their neighbors. The caste system assigns, among other things, a traditional hereditary occupation to each man, and families of priestly, argicultural, and craft castes supply each other with their specialized services by means of agreements that are expected to be so permanent that they can be passed from father to son. Many Indians continue to have their hair cut by the son of the man who cut their father's hair, and families jealously defend their right to inherit these traditional relationships. At the caste and village end of the social scale the inheritance of status and occupation still survives. At the other end of the scale, it once resulted not only in hereditary monarchies, but in the inheritance of many lesser governmental offices and chieftaincies. At all times except the very earliest period of the Maratha kingdom, virtually every important subordinate leader justified his position partly by heredity.

Shivaji had tried to create a state that could be closely controlled by the center, but as early as the reign of Rajaram (the third chhatrapati and the younger son of Shivaji), military requirements encouraged a return to a looser administrative control. Opposition from the Mughals had become more determined than in Shivaji's time, and while the various Maratha chiefs continued to acknowledge the symbolic leadership of Rajaram, each military commander now organized his own rather independent campaign. Their tactics were those of swift guerrilla sorties by which they chipped away relentlessly at the ponderous Mughal field army. The Mughals could concentrate huge forces and capture almost any position, but the Marathas were too swift and too dispersed for the loss of any single location to bring them final defeat. The military result was a long debilitating war which neither side could win, but which caused marauding armies to crisscross most of southern India. The political result for the Marathas was a radical decentralization of power. Each chief came to dominate his own area. He governed its population, collected taxes, and protected it when he could. He developed a vested interest in his domain. Rajaram's central Maratha government could not possibly maintain discipline over the far-flung commanders, and indeed it could not even supply the funds to pay them. Inevitably, the Marathas fell back upon the old jagirdari system. Military commanders were converted into jagirdars, and their jagirs were inherited by their sons and grandsons, even when the qualifications of the younger men were poor and their loyalty to the monarch dubious. As the jagirdar and his jagir grew in importance, the power of the central government inevitably diminished. This fragmentation of authority would have serious long-run consequences for the Marathas, but in Rajaram's time, the military tactics made possible by the jagirdari organization were quite successful in holding off complete Mughal conquest.

During later reigns, the tendency toward hereditary succession to office continued and increased. Chhatrapati Shahu, the fifth Maratha ruler and the grandson of Shivaji, had spent most of his childhood and youth in rather comfortable Mughal captivity. The Mughals hoped he might grow into a useful ally who would help them gain the loyalty of some Marathas, but when Shahu finally emerged from confinement, he acted as a largely independent ruler. He had to contest for power with his aunt Tara Bai, the widow of Rajaram, who, in the name of her son Shivaji III, had been directing Maratha affairs. Shahu faced very different problems in building power than had his grandfather Shivaji. Shahu had to build on his own hereditary claims, and in order to attract followers who had significant local power, he had to recognize their hereditary claims as well. Offices of the government soon came to be regarded as the property of particular families. It was during Shahu's reign that the office of peshwa, sometimes translated as prime minister and an office that had originally been filled by royal appointment, finally became securely hereditary. Even the office of senapati, originally the commander-in-chief of the armed forces, came to be felt to belong by right to the family of its occupant. The inheritance of office and status extended from the top to the bottom of the social system. Jagirs, offices of the central government, junior and regional offices, and military commands were all inherited.

BREACH OF INHERITANCE

Genealogical priorities can help to limit competition for the throne, but to the very extent that they define proper heirs, these priorities run the risk of designating an unsuitable or even an incompetent man. When rules of inheritance are carefully defined, even children may acquire formal office. Occasionally there may be no suitable heir at all. Others must then assume real power, and this leads immediately to a renewed power struggle in another guise. For such reasons, it is probably true that no hereditary system that results in the acquisition of real power can ever be completely defined or work with complete consistency. Always there must be ways of evading the hereditary rules. Even among the Marathas, where inheritance of offices pervaded the entire political system, there were times when inheritance

was circumvented. The most remarkable case was when power was transferred from the family of Shivaji, which ruled under the title of chhatrapati,
to the family of the peshwas, which ruled during the second period of the
kingdom.

When Shahu emerged from Mughal captivity in 1707, he had to build up
his own support at the expense of his aunt, Tara Bai. More than most Maratha rulers, Shahu was able to collect his own loyal following and appoint
some of his own people to office. One of his earliest and most loyal associates was a man named Balaji Vishvanath whom he appointed to the office of
peshwa. The office had been established by Shivaji, and until Shahu's time, it
had generally been filled by appointment with little regard for hereditary
qualifications. Shahu's first peshwa, Balaji Vishvanath, seems to have been
an exceedingly capable man and he has been credited with a good deal of
Shahu's early success in consolidating his administration. When Balaji Vishvanath died, heredity asserted itself and his son, Bajirao, was chosen to take
his place. Bajirao was a spectacularly successful general and under his leadership Maratha power expanded northward over wide areas of northern
India. Bajirao in his turn was followed by his son, who is generally known
by the name Nana Saheb, and who became peshwa in 1740 at the death of
his father. Nana Saheb was still in office when Chhatrapati Shahu died in
1749.

These three peshwas, Balaji Vishvanath, Bajirao, and Nana Saheb, were
all talented men, and they built up their office to a position second only to
that of the chhatrapati. Their rise was by no means without opposition on
the part of other powerful Maratha leaders, but they were backed by Shahu,
and as the Maratha armies expanded northward, the peshwas built up their
own power base by installing chiefs who were as loyal to them as to the
chhatrapati. As a result of the efforts of these three men, a cardinal rule of
power had been broken. As no supreme ruler should ever do, Shahu had
allowed a single man and a single office to emerge in unambiguous second
position. When Shahu died, the most powerful man remaining was Nana
Saheb, Shahu's third peshwa.

At first, nevertheless, there was a general assumption that an heir of
Shahu would take over. Shahu, however, had no sons by any of his four
legitimate wives. His first attempts to adopt a son had been unsuccessful,
but his aunt, Tara Bai, the widow of Chhatrapati Rajaram, finally presented
the world with a young man whom she offered as her grandson. Tara Bai
had once been Shahu's chief rival. As a woman, she had been able to rule
only in the name of her young son, but the son eventually proved to be mentally incompetent, and the Maratha chiefs had gradually shifted their allegiance to Shahu. Tara Bai spent many years in confinement, but she must
have been an indomitable lady, for at the end of Shahu's long reign, she was

still playing politics. She now claimed that her incompetent son had had a son of his own. Shahu's supporters expressed considerable skepticism about the candidate's genuine paternity, and some considered the matter to be an utter hoax. Nevertheless, Ramraja, as this young man came to be known, was eventually accepted, and Shahu died with the presumption that Ramraja would become the chhatrapati. Shahu did ask that his trusted peshwa, Nana Saheb, be allowed to continue in office.

Ramraja had been previously unknown. At the time he became chhatrapati, he was about 23 years old. For a time, he was certainly accepted as the grandson of Tara Bai, but inevitably, a three-cornered power struggle arose. The peshwa, with the support of some of his own powerful followers, worked to maintain his position. Tara Bai did her best to reassert her own will, and she surely hoped her "grandson" would be a compliant tool in her own hands. Ramraja, however, began to assert himself too, and unfortunately for Tara Bai, he did not prove to be as compliant as she might have wished. He refused to go along with her in many matters and he even showed signs of cooperating with the peshwa instead of with her. The peshwa set up his own administration in Poona in virtual independence of Tara Bai. Tara Bai then imprisoned the uncompliant Ramraja, and finally denounced him, declaring that he was not her legitimate grandson after all.

By that time, Ramraja had been married to a high family and he had been formally invested with the highest office in the land. It was difficult to dispose of him completely, but the revelation of his nonlegitimacy rapidly undermined any ideological claim upon which he might have built genuine power. At the same time, Tara Bai's statements also undermined her own claims. The peshwa was left in the strongest position and the solution finally reached was to reduce the chhatrapati to a figurehead and permit the peshwa to retain real power. The chhatrapatis became insignificant and, finally, they became virtual prisoners of the peshwas. Henceforth, serious power struggles would center upon the office of peshwa.

The circumstances in which power shifted to the peshwas were certainly unique. Shahu's first three peshwas were unusually able men, and since they led the northward expansion of Maratha power, the new northern chiefs owed their allegiance as much to the peshwa as to Shahu. Moreover, by the time Shahu finally died, the incumbent peshwa, Nana Saheb, could himself claim his office by inheritance from his father and grandfather, and these three generations were enough to give him some security in his office.

Even then, however, it is doubtful that he could have achieved complete power, if Shahu had had an adequate heir. Ramraja's show of independence suggests that a stronger man with a clearer claim to legitimacy might have been able to use the office of chhatrapati as a symbol around which to rally allegiance and compete with the peshwa. It was the doubt about Ramraja's

paternity that clinched the peshwa's new role. In that one instance, the circumstances were ideal for the transfer of power away from one family and
into the hands of another, but of course the shift left the patterns of power
largely unchanged. Since the office of peshwas was henceforth passed on
by the same rules as that of the chhatrapati, all the difficulties inherent in
hereditary transfer of power quickly affected the new office too.

The shift in power from the chhatrapatis to the peshwas was the most
dramatic occasion in which power escaped from hereditary transmission,
but there were other times, both in the royal families and in subordinate
chiefly families, when ministers or supporters began to exercise real power
behind the throne. In a curious way, even these shifts show the importance
of heredity. A man with no hereditary claim might rule more easily in
another's name than in his own, and the symbolism of inherited rank could
be maintained long after real power had slipped away to others. The chhatrapatis lost their power to the peshwas, but the now powerless office was
maintained until the very end of the Maratha state. The heirs of Shivaji
became virtual prisoners of the peshwas, but their high title continued to
be honored. Until the end of the kingdom, the peshwa went to the chhatrapati to obtain his symbolic robes of office, and in the confusion of the final
Maratha collapse, the chhatrapatis even made a brief bid for renewed
power, calling upon their ancient title as a rallying point. They were not particularly successful in their bid, but the British installed a man as chhatrapati
as late as 1818, hoping to give some sense of legality to their own rule, and
the office of the chhatrapati thus outlived that of the peshwa.

Lower offices, too, might be inherited without the substance of power.
The hereditary right to most offices was never quite so complete as that of
the chhatrapati or later of the peshwa, and strong rulers sometimes
appointed their own men. But to do so made enemies of the family of the
former office holder, and it was generally more politic to confirm a family
member in office. Since the new appointee might not be particularly competent, the administration might suffer, but more likely, the inherited office
would be gradually reduced to an honorary title as new offices with newly
appointed men were built up to take care of the practical affairs of state.
Authority was difficult to achieve without some hereditary claim to formal
status, but the inheritance of status without real authority was a common
occurrence.

By the end of Shahu's reign, the offices originally established by Shivaji
had been reduced to impotence. The hereditary incumbents retained their
honored titles, but they had lost their functions to newer and more dynamic
leaders. The result was a curious sort of circulation (or perhaps escala-
tion) of elites. Older families were continually moved upward to become
figureheads, while more vigorous men replaced them as real leaders. The

shift of power from the chhatrapatis to the peshwas was simply the most dramatic example of a pervasive and persistent process that operated at all levels of Maratha government.

Regencies, elevation of old offices to the status of figureheads, and the gradual transfer of real power from one office or family to another were all necessary if the reality of individual personal ability was to be allowed to assert itself in the face of hereditary privilege. The result was that real power tended always to be just slightly out of step with symbolic status. When power and status became too widely separated, the symbols of authority were gradually adjusted to fit the new and changing situation, but the symbols rarely quite caught up with reality.

KINSMEN

The rules of hereditary succession had be to flexible enough to allow maneuver, but the same flexibility that would keep incompetent men out of office, would also open the way for serious conflicts. Hardly a man succeeded to the Maratha monarchy without a challenge from other potentially qualified men. What an aspiring monarch needed above all else, therefore, was supporters, and the winner from among those qualified by inheritance would be the man who most successfully gained the loyalty of others. Or often, it is more accurate to say that the winner was the man whom the most successful group of supporters put forward as the figurehead for their own power play. From where might supporters come?

In a system that put such stress on heredity, kinsmen were an obvious possibility. Of course, dependence upon kinsmen raised all the same dilemmas that faced African rulers, but impressive cases of loyalty among Maratha kinsmen can be found. The second peshwa, Bajirao, seems to have had the complete loyalty of his brother Chimnaji throughout his term in office. Bajirao was a skilled military leader, while Chimnaji was better at administration and diplomacy, so their skills were nicely complementary. The sons of these two men, Peshwa Nana Saheb and his cousin Sadashivrao Bhau, continued to cooperate, apparently with little conflict. For a while, also, Peshwa Nana Saheb could count upon the reasonably faithful, if not very competent, aid of his brother Raghunathrao.

This brotherly cooperation must have been easier for the early peshwas, who had not yet achieved full power, than it could ever have been for the sovereign of the realm. Those in subordinate positions could achieve more power by cooperating with their kinsmen than by working independently or at cross purposes, so it would be to their mutual advantage to support one another. Kinsmen of the sovereign, however, were always potential claimants to the throne, and even a man with no personal ambition whatsoever would present an almost irresistible figure behind which any dissatisfied faction might try to rally opposition. The fear of such opposition forced every monarch to look with suspicion upon his close kinsmen. The very importance of inheritance made it dangerous to give them too much power, and the history of the Maratha monarchy shows clearly that kinsmen fought each other more often than they cooperated. Conflict among close kinsmen occurred from the earliest periods of Maratha power, when Shivaji imprisoned his own son, to the latest period of peshwa rule, when Raghunathrao contested the succession of his own nephews. For the Maratha monarchy, as for that of the Baganda, patrilineal kinsmen were almost always a source of more trouble than help.

Of course there are kinsmen other than those related by patrilineal ties. Diplomatic marriages are a means of securing kinsmen of another sort. By taking a wife from a powerful family, an aspiring leader might hope to gain a group of powerful supporters, but diplomatic marriages carried their own dangers. Shivaji took a woman of the powerful Shirke family as his second wife, and so consolidated under his own power the area which the Shirkes had controlled. After Shivaji's death, however, it was Sambhaji, the son of another wife who first gained the throne. The bitterness between the half brothers, and between their supporters, grew until finally the younger brother was imprisoned and his Shirke mother was executed on suspicion of complicity in a poisoning attempt on Sambhaji. Inevitably, the Shirke family became Sambhaji's mortal enemies, and they had their final revenge when they reported Sambhaji's movements to the Mughals with the result that he was captured and killed. What had begun as a political marriage led directly to a deep division within the kingdom.

To a monarch, the short-run advantages of diplomatic marriages might appear to outweigh their long-run dangers (if these were perceived at all), but there was another impediment to using marriage as a way of solidifying ties. Most high Maratha chiefs, including the chhatrapatis, claimed the status of Kshatriyas in the caste hierarchy, although they did not all admit equality with one another. The peshwas and a few other important families, however, were Brahmans. These caste divisions placed barriers upon intermarriage, so the families could not be linked closely together by ties of kinship. Since the two ruling families came from different castes, they could never intermarry, and the peshwas could not take their principal wives from the chhatrapati family as a means of legitimizing their own position. All these factors meant that neither blood nor marriage were of prime importance to a leader who looked for support. He had to look instead to nonkinsmen.

ALLIES AND SUPPORTERS

Broadly speaking, a monarch needed supporters with two kinds of skills and he had two kinds of rewards which he could offer in return. First, of course, the monarch needed military support. The century and a half of Maratha rule were years of incessant military competition. When Maratha armies were not out conquering their neighbors' territories, then the armies of the neighbors were invading the Marathas, or various Maratha factions were enthusiastically battling among themselves. The monarch also needed diplomatic and bureaucratic skills: the ability to keep accounts, to check on taxes and tribute, to handle disbursements, to keep order in a far-flung administration, and to engage in constant negotiations with both enemies and friends. The greatest Maratha leaders showed both military and bureaucratic ability. Some specialized in one or the other area.

To secure the loyalty of military chiefs and administrators, a monarch had to offer substantial rewards, either in the form of jagirs or movable wealth—money, jewelry, gold—that might come either from the booty of war or from taxes on the realm. Both jagirs and movable property were used to compensate subordinates throughout Maratha history, and it would be a mistake to draw too sharp a line between them. It would also be wrong to distinguish too sharply between central administrative figures, and the more dispersed or provincial military leaders. Nevertheless, there was a tendency for military chiefs to become established in hereditary positions on the land, while central administrators were more likely to be paid a cash salary. While their formal positions regularly became inheritable, these administrative titles could more easily become merely honorary than could those of the landed jagirdars. In other words, the central administrators were just a bit more like salaried bureaucrats than were the jagirdars, and to that extent they might be more responsive and loyal to the monarch whom they served. That did not, however, assure mutual agreement upon a successor, and indeed they were as likely to quarrel over a successor as were the jagirdars.

Two other subsidiary sources of support should be mentioned briefly, thought neither was dependable and both were particularly apt to lapse during interregna. Marathas sometimes followed the widespread Indian practice of leaving an established ruler in charge of a conquered territory with the understanding that each year this ruler would turn over to the conqueror a payment known as *chauth* which was often set at one-fourth the state's revenue. This system was simpler than the imposition of an entirely new administration, and it was a way of making conquered territories pay for their own conquest and contribute to the further strength of their conquerors. In return, the defeated ruler was able to retain something of his old position, for he had merely to acknowledge his tributary status and periodically he was supposed to pay up.

The system was sometimes justified by saying that conquerors were supposed to protect their tributaries from other enemies, but this side of the bargain was not always efficiently carried out, and so chauth was often a rather one-sided obligation imposed by the strong upon the weak. Of course, the tributary ruler could always hope to avoid paying, and from the conqueror's viewpoint, his schemes toward this end were the chief drawback of the system. Collection was always uncertain. Upon any evidence of central weakness, tributary states would drag their feet on payment, and indeed the Marathas had to wage almost unceasing warfare to enforce their claims for chauth upon various half-conquered territories. Each new monarch had the difficult task of trying to enforce the payments that his predecessor had claimed.

Support or opposition to a ruler might also come from mercenary soldiers, many of whom were foreigners. During the 18th century, Europeans imported new weapons and military techniques into India, and Indian princes were not slow to grasp their significance. They hired Europeans to organize artillery and they sometimes found it expedient to maintain mercenary battalions. During the latter part of the peshwa period, a contingent of mercenaries (north Indians, Pathans, Abyssinians, and Arabs) was attached to the central administration in Poona. They were paid entirely in money wages, and they acted as the palace guard and local police force. It was not a large contingent, probably no more than 5,000 men, but they were professionals and man for man were no doubt more effective fighters than most Maratha battalions. As foreigners, they had little political loyalty but would fight for whomever paid them. They became a threat to the monarchy only when the treasury became so weakened that their pay fell into arrears, but they did become embroiled in one succession struggle. Mercenaries were directly involved in the death of Peshwa Narayanrao, the only Maratha ruler to be murdered. More often, mercenaries acted as agents of others, not on their own initiative.

COOPERATION AND RIVALRY

To secure the monarchy, an ambitious man needed the support of as many administrators, jagirdars, and even mercenary leaders and foreign princes as he could find. Ideally, of course, a new monarch would like to inherit the loyalty of all his predecessor's supporters so that their collective energies could be directed outward toward the enemies of the kingdom instead of being squandered in internecine battles, but no new king could ever be so lucky. The very fact that a man had great power under one regime tended to make him seem a threat to the successor. Anyone who had wielded ancient and independent power might use it against a new man. Thus, each new monarch tried to collect his own supporters, men who would be personally dependent upon him. In this way the new man would try to limit any threat that might come from older established leaders. Successions, therefore, were times when everyone had to be vigilant, lest he be displaced by others, and at the same time they offered the best possible occasion for each man to advance his own interests.

In gaining support, the hopeful monarch had to offer rewards. Quite naturally, when given a choice, chiefs would support whoever offered the most in return. The king might be able to divide the land and wealth of defeated rivals or enemies among his own supporters, but these most desirable of rewards were always in limited supply. He could also promise greater independence to those who would help him, and chiefs might well throw their support to whichever side they felt would leave the greatest freedom of maneuver. A steady long-term trend carried Maratha administration from a system of paid officials under Shivaji to one of reasonably loyal jagirdars under Shahu and finally to what amounted to a federation of virtually independent chiefs. With each successive reign, the pieces from which the kingdom was built tended to become a bit less tightly joined together. The Marathas were no more immune to progressive fragmentation than were the Swazi or Bemba.

With the weakening of the monarchy, the chiefs not only grew less dependent upon the man above them, but they simultaneously grew more dependent upon those below. The direction of their responsibility tended to change. Decentralization of power was inherent in the decline of the monarch, and as they gained more independence of the central power, the chiefs had to rely more upon their personal relations with their own supporters. Then, when succession struggles for the high chieftaincies could no longer be successfully adjudicated by the monarch, all the same forces came into play in choosing the chief that had always affected the choice of the monarch. Subordinate chiefs began to maneuver their way to independence of the great chiefs, just as the great chiefs had maneuvered their way into independence of the monarch. An ever more radical decentralization of power was threatened.

To combat this trend toward dissolution, the monarch had few effective weapons, though he could try to take the interests of his subordinates into account and try to lead them in forming a common policy. Efforts in this direction found occasional expression in councils and conferences. It was common practice for Maratha leaders to meet in so-called *open durbar,* where they would publically and ceremonially acknowledge loyalty to their monarch. On rare occasions these gatherings became the occasion for more or less open debate upon issues and policy, though it was generally felt more seemly to consider such matters in private. When the disclosure of Ramraja's illegitimacy brought something of a constitutional crisis, the peshwa called the leaders together for a conference in the hope of working out a common policy through which the Maratha state could be preserved. The conference was hardly a model of democratic participation, but it did manage to achieve some degree of broad support for the final shift in power to the peshwa. At other times, too, important men conferred, and their common interests sometimes led them to seek a general consensus, but the councils were never more than ad hoc or emergency devices, and politics was more characteristically conducted by means of bilateral negotiations between the various parties. No council became institutionalized or lasted beyond the period of stress which brought it into being.

Indeed, the great men of the kingdom were never securely united. Their common interests were insufficient to overcome their rivalry, and the disputes of chiefs often became a threat to national unity. Land revenue was never enough to satisfy everybody. At each level of administration right down to the district and village, each official looked for ways to increase his own share. Jagirdars sought to expand their own territory, and if they could not expand outward, they had few scruples about doing so at the expense of their fellow Marathas. Added to these factors, there was always personal rivalry and mutual jealousy. Excuses for strife were never absent.

As each man sought to increase his own share, his interests could conflict not only with other chiefs, but with the monarch. Thus, a striking feature of Maratha politics was the uncertain loyalty of subordinate chiefs, and the history of the kingdom was marked by a long series of desertions of lesser chiefs from one faction to another. Some of these were followed by a redesertion and a return to one's original loyalty. Thus the monarch, almost like a Siuai big man, was always in danger of having his chiefs slip away from under his command. Shivaji's own son Sambhaji deserted to the Mughals and then later returned to his father. Shahu was able to build up his own power by attracting desertions from the forces of his opponents, but Shahu faced desertions from his own ranks as well. These desertions brought more than the loss of a single man, for the individual soldier owed his primary allegiance to his immediate chief, and he would follow his chief to another side. The resulting fragility of the military structure was a serious source of weakness to the state, but of course the weakness affected all sides, and Marathas were sometimes able to persuade enemy contingents to cross to them. Prince Akbar deserted his father, the Mughal emperor, and formed a temporary alliance with Sambhaji. In later wars Maratha contingents that were fighting for others sometimes defected to the Maratha state, and in doing so, they could critically affect the outcome of a battle.

A monarch might be expected to take a very dim view of desertion, but he had few means for punishing it. If his deserting subordinate was securely allied with his opponent, he would probably be out of reach, and he could be persuaded to return only with guarantees for his own survival. When a chief's power was based upon the control of his own jagir, the monarch might be safer to accept his unreliable protestations of loyalty than to risk the military venture necessary to replace him. Dealings between Maratha chiefs and their supposed enemies cloud the entire history of the kingdom. Chiefs came to act with such independence in allying themselves both with one another and with foreign powers, that the Maratha kingdom was finally converted into more of a confederation of chiefdoms than a centralized state. This was the steady direction in which the Maratha state moved.

As subordinate chiefs gained increasing power, they could become a threat to the monarch himself. One territorial chief, Mahadji Sindia, did become a serious threat to the central administration of his time, and the peshwas finally grew powerful enough to displace the chhatrapatis altogether. The only way to prevent any single supporter from gaining such a challenging degree of independent power was to balance him with rivals. The best time for the monarch was when his supporters had to compete with one another for their sovereign's favor, but when the monarchy was weak, the same rivalries would seriously undermine the ability of the state to act in unison.

At the king's death, hopeful successors would look for supporters, and at the same time the greater and lesser Maratha chiefs would conspire to put forward their own favorite candidates. Even the leaders of neighboring realms would get involved. In fact, it was a favorite game of Indian princes, as of princes throughout the world, to dabble in the succession disputes of their neighbors. The least they could hope for would be to weaken their neighbors and rivals; the most would be to put an ally into a position of power. The Nizam of Hyderabad once agreed to pay the Maratha chhatrapati a considerable sum each year as chauth, but for a period in the 1720s, he managed to maintain some ambiguity about whether this chauth was owed to Shahu or to one of his rivals. While "waiting for clarification" on this point, he did what he no doubt liked best: He paid no chauth at all. In other ways too, he attempted to prevent Shahu from monopolizing Maratha leadership and though he failed to dislodge Shahu, he surely strengthened his own position by playing off the Marathas claimants against one another. The Mughals practiced the same policy when they released Shahu and let him compete with his aunt, Tara Bai, and later, the Marathas themselves dabbled in Mughal succession struggles until finally the Maratha chief, Mahadji Sindia, became so powerful that he could place his choice of emperor on the throne of the decaying Mughal court.

SUCCESSION IN SUBORDINATE FAMILIES

As chiefly families achieved independence from any central control, they quickly encountered all the same kinds of succession problems faced by the monarchy itself, but to the degree that these families remained in a subordinate position, an additional factor had to be taken into account: the possibility that the monarch might intervene. The monarch's right to adjudicate arguments among his chiefs was widely accepted, and in particular, he was supposed to be able to decide disputes between rival claimants to the inheritance of a jagir. The extent to which he actually exercised this right to adjudicate, however, depended upon the details of each case, and especially upon the military strength of the various parties.

Interminable tales could be told of succession squabbles in chiefly families, but they would become tiresomely repetitive. Time after time, brothers quarreled over their patrimony. Time after time, the monarchs stepped in, sometimes successfully, sometimes not. The quarrels within the great Maratha families catastrophically weakened their houses. This weakening must sometimes have been welcomed by the center, for it fragmented the power of potentially insubordinate families, and at times the center deliberately encouraged the division of a jagir so as to weaken rebellious subordinates. New families which were more loyal could then be allowed to rise.

On the other hand, the interminable disputes within these satellite territories also had serious repercussions back upon the center. When the subordinate families themselves came to be divided into disputing factions, almost any claimant for the central throne was able to gain automatic support from dissident members of subordinate houses. In many cases, it is even difficult to know whether a challenger for the monarchy was gathering supporters so as to achieve his own ends, or whether the subordinates were using the candidate for the monarchy as a symbol behind which to advance their own interests.

In the final years of the Maratha government, the peshwa's family was divided into factions, as were the most important chiefly families. One faction of each family was allied with factions from the others. The factions intrigued politically and took to the battle field. The result can only be described as chaos. Splits and shifting alliances of this sort occurred repeatedly in the century and a half of Maratha rule, and they enormously confuse the political history of the kingdom. The implication of all these factors was that both superiors and inferiors could throw their weight into succession struggles. The monarchs could help decide the struggles within the subordinate houses, but the subordinate chiefs also helped to determine the outcome of struggles for the throne.

In spite of this apparent reciprocity, there was rarely any doubt about who held the symbolically superior position. The later Marathas always acknowledged the general overlordship of the Mughals. The chhatrapatis always retained their symbolic precedence over the peshwas, the peshwas were above the main chiefs, and the main chiefs were above more subordinate chiefs. In practical contention for power, this unambiguous hierarchy might make little difference. Thus, when Mahadji Sindia interfered in the Mughal succession, he did not act very differently from the peshwas when they intervened in the succession of their chiefs. But in principle, Mahadji was subordinate to the peshwa, who was subordinate to the chhatrapati, who was subordinate to the Mughal emperor. Mahadji was controlling an office three levels higher than his own. But the death of a man who held commanding power, whatever his title or symbolic role, left a kind of vacuum that was not left by a mere chief. A strong peshwa might singlehandedly decide the succession of one of his chiefs. When the peshwa himself died, the issues were more critical, and as long as the peshwa's strength was supreme, succession was unlikely to be easily decided. It could never be decided by a single person.

There was therefore a difference between the way in which the subordinate houses supported their choice of chhatrapati or peshwa, and the manner in which the latter intervened in the affairs of their vassals. If nothing else, intervention by the monarch was recognized to be proper behavior, and in favorable cases the parties to the dispute would accede gracefully to the decision of a single man. It was not so easy in the case of the monarch, where no single subordinate could hope to determine the outcome of a dispute. At best, he could do no more than throw his weight into a many-sided conflict.

IDEOLOGY

As one reads of the unending battles and intrigues of the Marathas and of the blatant self-seeking which seems to characterize the men who struggled, it is easy to fall into the illusion that Maratha politicians acted with no principles at all, that each man sought his own advancement so ruthlessly that no distinction can be made between deceitful and honorable methods. Such a conclusion would be unfair, for ideological principles that governed the quest for power do emerge from an examination of Maratha history, and it is well to take note of them.

First, there were the rules of heredity. Nothing but what was seen to be proper in the minds of men made it possible for a distant cousin or for an adopted son to inherit at the expense of an illegitimate though publicly acknowledged son. Nothing prohibited a daughter from sharing in the inheritance of power and property except the assumptions that people made about what is expectable and correct behavior. The rules of inheritance which so crucially affected the transmission of Maratha power were man-made rules, but they severely limited the choices that men regarded as plausible.

The acceptance of heredity was accompanied by an acceptance of rank. After Shivaji had consolidated his position, nobody challenged the right of his family to rule until the peshwas came along. The challenge of the peshwas had to be built up slowly and painfully, but once they succeeded, their claim to rule was as clear as that of chhatrapatis had formerly been. Other families ranked lower, and of these some were lower than others. Indeed the acceptance of varying rank was a fundamental principle of the society.

Ritual rank, defined by the caste system, placed some men at the top as Brahman priests and others at the bottom as workers in polluting occupations. The ranks of most men fell between these extremes. Partially coinciding with ritual rank, but partially contradictory, was a ranking in power. A non-Brahman family could far outrank some Brahmans in mundane governmental affairs, and families of more or less equal ritual rank could compete for political power. Over the long run, ritual rank probably tended to adjust to the realities of power. Those with enough power could make good their claim to Kshatriya ritual rank whether or not their ancestors had had any such pretentions, but in any event, differences in rank and in power were taken for granted. Marathas were never bothered by any such disturbing notion as a principle of universal human equality.

The firm acceptance of rank and of the hereditary access to status and power is clear, but other ideological principles also affected some men's decisions and, through these decisions, the principles affected the outcome of some disputes. To some degree, the early Marathas could consolidate power by asserting their common sentiments and their common destiny. Languages grade imperceptibly into one another in this part of India, and it is not really possible to say exactly where one language ends and another begins, but language and some other homely aspects of daily behavior did set off people of one region from those of others. These characteristics could serve for a time as rallying points around which to build loyalty to the Maratha cause, and Shivaji asserted that all territories where Marathas lived should come under his rule.

The Maratha armies were destined to sprawl over much of India and to incorporate territory far beyond the bounds of the Marathi language. As the kingdom grew, its leaders lost any claim to be building a nation of homogeneous people. But the Maratha ruling class retained some degree of cultural unity which set it off from other Indians, and even after the territorial expansion, an attempt could be made to substitute the appeal of Hindu unity for the narrower appeal of Maratha unity. Some Maratha leaders rather self-consciously made opposition to Muslim domination into a rallying point around which to generate military and political enthusiasm. The promise of support for Hindu sentiments and protection for Hindu shrines must have appealed to many non-Maratha Hindus who came to be incorporated into the kingdom. Too many reports tell of consultations between the monarchs and their Brahman teachers to let us suppose that Hindu ideals or the hope of freeing Hinduism from the Muslim yoke were merely a pretense designed to rationalize Maratha rule for the populace. Still, we must be careful not to project backwards from the Hindu–Muslim antagonism of more recent times, and to suppose that the competition between the two religions had the same meaning then as now. Muslims served the Marathas and Hindus served their Muslim opponents and there came a time when the fierce depredation of Maratha armies upon Hindu and Muslim populations alike negated any original appeal that their Hinduism might have brought.

The Marathas never constituted a state in the modern sense. Loyalties were always directed more to personal leaders and less to the abstraction of a political state than they are today. Nevertheless, the leadership had some ideal of unity which supplemented mere personal loyalty. They tolerated but never really acquiesced in a divided regime, and for the leaders, if not for the mute population, the ideal of unity may, at times, have slowed the kingdom's dissolution.

In spite of what can appear as fickle desertion, personal loyalty was certainly strong. Desertions by newly appointed officials and military leaders were not as common as desertion by their heirs. Personal loyalties were not so easily inherited as formal offices, titles, or property, but the followers and subordinates that each new monarch gathered around him were generally quite faithful. It was their sons who were more likely to desert and they were more likely to do so after the monarchy had also been inherited. Paradoxically, moreover, even desertion requires personal loyalty if it is to be successful. The deserting chief had to be able to take his loyal followers with him. The bonds of personal loyalty that really held the kingdom together were never fully or successfully harmonized with the presumption of inheritance to office and power, and the inevitable result was the final decomposition of the kingdom; but even as we survey the final wreckage, we should not forget the countervailing bonds of personal loyalty that allowed the kingdom to be built up in the first place.

Beyond sentiments of personal loyalty, Marathas also had more abstract ideas of proper and improper behavior. Murder, for instance, was certainly not regarded as befitting a monarch. On the battlefield Marathas killed each other and their non-Maratha enemies with enthusiasm, and Shivaji was admired for having personally killed an opponent in self-defense; but cold-blooded murder was rare, although it must have been a temptation to those faced with the never-ending machinations of political opponents. The Maratha monarchs surely knew that the Mughal emperors regularly consolidated their power by killing off their rival brothers, but the Marathas did not resort to such extremes. An unsuccessful attempt was made to poison Sambhaji I, but in the 150 years of Maratha rule only one reigning ruler was successfully assassinated, a record that some modern nations might well envy. The monarchs regularly imprisoned their uncles, brothers, and sons, but they stopped short of killing them. Even the reaction against the one murder that did occur bespeaks the Maratha attitude. Since Raghunathrao seemed at first to be the only surviving male member of the peshwa's family, it was difficult to know how to keep him out of office, but he was regarded as having been implicated in the murder, and his support quickly withered once an alternative heir was born.

Marathas also held notions of what constituted just and unjust rule, and these could have a bearing upon the success or failure of a ruler. Rule was certainly autocratic, but the rulers could not completely ignore an ethic that called upon them to rule with justice and with due consideration for the welfare of their people. A monarch might evade such obligations when he was strong and when his kingdom was united. Then the lower officials, to say nothing of the peasants, had little defense against his authority; but in periods of competition for power, even those rather far down in the hierarchy might, by their actions for or against a leader, help to tip the balance one way or another. The Marathas were able to expand at the expense of the Mughals partly because the Mughals had alienated their subjects by their arbitrary policies. Later, after Maratha power had spread over much of North India, it was their turn to lose the support of the local population by their ruthless exactions. The Marathas suffered a disastrous military defeat at the hands of the Afghans in 1761 at the battle of Panipat. The defeat was caused in part by the alienation of the population through which the Maratha armies had to move. The Marathas could get no logistic support except by force, and this simply sapped their popularity even further. Rivalry among their leaders might bring destruction to the lives and property of ordinary people, but these rivalries occasionally gave even the little man a chance to throw his support, however feebly, to the side that offered the greater justice.

PERSONAL ABILITY

In the end, each contender for power operated within the same system of rules and each could use roughly the same kinds of opportunities as his rivals. Where ideological claims were more or less balanced, we must finally recognize an element of personal ability that helped to decide the outcome of succession struggles. It takes skill to adjudicate the rival claims of contending chiefs and administrators, discernment to recognize and reward those with high qualifications, and careful judgment to know when to conciliate a potentially insubordinate chief and when to try to crush him instead. The most successful Maratha monarchs were astute judges of people, skillful administrators, and competent military strategists.

Such skills may require a native ability that is not given to all men, but careful training might have fostered the skills. The upbringing that potential rulers actually received sometimes did the opposite. So great was the danger of insubordination on the part of a monarch's kinsmen that potential heirs were often kept in confinement during their childhood. This was usually a rather comfortable confinement, by no means a rigorous imprisonment, but the restrictions did shield the heirs from the experience of the practical world into which they would be thrust. Shivaji restricted the movements of his own son. Madhavrao II was so sheltered in his childhood that his first attempts to assert himself in affairs of the state could hardly have been anything but erratic. Bajirao II emerged from confinement bitter at Nana Phadnis who had imprisoned him but otherwise little prepared for high politics. Few men could emerge from such restricted childhoods at all well prepared for leadership.

The longest unbroken series of successful Maratha rulers were the early peshwas. For four consecutive generations the peshwas offered skilled leadership to the kingdom, but only the fourth and last of these men grew up as the child of the first man of the kingdom. The first three grew up before the peshwas had yet surpassed the chhatrapatis in power, and even the fourth was his father's second son, and he was not regarded as the heir apparent until shortly before his father's death. The most successful Maratha rulers generally grew up under relatively free conditions with a chance to learn something about the world and to gain practical experience before being thrust into a position of power. Shahu was a partial exception to this generalization, since he achieved considerable success in spite of having spent most of his childhood confined within the Mughal camp, but Shahu was at least free to observe the operation of that powerful society, and the restrictions of his upbringing were probably less severe than were those of several other monarchs. The restrictions that so many monarchs placed upon potential competitors were intended to stabilize the monarchy and unify the realm. Paradoxically, they introduced instability instead. The future monarchs endured experiences that made them peculiarly unfitted for their duties.

INDIA AND THE MARATHAS

The Marathas arose late in the history of Indian kingdoms and they were provincial in origin, but many of the practices that affected Maratha succession rules had parallels at other times and places in India. Elsewhere too, land and offices were inherited by legitimate sons, and adopted sons inherited when there were no natural sons. Like the Marathas, other Indians expected their king to have a uniquely powerful position but recognized his need for counselors, clerks, and military chiefs. Legitimate succession to the throne was almost always to a surviving male relative, most often to a son, though occasionally to a brother; but the death of one king seems to have regularly triggered off a volent succession battle among the survivors. From the kingdom of Vijayanagar, which a century before the rise of Marathas controlled the southern peninsula of India, there are reports of confinement of the king's brother so as to keep him out of mischief, and on three occasions, high ministers usurped the throne by gradually taking over the powers of the reigning king, just as the peshwas took over from the chhatrapatis.

All Indian kingdoms seem to have been plagued with the same tendency to fragment that helped bring down the Marathas. Provincial chiefs would grow ever more independent and intractable. A strong monarch would beat his provincial chiefs into submission, but this always became more difficult with the passage of time. The chiefs would come to fight with one another until the kingdom became an easy prey to outside interference. All Indian rulers recognized this problem, of course, and while they had to cope with it in their own realm, they constantly dabbled in the internal quarrels, and particularly in the succession battles of their neighbors.

Like other Indians, the Marathas were fond of justifying their actions by citing ancient authority. It would be foolish to imagine that even the earliest Marathas represented some sort of pure and ancient Hindu tradition. Nevertheless, the similarity of many Maratha practices to those of other Indian kingdoms must raise the question of how much continuity the Marathas did show with the predecessors, and we can at least ask whether anticipations of Maratha practices can be found in classical accounts.

Many ancient Hindu texts refer in one way or another to governmental organization, but the most complete treatise on government is the *Arthashastra,* which is attributed to Kautilya, the chief advisor to the Emperor Chandragupta Maurya of the 4th century B.C., and which, in versions available today, dates from about 150 A.D. The *Arthashastra* includes extensive discussion of the organization of the state, the role of the king and his ministers, the conduct of war, the use of spies, sources of revenue, and virtually every other aspect of government. It constitutes a remarkable synthesis of the political theory and practice of ancient India. From this and other related texts, one can draw a good many inferences about the early political organization of India, and even more important perhaps, see the sources to which later Indians turned when looking for theoretical justification or occasionally even for guidance for their own actions.

The first principle to emerge from these texts is the crucial role of the king. He was seen in part as a military leader, and indeed military victories were one well recognized route to the monarchy, but he was also expected to be the supreme ruler of the realm, and the happiness of the kingdom was felt to be dependent upon the king's strength. Only the king was expected to have enough power to put down the anarchy that continually threatened mankind, so even an arbitrary and unjust king was regarded as better than no king at all. The king, to be sure, should rule in accordance with the higher divine law of the *dharma,* which imposed varying obligations upon all members of a society. The king's dharma should oblige him to rule justly and in the interest of his subjects; but if he failed to live up to his dharma, there were few practical sanctions that could be brought against him, or which would protect his subjects from him.

The author of the *Arthashastra* clearly recognized the danger that a king's own kinsmen might pose. He quotes a predecessor as saying "princes, like crabs, have a notorious tendency of eating up their begetter," and he was aware of the practice of confining recalcitrant sons, so as to reduce their threat. The *Arthashastra* describes the vital role played by the king's high ministers in the conduct of the government, and it recognized the possibility that they might take over effective rule in case the king should be incapacitated. Recognition is also given to the role of the ministers in proclaiming a new king after the old one had died. The new king was clearly expected to come from the family of the old one, and the most likely choice was the eldest son, though other sons or brothers were not ruled out. Certainly an incompetent older brother was not expected to succeed at the expense of an able younger brother, but the texts provide no clear mechanism for deciding the issue in ambiguous cases. In all these respects, Maratha practices seem to show considerable continuity from ancient times.

INDIAN "FEUDALISM"

A good deal of rather futile ink has been spilled debating whether or not Indian governmental practice such as that of the Maratha kingdom deserves to be called "feudal." The answer depends upon how broadly or how narrowly one cares to define "feudalism." Certainly Indian practices were never identical with those of Medieval Europe, and some differences are fairly obvious. The caste system gave India a more rigid social hierarchy than Europe ever had, but India has never had a single centralized religious hierarchy and it had no pope. Indians may have put less emphasis than Europeans upon the sanctity of the personal ties of vassalage. For Indians it was not so much sacred vassalage as practical monetary and material considerations—taxes on land and booty in war—that formed the essential cement that held kingdoms together. Yet in one respect, Indian "feudalism" outdid that of Europe. One essential feature of any system that we might call feudal is certainly the assignment of territorial domains to subordinate but hereditary offices, and the Indian acceptance of heredity as a means of access to status and office, went well beyond that of Europe, even in its most feudal or aristocratic periods.

The jagirdari system shows obvious parallels with European feudalism. Landed chiefs supported their own military forces, and passed their powers onto their sons. They were expected to use their forces to support their monarch, but their own power base gave them far more independence than mere appointed bureaucrats could ever have had. Classical Indian texts do not describe the jagirdari system and the way in which it arose is not entirely clear, but by the time of the Marathas, it was well established throughout the sub-continent. Shivaji made some efforts to counteract the jagirdari system, but it was too well entrenched in Indian thought and habit to be eliminated, and as soon as Shivaji died, the jagirdari system again rose in full force. Maratha practices came to resemble closely those of their predecessors and contemporaries elsewhere in India.

Perhaps the continuity with the past was due in some degree to the reverence in which the Marathas held the ancient Hindu texts, perhaps partly to the memory and example of less remote Hindu antecedents. But more important than these more or less direct effects of tradition in giving the Marathas characteristics that recall earlier kingdoms may have been the similar working out of unquestioned principles in the several times and places of Hindu rule. Like their predecessors for more than two millenia, neither Maratha leaders nor their subjects ever questioned the state's right to collect taxes from the peasants. Like other Indian states, the Marathas needed a mechanism to make the collection, and the jagirdari system was a convenient one. All Indians took for granted that the center of the state was the king, that he would be assisted by high ministers, that there would be a steep hierarchy of ritual rank and of power which separated man from man and family from family, that offices were hereditary in the male line, but that the realities of ability and of power kept the precise heir from being unambiguously designated ahead of time. Since the Marathas shared these assumptions with other Indians, it is hardly surprising to find that Maratha rules of succession recall those of other Hindu kingdoms. The instability which these rules helped bring to successive Indian kingdoms could not be permanently changed by a mere change of dynasty, or by conquest from a new center. So long as the assumptions that underlay the rules remained fixed, every new kingdom would suffer the same chaotic history as its predecessors.

CONCLUSIONS

By comparison with the four African tribes considered in the last chapter, our knowledge of the Marathas is abundant and it extends over many generations. This permits a more detailed understanding of the techniques by which succession was accomplished and of the impact of these techniques upon the society, but many of the same principles that governed succession in Africa appear as clearly among the Marathas.

A Maratha monarch could never allow another man, not even his son, to assume an unambiguous second position and, as always, this made repeated succession struggles inevitable. Principles derived from the Hindu classics and complex rules of genealogical priority were invoked to justify or rationalize the claims of contenders, and, as in many African tribes, the principles used at the royal Maratha level reflected quite closely those used in chiefly families. This meant that the principles were well known and broadly accepted, but they could never have been made unambiguous without presenting the monarch with a challenging second. With no possibility of appealing to a higher authority, the contenders for the throne sought to mobilize wide segments of their society. Their search for allies offered at least a glimmer of an opportunity for those well down on the political scale to make their interests felt, but their struggles repeatedly degenerated into violence. Usurpations occurred, but the principles of heredity were so well entrenched that these principles always governed the new office as tightly as they had the old, and so usurpations brought no fundamental change to the system. Kings struggled to concentrate powers into their own hands, but each new monarch had to barter away some of his authority in exchange for the support of other men. As the generations passed, this led persistently and irresistibly to the weakening of central control until the kingdom finally became so fragmented that it became easy prey to its enemies. The political organization could not, therefore, remain constant. It changed with the passing of each generation, and if we are to find stability in Indian politics, it can only be a very long-term stability in which the rise of new states and their breaking up into parts are seen as alternative phases of a single political cycle. All of this recalls the experience of African tribes.

It is not difficult to point to several specific characteristics of the Maratha kingdom that encouraged its own gradual disintegration. Three traits stand out most clearly: (1) the vested interest in jagirs and the independent power which the jagirs gave to the families of subordinate chiefs; (2) hereditary succession to subordinate offices, which allowed these vested interests to be consolidated and then led to progressively looser ties with the monarch; and (3) the ambiguity in the genealogical rules of royal succession, which left room for a struggle at almost every succession. The first two of these are characteristic of any political system that we would want to call "feudal," and in learning to avoid these, the Chinese developed a political system which, although dominated at the top by a hereditary monarch, was in most other respects the very antithesis of a feudal regime. The Chinese allowed no office of power, except for the throne itself, to become hereditary, and tendencies toward vested territorial interests were efficiently destroyed. Moreover, the Chinese even learned to designate the successor so clearly that succession struggles were eliminated. Thus, the Chinese avoided several of the weakest characteristics of Indian practice, and for this reason the "bureaucratic" Chinese succession system provides an excellent contrast to the "feudal" system of the Marathas. As we will see, however, the Chinese system had difficulties of its own, and in the end, these led to no less chaos than did the difficulties of the Maratha system.

CHAPTER 4

China of the Manchus

INTRODUCTION

Seventeenth and eighteenth century China shared much with contemporary India. The governments in both areas were led at the top by hereditary monarchies, and the emperor of China, like the rajas of India, was expected both to reign and to rule. He had ceremonial legitimacy as the head of state, but he was also expected to wield supreme temporal power. Both Chinese and Indian governments rested at the bottom upon their power to tax the agricultural majority of their population, and to use the income to maintain military and civil hierarchies. The army defended the realm and extended it when it could; the civilian bureaucracy kept the elaborate records without which control would loosen and taxation would fail. In the best of times, the government would repay its heavily taxed populace with peaceful civil order and public works, but the peasants were never asked whether they cared to participate and they usually contributed far more to the regime in taxes than they received back in services.

In many respects, of course, China and India differed profoundly, and after observing the chaotic political history of the Marathas, one must be impressed by the regularity and apparent ease with which the later dynasties of Imperial China managed to pass the throne from father to son. Succession struggles and palace coups were less debilitating than in India, and in the last dynasty, an unbroken sequence of nine rulers successfully passed their office to a son. All nine held predominant authority during at least part of their reigns. By any dynastic standard, this was a notable coincidence of genealogy with power.

The last dynasty, that of the Manchus, was foreign in origin. The Manchus conquered the Chinese capital in 1644, and by their willingness to master Chinese governmental techniques, the Manchus gained the support of many Chinese. These foreigners seemed to offer the best hope for maintaining Chinese civilization. Thus, Manchu rule gradually came to be Chinese in all essentials, and it exemplified both the strengths and weaknesses of the Chinese system. Because of their foreign background, however, Manchu succession practices can be seen as developing in three overlapping but distinguishable phases: (1) the original rise of Manchu power, and the progressive conversion of their political system to Chinese forms; (2) the period of the greatest strength of the dynasty, from the reign of the K'ang-hsi emperor through that of Ch'ien-lung; and (3) the period of decline beginning as early as the second half of the Ch'ien-lung reign, but gathering momentum from the time of the Opium War of the early 1840s. Each phase laid the basis for the one that followed, and each deserves some attention.

THE RISE OF THE MANCHUS

In the frontier zone of Manchuria, the world of the settled and agricultural Chinese gives way to the open steppes where non-Chinese have long supported themselves by migratory animal husbandry. Like other successful conquerors before him, Nurhachi, the founder of the Manchu dynasty, built his power by joining the military potential of mobile steppe warriors with the revenue base of settled Chinese farmers. Starting in the late 16th century with a small inherited territory, Nurhachi, like Shivaji the Maratha, progressively defeated his rivals and incorporated their men and land into his own growing realm. He grew powerful enough even to challenge the

---

[1]The sources upon which I rely for my account of the politics of Manchu China are discussed in the Bibliographic Notes (pp. 299–301).

provincial administration of the Ming government that had been ruling China for two centuries. Nurhachi laid the basis for civil administration in the settled agricultural areas, and since he occupied a commercially strategic region, he built a fortune by trade.

Nurhachi began as a military leader and one of his most enduring creations was his system of military "banners." Known as banners because of the distinctive colored standards that they flew, and modeled initially on the provincial military system of the Ming, the Manchu banners were destined to grow into one of the most distinctive organs of Manchu administration. They were, first of all, fighting regiments, but Nurhachi assigned all his followers, families as well as men, to a banner, and each banner received land that would give it an independent base of support. Nurhachi named a prince to lead each banner. The four senior banners were assigned to three sons and a nephew and later when four junior banners were organized, each was assigned to a younger son.

It would seem that Nurhachi was aware of the divisive threat that partially independent feudal realms might pose, for he did not allot each of his eight banners a single contiguous territory. Rather, he intermixed the territories among one another, and he also checked the danger of independent action by uniting the banner leaders, known as *Hosoi Beiles*, into a council of state. This council was expected to reach collective decisions that would make it difficult for any individual member to act independently. The four senior Hosoi Beiles, the leaders of the four senior banners, took monthly turns acting as a sort of temporary prime minister. Periodic responsibility for central administration not only gave them valuable experience, but reduced their exclusive commitment to their own banner.

In civil administration, Nurhachi closely imitated Ming practices. Following the Chinese example, he bestowed an imperial title upon himself as early as 1616. He also created a government secretariat in which jobs were to be open to men of talent, whatever their background, and he freely invoked the Confucian doctrines of the Chinese to give legitimacy to his administrative forms. By employing an increasing number of Chinese, he capitalized upon their tradition of bureaucratic skills, helped to gain the loyalty of the ever growing proportion of his subjects who were Chinese, and prepared his administration for its eventual capture of full imperial power. His Chinese supporters brought their own habits and their own conceptions of government, and the administration they helped Nurhachi to build soon came to be a close replica of the administration of the Ming.

Nurhachi had 16 sons by a number of wives and concubines. Many played important roles, but so long as Nurhachi lived, he was able to choose the most able of his kinsmen as his subordinates. Since Nurhachi had personally built his own realm, no one was likely to challenge his right to rule or his right to choose his chief lieutenants, but his sons, like the sons of other princes, quarreled. The eldest, Cuyen, had been a successful general and a powerful prince, but he was regarded as selfish and unjust, and several younger brothers asked their father to curb him. Cuyen was first reprimanded and later, when Nurhachi became convinced of his son's treason, he was imprisoned. Two years later he died, possibly executed. The remaining brothers cooperated without apparent friction as long as Nurhachi lived.

He died in 1626 and the three sons and the nephew who led the four senior banners assumed a sort of collective leadership. These four had been their father's chief lieutenants and had formed the highest council of state; and they claimed that Nurhachi had intended them to take charge after his death. As would be the case on many later occasions, however, the real intentions of the dying monarch were not entirely clear. Later Manchus came to agree that the wishes of the dying man were absolutely binding upon his surviors, but since successful claimants to power were always in a position to rewrite history, they may sometimes have tinkered with the monarch's testament to suit their own purposes. In Nurhachi's case, men would later suggest that his intent had been to name Dorgon, his 14th son, as his successor. Dorgon was not quite 14 at the time of his father's death, but he had already been given command of one of the junior banners. His age would seem to have militated against his immediate assumption of full responsibility, but his two full brothers were also slated by their father to be assigned banners. None of the other five banner leaders were full brothers, and the older men may have feared the potentially dangerous alliance that this trio might pose. The mother of these three committed suicide after Nurhachi's death. Such suicide was sanctioned by Manchu custom, and it was claimed that she acted in accordance with Nurhachi's request, but it seems more likely that it was done at the insistence of the senior brothers. They would have had special cause to fear the three brothers had their mother been on hand to help them. Manchu mothers, like Maratha mothers, were always tempted to intrigue on behalf of their sons.

Whatever Nurhachi's real intention, it was the senior banner leaders who held the power and it was they who assumed command. These four continued to take monthly turns leading the administration. As in some African tribes, the circulation of office among the top leaders was seen as a way of keeping the realm united. At the same time, however, they chose, ostensibly on instruction from Nurhachi, one of their own number as leader. The man they chose was Abahai, Nurhachi's eighth son, and the youngest of the senior four. The reasons for the selection of Abahai are not entirely clear. It is quite possible that by choosing the younger man, the others hoped they would run less risk of domination, but Daisan, the eldest of the four, seems to have consistently supported Abahai. Daisan never exhibited personal ambition to succeed to first place himself, and his support for Abahai may have been decisive.

At the start, Abahai was only first among equals, for all power and rights of decision making were shared with the other three senior Hosoi Beiles. A symbol of their equality was that all four Hosoi Beiles sat together at the same level, a practice very foreign to the Chinese, whose customs the Manchus were coming increasingly to imitate. Within a few years, however, Abahai emerged as the real leader. The independent power of the competing Hosoi Beiles was reduced by building up the power of both the civil and military staff officers in their banners. On the pretext that the senior men should not be troubled with excess work, various younger brothers and nephews were given a share of their responsibilities. Then the power of some of the leaders was directly broken. Amin, the cousin, antagonized many of the princes by his arrogance and independence during a military campaign in Korea, and Abahai was able to relieve him of his command. Next, Manggultai, Nurhachi's fifth son, upset some members of the court by losing his temper and threatening Abahai. Daisan then suggested that Abahai assume the higher position, while he and Manggultai accept a lower position in seating. Administration then ceased to rotate among the Hosoi Beiles.

Abahai, moreover, was a supremely successful leader in his own right. Under his direction, Manchu power penetrated far into China, and Abahai finally became the uncontested successor to Nurhachi. Abahai's moves to gain preeminence within the circle of his royal brothers, cousins, and nephews, can be seen as the first stage of a long contest between the power of the imperial office and that of the royal clan. Abahai's successors would gradually build up the position of the emperor and correspondingly undermine the competing role of the clan; but for the time being, the council of princes retained great authority. Abahai could reduce the power of some princes only by gaining the support of others.

Abahai died in 1643. Of the two men most strategically placed to inherit power, the most logical was certainly Abahai's eldest son, Haoge, then 34 years old. Haoge's succession was proposed, but he stood in fear of his uncle Dorgon who was 4 years his junior. Dorgon had proven himself to be a strong military leader and an excellent administrator. More than anyone else, he had organized and championed the newer Chinese style of government administration. Haoge had ample reason to fear Dorgon's power, for the uncle commanded a powerful banner of his own, and through his younger full brother, he could count upon the support of a second. Haoge, therefore, declined the inheritance, but a serious ideological barrier stood in Dorgon's way.

According to widely accepted Manchu custom, it was the members of the senior generation (the generation of the deceased ruler) who should gather in council and make the decision, but they had to appoint someone from the next lower generation as the successor. The logic of this rule was sound. The older and more experienced men were given the right to make the decision, but power was then entrusted to someone young and vigorous. Potential conflict among the older men was reduced by their mutual agreement not to seek office themselves. Dorgon, although younger than Haoge, was in the senior generation, and even if he had wanted to claim office, he would have risked the profound disapproval of his kinsmen, upon whose support he would finally have to depend. Too many commanders were devoted to Abahai personally or to the abstract rule requiring that the successor come from the lower generation to allow Dorgon to take over completely, but Dorgon was too powerful both in arms and in civil administration to permit a potential rival like Haoge to take over.

The result was a compromise, hammered out in a 17-day meeting of the clan leaders and the military commanders. Haoge's younger brother, then only 5 years old, was given the throne while Dorgon and his cousin Jirgalang were made co-regents. The child would soon be placed on the throne in Peking as the first emperor of the Ch'ing or Manchu dynasty, while Dorgon quickly emerged as the dominant member of the regency. Dorgon thus attained the substance of power, while preserving the traditional formalities of the succession rule. For the next 7 years, until his death in 1650, Dorgon was the effective ruler of the Manchus, and he was the real conquerer of China. In the year following his assumption of power, Manchu armies occupied Peking, and most of the rest of the country soon followed. For many generations imperial succession would proceed regularly from father to son, and there was never any ambiguity about who held the office of emperor. But there were many periods, like that of Dorgon's dominance, when the emperor did not himself exercise full control, so any account of the passage of power during the Manchu dynasty must take into account more than the single line of imperial succession. Figure 4-1 may help the reader to visualize the somewhat tortured course of Manchu power. The column immediately to the right of the dates lists the emperors and, except for Nurhachi and Abahai, who never ruled from Peking, gives their serial order. These emperors are connected to one another by arrows which extend across the years of each man's region, and which point downward from father to son. The right hand column gives the names of other leaders who wielded great power during the dynasty: regents, favorites, and other high officials, including the collective Hosoi Beile at the top, followed

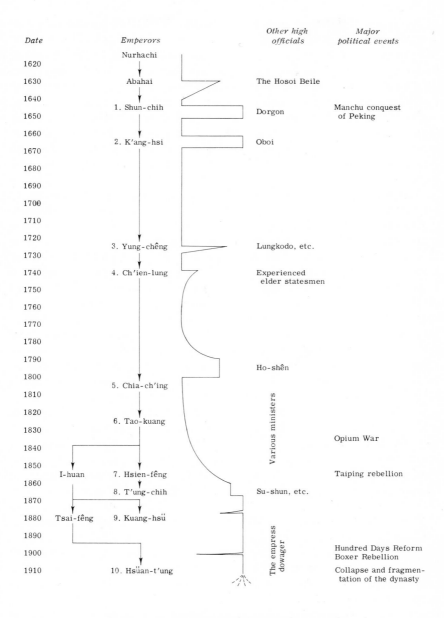

Date	Emperors	Other high officials	Major political events
	Nurhachi		
1620			
1630	Abahai	The Hosoi Beile	
1640			
1650	1. Shun-chih	Dorgon	Manchu conquest of Peking
1660			
1670	2. K'ang-hsi	Oboi	
1680			
1690			
1700			
1710			
1720			
1730	3. Yung-chêng	Lungkodo, etc.	
1740	4. Ch'ien-lung	Experienced elder statesmen	
1750			
1760			
1770			
1780			
1790		Ho-shên	
1800			
1810	5. Chia-ch'ing		
1820			
1830	6. Tao-kuang		
1840			Opium War
1850			
1860	I-huan 7. Hsien-fêng		Taiping rebellion
1870	8. T'ung-chih	Su-shun, etc.	
1880	Tsai-fêng 9. Kuang-hsü		
1890			
1900			Hundred Days Reform Boxer Rebellion
1910	10. Hsüan-t'ung		Collapse and fragmentation of the dynasty

Figure 4–1. Power during the Manchu dynasty.

by Dorgon just below. The waving line which wanders between the two columns of names, gives, in diagrammatic form, an indication of the locus of real power at any particular time. When the line lies close to the column of emperors, it shows that the emperor was in reasonably full control. When the line moves near to a regent, it suggests that the regent held power. The line wavers between the columns at times when power was shared or contested. Thus, it can be seen at a glance that during the first part of the dynasty, power tended to shift back and forth quite decisively between emperor and regent, while in the middle period the emperors more often monopolized power. In the end, real power shifted rather consistently away from the titular emperors.

Dorgon died unexpectedly in 1650 when the emperor, reigning under the title of Shun-chih, was still only 12 years old. Dorgon had acted vigorously, but high handedly, and he had made many enemies among the imperial princes. A struggle ensued over his replacement. Dorgon left no male heir, except an adopted nephew who was still very young, and the affairs of Dorgon's banners were left to several of his former lieutenants rather than to kinsmen. Some of these lieutenants claimed that Dorgon had left verbal instructions concerning their future part in the regency and had they acted with vigor, they might have assumed power. They were not decisive enough, however, and others, already disposed to view Dorgon's actions with distrust and skeptical of his verbal instructions, plotted with leaders of the other banners to take over the government in the name of the youthful emperor. The regency was formally abolished in 1651, and many princes rallied to the emperor. Dorgon's former supporters were displaced.

By the time Dorgon's regency ended, the foundations of the empire were well laid, and the Shun-chih emperor had the support of the many princes who had been antagonized by Dorgon. The army continued to push back the borders of the empire, and the emperor proceeded conscientiously, though unspectacularly, with his job. He embarked upon the study of Chinese and seems to have been strongly influenced by some aspects of Chinese civilization.

Shun-chih died suddenly of smallpox in 1661, still in his early twenties. Just before his death his third son, then 7, was designated heir, largely, it seems, because he had already contracted and recovered from smallpox, and was thus believed more likely to survive. Aided by the new child-emperor's mother, another regency was formed. It was dominated by a man named Oboi, who had been closely associated with Shun-chih ever since he had helped dispose of Dorgon's faction. Oboi now ruled in the name of Shun-chih's son, and he took the opportunity to settle a good many old grudges. He managed to make enemies of so many important men that the new emperor, K'ang-hsi, found wide and ready support when he was ready to displace his regent and assert power in his own right. This he did in 1669 when he was still only 14 years old. He had the vital help of Oboi's enemies, but the K'ang-hsi emperor soon asserted his own will. He inaugurated one of the most illustrious reigns of the Manchu era.

Already we can see a trend. With each new Manchu ruler, the assumption of effective power came a bit more easily or more decisively. Abahai, though a mature man, had to spend years of careful maneuver among his fellow princes. Shun-chih had to await the death of Dorgon, but then the symbolism of the imperial office was strong enough to bring him ready support. K'ang-hsi, admittedly a strong personality, did not have to wait for the death of his regents, but could displace them and assert his own rule when he was hardly more than a child. One can look upon this progression as a part of the increasing Sinicization of the Manchu government. A Manchu khan was placed in power by the agreement of his clansmen. A Chinese emperor needed no such sanction. As the government became more Chinese in form, the power of the royal Manchu clan declined, and the succession could then proceed by principles more like those of the Chinese.

As their territories expanded, the conquering Manchus, like the conquering Marathas, faced the problem of governing their newly won domains, and like the Marathas, they resorted to feudatory relations with powerful landed magnates. Chinese generals were given command over great stretches of southern and western China, just as Maratha jagirdars were given control over large tracts in newly conquered north India. In both China and India, the principle of direct rule from the center competed with the principle of less centralized "feudal" control by subordinate chiefs or generals. The difference lay in the theories of government available in the two areas. In India, Shivaji had tried to establish centralized control, but his descendants inevitably slipped back into the jagirdari system that Indians knew so well. In China, the Manchus had to resort to feudal control over some territories in the early decades of their rule, but Chinese governmental theory and practice gave every encouragement to a determined emperor who wished to crush his feudal subordinates and to centralize power in his own hands.

Early in his reign, the K'ang-hsi emperor determined, against the recommendation of his advisors, to crush the Chinese feudatories in the south, and substitute centralized rule. In 1681, after 8 years of bitter fighting, the feudatories were decisively beaten. K'ang-hsi, still in his twenties, was now the undisputed ruler of a united and centralized empire. There were further military engagements along the northwest frontier during his reign, but these never threatened the security of the nation or seriously interferred with its internal life. The Manchu emperors had triumphed.

CONSOLIDATION AND CENTRALIZATION

The consolidation of the empire under K'ang-hsi inaugurates the peak period of Manchu rule. Until K'ang-hsi's reign, the Manchu rulers had to compete with others, first with various rival border groups, then with the survivors of the Ming dynasty, and finally with rebellious Chinese feudatories. Now the Manchus were in undisputed control.

K'ang-hsi's success must certainly be attributed in large measure to his personal abilities. He was unquestionably a vigorous and dynamic leader. The assurance with which he displaced his regent Oboi and the vigor with which he pressed the campaign against the Chinese feudatories attest to his capacities. But K'ang-hsi also appeared at the very moment when the empire was ready for a single dominant leader, when his predecessors had made it possible for all threads of power to be brought together in one place. K'ang-hsi was the right man at the right moment.

The emperor's uniquely powerful position can be seen as a culmination of two separate developments: two millennia of Chinese history, and a half century of increasing Manchu power. The Chinese emperor had long filled a crucial role at the apex of a complex administrative and military hierarchy. All Chinese expected the emperor to provide centralized ceremonial, military, political, and administrative leadership. The Ming and particularly the Manchu dynasties exhibited the most thoroughgoing centralization of all, and in this the Manchus simply carried one step further the trends long evident in the Chinese political system. At the same time, K'ang-hsi's rule represented the culmination of the much more rapid development of Manchu leadership away from a chief of Manchu horsemen and toward an emperor of a centralized and bureaucratic state. The Manchus could change radically in the three generations separting Nurhachi from K'an-hsi, because they could follow the example of earlier Chinese dynasties, and because they were always ready to incorporate Chinese into their administration and their army. Thus it was Manchu military strength that first allowed Nurhachi's people to conquer, but by the time of K'ang-hsi, the emperor was ruling a Chinese nation with a Chinese type of administration according to Chinese rules. The centralization of power in the throne had decisive implications for later patterns of imperial succession, and so we have to consider the techniques by which this centralization was achieved.

As the examples from Africa and India have shown, a wise ruler must never let another man assume a clear second position, lest his own leadership be threatened. Every ruler must, of course, rule through subordinates, but he must keep these subordinates under control, and the most effective way to do this is to balance one against another. Each subordinate should have only such limited power as can be easily overcome by the opposing power of others. In this way, whenever one man begins to look like a threat, others can be called upon to dispose of him. When in efficient operation, the Chinese political system was as perfect a device as the world has ever known for fragmenting and for balancing all power except that of the top ruler. Each early Manchu leader took steps to further fragment his potential opposition.

Nurhachi had divided his army into the eight separate banners, no one of which was likely to pose a threat to his own central leadership, particularly since a single banner did not occupy a single contiguous territory. After Nurhachi's time the banners did temporarily serve as power bases for their royal commanders, but then the power of the royal commanders of the banners was gradually reduced, first by assigning them nonroyal staff officers, and then by bringing some banners directly under the emperor, until finally, under K'ang-hsi, royal clansmen were deliberately excluded from positions of high military leadership. Clansmen were consoled with high pensions and positions of honor, but they were carefully excluded from duties where they might accumulate too much power. Henceforth the highest military positions were always given to men who could be more easily removed at the will, or even the whim, of the emperor.

More important even than the army in securing the emperor's dominance was the Manchu acquisition of a Chinese-style bureaucracy. The rulers needed a vast administrative machinery to run the territories they conquered; the available machinery and the machinery to which the population was already accustomed was the traditional bureaucracy. Thus the government was, in a sense, formed from a Chinese bureaucracy that had been conquered by a Manchu army. Both the bureaucracy and the military regiments were responsible to the emperor, and in some degree they acted to check one another, or at least, the emperors could use the bureaucracy and the political ideology it represented as they strove to consolidate their dominance over the banners. The bureaucracy's strong ideological commitments included the recognition of the emperor's supreme position. An emperor who needed to assert his own will over his sometimes unruly and contentious fellow Manchus must have welcomed the ready support of scholarly and knowledgeable bureaucrats whose ideology granted him such a central position.

If the government had consisted simply of a Chinese bureaucracy and a Manchu army, the two divisions might have developed irreconcilable antagonisms, but in fact Chinese were incorporated into the army as early as Nurhachi's time, and many Manchus were brought into high bureaucratic positions. Chinese units were attached to the Manchu banners, though not completely merged with them, and this helped to further the fragmentation that the banner divisions had begun. Among civilians, Manchus were, of course, vastly outnumbered by Chinese, but Manchus were given privileged access to high government posts, restrictions were placed on intermarriage, and many Manchus lived in special encampments which were visibly set apart from the Chinese. Thus, by keeping the groups partially segregated and by granting special privileges to the minority Manchus while still admitting many Chinese to high office, the groups were kept in such balance that each checked the other and the emperor was left supreme. Manchu and Chinese, general and bureaucrat, all looked to the emperor for leadership, and any threat to the emperor from one quarter could be countered by pressure from another.

Army insubordination had been checked by keeping its various parts individually responsible to the emperor, but even more than the army, the bureaucracy was designed to have numerous internal divisions and so many mutual checks that no segment could pose a serious threat to the central power. Provincialism was discouraged by forbidding officials from serving in their home provinces, and rotating them constantly from assignment to assignment. The biographies of Manchu officials tell of long sequences of posts, with a move every few years from one province to another, and from one bureau of the government to another. An official would barely master one job before being thrown into a new one. If this lowered efficiency, it was also an exceedingly effective technique for preventing local or provincial concentrations of power.

Beyond this, the highest administration of each province was itself divided among several officials—the viceroy, the governor, and the commander general—and each checked the power of the others. Provincial army contingents were divided among the several different officials, no one of whom had full power. Rebellion by such units became impossible, but at the same time, local military operations became so cumbersome that the provincial battalions were rarely capable of putting down any more serious disturbance than petty banditry. When peasant or tribal uprisings occurred, as they did with increasing frequency, or when external enemies invaded, the central government almost always had to send out its own troops.

Like provincial administration, the central administration was fragmented. The Manchus adopted the six ministries of the preceding Ming dynasty, and each ministry reported directly to the emperor. No one without heroic stamina could attend to all the details of all the ministries, however, and the Manchus also took over the Ming office of the grand secretariat, attached directly to the emperor and intended to assist him with the manifold details of his office.

To check upon the rest of the government and to report any malfeasance, the Manchus followed earlier dynasties in maintaining a censorate as a separate branch of the administration. The censors were expected to busy themselves by looking over everybody else's shoulders, ferreting out cases of corruption, and reporting them to the emperor. They were supposed to be free to censor even the highest officials. The K'ang-hsi emperor also employed bond servants who were descendents of low-born retainers, and who submitted confidential reports about provincial conditions which by-passed the regular bureaucracy.

Thus, every institutional block within the government around which opposition to the emperor might have developed was thoroughly fragmented. Army was divided from civilian bureaucracy, banner from banner, province from province, grand secretariat from ministry, censorate from regular administration. At the top was the emperor, so powerful that he could fire any official or even abolish any office that seemed to threaten him, but such overwhelming power carried overwhelming dilemmas. The very magnitude of his duties forced him to rely upon subordinates to whom he could delegate at least some responsibilities, and inevitably those who took responsibility also acquired power. Moreover, to the extent that the power of others was fragmented, the ability of the government to act decisively and efficiently was impaired. Too much depended on the single unifying office of emperor, and the emperor could not do all things at once.

The Manchus had followed their predecessors in opening the bureaucracy to men who had passed the state examinations. The examinations were based upon the Chinese classics and they became exceedingly stereotyped in form, but in principle they opened government administration to men of talent, whatever their ancestry or political connections. The ideals of the examination system were clear, and so long as the examinations were well administered, they served as a check upon sheer nepotism or on the build-up of family or factional power. The system was by no means safe from corruption, however, and inevitably men sought other ways to advance their interests. With alternative power bases thoroughly fragmented, the only recourse left either for ambitious men who desired to advance their own interests, or for idealistic men who believed in particular policies, was to form loose and shifting alliances with others who had similar goals. The temptation to do so was irresistible. A man was supposed to be able to rise to ever higher positions through success on examinations, an exhibition of moral virtue and demonstrated ability. In fact, it was often more helpful to know the right people. Favorable mention by a patron might achieve more than years of devoted labor in minor provincial posts. Lower officials could use patrons in high positions; high officials could use henchmen from the ranks; everyone could use a friend. Networks of friendship cut across the organizational boundaries of the administration and they had a rather obvious potential for distorting the system, for they were regularly used to promote the self-interest of the members. From the top, these factions always looked like dangerous concentrations of power, and for this reason, they were repeatedly denounced. Time and again emperors issued edicts which demonstrated an almost pathological fear of cabals, and it was always assumed that they sought evil ends: the personal enrichment of the members or the advancement of incompetent or disloyal officials. The possibility that honorable and loyal men might band together to promote the policies they believed best for the nation was never acknowledged. It was assumed that good men need only support their emperor. To join a faction appeared to place oneself in opposition.

The mistrust of factions put reformers into a difficult position. Those seeking to reform the system found it difficult to organize themselves. As soon as they began to cooperate for the end they desired, they began to look like a faction. Their more opportunistic rivals, organizing to exploit the system rather than to reform it, had fewer scruples about their own organizing efforts, but they might find it useful to denounce the factionalism of the reformers. The ideals of the bureaucracy and of the educational system that fed it gave rise to repeated reform movements, but these were as often crushed when the emperors were persuaded that the reform faction represented an organized threat to their power.

The many divisions which crisscrossed the administration prevented any coalition from growing so powerful that it could threaten to overturn the government. A vigorous emperor could use the apparatus to keep the country at peace, to collect a bountiful revenue, and to build extensive public works. Foreign enemies could be kept at bay, and military expeditions could be sent thousands of miles from the capital. The machinery would even allow a weak emperor to survive. Once in office, the numerous internal checks would keep almost any man on the throne. With a weak man at the top, the government would continue to grind along in its cumbersome way, growing increasingly corrupt and moving toward decay, but during the reign of K'ang-hsi the system worked well. He was a vigorous and able man and he could control the machinery to his own ends. He consolidated the empire militarily; he improved the navigability of the Grand Canal and attended to flood control of the Yellow River; he toured extensively through his empire; he encouraged learning and sponsored the compilation of the history of the preceding Ming dynasty; he patronized the arts; he was interested in mathematics and science, welcomed Westerners, and valued their astronomical, geographical, and medical skills. The empire prospered. For present purposes, however, it is the implications of this extraordinarily centralized monarchy for the principles of succession that are important, and in this one respect, it must be said that K'ang-hsi failed.

THE MIDDLE PERIOD

K'ang-hsi could look back upon, and perhaps choose from, two different explicit traditions that governed succession. The Chinese expectation during the preceding Ming dynasty had been that the eldest son would succeed to his father's position, although occasional exceptions to this rule were allowed. Primogeniture conformed to the pattern of inheritance of ceremonial position at all levels of Chinese society. Even among the peasants, the eldest son ordinarily took over his father's ceremonial responsibilities and conducted the ancestor rites on behalf of his younger brothers and other members of the family. Noble titles were also normally passed to the eldest son. Ming custom, therefore, simply carried general Chinese practice right to the top, although this was a place where the choice of a qualified and skillful man was particularly important.

The Manchu succession rule upon which K'ang-hsi could draw granted no special rights to the eldest son. The Manchus expected a more equal division of responsibility among the sons, but when a single chief was needed, the members of the older generation would assemble to make the choice. The formal succession rule of the later Manchus was a compromise between their own earlier practices and those of the Chinese. The emperor came to designate his heir himself. This denied the earlier collegial rights of the clan as a whole, but it kept the choice in the senior generation and left the choice more open than allowed by the earlier Chinese expectation of primogeniture. As power was centralized under the emperor, it became difficult for anyone else openly to advocate his own choice of successor, for only the emperor himself could make such a decision. He alone could designate the preferred son.

K'ang-hsi publicly designated his second son Yin-jêng as his heir apparent, but not all of Yin-jêng's many half brothers acquiesced with good grace, especially when he showed signs of a violent temper, immoral conduct, and even of mental instability. His difficulties have sometimes been attributed to the overindulgence of an heir apparent, but in any case, they gave grounds upon which his brothers could dispute his position. As in many other kingdoms, the princes became bitter competitors. They formed themselves into factions, sought allies among the courtiers, and jockeyed endlessly for position. A long period of accusation and counter accusation among the brothers led at last to the removal of Yin-jêng from his role as heir apparent. Thereafter, the emperor refused to name a new heir apparent, having concluded that the practice led only to strife.

A dominant faction of brothers nevertheless emerged, and gradually they came to support the 14th son, Yin-t'i, and toward the end of the K'ang-hsi reign, it appeared that the emperor too had come to favor Yin-t'i. He never announced his choice publicly, but in 1717, Yin-t'i was given an important military assignment and the general presumption seems to have been that he was being given the chance to build up his reputation. He campaigned with some success in the west, returned to Peking in 1722 where he was received with great honor, and then set off again, leaving an elder brother and close supporter with instructions to keep him informed about developments in the capital. He seems to have been confident of inheriting the throne, and since his father was now approaching 70, he could expect to do so without inordinate delay.

Later that same year while Yin-t'i was still away from the capital, the emperor died. Another son, the fourth, was at his father's deathbed. Since this fourth son won out and became the Yung-chêng emperor, history came to be written from his partisan point of view, and his activities at the time of his father's death are not entirely clear. He seems to have cultivated the friendship of a number of high officials, and his subsequent harsh treatment of his brothers can be taken as evidence of some bitterness against them. The official histories state that K'ang-hsi's final testament provided for Yung-chêng's succession, though historians have guessed that the publicized will was fabricated. More to the point certainly was that Yung-chêng had the crucial backing of a man named Lungkodo, who was the commander of the Peking military garrison. Lungkodo kept the city under control while Yung-chêng was declared emperor. Yin-t'i, who had expected to inherit, was too far away from Peking to contest the outcome, and his allies at the capital were apparently caught completely off guard. Accusations have even been made that the old emperor was murdered, so as to allow Yung-chêng to seize control at the most advantageous moment. Such charges can hardly be proven, and they would almost surely have been whispered by those unhappy with the outcome, whatever the facts, but even if utterly unsubstantiated, the rumors do give evidence for the kinds of action then regarded as plausible for competitors for power.

The Yung-chêng emperor acted decisively to consolidate his own rule. He stepped into the role which dominated an otherwise fragmented power apparatus and he moved too quickly for any coalition to build up effective opposition. Two younger brothers were rewarded for their support, and a few others were tolerated for their neutrality, but Yung-chêng quickly found various pretexts for stripping those in Yin-t'i's faction of their rank and then of their freedom. Several died in jail, and others were not relaeased until after Yung-chêng himself had died years later. Any danger from his kinsmen was thus eliminated.

Within a few years, the new emperor also found pretexts for dismissing and then punishing the men who had helped him to power. A man who had spied for him against his brother, Yin-t'i, was removed from office, and

Yung-chêng then turned against Lungkodo, the Peking garrison commander, first accusing him of being too lenient with the spy and then of being too severe. Within 5 years of Yung-chêng's accession, Lungkodo was confined to prison where he died. If Lungkodo had known of irregularities by which the Yung-chêng emperor had achieved his position (it has been suspected that Lungkodo wrote the will designating Yung-chêng as successor), he had now been effectively silenced. Lungkodo had come as close to playing the role of kingmaker as anyone in the dynasty, but he died for his effort. The emperor's office had accumulated such power that a decisive and determined man could dispose of any one who presented any threat at all. Whatever the legitimacy of his accession, Yung-chêng consolidated his position much more rapidly than any of his predecessors. His speed and efficiency were no doubt partly a tribute to his own ruthlessness, and they were made possible by his greater maturity at the time of his accession, but he also benefited from the ever more centralized power of the throne. Whoever could make a sudden grab for the symbols of power could rally enough support to hold them.

The Yung-chêng period (1723-1735) was a relatively short interlude between the two longest reigns of the dynasty, but Yung-chêng proved to be a competent leader. He made some progress in weeding out the corruption that had grown rather serious in the later years of his father's long rule. He introduced reforms in the national finances, and he can be credited with laying the foundation for the splendors of the succeeding reign. He also took some final steps in centralizing the power of the throne, forbidding cliques or parties among his officials, and depriving princes of their power to control bannermen.

Having himself participated in a deadly struggle for the throne, Yung-chêng was well aware of the dangers of princely ambition. In order to minimize the next struggle, he kept the young princes inside the palace attending the palace school. Tutors instructed them in the virtues of obedience and loyalty, and from this time on, the indoctrination that princes received seems to have effectively limited their tendency to compete violently for the throne. It very likely also limited the dynamism and worldly knowledge which subsequent emperors could bring to their command over the empire. Though not imprisoned as closely as many Maratha princes, the Manchu princes did come to be secluded from the world over which they were destined to rule, and shielded from those men with whom they might be tempted to intrigue. Their ignorance of this world cannot have helped them to rule with skill. By careful education of his sons and by refraining from publicly naming an heir apparent. Yung-chêng succeeded in preventing fraternal strife. Of his four sons who lived to maturity, none but the one who became emperor amounted to much more than a nonentity. None of the other three seem to have nursed any serious ambition, and all acquiesced in their filial duty of accepting their father's will.

Yung-chêng placed the name of his choice of heir in a sealed box, the contents unknown to anyone else, a practice which then became standard. His chosen son, his fourth, and the second eldest of those who survived childhood, was publicly declared heir apparent as his father lay dying. This son became the Ch'ien-lung Emperor, and he shared with his grandfather, K'ang-hsi, the distinction of a long and glorious reign. Ch'ien-lung's accession was the first in the dynasty to follow entirely orderly and legitimate procedures. Even K'ang-hsi had to engineer what amounted to a coup against his regent before he acquired power, but Ch'ien-lung, 24 years old at the time of his father's death, seems to have had no challengers. He had the advice of experienced older statesmen, but as he grew older, he increasingly made his own decisions, those around him being reduced to yes-men and writers of eulogies. The Ch'ien-lung reign was notable not only for its length, but for its military successes and for its art and literature, and its first half marks the high point of Manchu power and the high point of political centralization. Before the end of the reign, however, the seeds of decay, in the form of pervasive administrative corruption, were clearly visible, and from that time onward, the political climate of China became ever more chaotic. No sooner had the succession problem been solved, it would seem, than the dynasty began to decline.

THE PERIOD OF DECLINE

Many factors contributed to the Manchu decline. Some were new, but others had beset earlier dynasties and had contributed to the seemingly endless cycle of dynastic rise and fall. Europeans were now arriving on the Chinese coast in increasing numbers, bringing pressures with which the Chinese had absolutely no experience. A more familiar problem was that of too many people. The very stability of the middle Manchu period had allowed a vast increase in population. Cut down drastically by the turmoil of the late Ming and early Manchu period, the population had climbed right back up to something on the order of 300,000,000 by late in the Ch'ien-lung reign. Resources were strained and poverty fomented unrest, but more than a reaction to Europeans or to an increased population, the Manchu decline was an administrative one, a steady decay in the ability of the government to cope with the gigantic task of running the country.

The traditional but simplistic Chinese explanation for the decline is to blame a wicked minister—Ho-Shên.[2] This man began as a low ranking member of the Imperial Guard, but he gained the confidence of the Ch'ien-lung Emperor, and rose rapidly from one position to another until during the last 20 years of the reign, he came to exercise enormous influence. Ho-shên accumulated a huge private fortune, no doubt at public expense, and he was able to place his own henchmen in many key positions in the empire. It was dangerous for anyone to refuse his wishes, for he could regularly gain the emperor's backing. During Ho-shên's sway, rebellions broke out in the provinces, attributable at least in part to the peasants' desperation at the exactions of Ho-shên's henchmen, but it was Ho-shên's men who were sent to put the rebellions down. Army leaders sent false reports to the emperor about the progress of their campaigns. They persuaded him that huge expenditures from the treasury were needed to raise and maintain the army, but they diverted the funds to their own private purses and failed badly in prosecuting the war. From top to bottom, the administrative hierarchy was riddled with corruption, and the Ch'ien-lung Emperor was quite incapable of dealing with it.

There is an attractive simplicity in blaming Ho-shên for the decay of the dynasty, but corruption was nothing new. Even from K'ang-hsi's reign, there is ample evidence of corrupt officials who built private fortunes at public expense and, rather than blaming an evil man, we must ask what it was in the Chinese system that allowed men like Ho-shên to gain such power. Perhaps we can find part of the answer by turning the question around and asking what there was that might have prevented corruption.

Fundamentally, there were only two impediments: the moral teachings of the educational system, and the internal administrative checks which were controlled by the emperor. It is a tribute to the moral power of the Chinese classics which formed the steady diet of the educational system that able and virtuous men continued to be found in the administration, but not even Chinese education could prevent an occasional rascal from slipping through. Honest men always had to compete with dishonest ones for imperial favor. This left it up to the emperor. But here lay a problem, for the very ease with which Ch'ien-lung and his immediate successors succeeded to the throne tended to make them prisoners of their own governmental apparatus. With little difficulty and with little chance to learn of worldly realities, the emperors slid into the seat of power. A flick of the emperor's vermillion pencil could decide the fate of millions. When-

[2]For my discussion of the role of Ho-shên, I depend upon David S. Nivison, "Ho-shên and His Accusers; Ideology and Political Behavior in the Eighteenth Century," *Confucianism in Action*, ed., David S. Nivison and Arthur F. Wright (Stanford: Stanford University Press, 1959), pp. 209-243.

ever he choose to exercise his power, he could appoint, promote, demote, or dismiss officials in any part of the far flung administration; but it became increasingly difficult for even the best intentioned emperor to make wise decisions. Surrounded by sycophants, the emperors were increasingly cut off from effective knowledge of the world beyond the palace gates. They were asked to choose between competing memorials from administrators asking for varying policies in a huge and complex realm. It was quite impossible for an emperor consistently to choose the most enlightened policies. Sooner or later, self-seekers would be certain to gain his ear.

According to well-accepted Confucian principles of government, an upright minister who believed another to be guilty of corruption should so inform the emperor, but if the one accused had well-established friends in the bureaucracy, and had access to the emperor, he might persuade the emperor that the accusor should be punished instead. As individuals and factions struggled for position, their one common interest was to prevent the emperor from knowing too much. More and more, the emperor came to be elevated out of touch with reality. He was protected by complex ceremonial restrictions. The highest ministers prostrated themselves and trembled in his presence. His actions became so unquestionable that even to criticize the decisions of his high officials could appear as indirect criticism of the emperor himself. In such circumstances, a Ho-shên who could get the ear of the emperor, who could flatter him and soothe his vanity, could come to wield enormous power.

But Ho-shên failed in one such dramatic respect that the omnipotence that latter generations attributed to him must be questioned—he failed to maneuver the succession to his own benefit. He must have known which of the emperor's sons would be best disposed toward him, and it is inconceivable that he would not have tried to influence the choice for his own advantage. But not only did an enemy of Ho-shên come to the throne; he was placed there even before his father died.

Ch'ien-lung lived to a great age, but a few years before his death, he announced that he did not wish to have a longer reign than his grandfather. He publicly declared that his heir should be his 15th son. This son was installed as the Chia-ch'ing Emperor, and Ch'ien-lung abdicated in his favor. The new emperor had been secretly designed as heir 20 years earlier, but he seems to have been treated equally with his brothers. The brothers had learned their lessions of filial piety so well that they never challenged Chia-ch'ing's accession. Only 2 of his 16 brothers played any significant political role at all. Chia-ch'ing asked these 2 to help with some administrative reorganization at the time he first took over power, but they were soon relieved of their posts on the explicit ground that too much responsibility should not be given to imperial princes. The problem of peaceful succession seemed to have been solved, but the brothers were all such nonentities that one must wonder if the 15th son was not equally fitted to be a nonentity. A stroke of chance rather than any demonstration of special ability thrust him into the emperor's seat.

For the first few years of his reign, from 1796 to 1799, Chia-ch'ing did not really rule. The same ethic of filial piety that kept his brothers from challenging his position kept him from displacing his father. Though his father was now growing senile, Ho-shên retained his position and made most of the effective governmental decisions. Chia-ch'ing could do nothing except watch from the side lines and quietly wait out his father's life. He did this with patience, but he must have long planned his moves, for within 5 days of his father's death in 1799, he had Ho-shên arrested and forced him to commit suicide. He was apparently backed by his brothers, for they received a share of Ho-shên's fortune. Ho-shên was gone, but the system that had allowed corrupt officials to gain power was not, and corruption continued to be a problem until the very end of the dynasty.

Chia-chi'ing took over control with little difficulty, but he took over an empire that was in a sad state of disarray. The administration was corrupt from top to bottom. The Yellow River flooded repeatedly, and allotments intended for flood control ended in the pockets of officials. The population had doubled in the preceding reign and food shortages, compounded by a corrupt and incompetent administration, drove the people to revolt. By this time, however, the military regiments had been carefully reduced in power. This had seemed necessary in order to subject them to the emperor's will, but in the process, they had lost much of their fighting potential. Instead of policing the countryside, the army's oppressive presence sometimes succeeded only in driving the peasants to further revolt. For the first time in the Manchu dynasty, peasant levies recruited by local officials proved to be more effective fighters than the government's standing army.

Chia-ch'ing met these problems with as much vigor as can reasonably have been expected. He made an attempt to remove some corrupt officials. He cut down expenditures wherever he could, but this built up resentment among those formerly accustomed to luxuries, and when he became unpopular among the officials, he compromised with them instead of ruthlessly eliminating those who were corrupt, as his grandfather Yung-chêng might have done. To balance the budget, he resorted to the old but corrupting practice of selling titles and positions. This partially undermined the examination system, and it allowed some self-seekers a more direct access to office. He was a diligent and conscientious emperor, and he did manage to bring the worst of the rebellions under control; but he had been trained only to be patient and obedient, and to follow the examples of his predecessors. It would have been too much to hope that such a man, thrust into such responsibility, could deal imaginatively with the manifold problems of the empire.

Chia-ch'ing died in 1820, and on his deathbed he named his second son, the eldest then living, as his successor. Tao-kuang was the third successive emperor to begin his reign legitimately and with little incident. The first few years of the reign were reasonably tranquil, but his treasury was low and Tao-kuang was unable to decide upon an effective plan to contain the Yellow River, which proceeded to flood disastrously. Tao-kuang had neither the skill nor the courage to take decisive action, and his administration relied upon anciently sanctioned but rigid practices. His indecision proved fatal in the Opium War of 1839-1842, when the British first exerted serious military pressure. Coming from over the seas instead of from the Asian steppes, the British and the other Europeans presented a new kind of menace to China, and the government had no idea of how to cope with these new barbarians. Locked within his own administrative apparatus, the emperor could hardly have any clear conception of what was involved, and his ministers tended to gloss over the difficulties. They feared the rebukes that might be provoked by candid reports of floods, bandits, or invaders. Tao-kuang vacillated between accepting the advice of those demanding vigorous action and those advising compromise, but his bureaucracy was not united enough or well disciplined enough to pursue any course consistently. The Opium War brought humiliation to China. Extensive Western penetration began, and local rebellions again broke out. Tao-kuang died in 1850, "leaving to his successor . . . a crumbling empire, a depleted treasury and four hundred million subjects in a state of unrest."[3]

About the only satisfactory aspect of the empire at the time of Tao-kuang's death was the peaceful accession of his fourth son, Hsien-fêng, whom he had secretly chosen as heir apparent. Within a few months of Hsien-fêng's accession, however, the Taiping Rebellion broke out, a major upheaval in which a jumble of mystical ideas, peasant unrest, and secret society techniques combined to produce an army and government that temporarily controlled much of South China. Hsien-fêng was young and inexperienced, and he could not cope effectively with the chaotic conditions. The decadent bannermen could no longer be relied upon, and the emperor allowed Chinese generals to recruit local peasant militia to suppress the rebellion. The militia served for a time to prop up the regime, but a local initiative was being allowed that earlier emperors had been careful to suppress, and in the end, this permitted war lords to build up the

[3]Fang Chao-ting, "Min-ning," *Eminent Chinese of the Ch'ing Period,* ed. Arthur W. Hummel, (Washington, D.C.: Government Printing Office, 1943), p. 575.

regional power that would shatter the empire. Fragmentation of all power and subordination of all officials to the Manchu throne had once served the emperor well, and it even helped to allow a placid series of successions. When the fragmentation of power finally undermined the emperor's ability to control internal rebellion or foreign invasion, it came to serve the emperor very badly indeed.

The Taiping Rebellion was finally suppressed, more through internal dissensions among its leaders than through any really efficient effort by the government, but complete internal peace was never achieved, and foreign powers continued to press demands. Hsien-fêng found the strain too great and he began to retire from active direction of affairs. An Anglo–French force reached Peking in 1860, and the emperor fled to Jehol where he no longer had the courage to face his officials or to grant audiences to foreigners. He finally abandoned all leadership, and left all questions of policy and administration to his officials. The dynasty survived for another 50 years, and through three more reigns, but from the time of Hsien-fêng's flight from Peking, no emperor would again exercise anything like full power. For the three reigns of Chia-ch-ing, Tao-kuang, and Hsien-fêng, each emperor had coped less effectively with his duties than his predecessor; each was more securely imprisoned by his own administration. The governmental appartus needed direction from a strong emperor on the top, but it is difficult not to conclude that the appartus had finally conquered the emperor.

The emperor died in 1861 and left only one son. There could be no question about the succession, but since the boy was only 5 years old, there was a very real question about the composition of the regency that would be needed during the new emperor's minority. The most powerful minister during the last years of Hsien-fêng's reign was a man named Su-shun and he and some other high officials produced a document that named them as joint regents. This document provided that edicts should be approved by the two dowager empresses of the dead Hsien-fêng, but it seems that the regents tried to bypass the empresses. Some reports even suggest that Su-shun, who controlled the expenses of the household, tried to starve the ladies into submission. At any event, the empresses, with the help of two younger brothers of the dead emperor, accomplished a well-executed coup d'etat, imprisoned Su-shun, and had him beheaded. With effective power slipping away from the throne, succession struggles were taking a new form.

The ranking dowager empress was Hsiao-chên. Her junior partner, later known as Tz'ŭ-hsi, or to Westerners, as "the old Buddha," had originally entered the palace as a low ranking concubine. She, however, was the mother of the new child-emperor T'ung-chih, and she was also the more literate and certainly the more forceful of the two women. Gradually asserting her own will, she became the effective ruler of China for most of the remaining half-century of the Manchu dynasty. In China, as in Indian kingdoms, women could rise to supreme political power, but the dowager empress, like Tara-Bai, the Maratha queen, ruled through her husband's family and in the name of a son.

The capture of power by the empresses dowager marks the final stage in the evolution of the Manchu throne. Insubordinate feudatories, rival royal princes, rebelling army contingents, and reform-minded officials had been progressively placed securely under the emperor's heel. Now, as had happened many times before in Chinese history, the emperor's power had finally been captured by members of his own household.

The empresses ruled for 12 years in the name of Emperor T'ung-chih, and they must be credited with more vigor and efficiency than anyone had offered in the preceding reigns. The worst of the rebellions were suppressed, bandits were brought under control, and the foreign powers, now knocking ever more insistently upon the gates of China, were kept appeased. Thus when T'ung-chih formally took over from his mother's regency in 1873, the empire was in a slightly improved state, but the emperor's personal situation was hardly enviable, for he could never escape his mother's confining presence. Having placed her own people in office, she retained their loyalty, and state papers continued to pass through her hands. T'ung-chih, moreover, was not a forceful person, and he was easy prey to the dissolute life which his position would allow and which some of those who surrounded him were ready to encourage. He did chafe at the restrictions placed upon him by his mother and they finally quarreled. In 1875, however, the young T'ung-chih Emperor contracted smallpox and the quarrels were resolved by his death.

The empress dowager Tz'u-hsi remained the dominant figure in the empire, and she was even able to defy dynastic custom by placing a cousin of T'ung-chih on the throne. T'ung-chih was the first of his dynasty to die without a son, and since he had had no brothers, he could have no nephews. Nevertheless, the proper mode of succession was anciently sanctioned and unambiguous: The throne should have gone to a man of a younger generation, the son, presumably, of a first cousin. By this time, however, the empress controlled the apex of all the converging lines of power, and her strength had grown so great that she was difficult to defy even on so clear a matter of principle. She adopted a child who was simultaneously T'ung-chih's clan cousin and her own sister's son, and by placing him on the throne, she retained her own position as the empress dowager. The new emperor, Kuang-hsü, was only 3 years old, and the dowager could look forward to many years of regential rule.

More than any earlier Manchu ruler, the empress dowager appointed eunuchs to high positions. Eunuchs had wielded enormous power during earlier dynasties, but they had been condemned by the early Manchu rulers for their evil influence which was believed to have weakened the government. Through most of the Manchu dynasty, their activities were restricted to the palace and the harem. Women of the palace were carefully sheltered, however, and the only men with whom they were likely to have close association were eunuchs. As a result, once the empress dowager came into power, it was natural for her to turn to them for assistance. Moreover, since eunuchs came from humble backgrounds, they were usually more dependent upon a royal sponsor than were high civil service officials or royal princes. From the viewpoint of the orthodox bureaucracy, however, they raised the threat of arbitrary interference by illegitimate up-starts who had bypassed the traditional paths to office.

The child emperor, Kuang-hsü, grew up, and he has been described as impetuous and ill-tempered, but he seems to have received some rather sound education and, given the circumstances of his upbringing, to have grown into a surprisingly conscientious young adult. He was declared of age in 1887, but the empress dowager continued to read important state documents and to make certain appointments, and the emperor long hesitated to go against her will. His foster mother even arranged his marriage to a woman 3 years his senior, who was certainly expected to check up on him, and to report to the dowager.

It was an anomolous position for a man who was supposed to be emperor, but his office did at least give him wide contacts in the administration. Finally in 1898, he came under the influence of a reform-minded official, and for a brief period, known as the Hundred Days Reform, he issued a series of edicts designed to introduce some measure of modernity into the government. These reforms can be seen both as a revolt of forward-looking Chinese who wished to modernize their government and make it competative in the modern world, and as a revolt of the emperor against the empress dowager. In the end, however, the ideological conservatives and the entrenched supporters of the empress were stronger than the reformers. The dowager emerged from her partial retirement and with the cooperation of many conservative allies, she virtually imprisoned the emperor and resumed full control of the government. She denounced the reformers and issued edicts in the name of the imprisoned emperor that begged her to resume control. The conservatives then let loose the Boxer Rebellion, which provoked renewed foreign intervention and brought renewed humiliation for China. But these convulsions ended just short of collapse of the dynasty. Local military leaders gained increasing independence from central control. The Emperor Kuang-hsü could do nothing except wait for his aged foster mother to die.

He died one day before she did, however, in 1908. As so often before, unconfirmable rumor suggested that he had been murdered, but it was the old lady who provided for the final dynastic succession. Another child was now named emperor. He was a nephew of the dead Kuang-hsü and he reigned under the title Hsüan-t'ung. His father, Tsai-fêng, the brother of the late emperor, was to be regent, but these were now empty privileges in a crumbling realm. In 1911, the emperor and his regent were forced by the revolution to flee Peking, and in the following year, the child's abdication was submitted. The Manchu dynasty had come to a ragged end.

THE CHALLENGES TO LEGITIMATE SUCCESSION

This sketch of Manchu political history may seem to have strayed far from the narrow question succession, but the organization of the imperial household, the methods by which princes were educated, the techniques by which lesser officials were appointed, and indeed every aspect of the organization of the far-flung government all had a direct bearing upon the way in which power was transferred. The techniques of selection, in turn, directly affected the ability of the men chosen to deal with day-to-day problems, and all these were bound up with the degree of stability and of chaos found in China at various periods. Together, they contributed to the cyclical rise and fall of dynasties.

Perhaps the most notable single aspect of the Manchu dynasty, particularly when compared with dynasties in most other parts of the world, was its staying power. A dynasty of 12 rulers spanning two and one-half centuries was no mean achievement, but the Manchus were not the only Chinese dynasty to achieve this record. The preceding Ming dynasty, with 16 emperors, lasted as long, and some earlier dynasties had been nearly as enduring. By most dynastic standards, these were long and stable regimes, and the ability of emperors to follow each other peacefully to the throne was an essential element in their stability.

We can begin to understand how the Chinese could achieve such regular imperial succession by looking for directions from which threats to the dynasty might have come. If we can understand how these threats were minimized, we will have gone far in understanding the factors that made Chinese dynasties so much more enduring than those of India. Several quite different sorts of threats presented themselves at different periods, and they were countered by corresponding different means of defense.

Male Agnates

Male kinsmen, particularly brothers, posed the first threat to orderly succession in China, just as they did in India. The Marathas never found a way of controlling the rivalries among brothers, but the Manchus, with the lessons of two millenia of Chinese history upon which to draw, recognized and countered their threat. The danger of large-scale armed combat between the brothers was soon reduced by depriving the princes of individual control over any power base, such as a banner or a geographical area, but the threat of palace coups instigated by or on behalf of a brother remained a threat until Yung-chêng was able to instill a serious filial piety into his sons. By the end of the dynasty, the right of the father to name his successor was so thoroughly accepted that brothers no longer challenged his choice. To deprive them of the means for making a challenge, the princes were prevented from forming too close an association with powerful officials, and brothers who did not succeed to the throne were generally denied any significant office of their own. The cost of such measures, of course, was to bring poorly trained men to office and to make cooperation between a new emperor and his officials difficult; but brothers were effectively kept out of mischief.

Feudatories

The most serious rebellion against the early Manchu emperors was that of the Chinese feudatories early in the K'ang-hsi reign. Several Chinese generals had helped the Manchus to gain power. Their efforts were rewarded and Manchu hegemony quickly extended by assigning them large tracts in southern China which they were able to rule in virtual independence. No fully centralized state was possible so long as the generals could defy the central government, and it took a long war finally to dispose of them. Once put down, however, the habits of the centralized bureaucratic system prevented any other feudal power from building up in later reigns.

Incipient decentralization had been characteristic of the early periods of other dynasties. In the turmoil of setting up a new government, it was always an easy expedient to assign a territory's administration to an able kinsman or general. Once, early in the Ming dynasty, a territorial magnate, Yung-lo, who happened also to be a prince, successfully rebelled against a nephew and seized the throne for himself. Yung-lo was both a prince and a territorial ruler and his rebellion was both that of a kinsman and of a general. The Manchus, profiting perhaps from Ming mistakes, never let a prince control a large contiguous territory. By denying their banners a single geographic base, the Manchus showed administrative genius. Princes had power over various banners, and a few Chinese generals would temporarily dominate large contiguous territories. No one in the early Manchu period was ever allowed to combine genealogical claims with a territorial base of power. Once the early territorial chiefs were surpressed, the Chinese tradition of administrative centralization again became dominant. During the remainder of the Manchu dynasty, as in the latter part of earlier dynasties, territorial rebellion of the sort that had played such havoc with the Maratha kingdom, was never a problem. Here was perhaps the most profound difference between the "feudal" Maratha state and the centralized bureaucratic state of the Chinese.

Families of the Empresses

In earlier dynasties, kinsmen of the empresses had sometimes amassed great power, and occasionally they were even able to usurp the throne. The most famous example is Wang Mang, a nephew of an empress of the early Han dynasty. Wang Mang worked his way into the highest position of the bureaucracy, and he dominated the government during the reigns of two child-emperors. He finally took the throne for himself, founding the Hsin dynasty in 8 A.D. In the Manchu period, a male kinsman of one early empress climbed temporarily to considerable power. Songgotu, an uncle of the young K'ang-hsi's empress, had helped the emperor to displace his regents, and he thereby put the emperor in his debt. K'ang-hsi was too strong a man to suffer competition for power, however, and he later accused Songgotu of meddling in the struggle among his sons. Songgotu then lost his influence.

At other times, the Manchus had little trouble from the kinsmen of empresses, and they were usually careful to exclude the empresses' relatives from official position. To avoid such entanglements, they even declined to take their consorts from powerful families, and they kept the women secluded in the palace. Many of the empresses had quite humble backgrounds. Yung-chêng's mother had come into the palace as a maid-servant, but this did not prevent her son from becoming emperor, or herself from later attaining the rank of empress dowager. Tz'u-hsi, who as a later empress dowager dominated late 19th-century China, was the daughter of an undistinguished Manchu official, and she entered the palace as a low-ranking concubine. The Chinese, unlike the Marathas, regarded the original rank of one's mother as quite irrelevant in determining the right of a man to succeed. They would merely adjust the rank of the mother retroactively, or even posthumously if necessary, to accord with the subsequent facts of succession. Since low-ranking women who lacked important kinsmen could be brought into the palace, any danger that might come from a woman's powerful relatives was reduced to the vanishing point.

Usurpation by a Minister

In early dynasties, ministers had sometimes grown so powerful that they stopped the pretense of ruling in the name of a figurehead emperor and themselves assumed the throne. Wang Mang, the founder of the Hsin dynasty, was one such minister, and in 265 A.D. another minister, Ssu-ma Yen, was similarly able to usurp the throne and found the Western Chin dynasty. In fact, usurpation by a minister can almost be said to have been a normal way of founding new dynasties in early China, just as it was in some Indian kingdoms. The Manchu defense against such usurpation was simple: Never let a minister gain so much power that he might become a threat. No dynasty so consistently kept its ministers in a subordinate position. This might prevent an able minister from pursuing firm and vigorous actions in pursuit of good government, but it kept the emperors on their throne.

A number of high Manchu officials did wield great power, particularly Ho-shên in Ch'ien-lung's reign, and Su-shun for a brief period in the reigns of Hsien-fêng and T'ung-chih, but these men attracted as many enemies as supporters, and they hardly endangered the throne. Each new emperor usually took pains to remove the powerful members of the previous administration, men who might present a threat to a younger and less experienced man. Each emperor built up his own circle of loyal assistants. Emperors could dispose of even their highest ministers quite ruthlessly when they cared to do so, and many a high minister's life ended with the executioner. The dangers of high office unquestionably dampened the enthusiasm of many officials, and made them hesitate to climb to the highest positions. Moreover, ascent through the bureaucracy was so slow that those who reached the top had generally passed the years of vigorous youth. They were more likely to opt for the relative safety of loyal service than for the risks of competition with an emperor. No minister came close to usurpation, either in Manchu times or during the preceding Ming dynasty. Here is one place where the experience of late dynastic China diverged sharply from that of India. There, ministerial usurpation continued to be quite common until the end of independence. The different opportunities of usurpation rested upon a fundamental contrast in Chinese and Indian governmental organization.

In Hindu India, every office tended to become hereditary. In China, no office with real temporal power, other than the throne itself, could ever be inherited. Only during their earliest reigns did the Manchus extend power to royal kinsmen. As they adapted themselves to Chinese practices, they learned to rigidly exclude royal kinsmen from office, and no other families were ever given hereditary access to power. To be sure, many elegant sounding titles were hereditary, but these titles carried no power, and they served to pension off men who might otherwise mount a challenge, rather than to legitimize or confer authority. Except for the throne, all positions of power were gained either by climbing through the regular bureaucracy which was explicitly designed to counter the influence of heredity, or else by gaining the emperor's confidence by less formal channels within his household.

In both China and India, real power occasionally slipped out of the hands of the titular ruler when ministers dominated the government. The difference between the areas, and the factor that made usurpation far more difficult in China, was that none of the secondary Chinese offices were hereditary. Thus, they were sharply differentiated from the office of emperor. In India, the other offices could be as hereditary as that of the king, and once power shifted to a new man, it also shifted to a new family. Such power could then pass on by heredity, as it never could in Manchu China. Of course all the dilemmas and all the internal contradictions of hereditary succession effected the new office and the new family in India, and from this point of view, the situation had not much changed; but certainly the ruling family had changed, and a usurpation had been consolidated. A Chinese official might usurp the power of his sovereign, just as a Maratha official might, but since it was impossible in China to pass that power on to a son, the official could not found a dynasty. Sooner or later the rights of the Imperial line would be reasserted. Usurpations in China could only be temporary. Indian usurpations were sometimes quite final.

Temporary Usurpation by a Regent

No high minister was able to usurp the throne during either of the last two dynasties, but effective power was often put in the hands of men other than the emperor. In particular, several Manchu emperors came to the throne during their childhoods, and once slightly different circumstances might have allowed a regent to effect a more permanent transfer of power. The most likely candidate for usurpation was Dorgon who, as regent for the first Manchu emperor, had conquered most of China. Dorgon was cautious, however, and ruled only in another's name. He seems to have made no attempt to assume the throne himself. Two centuries later, the empress dowager grew powerful in another regency, but as a woman, she could never take the throne. A third powerful regent, Oboi, who ruled at the beginning of the K'ang-hsi reign, was not a member of the imperial family, and he was efficiently displaced by the rising K'ang-hsi.

Crown Princes

In some parts of the world princes have challenged and even displaced their fathers. The king's sons were seldom a danger to the Manchu ruler, although the struggles among K'ang-hsi's sons and the rumors that his death might have been hastened by his son Yung-chêng show that a threat from that quarter could not be entirely ruled out. Manchu emperors kept their sons under control in two ways; first by refusing, until they lay on their deathbeds, to name a crown prince; and second by inculcating an intense filial piety. So great was the deference paid to the older generation that when Chia-ch'ing was named emperor, he could not really rule as long as his aged and senile father lived. The Emperors Hsien-fêng and T'ung-chih were unable to capture effective power from the empress dowager. Even if the later princes were not themselves sufficiently awed by filial reverence to force them to defer to their father, everyone else at the court would expect them to behave in a filial manner. With such a firm expectation surrounding him, it became impossible for a son to defy his father's wishes.

The Household

The Chinese political system effectively deprived challengers of any power base that might have been used to threaten the emperor, but the emperor was left isolated. Smothered with the ethic of filial piety and denied wide contacts throughout the empire, potential heirs could be intimate only with their palace staff. In the end, this would allow eunuchs and palace women to gain great power. It was always a temptation for emperors to rely upon eunuchs. Eunuchs were men of humble background who, by renouncing their duty to bear heirs, had abandoned their families. The kinsmen of eunuchs could pose no threat to the throne, and the eunuchs themselves were peculiarly ill-equipped to found a dynasty. Thus, they were completely dependent upon the good will of the emperor, and they were regarded as the most loyal of servants. Since they were the only men allowed contact with the palace women, eunuchs also had an opportunity to influence the women of the court and these, either as mothers or consorts of the emperor, might influence the great man himself. As a result, eunuchs repeatedly rose to enormous power and they sometimes became the virtual rulers of China. Held in contempt by the scholar–officials, there can be no question that some eunuchs were utterly corrupt. Others were able men, but they rose to power through flattery and by means of an irregular access to the emperor. They bypassed the orthodox system of recruitment, with its examinations and its built-in checks against ineptitude and venality. Of course it was the scholar–officials who wrote the histories, and they unanimously condemned eunuch government.

The founders of both the Ming and Manchu dynasties forbade the use of eunuchs except for palace duties. The Ming emperors soon forgot this injunction, and eunuchs came to wield great power during much of the dynasty. The early Manchus were contemptuous of the eunuchs who ruled during their predecessors' era, and they succeeded in keeping them in check for a longer time. Their success was not merely a matter of good sense, however, for it was also made possible by an available alternative. Subordinate Manchus could fill somewhat the same role that enunuchs had filled earlier. Manchus were set apart from the Chinese majority and they were recruited into government service by shorter steps than other officials. If eunuchs and scholar–officials had served to counterbalance each other in earlier dynasties, Manchus and Chinese officials similarly balanced each other in the last dynasty. Partly from good planning, therefore, but partly because the Manchus could draw upon an alternative source for servants, eunuchs did not become really powerful until the rule of the empress dowager. Then, at the end of the dynasty, when the distinction between Manchu and Chinese was beginning to blur, and under the rule of a palace woman whose position would bring her close to eunuchs, several rose to high and responsible positions. Even then, none came to exercise the sort of power they had held in previous dynasties.

Eunuchs have often been blamed for the evils that brought the collapse of dynasties, but it is more just to blame a system that isolated the emperor from everyone except the menial members of his own household. Those with whom an emperor had close contact, women, eunuchs, or an original low-ranking guard like Ho-shên, might acquire great power, and the checks of the traditional bureaucratic system were quite unable to prevent the abuse of such power. The destruction of all sources of power that might compete with an emperor allowed members of the household to abuse their position. It was the capture of the emperor by his household that repeatedly brought the decay of Chinese dynasties.

Warlords

When the imperial military system grew soft and when peasant uprisings broke out, the only force that could put them down were locally recruited peasant militias. More effective in suppressing revolt than the regular army, they also presented their own threat to the central power. If peasant militias became too strong, their leaders, now turned into warlords, could assert increasing independence. Separatist tendencies could then arise in a new guise. In the turmoil of Manchu decline and during the succeeding "republican" decades, effective local power often came to be held by warloads who could act quite independently of any central government.

Revolution and Invasion

The concern of this chapter has been with the succession within a dynasty, with the alternatives by which power could be transferred within the limits of what has usually been looked upon as the same government. However, no account of Chinese succession would be complete without a comment about the switch from one dynasty to another. With all legitimate opposition to the established emperor proscribed, any serious opposition had to be kept strictly secret, or else assume the form of open rebellion. Secret societies which periodically emerged to inspire or support armed uprisings seem to have been a more or less permanent feature of Chinese political life, and like earlier dynasties, the Manchus suffered a long series of peasant rebellions. These grew in intensity as the central government became less effective. Similar rebellions had toppled earlier dynasties and put new men into power.

A weak central government also presented a tempting target to the outside. The Manchus themselves had seized their opportunity in the period of Ming decline, and when it became the Manchus' turn to stagnate, China became an easy prey for the Western powers and for the Japanese.

In a sense, a change in dynasty, whether it results from invasion or from internal revolution, is a less legitimate and less orderly succession than the transfer of power within a single dynasty. Changes in Chinese dynasties were not usually effected without extensive warfare. But Chinese history is long, and even the switch in dynasties came to have a legitimacy of its own. It was well recognized that one dynasty could lose its Mandate of Heaven, and the very success of a rival dynasty in asserting its own power would demonstrate that the Mandate had shifted. It even seems that the complete success with which those who governed centralized all power into a single office, and the success with which they destroyed all competition, finally necessitated the convulsive renewal that only a change in dynasty could bring.

DYNASTIC SYSTEMS

Many aspects of Chinese dynastic succession recall features also found in Africa and India. The Chinese passed the throne down in the familiar male line. They learned to keep any man from assuming an unambiguous second position. They evolved new and changing patterns as one generation followed another. In these and many other ways Chinese practices seem familiar. But Chinese politics also had some unique characteristics, and these stand out with special clarity when seen in contrast with the African and Indian examples.

Among these uniquely Chinese traits was the restriction of heredity to the throne. Subordinate Marathas and African chiefs might acquire their posts by the same hereditary rules as applied to the king, but all subordinate governmental posts in China were appointive. The Chinese, in fact, went the absolute limit in centralizing appointments, and in the end, when the emperor gained the unquestioned right to appoint his own successor, even the throne became appointive.

By allowing the throne to become appointive, the Chinese can be said, in a sense, to have "solved" the succession problem. The last several emperors gained their office without a struggle. This closed the political system to the kind of periodic renewal that regular succession struggles have brought elsewhere. No longer did each generation experience a time when contenders for the throne sought allies. No longer were there times when other men could bargain for their own rights by selling their support in return for some degree of power or security of their own. Certainly this "solution" brought stability of a sort, but by constructing a system that avoided regular succession struggles an ever less efficient, less responsive, and less realistic government was enabled to stay in power. The price of this stability and of the sequence of peaceful successions was the utter chaos in which the dynasty finally fell. It was as if all the chaos that other political systems distribute over several separate periods of succession had all been saved up for one overwhelming period of chaos at the end.

A system in which all offices are appointive represents a sort of logical extreme of centralization, and the Chinese system had characteristics that will appear again when we consider more modern centralized systems. Appointment from above is made possible by so thoroughly breaking up all competing bases of power that everyone is dependent upon the center. Officials must then be delicately responsive to those above them, and this can easily slip over to a sycophancy that deprives the center of realistic contact with the outer reaches of its own domain. At the same time, officials deprived of secure but legitimate power bases of their own are driven to seek alternative means of advancing their own interests, or at least of maintaining their own position. They seek alliances with others like themselves. Networks of friendship, of influence, and of mutual help begin to crisscross the administration. Before long, these will look dangerous to the top man, and he will denounce them and destroy them when he can, but new networks will inevitably form.

The strongest Manchu leaders were those who had to struggle for their position. The struggles probably served both as a selecting device which eliminated those not qualified to lead and also as a training ground in which the eventual winner learned enough about the system to guide it with some skill. Until the accession of Ch'ien-lung, every emperor had to maneuver or intrigue to gain power, either by gradually asserting himself over competitors as Abahai had done, by displacing his regents like K'ang-hsi, or by disposing of his brothers like Yung-chêng. Even the empress dowager Tz'u-hsi, who at the end of the dynasty emerged as a strong force in an otherwise chaotic sea, had to struggle for her power. The reigns of Chiach'ing, Tao-kuang, and Hsien-fêng were all inaugurated by peaceful and uncontested succession, but these emperors were weak, and their reigns saw progressive administrative deterioration. The one apparent exception to the generalization that strong rulers struggled for their place was Ch'ien-lung. His succession was the first in the dynasty to be fully orderly, and his reign was undeniably long and illustrious. But Ch'ien-lung took over a unified, well-managed empire from his forceful father, the man who may have done more than anyone in the dynasty to root out corruption. Six decades later Ch'ien-lung left a government that was shot through with corruption from top to bottom. In this sense, the Ch-ien-lung reign hardly deserves to be counted as successful. The glories of his reign were based very largely on the accumulated capital of his predecessors, and the collapse of the following reigns was at least partly attributable to his own failures. No sooner had Manchus begun to inculcate their princes with enough fiilial piety to insure peaceful acceptance of their father's will, than the emperors began to weaken. Honesty and efficiency required a strong emperor, but an emperor who gained power smoothly, easily, and legitimately could not be strong.

CYCLICITY AND CHANGE

The repetitive rise and fall of Chinese dynasties has encouraged a cyclical view of Chinese history, but a comparison with tribal dynasties in Africa or with Indian kingdoms like that of the Marathas makes it clear that cyclical rise and fall was never a monopoly of the Chinese. It may even seem that dynasties have inherent properties that severely limit their endurance.

Repeatedly, it seems, solutions to problems that arise in the early phase of a dynasty create new problems for the later phases. Thus, elimination of all competition for the throne allowed the household to capture the Chinese emperor. Military requirements encouraged the early Marathas to accept the jagirdari system, but this led in turn to the dismemberment of the kingdom. Among the African Baganda, a fraternal succession rule led to furious struggles for the throne, and these were resolved only when all the unsuccessful brothers came to be murdered. Perhaps every rule of succession is so imperfect that it leads to the establishment of a revised rule.

Changes of this sort are difficult to perceive in the short periods of observation that have been typical for field anthropologists. Unable to see long-term trends, anthropologists have imagined more stability of rule and custom than events can really justify. We have too often supposed our societies to be rather static and unchanging or supposed that such changes as do occur are reactions to external pressures. The idea that changes come about as a means of solving internal problems—the Hegelian notion of the resolution of internal contradictions—is certainly an old one in Western thought, but anthropologists, with their "functional" biases that have led them to look for coherence and order, have only rarely looked for the contradictions, and have only rarely seen the resulting changes.

When evidence of change becomes inescapable and when it seems that patterns of one generation lead inevitably to the new patterns of the next, the anthropological bias in favor of stability can only be salvaged by discovering a cycle that eventually brings the system back to its starting point. The varying patterns can then be seen simply as varying phases of a single larger pattern. Thus, the patterns which followed each other in the course of the Manchu dynasty can be seen as alternating phases of one overarching Chinese system. The phases may repeat themselves almost endlessly, but all may seem to contribute to a long-run Chinese stability. Similarly, the centralizing and disintegrative phases of Maratha rule can be seen as complementary processes that have repeated themselves many times in Indian history, as areas have coalesced under new and vigorous kingdoms, only to split up again as these kingdoms weakened. In Africa, the Bemba may have oscillated between short periods of reconcentration of titles among a small group of kinsmen and longer periods when the titles again drifted apart among more and more distantly related people. In all these cases, we might argue that the essential structural features of a political system would be preserved through all the varying phases of the cycle, so long as the phases follow each other with some regularity.

Such cycles are intriguing, but they are capable of a disturbingly wide application. The Bemba may have gone through alternating periods of broadening and narrowing the range of their title-holding elite, but, as was pointed out earlier, (p. 46) it is also possible to relate the people of the centralized Bemba state with their neighbors who lack a central state, and say that they exhibit two different phases of the same political system. No faith in equilibrium or in political cycles can help us to decide whether a state like the Bemba is more likely to tighten up by narrowing its range of title-bearing kinsmen (and thus follow one kind of cycle), or instead to shatter into smaller pieces (and thus follow a different cycle). No cyclical theory of Chinese history would ever have allowed us to predict future events. When, early in the Manchu dynasty, the Chinese feudatories rebelled, we could not have predicted that the Manchu emperor would emerge victorious and so allow his dynasty to complete a full dynastic cycle. Had a Chinese general been victorious instead, he might have established his own dynasty, and we would then look back upon the Manchus as filling a mere interlude, as a frontier tribe which had once been used by the founder of a Chinese dynasty in his struggle to achieve first place.

Thus, however intriguing political cycles may be, they can be applied only after the event. They can be too easily fitted to too broad a range of phenomena to be of any use in predicting the future. One who becomes too entranced by abstract cycles and by presumed structural continuities through these cycles may miss the change and the variability that occur within each cycle and which involve quite different kinds of human relationships. If all particular systems are seen as phases of an all-embracing system, it becomes difficult to compare the particular systems that have been observed and to assess their varied strengths and weaknesses.

The lesson of Chinese history for our understanding of succession, then, is not that there was some sort of long run stability, but rather that there was after all, short run instability. No single set of practices that the Chinese or Manchus developed was capable of being perpetuated unchanged over a span of several generations. Yet, the Manchus did stay on the throne for more than two centuries, and their Ming predecessors had held power even longer. The Chinese system did provide stability of a sort. At the very least, it allowed an unbroken sequence of nine sons to succeed to their father's throne, and more of these successions were peaceful than in many of the world's kingdoms.

Finally, if there was one single factor that united the many techniques by which the Chinese provided for peaceful succession, it lay in the profound historical knowledge held by many officials and even by a few emperors. More than any other people, the Chinese were acutely aware of the structural problems that might interfere with orderly government and with orderly succession to the throne. All officials were supposed to be trained in the ideology and history of the Chinese political system. They could recall vividly how earlier rivals had struggled for power, and how earlier dynasties had fallen. They could cite clear examples that showed the dangers of high officials, of feudal princes, of women, of eunuchs, and of every other conceivable threat to the throne. The Manchu rulers listened to their officials, and they took effective means for holding such dangers in check. Every conceivable techniques for achieving peaceful hereditary succession was known and used by the Manchu heirs to the Chinese civilization. They can be credited with developing the ultimate hereditary monarchy.

Modern scholars who would like to suppose that their patient investigations of the past might actually be taken seriously enough to affect the future ought to be able to take some comfort in the importance that scholarly knowledge had in keeping emperors on the throne. Historical knowledge really did mean power. That in the end the Manchu government weakened and fell means only that the exercise of power and its hereditary transfer are difficult problems which not even the Chinese with all their historical knowledge could completely solve. They did better than most of mankind.

CHAPTER 5

The Decline of Heredity

ALTERNATIVES TO HEREDITY

One searches almost in vain through the two millenia of Asian history that preceded the European expansion for times or places where top rulers were habitually chosen without regard for heredity. Men without distinguished antecedents often fought their way to power, of course, but heredity always tended to sanction the selection of their successors. Hereditary monarchs have played an important part in European politics too, but once we become aware of the virtually complete absence of alternatives to heredity in other parts of the old world, we must be struck by the fact that European rivals to heredity have existed for a very long time.

We think first of ancient Greece. Athenian democracy seems all the more miraculous when seen in worldwide terms rather than simply in European terms, for nowhere else at such an early date and nowhere else until many centuries later was heredity so completely overcome. Through a long and tumultuous process, Athens extended political participation to wider and wider segments of its population. Royal leadership first gave way to an aristocracy of land and sword. Then, progressively, merchants, artisans, and small traders, and finally even farmers and foot soldiers won the right to participate in government. The admission of new groups often came when tyrants competed for power and called upon progressively wider segments of the population for help, but as the process continued, a complex set of democratic institutions were evolved. The citizens met in huge assemblies, but where special tasks had to be performed these assemblies chose magistrates with strictly limited powers. Some magistrates were elected and some were chosen by lot, but all had short terms and none was allowed to gain the predominant power that monarchs held in other parts of the world. In extending political participation to a wider body of its citizens than any civilized state had previously done, the Greeks, and, above all, the Athenians devised orderly though cumbersome political procedures which helped to provide a setting in which civilization could flourish as it has flourished only in rare periods of human history.

For later generations of Europeans, the Greeks set an example that has never quite been forgotten. In Asia, the few governments that lacked hereditary monarchies offered far less prestigious examples than the Greeks. Indian philosophers knew about and described tribal democracies and oligarchies, but these philosophers were always more concerned with the dangers of anarchy than with the dangers of tyranny. They tended to look upon nonmonarchical tribes as weak and upon their governmental forms as undesirable. The governments that Indian politicians and philosophers pointed to as pragmatic examples that were worthy of emulation were always hereditary monarchies. For Europeans, Greek democracy offered credible alternatives. Their governmental forms might not be viewed with uniform admiration, but it was impossible to dismiss the Greek city-states as mere backward tribes.

The Greeks, moreover, left traditions both of empirical description of government and of political speculation that were never entirely lost. Plato's *Republic* was but one of many Greek works that treated the desirable form of government. Aristotle supervised the collection of historical and descriptive accounts of no less than 158 city constitutions. Most of these accounts have been lost, but Aristotle's *Constitution of Athens* survives, and in it and in his *Politics* we can see the beginning of a comparative science of government that ranged across a far more varied range of political forms than would have been possible for an author whose experience had been limited largely to monarchy. The times and places of later Europe where republican or democratic governments have flourished have been relatively few and brief, but knowledge of Greek political description and speculation was never quite forgotten. Ever since Plato and Aristotle, Europeans have been debating the principles of government. These debates have ranged more freely, and have been less bound by limiting assumptions than have the corresponding debates of Asians. The debates over principles have helped to make possible a wider political experimentation in practice. Here lies much of the political uniqueness of Europe.

It is difficult to judge the extent to which Roman politics was directly influenced by Greek examples and the extent to which it developed along similar lines because of similar conditions. In either case, Rome did follow Greece in developing a nonmonarchical government. As in Greece, the politically active proportion of Rome's population gradually expanded as the government opened to progressively wider circles, and the Romans even surpassed the Greeks in the development of representative institutions. They were, moreover, the first to demonstrate that nonmonarchical government could be adapted to the rule of a larger nation than that of a single city and its hinterland. The genius of Rome was to adapt some elements of Greek democracy to a territory as wide as any of her monarchical predecessors or contemporaries.

Eventually the Roman republic gave way to the Roman Empire, in part because the republican institutions were never fully successful in providing the kind of strong centralized leadership that a large nation required in an emergency. Even under the Caesars, however, heredity never played the exclusive role that it did in the Eastern empires, and the Roman monarchy continued to be decked out with the trappings of the older republic. The magistrates of the republic had always been appointed, and the rulers of the empire continued to seek formal appointment by the senate. Appointment finally was reduced to little more than senatorial confirmation of de facto power, but even this residual ability to grant the final seal of legitimacy kept heredity from the exclusive role that it had in both China and India.

In China, the great watersheds of history were the times when heredity broke down, the times when dynasties changed. In Rome, new men were sometimes able to take over the imperial office from their fathers or brothers, and the imperial line included a few longer dynasties when several men from the same family ruled in turn. Far more often than in China, however, new men, unrelated to their predecessors, arose to claim the office, and this constituted a less decisive break with the past than it did in China. The openness of competition implied by the weak claim of heredity certainly contributed to the political turbulence of the Roman Empire. Rivals often had to fight to establish their claims. At the same time, the less restricted competition and the corresponding ability of new men to rise to power may have postponed the kind of internal decay that was the eventual fate of so many Chinese dynasties. Before a Roman dynasty could decay so far, it would be overturned by more vigorous and capable men. These could quickly gain a kind of legitimacy by having their new position duly ratified by senatorial appointment.

The examples of Greece and Rome were never quite forgotten, but later Europeans could also turn to less remote instances of the nonmonarchical transfer of power, and Medieval Europe provided prestigious examples— none more striking than the papacy. The early popes had been selected by a bewildering variety of techniques. In the face of clerical celibacy, the single principle by which the papacy could never be claimed was heredity, but the office was perpetually fought over by rival Roman factions, and, at the same time, it was long subject to confirmation by the temporal rulers of Rome. At times the office became virtually appointive. Even after the collapse of the Roman Empire in the West, the bishops of Rome long continued to seek confirmation of their appointment from the eastern emperor, although the distance between Rome and Constantinople and the feeble temporal power available to the distant emperor gave considerable practical independence to the papacy.

The reforms of Hildebrand in the 11th century stabilized the papacy and secured its independence. Henceforth, the pope was to be selected by regular elections by the high clergy of Rome—the college of cardinals. Papal selection was thus removed from lay control, and the electoral system worked with such striking success that its essentials have survived until today.

With the establishment of the college of cardinals as the legitimate body of papal electors, western Europe acquired a ruler who had extensive temporal power, but who gained his office by well-defined electoral principles rather than by heredity. Even in the period when heredity was the predominant justification by which kings and feudal magnates assumed their offices, the papacy provided an example of a different principle of selection. Nowhere in the Islamic Middle East, in India, or in China was such a powerful temporal ruler selected in this way. Only Europeans had such an example before them.

Nor was the papacy unique. In the North, another high elective office arose—that of the Holy Roman Emperor. In medieval Germany, as elsewhere in medieval Europe, most kings and nobles gained their offices by heredity, but the Germans had not always given an exclusive role to heredity any more than the Greeks or Romans had. The Romans had described German leaders of an earlier era who would announce their willingness to lead a war party. They would collect a *retinue* of those willing to follow them in hopes of successful raids and ample booty. Such leaders can be compared with the big men of Melanesia, for both in Germany and Melanesia men rose to power on the basis of their personal ability to attract and hold supporters. Heredity was as unimportant to the retinue leader as to the big man, and the retinue leader's power, like that of the big man, would quickly dissolve if he lost support. The ability to desert was an effective if rather negative form of election.

For several turbulent centuries, German chiefs retained power only so long as they held the loyalty of their followers, but with more settled times, their leading offices came increasingly to pass from father to son. As the German tribes settled down and coalesced, the discontinuity implied by older political forms had to give way, but even after more enduring kingdoms emerged, the idea of election would long continue to coexist with the idea of heredity. Each had a claim upon legitimacy. Accidents of birth helped to allow heredity to win more decisively in the area that became France than in the area that became Germany. The French royal line happened to produce sons for many consecutive generations, while several German emperors died without heirs. As a result, the German crown had to pass to new families. Beyond these accidents of birth, moreover, the German emperors began to make claims of being more than mere kings. Once they asserted the additional claim of being the Holy Roman Emperor, the appeal to mere heredity seemed rather questionable. When the king of the Germans became the emperor of Rome, succession had to be a more complex matter. The need to assert that the emperor was indeed something more than a king, made it seem necessary to legitimize the office by some special means.

Papal approval was one possibility, but this implied an undesirable subjection to the pope. Other than papal selection or heredity, however, the only other source of legitimacy seemed to be some type of selection by the other princes of Germany. Princes first played a part in choosing their king through influence, intrigue, and the application of military might, the familiar techniques that princes used everywhere, but the dangers of ill-defined rivalry combined with a groping toward a greater legitimacy to encourage ever more orderly electoral procedures, until certain princes gained the recognized right to make the selection. At first, these were simply the princes who had the predominant temporal power but, later, traditional rights became well defined, and seven electors finally gained an uncontested right to elect the new monarch.

Thus, in the North as in the South, there emerged by the end of the Middle Ages an important leader whose position was legitimized not by heredity, but by an election. The right of the electors to designate the emperor, like the right of the cardinals to designate the pope, serves as a curious link between the ancient and the modern worlds. The idea of election reappeared at the very top of society. The examples, both of the throne of Saint Peter and of the throne of the Holy Roman Empire, stood as alternatives to hereditary selection, alternatives to which all Europe could look.

THE CONSTITUTED BODIES

If Europe of the Middle Ages was unique among the civilizations of the old world in providing prestigious examples of high electoral office, so was it unique in its reliance upon representative councils. At the close of the Middle Ages, "constituted bodies" were found everywhere in Europe west of Russia. These constituted bodies were the councils, diets, and assemblies where men gathered to debate the issues of their times and to seek to forge a common policy for their territory. Rulers regularly called together the influential members of their town, their region, or their nation, and they sought, thereby, to associate these men with their own plans. With time, the councils often gained a sanctity of ancient tradition and they sometimes could exercise extensive power. Constituted bodies have formed such a regular part of European government that westerners may not grasp just how unique they were. Nowhere in the empires of Asia were there councils or assemblies that met with the regularity, or that wielded the kind of influence, that they did in Europe.

The constituted bodies assumed an infinity of forms. Some consisted only of nobles, some included burghers, and others had clerical or even peasant representation. Some covered what we would think of today as a nation; others were restricted to a province, still others to a single town. Membership might be appointive or it might be hereditary, and occasionally it could be purchased. In some places, offices were gained through election, though only in a few cantons of Switzerland did anything approaching a majority of the adult males participate in the elections, and even in these cantons, the electors traditionally bestowed their choice upon the men of a limited number of families. Almost everywhere, whatever their formal composition, the constituted bodies tended toward more or less self-perpetuating councils of nobles, landowners, or merchants—notable men from notable families.

Often there was some degree of competition between the monarchs on the one hand, and the men and interests who were represented on the constituted bodies on the other. The outcome of this competition varied in different parts of Europe. In Poland, the diet of noble landowners became so completely dominant that the throne was reduced to insignificance. By contrast, the constituted bodies of Spain, both the national Cortes and the urban cabildos, came to be dominated by the throne. In some areas, a more even balance between throne and constituted bodies was longer maintained, but, for all their variability, nothing more clearly delimits the geographical range of Western civilization in the early modern era than the existence of some sort of constituted bodies. Further east, in Russia and in the Ottoman Empire, they did not exist at all.

Important among the constituted bodies were city councils, and it was in the cities, above all, that Europeans conducted the experiments and worked out the techniques that would provide the first modern examples of republican governments. In the cities men learned to avoid hereditary leadership, and they demonstrated that other techniques of choosing were possible at a far humbler level of society than that of the papacy or the Holy Roman Empire.

From the beginning, the organization of the nascent cities diverged sharply from the practices of the rest of the feudal world. While other men were organizing themselves into the strict hierarchical relationships characteristic of feudalism, the craftsmen and merchants of the cities organized themselves instead into mutual help societies—guilds and communes that directly countered the hierarchical spirit of feudalism. The merchants and craftsmen of these new cities were useful to the princes, for they could offer a welcome source of wealth, but the mechanical and entrepreneurial techniques upon which cities depended were generally so mysterious to the feudal rulers that cities flourished best where rulers meddled least. Higher temporal rulers would grant charters to the cities and, with luck, they might then leave them alone and allow them to conduct their business in considerable independence.

The details of governmental forms were extremely varied. City charters often reserved to the territorial ruler the right to appoint the city leaders, but in some cases the right of appointment was relaxed, and then the feudal lord might merely confirm the men first proposed by the burghers themselves. It could even come about that no outside confirmation was needed any longer. Urban privileges thereby became transformed into urban rights, and a few cities finally gained virtual independence of any higher power. First in northern Italy, and later in northern and western Europe, these cities served as laboratories for experimentation with various republican forms.

For a study of succession, the most striking single fact about Europe is its long history of offering alternatives to heredity. As they devised other methods of selecting leaders, Europeans faced many of the same problems that hereditary systems faced, but they faced a few new problems as well. Among their recurrent problems was whether or not to have a single dominant leader at all.

THE NEED FOR A SINGLE LEADER

Since the time of the Greeks, Europeans have struggled with a recurrent dilemma: how to get effective leadership without tyranny. This is a question that seems rarely to have bothered either Indians or Chinese. There, kings and emperors were expected to be tyrannical. Order seemed to demand a strong monarch, and the Indian and Chinese philosophers worried far more about how to prevent civil chaos than how to prevent tyranny. Starting with the Greeks, however, European philosophers have worried a great deal about tyranny, and practical men have often justified their actions by claiming that they were working to prevent another man from gaining too much power.

Often, the most effective way to prevent tyranny has seemed to be to deny a dominant position to any single man or any single office. The Greeks and the early Romans gave responsibility to a large number of magistrates, but they did not allow any single magistracy to have more than a small share of total power. Many of the Greek and Roman magistracies, moreover, were collegiate. Two or more men would share the post and each would check the power of his colleagues. The terms of the magistracies were also kept very short, generally no longer than a year, and the Greeks went so far as to fill many of their posts by lot.

The dangers of such heroic efforts to distribute power widely are obvious, and crises repeatedly arose that seemed to call for a firm hand. Tyrants might be able to manage affairs behind a facade of democratic or republican forms, but there was always a danger that such a tyrant would subvert the system entirely.

To cope with emergencies, the Romans allowed two of their magistrates, the consuls, to appoint a dictator to a limited term as chief of state. The dictator was unique among the officials of the Roman republic in ruling alone. Unlike other magistrates, he had no partner of equivalent rank who could veto his actions. The dictator could act more decisively than either the Roman assemblies or the collegial magistrates of the regular administration, and the risk that the dictator might turn into a tyrant was lessened by severely limiting his term of office. He was supposed to have time enough to deal with the crisis, but not enough time to convert his office into permanent tyranny. In the dictator, the Romans had a single powerful ruler, but he was a ruler who differed profoundly from any hereditary monarch. Not only was his term of office more limited, but his method of appointment was entirely different. He was unambiguously appointed by those over whom he would assume authority, and hereditary qualifications were quite irrelevant. At the same time, the dictator had a legitimacy that escaped a mere tyrant who had either to manipulate politics from behind the scenes, or else to seize office by extra-legal means.

Later republics repeatedly struggled with the same problem—how to get leadership without tyranny. The cities of medieval Italy were first governed by councils of various sorts, but these could not consistently control internal strife. Families battled for control of the councils and the threat of civil war hung over each annual election. What seemed to be needed was a single leader who would keep order, and in the latter half of the 12th century, the first cautious moves in this direction were made when a number of Italian cities began to choose an executive known as the *podesta*. The podesta was not usually a native of the city he administered. Only if he came from elsewhere would the local factions be able to trust his neutrality, and his term, like that of ancient Greek and Roman magistrates, was usually limited to a single year. The podesta was supposed to be a sort of town manager and legal expert, but he was hardly a strong leader. Repeatedly the cities needed someone with more authority.

When war threatened, there was always a temptation to call upon a more vigorous man, but it was sometimes difficult to dispose of him after the emergency was over. The merchants who became dominant in the Italian cities had neither the skill nor the desire to assume a military role themselves, so they turned to mercenaries. The men whom they hired to give them military defense, however, began to dominate the people they were supposed to serve. In a number of the cities, where there had been relatively free governments in the 12th and 13th centuries, autocratic military chiefs arose in the 14th. Pisa hired an army commander who, in 1314 turned to arrest some of his merchant employers and then persuaded the public parliament to confer upon him a 10-year term as the lord of the city. Florence, faced with an emergency, appointed King Robert of Naples to a 5-year term as the city's signore. The limits of the signore's power were carefully defined, however, so that Florence retained its other institutions intact, and at the end of his second term, Florence succeeded in dismissing Robert. Later emergencies persuaded the Florentines to appoint first a Spaniard, Raymond of Cardona, to the post of war captain, and later Robert's son, Charles, to a 10-year term as regent and protector. Charles was given the privilege of maintaining troops, and of making peace and war, powers considerably greater than his father had been given, and Charles even persuaded the Holy Roman Emperor to confer upon him the hereditary title of Duke of Lucca. He had ambitions of extending his rule over all of Tuscany, and Florence was saved from his permanent rule only by his timely death.

In a later century, the Dutch republic faced the same problem as the

Italian cities. In the 16th century, the cities of the low countries were only weakly united by their war of independence against Spain. In the emergency, military imperatives took precedence over the fear of tyranny and the Dutch turned to a local nobleman, William the Silent of the house of Orange. They first chose him to a post known as the *statholder,* and he was intended to be their military leader, but for several generations he and his descendants competed with the constituted bodies for power. At times the statholders came to dominate the very councils that claimed to have originally appointed them. When there was peace, the councils sometimes managed to do without a statholder, though they usually had to wait for the incumbent's death before unburdening themselves of their own chosen leader, and as soon as war threatened once more, they would again be forced to call upon more centralized leadership.

The same problem arose when the American colonies first declared their independence from England. In most of the colonies, the governors had been appointed from England, while the legislative assemblies were locally elected. Inevitably, the governors tended to represent English interests, while the assemblies were more responsive to local wishes. Quite naturally, many colonists placed their greatest trust in their assemblies. With the assertion of independence, the governors were forced to leave, and in most of the new states the assemblies found themselves ruling alone. Mistrusting strong executives, the revolutionary radicals first tried to run their new states with weak governors or with no governor at all. Those states that did choose governors restricted their powers, and made them directly accountable to the assemblies. The governors were surrounded by executive councils that were appointed by the assembly and intended more to keep them under a watchful eye than to assist them. Pennsylvania, Delaware, New Hampshire, and Massachusetts first tried to do without any real governor at all, and executive power was given to a council instead.

The American states, like the Italian and Dutch republics before them, soon discovered that managing a government was difficult unless a single person was given clear executive responsibility. Earlier, they had experienced what they felt was executive tyranny, but they now faced the complementary problems of disunified legislative leadership. Experience with their experimental wartime governments soon began to convince Americans that executive tyranny was not the only danger that had to be forestalled. Legislative tyranny and just plain legislative bungling could also be serious problems.

Practical experience gradually convinced the men of the revolution that a reasonably strong single-man executive was needed, and a trend developed that favored popularly elected governors so as to make them partially independent of the assemblies. They also came to be granted a greater right of appointment and a greater power of legislative veto than had t thought wise. When the time came to write a constitution for the government, its authors were prepared to accept a president who l.... ....siderable independence of congress. Like many other men who had feared the tyranny of a single strong executive, the revolutionary Americans also learned to fear the chaos that threatened when the executive was too weak.

CENTRALIZATION AND DECENTRALIZATION

Without an adequate executive, the dangers both of conquest from the outside and of chaos on the inside are very real, but the danger that too strong a leadership may turn into tyranny is just as real. Whenever a man gains predominant power, he seems driven to consolidate his position. Many men have gone much further in the acquisition of power than had ever been intended by those who first put them into office.

Pressures toward the centralization of power, however, face compensating forces that serve to decentralize, and times of succession are often the most favorable periods for renewed decentralization. At successions, men are likely to have to compete for power, and when they compete, they must search for allies. To obtain the support he needs in order to gain office, a man may need to barter away some of the strength of that office. The promises he makes as a candidate constrain him later. Even after a man has secured the top post, moreover, similar forces may still operate. The top man will still have rivals, and often his most dangerous rivals are those who are closest to him in power. The ruler may find it tempting to secure his own position by appealing over the heads of those nearest to him and calling for support from those beyond. In this way, the man at the center and the more or less democratic or popular outer sections of the political system may become allied against the aristocratic or oligarchical middle ranges. Superficially, the relatively balanced rivalry of contenders for the top office seems quite different from the appeals of the top man for popular support. Nevertheless, both involve rivalry at the top; both involve a search for support; both serve to open the political system to participation by those formerly on its outer margins.

Logically, centralization and decentralization are opposites. The one implies an increasing power at the center of the system so that more and more decisions can be made by a smaller and smaller range of men; the other implies the opposite. When the top man appeals over the heads of those closest to him, however, centralizing and decentralizing pressures work together. The top man usually hopes to centralize power into his own hands by undercutting his nearest rivals, but his plebeian allies hope to gain a more secure political role for themselves and they are thus working to decentralize. The aristocrats or oligarchs, who occupy the middle, see their power threatened from both sides. The precise distribution of power among these varied groups comes only as the resolution to many competing forces. Concrete examples can illustrate some of the possibilities.

Among the Marathas, each succession tended to loosen the bonds that held the kingdom together because the contenders for the throne had to barter away their powers in return for the support that would gain them their office. Where more explicit electoral procedures have been used, the same processes can sometimes be observed. No example is more striking than that of the Holy Roman Emperor.

By the 12th century, certain princes of Germany had firmly established, by custom and by law, their right to elect the emperor. Emperors frequently maneuvered to have their own sons elected, but persuading the electors proved to be costly. In order to win, each new emperor had to make concessions to the electors. Since the electors might be more interested in securing their own positions than in ensuring the continued power of the throne, each election saw the emperor bartering away some of his real power in return for the symbols of office. During the same centuries, when the monarchies of France and England were growing stronger and more centralized, the most august monarchy of all was frittering away its power. The throne was finally so weakened that Germany came to be divided into independent states.

A broadening of power is inherent in the rivalry among successors, but in the Holy Roman Empire it went no further than to distribute power among the princes. In some European cities, rivalry led, over the course of centuries, to much more open political systems and to far broader participation. Both Florence and the Dutch republic illustrate the manner in which power has sometimes come to be gradually decentralized, and both recapitulate, to some degree, the events that at a much earlier era had brought democratic and republican government to Greece and Rome.

In the 12th century, Florence was ruled by a 12-man council whose members represented both the local petty nobility and the wealthiest of the rising merchants.[1] The council, however, was torn by rival factions, and their struggles opened the way for two different and in some ways contradictory tendencies. On the one hand, centralization was encouraged by the need for firm leadership, especially when external enemies threatened. In emergencies, the Florentines buried their differences and appointed military leaders who promised to defend them, and on several occasions, these leaders tried to convert themselves into permanent rulers. Decentralization,

---

[1]Ferdinand Schevill, *History of Florence* (New York: Harcourt Brace, 1936).

on the other hand, was also encouraged when the rivalries among those with predominant power offered those on the fringes of the political system a chance to make their desires felt. Not infrequently these two superficially contradictory tendencies worked together.

The first step in the broadening of participation occurred when rivalries among the nobility allowed the most powerful merchants to gain the dominant political position. By the end of the 13th century the merchants, through the mechanism of the seven leading guilds into which they were organized, were directing the city affairs. Members of these guilds elected a council of six priors which was the dominant organ of the city government. The members of these major guilds were no more united than the older nobility had been, however, and soon the lesser guilds were agitating for more representation on the priorate. Early in the 14th century, the lesser guilds extracted concessions from the major guilds and prevented a hardening of the oligarchical boundaries. Occasionally the lesser guilds even unseated the oligarchs from their position on the priorate and, always, they forced the oligarchs to be on their guard.

The possibility of alliance between popular or more "democratic" sentiments, and the narrow and tyrannical forces of a single leader is shown by the experience of Florence with an adventurer. In 1342 the priorate felt obliged to call in a Frenchman, known as the Duke of Athens, to command the army. Florence was in such a financial crisis at the time that the priors felt they had to let the Duke take strong measures. The Duke, however, played local politics, and, allying himself with relatively popular segments of the population, he encouraged anti-priorate sentiments. Plotters urged him to make himself signore, and the priors were cornered into giving him a life appointment. The Duke was not successful in solving the city's problems, however, and he so far alienated the various classes of the city that they finally rose and deposed him. The right of the city to choose its own leaders was still too strongly entrenched to permit a man such as the Duke of Athens to retain power without broad local support.

The financial crisis of the 1340s, together with the calling and dismissing of the Duke, did open the way for the lesser guilds to seize a larger share of power. For a time the priorate was dominated by the smaller merchants, but even this government continued to exclude the even larger proletarian masses, in particular the textile workers. Now, for the first time, they too began to organize and to seek admission to the ruling circle. However broadly the ruling circle was drawn, there seemed always to be others just outside, clamoring for admission. When noble factions had squabbled, rich merchants and bankers had found it possible to work their way to power. When rich merchants squabbled, the lesser merchants were able to rise. Now that upper and lower merchants were in competition, the moment had come for the textile workers to agitate, and they had their hopes raised by encouragement from the Duke of Athens. This was the high point in the trend toward a democratic political system, and the democratic trend was carried further in Florence than in any other Italian city. The result, however, was chaotic rivalry and kaleidoscopic shifts of power, until democratic hopes were finally thwarted by the lack of skilled leadership and inadequate economic power.

In the end, the democratic trend in Florence was reversed. By the latter part of the 14th century, the old oligarchy was again triumphant, and a clique of top merchants ran the city. For a time they were content to rule through republican forms, but initiative was becoming narrowed and republican techniques of selecting leaders were slowly subverted. Finally, after 1429, when a badly managed war undermined respect for the ruling clique, favor fell upon the Medici family. They had occupied a position on the fringe of the oligarchy, just far enough from the center to gain a vague aura of popular support, and, for the last time, some sort of broad support played a part in a shift of Florentine power. As the Medici took over, however, Florentine government was finally converted from a republic to a renewed hereditary state.

Many elements of the Florentine experience came to be repeated in a later century when the Dutch faced the same contradictory pressures.[2] As in Florence, the merchants of each of the principalities of the low countries along with a few members of the local nobility were organized into constituted bodies, known here as the Estates. Just as the priorate of Florence turned to the Duke of Athens, so the Estates of several of the Dutch principalities called upon William the Silent to lead their armies. When they called him their "statholder," they used a title that had formerly been bestowed by the monarch upon his local representative, but now it was the Estates that conferred it upon their own chosen leader.

Under the monarchy, the statholder had been responsible for selecting the officers of each town from a list which the leading members of the town had drawn up. These leading townsmen were known as the regents and, in principle, it was they who now appointed the statholder. The force of tradition was strong, however, and the statholder, even when appointed by the regents, continued to select the officers for the towns. He was thus able to play a large part in selecting the very people who were, by one interpretation, his masters. Clearly there was ample scope for rivalry between regents and statholder.

Williams's son Maurice was appointed to follow him as commander in chief of the federal army and navy. The Estates did their best to assert that

---

[2] See G. J. Renier, *The Dutch Nation* (London: George Allen and Unwin, 1944).

the appointment came from them and that it was not the result of the automatic working of heredity; but in the late 17th century, it would have been impossible for the scion of a noble family not to seek dynastic aggrandizement. In an age when kings were growing more powerful in the neighboring states of Europe, Maurice was inevitably pushed to act more like a monarch and less like an appointee.

The townsmen, of course, were never completely united, and this gave an ambitious leader like Maurice the chance to play one group against another. Maurice came to ally himself with nonregental, even vaguely "democratic" elements. Here again was the alliance between an ambitious leader at the top with the more or less democratic interests at the bottom, against the oligarchical middle. It was the sort of alliance that has often led to a broadening of political participation and in this case, by intelligent maneuver and some straightforward application of military force, Maurice succeeded in changing the composition of the towns' regents and thereby broadening the oligarchies. The forms of the regential government were left intact, however, and once Maurice had placed his supporters into the regencies, it was clear that he hardly sought a democracy. The familiar forms of government remained intact, while the House of Orange gained some identification with relatively democratic sentiments at the same time that it continued to cooperate with the business interests of the towns. Maurice died in 1625, and his brother Frederic-Henry became statholder. Frederic-Henry cooperated closely with the regential regime, stayed in office until his death in 1647, and was then followed by his son, William II. Clearly, whatever the theory of regential appointment may have been, a hereditary dynasty was becoming established.

William II, however, died during an interval of peace, and this gave the Estates courage not to appoint a successor. They were able, temporarily, to divest themselves of a statholder, and to gain experience in governing themselves in what has come to be known as the first statholderless period. Later, however, a new military threat arose and the situation reverted to its earlier state. In 1672, a mob demanded a change in the regents, and the reinstatement of a statholder. The son of William II now became Statholder William III, helped into office by a bit of mob action. This represented a rather broader section of the population than that of the regents, and so here again was the alliance of the powerful leader at the top with the wider groups below. The same cycle was repeated yet another time. A second statholderless period came to an end in 1747 when the War of Austrian Succession brought still another statholder, William IV, to office on another wave of popular agitation against the oligarchs of the regential party.

In each of these cases, relatively popular pressures brought a strong man to power, and in each case, the strong man proceeded to back away from his more popular supporters and to cooperate with the established regents. The long-term trend, however, was for political participation to broaden, and over the course of the centuries, the originally narrow oligarchy was gradually opened to a wider and wider proportion of the population.

STABILITY AND THE DEFINITION OF PARTICIPATION

Florence and the Dutch republic were in an almost endless state of political turmoil, and the definition of exactly who should and who should not be admitted to participation in the political system was usually one important issue under dispute. The Venetian republic provides a remarkable contrast.

Venice was one of the first Italian cities to gain political independence. The city leaders maneuvered adroitly between the declining power of Constantinople and the growing power of the papacy and then that of the Holy Roman Empire. Located on the border between the realm of fading eastern influence and the slowly reorganizing territories of western Europe, Venice maneuvered her way to independence from both. Never succumbing either to a personal tyranny or to hereditary rule, as so many other cities finally did, Venice survived for centuries until its frame of government came to be older than any royal house of Europe. Venice became a political wonder of stability and apparent immortality, a demonstration to all who cared to look that republican organization could work.

Venetian leadership was exercised by its Grand Council. Formed in 1142, the council originally included all prominent Venetians, but its membership was gradually restricted until it came to be strictly hereditary and firmly closed to all outsiders. All men who came from families with the hereditary right to sit on the Grand Council were considered nobles, and, whenever they were in Venice, most of the nobles seem actually to have attended the regular Sunday meetings. Altogether as many as 2,500 men of office-holding age might belong to the Grand Council, and while Venice can hardly be called a democratic state in any modern sense, this large council did provide a far more broadly based political system than the hereditary monarchies of its era. The Grand Council chose men from among its membership to hold the approximately 800 government offices. As in earlier Greece and Rome, terms of office were short. Every nobleman could expect to have terms in several offices during his career, but offices could be as much an obligation as a privilege, for the real interest of many nobles always lay in commerce. Participation in the political system was a duty of citizenship necessary to maintain a climate in which business could flourish, but it was not usually an end in itself. Some nobles, of course, were politically more ambitious than others, but all shared in the responsibility of filling the bewildering maze of committees, governorships, embassies, and judicial bodies that made Venice a viable state.

The secret of Venetian stability was certainly its Grand Council. Its noble members were too jealous of the privileges of their class to admit outsiders, but at the same time, they were too jealous of one another to allow any single man or small clique to gain dominance. Those with political ambitions could rise slowly through the hierarchy of offices subject always to the approval of the Grand Council. At the top was the doge, the titular head of state and the occupant of the most prestigious office, but the doge did not rule Venice. That was the collective responsibility of the Grand Council and of the many officials it appointed. The nobles of Venice would no more let a single tyrant usurp their privileges than they would open their membership to the rabble. Venetian stability depended above all on a rigid definition of who could and who could not participate in the political system. The Venetian nobles were consistently unwilling either to let power be shared more widely or to be concentrated into fewer hands. The oligarchies of most other Italian cities succumbed alternately, or even simultaneously, to the twin threats of wider and more democratic political participation or to narrower and more tyrannical rule. By rigidly defining its own boundaries, the Venetian oligarchy protected itself against both the centralizing pressures of one-man rule and against the decentralizing pressures of elements that might hope to gain a greater political voice.

The example of Venice shows clearly that stability is possible at an intermediate level of participation, but it is a level that is not readily available to modern men. We are no longer willing to justify a ruling aristocracy of the sort that led Venice. Today, the only viable possibilities seem to be either an extreme centralization, or a democracy based upon universal franchise. When neither of these works very well, a nation is more apt to endure violent swings between the two extremes than to settle on a stable compromise at some midpoint, such as was once possible in Venice.

USURPATION

When the Maratha chhatrapatis grew weak, the peshwas were able to usurp their power. When the emperors of Han dynasty China grew weak in 8 A.D., the minister Wang Mang was able to found the Hsin dynasty. In 751, when the Merovingian kings of the Franks grew weak, their mayors of the palace were able to usurp the throne and found the Carolingian dynasty. In all three cases, men came to the throne without the sanction of heredity, but since all three then proceeded to pass their throne on to hereditary successors, very little in the political system had changed. The same weaknesses, the same inherent contradictions, would plague the new dynasties as plagued the old. When the kings of England and the statholders of Holland grew weak, their power was also usurped, but because the usurpers then passed their offices to their successors by entirely different procedures, a profound mutation in the political system had occurred.

During the statholderless periods, the constituted bodies of the low countries gradually learned to manage their affairs without a statholder, but they could not manage without a responsible man, and a new office arose which assumed some of the statholder's former responsibility. This new office was that of the grand pensionary of Holland, the most important of the constituent states of the Dutch Republic. At first, the grand pensionary was a sort of legal advisor to the Estates of Holland, but the other members of the Estates could absent themselves only for short periods from their businesses and private affairs in their respective towns, and the grand pensionary became the only permanent member of the council. He presided at the meetings of the Estates, ran its business between meetings, and became the chief civil officer of the state. Clearly, the grand pensionary was in a strategic position to lead if he chose to do so, and some grand pensionaries became, in effect, the presidents of Holland. Furthermore, since the state of Holland had such a predominant position within the Dutch federation, the grand pensionary became very nearly the president of the entire Dutch Republic. Since the grand pensionary was unambiguously chosen by the regents and since the office never became hereditary, the Dutch had evolved a very different type of leadership than a monarchy.

A somewhat similar development took place in England when the prime minister replaced the monarch as the most powerful figure in the government. King and Parliament had competed for hundreds of years. When the kings were strong, they could use Parliament for their own ends, but when the monarchy was weak, Parliament could assert its own will, and it even came to offer a continuity to the government that no sequence of monarchs could provide. During the republican period Parliament made an early attempt to rule with no monarch at all, but Cromwell's ability to assume dictatorial powers offers us still another example of the need for centralized leadership and of the tendency for a single man to assume the leading position. The monarchy was eventually restored, and both under the relatively strong rule of Charles II, and later and more modestly under William III of Orange, royal power tended once again to increase at the expense of Parliament.

Parliament was always there, ready to fill any breach, however, and when the throne weakened even more decisively under the early Georges in the 18th century, Parliament was ready to assume full control. Once again, a single dominant ruler was needed, and now the office of the prime minister was evolved. Ministries continued to be described as if they were responsible to the king, but real power was henceforth securely lodged in Parliament. A usurpation had taken place, but it left the political system in a radically changed form. Since nobody ever imagined that the prime ministry should become hereditary, the chief position of power has had to be pursued by other means.

THE END OF HEREDITY

Through more than two millenia of European history, hereditary offices competed with offices achieved by other means. For much of that time heredity must have seemed to have the decisive advantages. From the fall of the Roman Republic through the Middle Ages, republican institutions faltered, and the feeble representative institutions of the first cities of modern Europe could hardly have looked capable of competing with and finally subjecting the monarchies. Nevertheless, the Italian city republics had their days of greatness, and later the Dutch and the British demonstrated that it was possible to govern a territory wider than a single city by means other than a monarchy. Finally, the practical examples of the American and French revolutions, together with the new political philosophy of the Enlightenment, so far undermined the legitimacy of heredity that men ceased to claim serious political power on the basis of their ancestry.

The turmoil that erupted in France and that then spread over most of the Continent hardly brought an immediate acceptance of republican or democratic government, but it rapidly destroyed the legitimacy of hereditary succession. Where European kings survived, they were reduced to mere figureheads. In other parts of the world, monarchs stayed in power somewhat longer, but one of the truly revolutionary changes that man has undergone since 1800 has been his loss of faith in heredity. The decline of heredity has been one aspect of the spread of European ideas over the rest of the world. Heredity often gave way first under the impact of colonial conquest, but the collapse of the colonial empires has only confirmed its disappearance. A search for hereditary monarchs who retain any significant power in 1973 is about completed with Haile Selassie of Ethiopia and a few Arab kings.

In earlier centuries and in other parts of the world, the dangers of anarchy had justified rule by a single man, and the surest way to select that man usually seemed to be heredity. When heredity goes, the need for leadership remains, and a large part of politics now revolves around the problem of how to select leaders in the absence of heredity. Without the limitations on the struggle that heredity provides, the way is open to much wider competition. This carries the danger of destructive struggles, but the nonhereditary regimes that Europeans learned to organize also had some important countervailing advantages. Most important has been their relative openness to new men with new ideas.

For all the many reasons that appeared in the Maratha and Manchu examples, dynasties must inevitably decline. Sooner or later they will grow weak and need replacement. The replacement may come fairly quickly when a usurpation like that of the peshwas allows new men to take over, or it may be long delayed when it must await a debacle of the sort in which the Manchu dynasty of China finally collapsed. The longer replacement is postponed, the greater the final convulsion is likely to be. Without heredity, renewal must come more often, and if some sort of reasonable orderly electoral process can be evolved, it may even come fairly peacefully. Republican regimes, being more open to challenge from a broader range of participants, can renew themselves regularly and with far less turmoil than hereditary regimes, and the men who reach the top are less likely to have endured the debilitating periods of imprisonment or confinement in the smothering safety of a protective household than are princes, who have to be treated like potential heirs and thus as potential rivals. New leaders in a republic are less apt to have been cut off from worldly knowledge. Some degree of open and, in the best of times, peaceful competition is allowed. This may soften the violence of competition that must sooner or later come to any political system.

Thus, in spite of the many advantages that once made it the first choice of most of mankind's political systems, heredity has come to an end. It has given way to more successful political systems, and it is even tempting to see the decline of heredity as one important factor in the 19th and early 20th century dominance in the West. By then, Europeans and North Americans had developed political systems that did not have to endure quite the same degree of debilitating succession struggles that were endemic in the rest of the world. Of course, Europeans struggled over succession, but their struggles were sometimes damped down. Instead of a major struggle once each generation, Europeans had minor electoral struggles every few years. Pressures did not build up so long waiting for the release of the final convulsion. One president or prime minister might fall, but another would quietly take his place. ·

As long as India remained reasonably united under the Mughals and as long as China remained united under the Manchus, European powers could gain no more than a foothold along the edges of their realms. Real power in Asia came to the Europeans only when the native governments grew weak and this happened when their succession systems failed to provide the single strong leader that their political systems required. The British could defeat the Marathas only when various Maratha factions were completely at odds with one another. Then, the British could ally themselves with some Maratha contingents to defeat others. In its rise to dominance, the new British government did exactly what all earlier Indian governments had done: played off its opponents against one another, insinuated itself into the divisions that beset its enemies, and gradually assumed more and more power for itself. Unfortunately for the Indians, however, the new British government was far less subject to internal divisions than were its Indian predecessors. When a ruler left office in England, or when the representative of the British government left office in India, there was no sudden weakening of British power that other princes could exploit. There were no sudden divisions in the Empire when struggling contenders bargained with potential allies. Instead, a new prime minister or a new viceroy simply stepped into the old office. There might be a slight shift in policy, but the essential nature of the regime would continue. India could not gain independence again until her people had learned to play for power under entirely new rules. No hereditary monarchy could be a match for the new European style of government.

AN ALTERNATIVE TO HEREDITY

Since the time of the Greeks, a leading European competitor with heredity has been some form of election. By the end of the 18th century, a solid theoretical basis had been laid for republican government, and the philosophical and political doctrines that helped to inspire and also to rationalize first the American and then the French revolutions became the common property of the Western man: representation, natural rights, the separation of powers, federalism, government by contract, the people as sovereign. These abstract doctrines, however, needed to be given a practical application and nowhere were they applied earlier or more successfully than in newly independent North America. Three practical devices by which the Americans put the new theories into practice deserve comment: the expansion of the franchise, the development of practical techniques for creating new constitutions, and the invention of mass political parties.[3]

First came the expansion of the franchise, and it came almost by accident. The colonies were ruled under charters granted by the throne and it was taken for granted, as it was in Britain, that men of property would take the leadership in public affairs. Only men with the stake in the community that property represented were expected to have either the interest or the

---

[3]The sources upon which I have relied for my comments on American developments are listed in the Bibliographic Notes (pp. 302–303).

right to help make governmental decisions. In England, property requirements kept the electorate small in proportion to the population, but far more
men held property in the colonies. The same requirement that kept the
electorate small at home opened it relatively wide in America. A considerable proportion of the colonists grew accustomed to participating actively
in town and county government and to voting for representation in the
colonial assemblies.

In a land where suffrage was already extensive, the first years of the
revolution saw its considerable further expansion. Two main groups had
formerly had their franchise limited: farmers in the more recently settled
western regions of some colonies, and the "mechanics," or workers of the
seaboard cities. In the former case, legislative apportionment tended to leave
the western counties underrepresented, while, in the latter, property requirements were often too high. Extending the franchise to these groups,
both by creating new legislative seats for western counties and by lowering
property requirements, was one way by which power might be shifted away
from those who were most inclined to be sympathetic to the crown. Thus,
as radicals who favored independence gained control of the legislatures,
they sought to consolidate their position by extending the franchise. Here is
a very concrete example of the way in which rivalry among leaders—in this
case between revolutionists and loyalists—can lead to the expansion of
political participation. The radicals usually stopped short of extending the
vote to all adult freemen and, of course, they never even considered extending it to the slaves. Nevertheless, the American franchise became very much
broader than it ever had been in Britain, and the broad political participation that this implied had a profound influence upon every subsequent
political development in America.

As the franchise was expanding, Americans also groped their way toward
a new conception of constitutional law and toward new techniques for
framing constitutions that would give legitimacy to their governments. The
colonists had come to look upon their colonial charters with some degree of
pride and even reverence. They were seen as written guarantees of their
rights as Englishmen, and with the assertion of independence, they felt the
need for new written documents. This time they would draw up the documents themselves rather than accept them from the crown, but the new
charters, like the old, would guarantee their rights and set out the frame of
their government. As a result, in the midst of war, the Americans busied
themselves with the complex task of writing new constitutions for their new
states.

This wartime exercise in constitution writing gave Americans extensive
practical experience with organizing new governments, and some clear
principles gradually became established. Constitutional law came to be seen

as resting upon the explicit mutual agreement of the constituent population, and it came to be seen as different and more basic than ordinary legislation which ordinary assemblies might adopt. It also came to be widely accepted that constitutional provisions, unlike ordinary legislation, had to be submitted for ratification to a broader constituency than the body which actually drafted the documents. Ordinary legislation could be adopted by an assembly; constitutional legislation needed ratification. Thus, the Americans worked out practical devices for constructing new governmental forms and practical means by which to gather a broad expression of support for the forms. A new kind of legitimacy was created, a legitimacy that rested neither upon the hereditary principle of monarchy nor upon the kind of hallowed tradition that supported the British Parliament. Legitimacy now rested instead upon the explicit consent of the governed.

A third important American contribution to the practical running of a modern republic was the development of the modern mass political party, but the acceptance of parties would not come until a generation after the revolution. The founding fathers had hoped to avoid parties or factions, and indeed they denounced them vigorously. What they knew of party politics had seemed divisive and petty, a jockeying for personal advantage rather than organization to promote the common good. The parties that had developed earlier in Britain or in some of the colonies would hardly have inspired anyone's confidence. Rather, they looked conspiratorial and subversive, and the role that parties would come to play in organizing the electorate and seeking to put together winning coalitions was completely unanticipated. At best, the writers of the American constitution saw parties as inevitable though unpleasant concomitants of a free society. They were to be held in check as much as possible.

The national parties of later years did have colonial anticipations, particularly in Pennsylvania, which, in a number of respects, had a precocious political development. Nascent parties competed to build up their respective positions within the Pennsylvania assembly and they developed a remarkably modern electoral style. Pamphleteering became common, and men sought election on specific issues. They formed alliances which sought electoral support very much in the manner of our modern political parties.

The Pennsylvania experience was repeated on a national level once the federal constitution went into effect. Parties may have been unwanted, but some means had to be developed for bridging the gap between the government and the people, between legislative factions and popular interests. Without planning and against everyone's better judgment, national parties began to coalesce early in the first administration. First, Hamilton put together a congressional coalition that would support his program, and thereby helped to bring order out of an initially chaotic congress. He took the lead in reaching out to the states, seeking an alliance of moneyed men who had an interest in orderly government and who would support his program. Hardly realizing what he was doing, Hamilton was helping to weave together a web of friendship and common interest on both the national and state levels that would ultimately come to be known as the Federalist Party.

The vigor of Hamilton's faction stimulated opposition, and with Jefferson as their symbolic leader and men like Madison taking the organizational initiative, the "Republican" opponents of the Federalists appealed directly to the electorate and mobilized popular support. Organization proceeded at all levels. Local factions oriented to local issues would align themselves with similar factions in other states and with the congressional parties. Alliances formed among a complex network of economic, class, regional, and ethnic interests, and they worked their way toward coalitions that could contest elections. With the wide suffrage now available in America, these alliances were essential if the local politics of the courthouses was to be integrated with the national politics of the congress. The Republicans became the first modern political party, an organization in which power rested upon superiority in numbers and its ability to get out the vote.

Even while busily organizing, neither Federalists nor Republicans could at first accept the idea that organized parties could play a legitimate or useful role. The very notion of an opposition seemed to imply subversion. The old Chinese ideas that all factions were self-seeking and destructive and that loyal men need only support and work for the government would not have seemed so strange to the founding fathers as they do to us. A generation would pass before the idea of a loyal opposition became acceptable and before the suspicion of sedition would be removed from men who organized to oppose those who held office.

The Republicans were able to use the machinery provided by the constitution to gain office, and the Federalist party went into a decline. The country was then left with a single party. Inevitably, factions soon developed which fragmented the dominant Republicans. Intraparty wrangling rose in direct proportion to the weakening of Federalist opposition, until all that was left were a number of personal factions, none of which had nationwide organization. There was an unruly and multi-sided scramble for the presidency. Factions, it seems, are inevitable in a dominant party, and complete dominance must be followed by complete chaos.

Finally, the time came for a renewed cycle of party formation. In the 1820s, with John Quincy Adams in the presidency, an organized opposition again began to form. Men, like Martin Van Buren of New York, who considered themselves the true heirs of Jeffersonian Republicanism, organized in opposition to President Adams, just as an earlier group had organized opposition to the Federalists. Now for the first time, men like Van Buren began to argue that party organization was not simply an inevitable evil of a republican government, but a desirable and essential part of it. Being able to look back to the now revered generation of Jefferson, whose activities were almost by definition accepted as high-principled, Van Buren and his contemporaries no longer had qualms about their own organizational activities. They even argued that an organized party of opposition was desirable. Parties came to be recognized as the means of bringing order where there would otherwise be chaos, and as a means by which the party in power could be held in check. The new Democratic Party was supported by a coalition of highly professional politicians, and it rested upon a broad base of local organization. The result was the triumph of Andrew Jackson in 1828.

Without conscious design, and indeed in the face of general disapproval, party organization had grown up to bring order to the rivalry that seems inevitable in any political system. It is hardly too much to suggest that the American constitution could never have been made to work if parties had not been organized. Where the franchise was so extensive, some mechanism had to bridge the gap between congressional factions and courthouse cliques. Only party organization could give the voters a choice among plausible alternatives. From the launching of the Federation, the American electorate was far more extensive both in geography and numbers than any electorate in previous human history. Without parties to organize this electorate, the machinery of government could not have long survived. Since the time of Jackson, parties have played a crucial part in the selection of American leaders. The American succession system depends heavily upon them.

The American and French political experiments and the political philosophy that supported them had a profound attraction for the men of that era. To many men then, and to many western Europeans and Americans ever since, it has seemed only reasonable to suppose that elections would become the dominant way of selecting leaders. We ought, however, to be at least as impressed by the failures of electoral regimes as by their successes, not only by their failure to live up to their promises of liberty and justice for their people, but also by their institutional failure to survive in the face of competing forms of government. The 19th century saw the establishment of a few stable electoral regimes in North America and western Europe, but in the majority of nations where elections have been tried, the elected governments have come to grief. Today, heredity regimes are gone, but most of the world still lives under rulers who have gained their position by other means than the popular vote. Where heredity is gone and republican government has not taken its place, we must ask what has arisen instead. Are there other systems that work better than our own imperfect electoral system? The final chapters of this book are devoted to the alternative political systems that seem to be available to modern man, and to the means by which men seek power in these systems.

CHAPTER **6**

Latin America

INTRODUCTION

When, in the early 19th century, Spanish America followed Anglo–America into independence, the new nations could call not only upon the abstract ideals of the Enlightenment as guides to political action, but look also to actual governments in both Europe and North America that stood as reasonably successful examples of electoral regimes. A century and a half of independence, however, and a century and a half without monarchy, have not been enough to bring stable electoral regimes to most of Latin America. Elections have often been held; sometimes they have been honest; occasionally they have even brought the man with the largest number of votes into office. But honest or not, the results of elections have often been nullified by armed men who have taken the decision into their own hands

148

and forced it upon their country. The coup d'etat rather than the election still seems to be the characteristic Latin American path to high office.

From a North American vantage point, it is easy to conclude that Latin American politics is simply pathological. North Americans seem to imagine that political stability is the norm and that it is instability that needs explanation. Yet the example of the newly independent nations of Asia and Africa in the decades following the Second World War must make the Latin American kind of "instability" look rather like the normal political condition of modern man. Latin Americans are not the only people to lurch from military coup to military coup. During the decade of the 1960s, for instance, no less than 20 coups overturned governments in the newly independent nations of sub-Saharan Africa. Rather than asking why these nations have failed to find stability, we might do better to ask the more neutral question: How do their political systems work? Hereditary offices have disappeared from Asia, Africa, and Latin America as completely as they have from North America and Europe, but heredity has not been consistently replaced by elections as a means for legitimizing leadership. What has been substituted? How is top office achieved where heredity is no longer taken seriously, but where elections seem not to be taken very seriously either?

Latin America has an advantage over the many other parts of the world where one might ask these questions, for it has had what might be called a precocious underdevelopment. Since the early 19th century, much of Latin America has consisted of poor, ex-colonial, and underdeveloped nations. These have had a century and a half more experience with underdevelopment than nations elsewhere in the world. We can, therefore, examine their political organization over a much longer time span than is possible with the newer nations of other continents. The politics of much of Africa and a good deal of Asia, however, now seems to be falling into patterns reminiscent of Latin America, and any hope that the military coup is merely a transitional stage through which only newly independent nations pass should be tempered by our knowledge of Latin American history.

THE LEGACY OF SPAIN

Spanish America fought its way to independence in the early decades of the 19th century, but since the new nations inherited the indelible imprint of three centuries of colonial rule, it is quite impossible to understand post-colonial politics without first examining the Spanish regime.[1] Spain was

---

[1] Hubert Herring, *A History of Latin America* (New York: Alfred A. Knopf, 2nd rev. ed. 1961) provides a broad and general framework of Latin American history.

governed through a centralized and hierarchical administration. Viceroys, the direct agents of the king, held jurisdiction over the largest territorial divisions, but below them were the lesser officials of the smaller presidencias and captaincies general, and a fleet of administrative, judicial, and investigatory officials who were expected to protect the natives, administer justice, insure a sound financial return to the crown, and keep watch over one another. In its centralization, in its subordination to the monarchy, and in its network of mutually counterchecking bureaucrats, this administration can be justly compared with that of Manchu China.

The administrative structure was also not unlike that of Spain itself. Strictly speaking, the Spanish dominions in the New World were not colonies at all, but were possessions of the king, equivalent to, rather than subject to, the kingdoms of the Iberian peninsula. Nevertheless, the special conditions of America could never allow a simple duplication of Iberian practices, and American administration came to be even more centralized than administration at home. The American lands were new, and they were first opened and ruled directly by the king's agents. Throughout the colonial period, top officials were almost always "peninsulares"—Spaniards from the peninsula, who however competent or incompetent they may have been, were, with remarkable consistency, firmly loyal to the crown.

At the same time, the distance from Spain and indeed the distance from one American possession to another made central supervision of every detail entirely impossible. At the lower levels of administration, considerable local responsibility had to be granted, and at the lowest level of Latin American government were the cities. These quickly assumed a more important role than did cities in British America. Cities were laid out more promptly, and their administrations were given jurisdiction not only over the city nucleus itself, but over a circle of surrounding territory that might stretch out until it met the territory of the next city. Perhaps "city-state" would better characterize these domains than the simple term "city," though of course they were never, in any way, independent.

Some aspects of local administration were entrusted to the *cabildos* or city councils. These were the Latin American equivalent of the "constituted bodies" long known in Europe. The constituted bodies of Spain came to be subjected more firmly to the crown than did those of many parts of Europe, but they were not abolished even in Spain, and the Spaniards in America faithfully duplicated the city administration of the Iberian peninsula. The cabildo proper of a city consisted of a relatively small body of men who held formal office, but occasionally larger councils were convened, the so-called *cabildo abiertos,* at which all substantial townsmen were entitled to discuss particularly important issues. The great distances and sparse population of Latin America allowed and even forced the cabildos to assume a good deal of local responsibility.

Membership in the smaller cabildos was gained in various ways. In some cases, membership was quite permanent or even hereditary, but more typically it changed regularly, sometimes every year on January 1. Often, especially in the early years, the members were appointed by higher administrative officials, but in some cities the substantial men of the community elected their councilmen and in others the offices could be bought and sold like property. In Buenos Aires, the members of the cabildo nominated their own successors, though their selection had to be approved by the governor. In colonial Venezuela, the leading citizens elected their cabildo every January first.

Each cabildo was charged with governing the city and its surrounding territory, but it would be a misconception to imagine that even the elected cabildos amounted, in any sense, to democratic governments. Whatever the formal rules by which membership was gained, the cabildos always represented the interests of the leading local families, and these families formed a similar class with interests similar to the oligarchies of many earlier and contemporary European cities.

Men of Spanish descent who were born in America, the *creoles,* were generally excluded from the highest administrative posts. These were reserved for natives of Spain, and as a result, the able, wealthy, and ambitious creoles could find scope for politics only in the cabildos. Thus, although the cabildos were never so democratic as to represent anything like the total population of their territories, they did come to represent the viewpoint of the more substantial of the men who had been born in America. Since they represented local interests, the cabildos could handle routine local problems in a way more responsive to local needs than could foreign appointees, and they helped to keep the administration informed about local conditions. They also served as a political training ground for a few ambitious individuals.

For three centuries of Spanish rule, the cabildos served as a useful and generally loyal bottom rung of government and they helped to maintain the stability of a notably stable regime. During these centuries there was never any doubt that absolute and final authority lay with the central administration that was appointed from Spain and dominated by peninsulares. The cabildos never made the kind of challenge to this central administration that was made by the colonial assemblies of British America. Nevertheless, when independence came to Spanish America, the only governmental bodies that were in any way responsive to American interests were the cabildos. Almost by default, it was the cabildos that usually took the first steps in organizing independent governments. The estates of the Nether-lands, the parliament of England, and the assemblies of the North American colonies had all, at one time, found themselves ruling without a statholder, king, or governor. The day came when the Latin American cabildos found themselves in the same position.

Beyond the bounds of the city proper, central administration in colonial times was tenuous. The more remote sections of America, of course, were never administered at all, but between the unadministered Indian territories and the organized urban centers were large stretches of rural land. Here was found the real wealth of Spanish America, and here haciendas brought riches and power to a few owners, and poverty to the bulk of their workers —whether these were Indians, African slaves, or men of European descent. Here, beyond the limits of the city, an almost feudal political system de-veloped. Large land owners monopolized not only the wealth of the land—export crops and livestock—but political power as well. At independence, when the overarching Spanish administration was removed, rural political leaders emerged as one of the dominant forces in the new society. They sometimes dominated and sometimes collaborated with urban interests, but they had to be reckoned with in any political calculation. Besides the urban cabildos and a species of rural feudalism, Spain willed much else to her independent daughters, among other things the Catholic Church and a restricted but lively intellectual tradition. The power of the church was thoroughly entwined with that of the government, but the church did not disappear with the Spanish administration. It remained to complicate and occasionally to dominate the politics of the newly independent nations. The intellectual tradition found expression in the nucleus of a system of higher education and in a small but sophisticated educated elite. At the beginning of the 19th century, the members of this elite, many of whom had been educated in Europe, were well acquainted with the political doctrines of the United States and of revolutionary France. Once independence was achieved, these doctrines helped to foster democratic sentiments and ex-periments.

INDEPENDENCE

Independence came to Latin America only after Napoleon's armies had conquered Spain and overturned the only Spanish government to which American dominions could direct their unambiguous loyalty. The lack of enthusiasm for independence is shown by the fact that the first independent actions were made in the name of loyalty to the deposed Spanish king. To be loyal to the deposed king, however, implied local initiative in defying the Napoleonic regime in Spain and this initiative came at a time when the central administration was collapsing. Increasing local initiative, declining central power, and the encouragement offered by the revolutionary doctrines then popular in both North America and Europe, led inexorably to declarations of complete independence on the part of one after another Spanish American territory.

It was often the cabildos that first tried to organize local administration and that first took the initiative in building independent political structures. The cabildos, however, were neither very representative nor very unified. The jurisdiction of each cabildo was limited to a single city and its hinterland, and each cabildo was often split among disputing factions. Nevertheless, in the absence of more broadly based representative institutions only the cabildos could take initiative. In Buenos Aires, for instance, the cabildo succeeded in forcing the Spanish viceroy to summon the cabildo abierto in 1810, and this larger assembly of 250 people then chose to evict the viceroy. They made this move in the name of Ferdinand VII, the Spanish king, but their action was clearly a revolutionary one. Viceroys had always been appointed from above, and their appointment had never been subject to any sort of local approval; but neither the viceroy nor the now deposed Ferdinand had the power to suppress this local initiative. The only logical outcome was a final assertion of complete independence and, in fact, the Argentines date the birth of their republic from the departure of the last viceroy.

The cabildos of Buenos Aires soon ran into problems, however. The cabildo abierto was large and cumbersome, and it lacked any settled procedural traditions. It could not possibly assume effective rule itself, and could really do no more than grant or withhold its blessings from various more personal rulers, though even this gave it something of a legitimizing role. The smaller cabildo, on the other hand, never gained consistent recognition as the legitimate governmental authority. Men sought offices within the cabildo and the offices could be used temporarily to rally public opinion and encourage one's favorite policies, but those who disagreed felt few qualms about defying the cabildo, and no consistent set of rules emerged by which cabildo offices might be peacefully acquired.

These ostensibly representative bodies, in fact, came increasingly to serve as fronts for military commanders. Strong men more or less openly dictated terms to the members of the cabildos, or placed their own men in cabildo offices. In principle, the military commanders were appointed by the cabildos and were authorized by them to lead the troops which cabildos organized for defense. In fact, the commanders came to dominate the cabildos as often as the reverse. Here in the new world, the representative bodies faced the same problem that many others had faced in the old world—military leadership was needed, but it easily got out of control—

and the cabildos were even less prepared to defend themselves against military domination than were some of the old world constituted bodies.

Here at the very beginning of independence was a clash of political principle, for the legitimate authority of a representative body came to be challenged by the real power of men on horseback. It is a conflict that has bedeviled Latin American politics ever since. Neither the representative bodies nor the men on horseback have been consistently able to provide adequate government alone. The cabildos and their more representative successors have often lacked the worldly strength to enforce their decisions. The men on horseback have had the firepower, but in the search for some kind of legitimate mandate that would allow their governments to be stabilized, they have usually felt obliged to claim support from a representative body. It was to the cabildos that military leaders first looked in seeking this legitimacy.

Under Spain the cabildos had never controlled more than a single city, but, with independence, efforts were soon made to bring representatives of neighboring cities together. Something had to replace the central Spanish administration which had formerly been the only government authority above the cities. Assemblies of representatives of a wider region than a single city were called together, sometimes on the initiative of a single leader, and these struggled to find some sort of general agreement and to bring some sort of order into the governmental system. Simón Bolívar convened a number of congresses, some quite ephemeral, in the areas he liberated from Spain—Venezuela, Colombia, Ecuador, Peru, and Bolivia. Augustín de Iturbide called a congress in Mexico in 1822, the year after his forces had expelled the Spaniards from Mexico City. In Argentina soon after the deposition of the last viceroy, Buenos Aires led the cabildos abiertos of the cities and towns of Argentina in organizing the first congress of cabildo representatives. Other congresses followed.

These congresses had no precedents, and not only were they unable to agree on policies, they were unable even to agree on the rules by which their members should be chosen and admitted. When the congresses did not simply founder, they most often had the same fate as the cabildos—they became fronts for rising strong men. It may seem that the most notable characteristic of the earliest congresses of Latin America was their complete failure to provide for consistent and orderly governments, but it is at least as noteworthy that congresses were so widely attempted. Most of the nations of Spanish America finally found unity at the hands of a strong man who simply rose up and impressed his will upon a territory, but this happened only after the failure of many experiments with more orderly processes of government formation.

Those who struggled for independence quickly faced the problem of finding a mechanism by which to choose the head of govermnent. Latin Americans had been accustomed to a centralized monarchy, and sentiment in favor of a new but locally based monarchy was strong. Signers of the Argentine Declaration of Independence searched for a monarch among members of the Spanish, Portuguese, and French royal families and some even suggested that a prince of Inca descent would be appropriate. Iturbide assumed the title of Agustín I, Emperor of Mexico, but since he was deposed in less than a year, his dynasty can hardly be taken very seriously. Later, in 1864, Mexico endured another brief royal interlude when Napoleon III imposed Maximilian, a scion of the Hapsburgs, as Emperor. Maximilian, however, came to an ignominious end. He was shot in 1867, and that ended monarchy for Mexico.

Brazil underwent a more serious monarchical experiment. When Portugal fell to Napoleon, the British Navy helped the Portuguese royal court to move to Brazil, and when Portugal later became independent again, some members of the royal family stayed in Brazil and gave it 70 years as an independent monarchy. The result was a far smoother transition to independence for Brazil than for its Spanish neighbors. Nowhere in Spanish America could the various contending parties agree upon a royal candidate.

Incipient family dynasties have arisen from time to time in Latin America. Two brothers dominated Venezuela in the mid 19th century, and their dynasty might have continued had a son and a nephew not quarreled over the succession. When the Paraguayan dictator Carlos Antonio López died in 1862, his son Francisco Solano López successfully assumed office, but the son was soon ruined in a war against Argentina, Brazil, and Uruguay and that dynasty thankfully ended. More recently, the Somoza family managed temporarily to perpetuate its dictatorship in Nicaragua when, in 1956, rulership passed from father to son in comfortable hereditary succesion. Even as recently as 1971, François Duvalier was able to arrange his son's succession to the presidency of Haiti.

These examples demonstrate that the forces that encourage hereditary succession did not suddenly evaporate when Latin America became independent, but hereditary patterns have never been consolidated, and other techniques for achieving office have been used far more often. In fact, even in the early 19th century, the ideological foundation upon which hereditary succession could be justified had crumbled so far that a man could rarely claim office simply by virtue of his ancestry. Other principles had to be appealed to. At independence, as today, the problem was to find an acceptable alternative principle.

The obvious alternative was some sort of electoral system, and throughout Latin America republican assemblies convened, debated, and wrote constitutions. The constitutions expressed the highest republican ideals, but these immediately collided with the reality of social conditions in the territories to which they sought to bring law. Population was often sparse, and the discipline of the Spanish imperial authority was gone. The most experienced administrators had often been exiled. Lawlessness became an almost permanent condition. Security in the rural areas declined, people fled to the cities, and agricultural productivity dropped. The mass of the population was miserably poor and utterly lacking in the kind of education or experience that could have supported orderly republican procedures. If these ignorant masses had been asked to choose their own governments they could hardly have done so with enlightened intelligence. At best, they would have followed the lead of their landlords or their bosses. In fact, of course, they were rarely given anything like the general franchise. Debates about governmental forms and contests among ambitious rivals were confined to a small minority of the population. The high ideals expressed in the republican constitutions foundered upon the reality of the general lack of political experience.

The collapse of the Spanish administration was followed by the wars of independence, and these left behind them a turbulence verging on anarchy. Some men came to feel the need for a strong executive who could take decisive, even dictatorial, action. Yearnings for a renewed monarchy were one expression of this feeling, but there were other expressions too. Simón Bolívar, for instance, once advocated a constitutional provision that would give a man the presidency for life and the power to appoint his own successor. Such a system abandoned the hereditary principle, but it would have amounted almost to a monarchy since it would allow life rulership and remove the choice of appointment from the people.

Bolívar's scheme was never actually built into the constitution of a Latin American state, although both life tenure and the power to appoint one's own successor have had an important place in practical Latin American politics. They have, however, been de facto rather than de jure practices. Many dictators have become so strong that they could be removed only by death, and some have been able to impose their own choice as successor. But neither life tenure nor the attainment of the presidency by appointment of one's predecessor is the sort of principle that most men have wanted to enshrine in their constitutions. The fear of anarchy might persuade men to accept as realistically necessary the dictatorial powers implied by these principles, but they would not accept them as ideal.

In an area with no tradition of representative government beyond the limited representation of the oligarchical cabildos, with no experience in cooperation even between neighboring cities, with massive illiteracy, with widespread lawlessness and banditry, with war and economic disruption, and with meddling intervention from foreign governments, it is no wonder that representative and constitutional government failed to take immediate hold. The wonder may be, instead, that representative institutions held such a strong attraction.

A TYPOLOGY OF LATIN AMERICAN REGIMES

In its century and a half of independence, Latin America has had a kaleidoscopic succession of governments. They have included almost every political form that man has ever devised, and any typology of these governments must amount very nearly to a typology of all governments everywhere. Any such typology must inevitably gloss over the infinitely varied details by which men can organize themselves. Still, I want to argue that each kind of government has had its own internal contradictions and that the changes in patterns of succession have been brought about by these contradictions. If the discussion is to be manageable, some rough typology is needed, even if its risks doing violence to the details. While acknowledging the difficulties of any typology, it seems plausible to distinguish five important varieties of Latin American leadership, each of which comes to power by its own characteristic techniques: (1) the caudillo—the "man on horseback" who seizes power by his personal military might; (2) the self-perpetuating oligarchy; (3) the presidential system with contested elections; (4) the military or military–civilian junta; and (5) the dictator. This typology leaves out a few aberrant forms, such as the early Brazilian monarchy, the committee executive that once led Uruguay, or the traditional parliamentary system of Chile that has often been compared, in both its organization and in its instability, with that of France. The modern one party system of Mexico, moreover, fits the typology only with difficulty. Neverthless, most Latin American governments can be assigned reasonably well to one or another of these categories.

These governments have come to power in different ways, and where different forms of government have followed each other, so have different patterns of succession. If it is true that each type of government has serious inherent difficulties and that none has been able to provide permanent stability, then each type would tend to encourage succession patterns different from those which first brought it to power, much as each pattern of dynastic succession in Baganda, India, or China seemed to entail difficulties that could only be resolved by a modification in the succession practices. Latin Americans, like Baganda tribesmen, have had difficulty settling down to any one single type of government or to a single accepted style of succession. Instead various types of government seem to have followed each other like the horses on a merry-go-round. It is worth considering each of these five types of government together with examples of the problems that each faced.

To make the discussion as concrete as possible, I will emphasize certain examples, but I do not want to imply that these examples are typical in all respects. I will draw in particular upon the history of Argentina, and while that country offers a satisfyingly diverse range of governmental forms for our inspection, it is certainly not "typical" of all Latin America. Rather, it is one of the most industrialized nations of the continent with one of the best educated populations, and it has in some ways been at the forefront of Latin American developments. One must conclude that if Argentina has had so much difficulty settling down to a stable governmental form, the difficulties of the less bountifully endowed nations must have been that much greater.

I will emphasize internal politics and internal rivalries, and in the process I will certainly fail to do justice to the meddling of foreigners. One cause of Latin American instability has certainly been the willingness of North Americans and Europeans to interfere. They have repeatedly helped old governments out of office and helped new ones in. At the same time the foreigners could hardly have interfered so successfully, had the internal political climate not invited that interference. It is unquestionably true that foreign meddling has helped produce political instability. It is equally true that political instability has allowed foreign meddling. Since my topic is the internal forces that bear upon succession, it is to these that emphasis will be given in the following examples.

THE CAUDILLO

In the countryside, even more than in the cities, the collapse of Spanish power left a political vacuum. Away from the cities, not even the minimal order and continuity provided by the urban cabildos was available, and here strong men, self-appointed local chieftains, arose to fill the void. Village and tribal chiefs, bandit leaders, army officers, and feudal land owners (and the distinction among these is sometimes difficult to draw) who could attract men through the force of their personality, their example of manliness and horsemanship, or offers of protection or patronage could become a power in the countryside. Those who controlled the land and its produce, and above all those who could direct the use of arms, could gather followers and build petty domains. Such men could reward their more loyal henchmen with power and with the loot of battle.

Here, with the collapse of Spanish rule, a rudimentary political system arose that recalls the much earlier time when German retinue leaders gathered followers and organized raiding expeditions. Like the German retinue leaders, the 19th century Latin American boss—the *cacique*—had to give his henchmen tangible rewards, otherwise the cacique, as much as the retinue leader or even the Melanensian big man, would find his followers drifting away. His power would collapse. So long as the cacique could keep his followers satisfied, he could deliver their votes when they were needed, or he could mold them into a small army. In an area where national patriotism emerged only slowly out of the debris of the Spanish empire, personal loyalties to regional caciques were often intense. The strong man and his followers formed a kind of primitive political force that would be unlikely to accept the ballot box as a realistic method of settling a dispute. A lost election was too easily overturned by bullets.

In their dependence upon supporters who might desert at any time, the caciques recall German retinue leaders and Melanesian big men, but the caciques faced another constraint less in evidence in those distant times and places. Mobility, and above all fire power, were more extensive in 19th century Latin America than in Melanesia or early Germany. Inevitably, neighboring strong men fell into competition with one another, and there had to be some sort of accommodation among them. Rival caciques might fight and try to defeat and displace one another or they might form alliances, but in the long run, whether through conquest or through alliance, the logic of these struggles was gradually to build larger power blocks. Larger units were formed until one man could finally lead a coalition of chieftains that could take over the national government. This is what happened in several parts of Latin America, and often it was such a man who finally imposed unity on the territories that became nations.

In Argentina, unity was imposed by Juan Manuel de Rosas.[2] Central government had collapsed in a decade of anarchy following 1819. Only a strong man could stifle the disputes and Rosas had many qualities that suited him ideally for this role. Scion of a prominent Buenos Aires family, he nevertheless became a master gaucho, a horseman skilled in the manly arts of the Pampas. He was able to organize his followers into a private army of terrorists and thugs who would carry out his will, and this man of comfortable urban background became the champion of the masses. Early in his career, he was able to impose his will on Buenos Aires by cutting off its sources of supplies in the outlying districts. In 1829, the provincial legislature of Buenos Aires elected Rosas governor and from that base he went on to subjugate the rest of the country. He eliminated the unfriendly caciques of the various provinces until he finally became the undisputed caudillo of the whole country. His rule was tyrannical and bloody,

---

[2]The sources upon which I draw for my Argentinian examples, which are scattered through the next several sections, are discussed in the Bibliographic Notes (pp. 304–305).

for he brooked no opposition. His secret police spied on his enemies and when they did not flee the country, he imprisoned or killed them. Rosas also understood practical economics, for he gained a tight control over meat supplies and a monopoly over the butcheries of Buenos Aires. The man who posed as champion of the masses enriched himself bountifully as he climbed to power.

Rosas left a violent legacy, but whether Argentina could have been unified by less brutal methods is open to question. If Rosas had not been there, somebody else might well have done the same job. Certainly Argentina was not alone among the Latin American nations in submitting to a man on horseback who exacted his tyrannical price for resolving his nation's anarchy. Rosas was but one of many 19th century caudillos. Porfirio Díaz, for instance, came to power in Mexico in 1876, after 66 years of almost unrelieved strife and more than 70 switches in the office of the chief executive. Díaz suppressed banditry, stifled the opposition, and imposed his peace upon Mexico. In some places, periods of anarchy alternated with periods of personal tyranny. José Antonio Páez imposed some order upon Venezuela, but when he was ousted in 1863, chaos descended. Only after 7 years did Antonio Guzmán Blanco finally impose a renewed peace. Ecuador experienced a similar interval of anarchy between 1845, when the regime of Juan José Flores and Vicente Rocafuerte ended, and 1860 when the theocratic dictatorship of García Moreno again brought order. One could easily conclude that only two political options were available in 19th century Latin America: chaos and personal tyranny.

The caudillos who imposed their tyrannical peace came from a bewildering variety of social backgrounds: aristocratic, creole, and Indian; educated, and illiterate; professor and cowboy. They varied from bloody bandits concerned with little but booty, to idealistic and more or less honest nationalists. What they had in common was neither their backgrounds nor their motives but a kind of personal ability that could hold supporters in a social milieu that permitted the expression of personal power.

Perhaps Latin America in the first half of the 19th century could have moved in no other direction than the imposition of caudillo rule, but from the beginning, the caudillos faced a fundamental dilemma: The naked techniques by which they gained and maintained power could never be clothed with a decent legitimacy. They did grope for legitimacy. They tried to buttress their armed might by various ideological appeals and in particular, they conferred constitutions and they sponsored elections.

In its first decades of independence, Latin America underwent an orgy of constitution writing. Most of the resulting documents were modeled more or less closely upon the constitution of the United States, but their relationship to the actual behavior of political leaders was often tenuous.

Constitutions were expressions of intent, evocations of ideals, rather than blueprints for practical action. The constitutions all provided for some form of election—indeed it was difficult to invent any alternative foundation upon which legitimate occupancy of office might be based—but elections could be manipulated and they generally were. Elections were not always secret, and political bosses were generally able to deliver the vote so successfully that fraudulent counting was hardly necessary. Rosas managed to win a plebecite in Buenos Aires by the satisfying margin of 9,320 to 8. With no long tradition of free elections, and no large educated public to keep watch upon the polls, elections were a far from perfect technique for sounding out public opinion.

It would be a mistake, however, to dismiss the constitutions and elections as meaningless, for if nothing else, they were a concession to the beliefs of a good many prominent citizens. Even if the leaders themselves had no intention of conducting or honoring serious elections, the mere fact that the constitutions provided for elections gave anyone opposed to the government firm grounds for objecting when elections were not held or when they were too blatantly fraudulent. The methods by which the caudillos ruled could not help but arouse antagonisms, and there were always people ready to seize upon the ideological weakness of leaders who failed to follow their own rules. The caudillos could clamp a lid upon political dissent, but they could not possibly win everyone's genuine support.

Economically, the rule of the caudillos could be disastrous. Men who rose to power through force of arms might have little clear program for economic improvement, and they were more likely to be interested in enriching themselves and rewarding their henchmen than in promoting the general welfare. Even if they had only the best economic interests of the nation at heart, their economic policies would be likely to be inconsistent and clumsy. Their background and training hardly prepared them to direct economic development. Even the idea that economic development was a desirable or possible goal was not yet clearly formulated. The tendency was always for a small ruling group to become enriched. Land might be bestowed in great parcels upon a few great land owners. The elite could vacation in Europe and send their sons abroad for a European education while the mass of the population stagnated in illiterate poverty.

Few caudillos had qualms about enriching themselves. Indeed, the possibility of enrichment was a prime motive for seeking office. The caudillos knew their term might at any time be ended by rebellion, so they usually took the sensible precaution of storing resources abroad where they could live in comfortable retirement should that become necessary. Examples of corruption at the top provided inspiration to those below. There was a vast leakage of government resources into the pockets of politicians. After all, the caudillo had to reward his supporters. It came to be assumed that politicians took office for gain. Corruption was expected, but when it became too blatant, it could still arouse the anger of those not sharing in the bounty.

The inequities of the system inevitably drove some men into opposition. Some, in self-interest, resented their own exclusion from the ruling group. Others held more abstract ideals of justice. Opposition might inspire repression from the government and this, in turn, could bring more opposition. When a Latin American government has fallen into such a spiral, it has been only a matter of time until its leader has been forced out of office. A few caudillos managed to stay on top long enough to die a natural death; a few stepped out of office more or less gracefully to make way for a successor; many were removed only by rebellion.

Whatever the outward appearance of national unity, the caudillo in reality sat on a powder keg. He controlled the weapons and much of the economy. He could reward his henchmen and try to keep them loyal. He could enrich himself. But on both ideological grounds and from self-interest, he collected enemies. Sooner or later, these enemies were likely to join forces and evict him.

Caudillos fell in various ways, but their fall was often sudden. Rosas drove many of his opponents to exile, many of them to Montevideo, Uruguay, just across the river from Argentina. Here they agitated for reforms and conspired to displace him but, in the end, it was from the inside and at the hands of one of his lieutenants that he was overturned. Justo José Urquiza was the leader of the province of Entre Rios, but when he rebelled in 1851, all of the many enemies of Rosas rallied to his side. Rosas' supporters melted away, Urquiza was able to take over with relatively little difficulty, and Rosas left for exile in England. Although achieving power through the same kinds of personal loyalties, alliances, and violence that Rosas had used, Urquiza turned out to be a less violent and tyrannical leader than his predecessor. In this, Argentina was more fortunate than some other Latin American nations where one tyrannical caudillo followed another with little clear movement in the direction of more representative government or more orderly patterns of successions. A new set of henchmen would help themselves to the treasury, a new set of slogans would be rung about the nation, but no real change would come to the political structure. Each new man, of course, would face the same difficulties as he tried to legitimize his own role and suppress the inevitable opposition.

The rare caudillo who stayed in power long enough to plan his own peaceful retirement had to think about a successor and here the dilemmas of caudillo rule became most acute. In arranging for the succession, the caudillo's obvious course of action was to attempt to impose his own choice, but to do so would deprive the new man of the chance to prove himself by fighting his way to dominance, as the older caudillo had done. The man who would succeed peacefully cannot rely so strongly upon fire-power, and he is forced to rely more heavily upon constitutional formalities —or at least upon the appearance of constitutional formalities. This makes it exceedingly difficult for one man to take over the power of his predecessor intact. Like a Maratha prince who must negotiate for power among his father's old chiefs, a new president must make his peace with at least some of the other supporters of the former president. What may emerge is an oligarchy, a government in which no single man is as clearly dominant as the caudillo had once been. Now, a group of powerful men may try to agree on some division of the power and of the spoils. Latin American oligarchy has not implied that a set of men have literally held joint office or ruled together through some formal process of collective decision making. The turbulent conditions of 19th century Latin America seemed to require a single man to assume responsibility for the final decisions, but a number of forces encouraged the broadening of the power base beyond the purely personal and individual kind of government of the fighting caudillo.

OLIGARCHIES

The half century between 1862 and 1916 in Argentina is reckoned as the period of the conservative oligarchy. This was a longer and on the whole a more orderly period of political and economic development than most other Latin Americans achieved in the 19th century, but it gained stability only after some initial fumbling. With the departure of Rosas, Urquiza was the strongest man in Argentina, but he never achieved the towering position of his predecessor. As soon as Urquiza had taken over, the exiled opponents of the former caudillo flooded back to Buenos Aires, and they did not care to see another man become so dominant. Antagonism soon flared up between the wealthy urban leaders of Buenos Aires, led by Bartolome Mitre, and the new caudillo whose power rested in the provinces. So strained were relations that Buenos Aires actually managed to secede. It remained independent for 8 years, while Urquiza was left in command of the rest of the nation. The armies of Buenos Aires and the provinces skirmished now and then, but the war was only intermittently bloody. The armies directed from the capital finally gained a decisive advantage, and in 1862 Urquiza retired. Buenos Aires was reunited with the provinces, and Mitre, the leader of Buenos Aires, became president.

Mitre gained the presidency largely by force of arms, but his position was soon given legitimacy by an election under the provisions of a constitution that Urquiza had sponsored. This constitution, like many other 19th century Latin American constitutions, was sponsored by a strong man who needed to give legitimacy to his rule. In form, it was modeled closely upon that of the United States, though it provided a 6-year presidential term and banned immediate reelection. The principle of limited presidential terms and the prohibition upon reelection gained widespread support among thoughtful Latin Americans. These came to be seen as a means by which to set bounds upon tyranny, while still allowing a man to rule with strength for a limited time. Experiments with limiting terms of office are as old as the ancient Greeks and Romans, and in Latin America, limits have been incorporated into constitutions and taken rather more seriously than some other constitutional provisions. The prohibition on reelection is a convenient principle to use against a man in power or to assert when trying to legitimize one's own position, but a president who has himself asserted the principle too loudly can find himself trapped by it as his own term comes to an end.

Thus, by the end of his term in 1869, Mitre, who had consolidated his own position by accepting Urquiza's constitution, felt he had to step out of office. By then, too, Mitre's party had split and Mitre's own popularity had declined. He was willing to acquiesce in the election of Domingo Sarmiento, who had formerly been one of his associates but was now supported by the opposite faction of the party. Six years later, Sarmiento's faction put forward Nicolás Avellaneda, but Mitre now offered himself for office again, too. The election contest between Avellaneda and Mitre was utterly fraudulent, but Avellaneda's party controlled the election machinery and he was declared the winner. Mitre, the loser, charged fraud, raised an army, but was then defeated. In gentlemanly fashion, the winners granted Mitre amnesty, and in return Mitre accepted Avellaneda's presidency. At the end of his term, Avellaneda supported General Julio Roca against a powerful challenger, and after a show of military strength, Roca was properly ratified by elections. Roca, in his turn, was followed more easily in 1886 by his brother-in-law, Juarez Celman. Presidents were coming to power with less and less violence. Mitre gained office only after a lengthy war. Avellaneda had to defeat Mitre in battle, and Roca had to use his troop to capture Buenos Aires. Celman gained office peacefully.

The patterns of power now emerging in Argentina were clearly quite different from those that dominated the regime of the earlier caudillo. No longer was a single man so clearly dominant. Rivalry for power was not quite so bitter, and the rivals, even after fighting, were sometimes willing to grant each other amnesty and pardon. Mitre allowed Urquiza to retire in peace and Avellaneda granted amnesty to Mitre. What now led Argentina, was a circle of powerful men whose common interests ran deep enough to temper their rivalry and encourage adherence to at least a few gentlemanly rules. Though public opinion in the modern sense hardly mattered, the opinion of the men of this leading circle mattered very much. No president could ignore the quickly accepted rule against immediate reelection, and any who acted too vindictively against his defeated opponents risked losing more in alienated support than he gained in eliminated enemies. Few men, after all, can be confident of benefiting from a violent resolution to political rivalries. People can get killed in the rebellions, and many who are not killed may still be thrown into prison or exiled. Most men who compete for power would surely rather work out some sort of gentleman's agreement about the conduct of government than resort to guns.

Once such desires become effective in the brokerage of power, an oligarchy can be said to have replaced the earlier and simpler rule of a single man. Of course, the threat of violence always lurked in the background, and the temptation to use force arose repeatedly, but as in the cities of Greece more than 2,000 years earlier, and as in the republics of Italy or the Low Countries, there was a tendency in Argentina and in a number of other nations of Latin America for governments to broaden from the complete domination by a single man to domination by an oligarchy.

As succession to the Argentine presidency grew more orderly, the dominant elements in the selection came to be the choice by the incumbent president and a narrow circle around him, and the subsequent manipulation of an election to legitimize this choice. We can see parallels between trends here and similar trends in the Manchu dynasty of China where the choice came to be made even more decisively by the predecessor. In Argentina as in China, the tendency was toward ever more peaceful and decisive successions, but the increasingly peaceful climb to power removed the contest from any sort of public participation. Even a military contest offers some chance for a wider public to take part. Comfortable arrangements made at the top excluded all but a tiny number of citizens. Thus the expansion from one man rule to oligarchical rule in Argentina implied an even greater exclusion of the public. Without armed battles, the wider public could no longer make its interests felt, even at the time of succession. Much the same narrowing of participation took place in China, but the process was far more rapid in Argentina, for a new president was needed every 6 years, rather than just once in each generation.

The very ease with which each president imposed his choice removed the contest from the public domain. The people as a whole had no effective voice at all in choosing their leaders and so the leaders hardly needed too be responsive to public desires. Under Avellaneda, Roca, and Celman there was progressive deterioration in public service. Huge profits were extorted from government contracts, and extravagance and corruption knew few bounds. Presidents followed each other in and out of office with little deference to public opinion until their behavior finally aroused such outspoken criticism that an opposition could form. The opposition included those who, whether from idealism or jealously, did not like to see President Celman and his collaborators grow so rich. Some units of the army had their own reasons to be dissatisfied with Celman, and a revolution was mounted. It was soon put down, but the episode undermined support for the regime. The reformers advocated free and honest elections, but the old guard was able to cling to power until 1910. At the end of each term they would manipulate elections so as to bring the man of their choice into office.

Once again, it is worth making comparisons with dynastic China. Certainly the ideological and economic bases upon which the Chinese and Argentine regimes rested could hardly have been more different, yet both regimes changed with time, and both tended to change in the same direction. Starting, like a Chinese dynasty, as an autocratic conquest state under its caudillo, Argentina settled down under a centralized and self-perpetuating regime. Legitimate internal challenges to the regime came to be almost as impossible as in China. Then, with no need to appeal to broad support, the regime itself became ingrown. It was sheltered from direct responsibility to popular demands, and corruption was rampant.

As long as they were denied the freedom of the ballot box, the radicals had to rely upon conspiracy and revolt, and a radical revolution was crushed in 1905. Nevertheless, in 1910 the old guard finally yielded. They had taken turns with the presidency for half a century, but they faced increasingly vociferous demands for reforms, and they now allowed Roque Sáenz Peña to become president. He was known as a reformer, but his family connections were impeccable and he came in as a candidate of the old guard. In the face of radical agitation, Sáenz Peña probably seemed to represent a fairly safe compromise. He was enough of a reformer to support honest elections at the end of his term, however, and this made it possible for Argentina to hold its first open presidential election in 1916. At last the radicals were able to gain office, and the long rule of the oligarchy came to an end.

The reign of Argentina's conservative oligarchy was unusually long and uninterrupted by Latin American standards, but it was by no means unique. The government of Costa Rica before 1870 consisted fundamentally of an alliance among the principal landowning families. These would agree among themselves to choose a president who would protect their interests. The rulers of Peru, known as "the forty families," controlled the government just as they controlled the best land and the largest businesses. In Columbia, there was a greater appearance of party competition, for power occasionally passed back and forth between the so-called "liberals" and the so-called "conservatives," but in the 19th century neither of these factions was by any means representative of the general population, and the leaders of opposing factions had more in common with each other than with the mass of the population.

Even a small oligarchy has to designate particular people to make particular decisions and, with the exception of the Uruguayan experiment with a committee executive, Latin Americans have always vested the office of the president with predominant power. The business of the oligarchy, then, is first of all to find a suitable candidate for the presidency and then to make sure that he gets into office. When there is a reasonable consensus among the powerful men, elections can easily be manipulated so as to legitimize their choice. The president may not always please all members of the oligarchy but he may share their interests closely, and he may be sufficiently beholden to them not to betray them. Some Latin American presidents have been faithful front men for others who have pulled the real strings from behind the scenes.

The desperate Latin American need for a center of decisive action, however, has generally given the presidential office great political leverage. Once in office, a president may be able to build up considerable personal power, and some have managed to transform their role into something hardly different from that of a personalistic caudillo. The line between a caudillo and a leader of an oligarchy is by no means sharp. Even a man who does not aspire to the personal power of a caudillo is likely to lead the oligarchy for his term of office, and he is likely to have the largest voice in choosing the next president.

As a result, oligarchies tended, at times, to approximate a system where each president, like each Chinese emperor, appointed his own successor. An appointment that comes too easily, however, tends to make a man a captive of his appointer. Indeed, some presidents have perpetuated their own rule by choosing a loyal supporter to act as their figurehead. Sometimes this system has worked so well that a man has been able to assume the presidency in alternate terms. He simply steps aside during the other terms in favor of a henchman. But this is a risky maneuver, and some appointed successors have proven to be far more ambitious than their sponsors had intended. An originally faithful henchman, once placed in office, can begin to maneuver his own men into positions of power and to displace his rivals. If the older leader feels sufficiently threatened but is still unwilling to retire, violent rebellion may occur, for the outcome of this rivalry may depend as much upon the skill with which men direct military force, as upon their skill at political in-fighting. Here is the classical conflict between one leader and his own chosen successor.

When the successor does not actively work to free himself from dependence upon the appointer, he is in danger of remaining a mere figurehead, but too easy an appointment also removes him from any close dependence upon the broader masses of the nation, and it deprives him of an important means for consolidating his own personal power. As always, therefore, too easy an acquisition of office is likely to result in weak leadership, and this has meant that appointment by a predecessor has seldom been a consistent means of arranging Latin American successions. The possible complications that can interfere with successful appointments have always been so great that a simple progression of appointees has rarely been successful. The preference of the predecessor is but one of several elements that have entered the puzzle of choice.

OLIGARCHICAL WEAKNESSES

The advantages of the oligarchies over the caudillistic regimes are clear. Oligarchies have a slightly broader support and since they draw upon a slightly wider circle of opinion, they may be a bit less likely to run to policy extremes. No single member of an oligarchy has quite so much potential for mischief. They provide a better prospect for continuity from one presidential term to the next, and they can sometimes avoid violence when transferring power to a successor. On the other hand, the Latin American oligarchies faced serious problems of their own, and, of these, three deserve special attention: legitimacy, corruption, and internal disputes.

1. Legitimacy

Oligarchies, like caudillos, have had difficulty legitimizing their rule. In groping toward collective decisions, the members of an oligarchy find it difficult to govern without some reasonably coherent set of rules, and without at least lip service to constitutionalism. However shamelessly the Argentine oligarchs manipulated elections, they never felt they could do without them. Without elections they would have had an even less persuasive claim to power than the charismatic caudillo. It is harder for a clique than for a single man to inspire personal loyalty. Honest elections can quickly remove an oligarchy from power; no elections at all would leave them with no claim to legitimacy whatsoever. Managed elections are an uneasy compromise between the need for legitimacy and the desire to retain power. Yet by accepting elections, even managed elections, an oligarchy gives all who are opposed to the regime a clear and persuasive principle around which to rally their opposition. To the very extent that an oligarchy can present itself as more constitutional and legitimate than a simple caudillo, it also arouses higher expectations. It becomes difficult both to satisfy these expectations and to stay in power.

2. Corruption

Those opposing an oligarchy can express their opposition through an ideological appeal for open and honest elections, but ideology, by itself, is rarely sufficient, and the challengers may also be able to arouse sympathy for their cause by pointing to the corruption of the rulers, for by most standards the oligarchical rulers were ruthlessly corrupt. Nineteenth century Argentine presidents and their contemporaries in neighboring countries were able to profit handsomely from their offices and they helped their allies and henchmen to do the same. Great wealth came to Argentina as cattle and grain empires were built up. Much of this wealth found its way into the pockets of the political leaders, and there was little to prevent even the most blatant corruption. Certainly righteous indignation on the part of an outraged electorate would have counted for little at the polls, even if the electorate had been educated enough and knowledgeable enough to become outraged.

Perhaps it is only by the judgment of an outsider that this self-enrichment can be called "corruption." The men who ruled may simply have thought of themselves as conducting their business by all available methods, and controlling the government was surely a profitable way to conduct business. But the system certainly perpetuated and exaggerated a gross inequality of wealth. This encouraged a few men of high ideals to point to the inequities of the regime and call for its overthrow. Their voices were added to those who called for open elections, and to the many others who had few high ideals but who could hope for a larger share of the bounty. It was of such elements, both idealistic and opportunistic, that the radical challenge in Argentina was formed.

3. Internal Disputes

It was, however, neither their lack of legitimacy, nor their corruption that gave the oligarchs the most trouble. Their most serious problems came from their internal disputes. If an ideal oligarchy should serve as a peaceful means for choosing leaders and for adjusting and compromising power, then most oligarchies were far from ideal. Not only in Argentina, but elsewhere as well, the oligarchical periods saw almost unceasing internal quarrels among those in government and among those aspiring to rule. The supply of power was, of course, limited so that when one man gained power, others lost. Some men were bound to be disappointed, and disappointment led sooner or later to dissention. It was impossible to keep competition permanently within peaceful bounds.

Men used whatever means they had: personal influence, economic pressure, military force, and when other methods seemed doubtful, Latin Americans like political competitors of all eras would even appeal to groups outside the normal oligarchical circle. Since Latin Americans have never been able to define the limits of the oligarchy with precision, as the Venetians had once done, those on its fringes or those just outside could always hope to exploit the dissentions within the narrower circle. Some of those close to the center might hope to advance their own cause by an alliance with more popular groups. Thus, Mitre, the protoype of the Argentine oligarch, once allied himself temporarily with the radicals. Many an oligarch has sought allies among the military. Others have rallied the rural poor to arms, or stimulated the urban mobs to riot on their behalf. As was the case with their European predecessors, the internal divisions within the ruling circles of Latin America have offered the best hope for those who pushed for broader participation.

Thus the oligarchical regimes, like those of the caudillos, had internal contradictions that made their perpetuation difficult. Depending less upon the charisma of a single man, they had to depend more upon an appearance of constitutionalism, but this immediately opened the door to an ideologically based opposition. The inevitable disunity within the oligarchies always made them unstable, and it has been difficult to establish any clear pattern of succession within them. Rather, they wobbled uneasily between simultaneous but partially contradictory pressures: to resolve the conflicts by submitting to one-man rule, or to broaden the power base and allow more popular participation. As always, these two pressures sometimes worked together, for it has been aspiring autocrats who, trying to undermine the position of their oligarchical competitors, would appeal most loudly for popular support.

A few Argentine presidents who are counted as members of the oligarchy came close to reimposing one-man rule, though none ever governed with the single-minded ferocity of Rosas. Elsewhere, men who were chosen by an oligarchy and who were expected to lead the consensus of the ruling elite sometimes became tyrannical masters of their nations. When no dictator emerged from an oligarchy, the tendency was instead to drift and weaken. This might give an opposition the chance to gain enough power to mount a successful rebellion and replace the government, and some such revolutions have brought new social or economic elements to leadership. The urban bourgeoisie, for instance, has sometimes replaced the landowners as the dominant power. It has been rarer for a new philosophy to have guided those in office. Often, the new group manages power in ways not so different from those of the old oligarchy. The new oligarchy simply replaces the old and comes to be subject to the same sorts of internal strains. It will finally drift toward the same kinds of corruption and oppression, and it will again invite another revolution.

Convulsed with internal conflict and challenged by idealistic reformers, there is one final possibility for a hard pressed oligarchy—hold an honest election. Driven partly by idealism, partly by despair with any other course,

Latin American rulers have periodically decided to sponsor real elections. Presidents who, like Roque Sáenz Peña, came to power by the choice of the oligarchy and ratification of a fraudulent election sometimes still believed in the principle of free elections. If at the same time it seemed that any other course could lead to civil war, a president and his colleagues might have strong motives for carrying out a "revolution from above." A president may even hope to pass on the reigns of government by such honorable means as to be allowed an honorable retirement in his own nation and not be forced into exile as so many other ex-presidents have been. A combination of personal self-interest, despair with alternatives, and democratic idealism has at one time or another brought open elections to most of the nations of Latin America. Of course, no absolute line separates an honest election from a fraudulent one, but the real test is whether a government is willing to turn over power to an opposition after being defeated at the polls. Governments have been known to nullify unfavorable election results, even after permitting honest elections, but sometimes they have bowed to the decision of the voters and allowed new men to come to power.

ELECTED GOVERNMENT

North Americans, convinced of the feasibility and virtue of popular elections and universal suffrage, may fondly hope that once elections are held, all problems will dissolve, honesty come to government, and peace ensue. Of course, elections have not always worked so perfectly even in North America, and in Latin America the problems of making a success of an electoral regime are considerably greater. The problems are not insuperable. Costa Rica and Uruguay have had many decades of reasonably honest and nonsanguinary electoral democracy, and no mysterious quality of Latin mentality makes electoral government forever impossible. But it must be admitted that Uruguay and Costa Rica are exceptions. Elsewhere in Latin America, elections have been held less regularly; they have not always been honored even when held, and when freely elected governments have come to power, they have often later come to grief.

The Radical party of Argentina replaced the Old Guard in 1916 as a result of the first honest election in the nation's history. The new president was Hipólito Irigoyen, the leader of the Radicals, and his election amounted to a peaceful revolution at the polls. He was welcomed enthusiastically by a large portion of the population, but Irigoyen had, of necessity, spent most of his political life conspiring against the old oligarchy. He had become the undisputed leader of the Radicals, but he was always more skillful at conspiracy than at the practical business of running a government. Once in power, he tended to panic in a crisis. Irigoyen seems to have been a charming if almost mystical man, but his rule was a personal one. He had no skill at delegating authority and he could develop no positive program out of the contradictory elements of his own Radical party. To his credit, Irigoyen was scrupulously honest. Nothing so clearly sets him apart from all earlier presidents as his death as a poor man. Unfortunately many of the Radical politicians who came to office with him were as rapacious and as single-minded in pursuit of their own self-enrichment as their Conservative predecessors had been.

Irigoyen, moreover, had no scruples about political intervention on behalf of his supporters. He brought Radicals into many offices of the government and he even intervened in the army, rewarding officers who had supported his party. Thus, the army was politicized and it would be difficult to keep it neutral later. He allowed the press great freedom, but he did his best to undermine his political opposition, and at the end of his term, like earlier presidents, he was able to have his own choice of successor elected and installed.

Marcelo T. de Alvear, president from 1922 to 1928, was intended to be Irigoyen's front man, but Alvear insisted on picking his own cabinet and the result was a split in the Radical party between the followers or Irigoyen and the *anti-personalista* radicals who supported the new president. The Radicals proved to be as subject as the Conservatives to disputes between one president and his hand-picked successor. Alvear's term was reasonably successful and calm and at its end, he sponsored the most honest election in Argentina's history. Two years later, the results of this election were overturned by the military. What went wrong?

The election of 1928 turned into a contest between the supporters of Irigoyen and the anti-personalista radicals who now allied themselves with the older conservatives. Irigoyen, who had been out of office for a term, was again eligible, and his supporters backed him for a new term. Irigoyen, the old hero of the Radicals, had a far broader personal appeal than the relatively colorless anti-personalistas, and he was swept back into the presidency by a 2 to 1 margin. But Irigoyen, never a dynamic administrator, was, by 1928, declining into senility. He became suspicious, isolated, and nothing but a figurehead for lesser men who shamelessly abused their power for partisan purposes. The bureaucracy became tangled, finances were in confusion, and Irigoyen apparently had no idea of the chaos about him.

Then came the financial crash of 1929. During the First World War and the 1920s, general prosperity had cushioned the effects of incompetence and corruption in the radical government. Now, even worse incompetence and corruption coincided with the effects of the crash, and the result was disaster.

Earlier labor supporters of Irigoyen deserted him. So did the students. Radicals were defeated in local elections in Buenos Aires, and there was public talk of a possible coup. Irigoyen was finally persuaded to resign in favor of his vice-president, but affairs had already drifted too far. On September 6, 1930, a military coup disposed of the radical government and placed General José F. Uriburu in the presidency. There was immense popular rejoicing.

In retrospect, it is possible to see the coup of 1930 as a critical turning point in Argentine history. Uriburu's coup followed a long period of growing political order and democracy. For more than half a century, presidential terms had followed one another with considerable regularity, and since 1916, the trend toward honest elections seemed clear. However, the strength of Argentine democratic habits should not be over-estimated. Until 1916, elections had been regularly manipulated, and military uprisings had occurred as recently as 1890, 1893, and 1905. These three had been unsuccessful, but in early times political disputes had been regularly settled by military force, and the memory of even unsuccessful military uprisings made further attempts seem a reasonable expectation to Argentinians. The fact that the most recent military uprisings had been led or inspired by the Radicals made them very nearly respectable in some circles.

The coup of 1930 was only the latest of a long series of military interventions, and we have to try and understand why electoral governments were so weak as to be subjected to military overthrow, and why so many citizens did not merely acquiesce but cheered the army in its intervention. Like caudillos and oligarchies, electoral governments seem to have had internal weaknesses that have made them subject to subversion. Why have they been so fragile?

First, few Latin American countries have had a well-educated electorate. Attempts were once made to use property requirements as a means by which to exclude a portion of the citizenry from voting, and literacy requirements are sometimes still applied. Literacy requirements, of course, are subject to serious abuse, and when they are honestly administered in Latin America, they disenfranchise a large portion of the population. Elected legislators are naturally more responsible to those qualified to vote, than to those who are not. Thus, elections present a dilemma: When the franchise is widely extended, ignorant votes are cast; when the franchise is restricted, the poorest segment of the population cannot make its interests felt.

Property and literacy qualifications for voting resulted in the rule of the "gentry." Land owners and urban professionals have sometimes been well represented in government at the same time that the rural masses were rather efficiently excluded. Elected gentry governments of such nations as

Chile, Brazil, and Colombia have sometimes showed considerable respect for legality, but they failed badly in the task of integrating the various segments of the population, and it is little wonder that many of those excluded would welcome any change at all. With no role in elections anyway, many would be pleased to see a junta or a strong man take over the government. One weakness of Latin American democracy has been that many electoral governments have been less responsive to the desires of the masses than have some dictators. The most honest of elections have sometimes brought the most reactionary men to power, and their governments have sometimes lacked efficiency or even a clear set of policies.

When given the opportunity to vote freely, moreover, it must be admitted that Latin Americans have sometimes demonstrated a profound ability to choose colorful but disastrous candidates. Irigoyen's reelection in 1928 by the best educated nation in Latin America is an outstanding example. Another is the repeated insistence of Ecuadorians upon reelecting Velasco Ibarra. A colorful figure and a spell-binding orator, Ibarra ruled briefly in 1934–1935 and then in 1944, he engineered a rebellion which brought him back into office. He brought his nation little except economic chaos, and in 1947 the Ecuadorian army sent him into exile. A calmer period ensued leading to honest elections in 1952 when Ibarra came back by popular vote. Again, there was economic decline and political repression, but Ibarra served out his term this time and left peacefully in 1956. By most criteria the next administration was more competent, and some economic progress was made. The Ecuadorian voters seemed determined to learn nothing, however, for in 1960, they again voted for Ibarra. Now in office for the fourth time and no more able to carry out his campaign promises than on earlier occasions, Ibarra soon became the target of protests and demonstrations by students and workers. This time the army deposed him rather than letting him serve out his term, but he was permitted to stand for election again in 1968 and, after nosing out his two opponents in a closely contested three-cornered election, the 75-year-old Velasco Ibarra came to office for the fifth time, only to be deposed once more by the army in 1972. By any standards of honest, efficient, or purposeful government, his regimes had been utter failures, but he could not be put down by free election. It is hardly to be wondered if some Ecuadorians were to become disillusioned with the electoral process itself.

In truth, however, the electorate has not always been offered very promising alternatives. Under a caudillistic or oligarchical government, the potential opposition is forced to act conspiratorially. Their overriding concern is to overthrow the old government. When suddenly given the chance to compete in a more or less free election, they may have trouble presenting a sound positive program. Personalities may count for more than policy, and the major appeal of the challengers is the promise to throw the rascals out. Once in office, however, they may act in ways not at all unlike those very rascals. Where government leaders have always enriched themselves, the new men may not be able to resist temptation. When there is a general expectation of corruption, the population may be relatively cynical and resigned if the new turn out to be as corrupt as the old. Why should a man remain honest in electoral office when, no matter how he behaves, everyone presumes he will enrich himself?

For these many reasons, electoral governments have not been consistently less corrupt or more enlightened in their social and economic policies than other governments. Moreover, it is in the nature of electoral politics that government activities are relatively open to public inspection. If rival politicians can scrutinize each other's behavior and publicly accuse each other of malfeasance, then an electoral government may give the outward appearance of far more corruption and disorganization than a more tightly controlled dictatorial regime where the dirty laundry is more easlly concealed.

The results of elections must almost always be disappointing. The promises of the candidates are likely to go beyond any reasonable means of fulfillment, and repeated disappointments confirm the suspicion that politicians are in the business only for their own enrichment. Economic chaos aggravated by governmental mismanagement, bureaucratic immobility, and a history of rigged elections, all conspire to produce disillusionment, not only with a particular election, but with the electoral process itself. It is not difficult to find fault with every government that elections bring. Where many are disenfranchised and where poverty makes postponement of needs impossible, people cannot wait patiently while a democratic opposition painstakingly builds a program. There is no time. Or at least there seems to be no time, and the short-cut of revolution seems always to hold out hope. A country in turmoil, caught between quarreling politicians, none of whom are able to take effective action, may seem in desperate need of a housecleaning. Large parts of the population may be eager to support those who promise to do the job. A population seething with grievances against one government may welcome a new government and its new promises.

Troops must participate in the final overturn of the government, but many other segments of the population may back them or even lead them to action. Land owners and conservative business leaders may see in strong government a means of protecting their own class privileges and some hope for retrieving lost national prestige. The large and inept bureaucracy may suppose that a military regime will be less worried about expenses than a civilian regime, and if the generals know little about practical government, the bureaucrats can hope to be left to carry out their jobs unmolested. Even the working class may yearn for a sort of a military messiah, a man who will decree benefits for the common man. Everyone may indulge in a bit of wishful thinking. Everyone may hope that the military will be efficient enough only to knock *other* heads together. The tradition of military intervention makes some people relatively willing to cooperate in planning another intervention, and makes others willing to accept it once it has occurred. North Americans who tend to be contemptuous of military leaders ought to realize that their popular backing has often been very broad indeed.

MILITARY INTERVENTION

When inclined to despair at the willingness of military leaders to intervene in the affairs of their governments, we might do well to remember that military governments are nothing new. The Italian and Dutch republics were regularly threatened by their own army commanders, and many regimes of earlier centuries were imposed by military might and directed by military leaders. Roman generals fought their way to the imperial throne, aristocracies have been formed of the fighting elite, and many dynasties have been founded by men who were first of all army commanders. Both Shivaji, the Maratha, and Nurhachi, the Manchu, directed armies and imposed their authority by the sword. We might even conclude that what is new in today's politics is the possibility of civilian government, or, more accurately, what is new is the distinction between a civilian and a military regime. However natural the distinction may seem to us today, it can hardly be made for many of the governments of our predecessors. Governments have usually been led by those who control the weapons.

Nevertheless, modern armaments and modern communications have certainly given a new quality to military intervention. Where the would-be ruler of an earlier day had to combine political skill with military might in a slow accumulation of power, the modern military man may be able to use his position in government and his control of the arsenal to overturn a government in a matter of hours. In many nations today, not only in Latin America but in other parts of the world as well, civilian regimes are constantly threatened by their own armies, for the modern army has many sources of strength. Not only does it have the firepower, but it must be organized to use its firepower effectively. This implies a clear chain of command and a tradition of tight discipline. Officers, often educated together but somewhat isolated from the rest of the nation, develop an esprit de corps, and as they learn to assert the manly virtues of courage, fortitude, and honor, they may become contemptuous of their flabby civilian contemporaries. Central direction and the habit of discipline, to say nothing of the heavy artillery, cannot help but give the army important advantages when it finds itself competing with mere civilians.[3]

Men who have spent their lives within a military system can easily come to see themselves as possessing unique virtues. Civilian politicians seem always to be squabbling among themselves, always compromising with their opponents. Politicians lack the clear chain of command and the clear means of reaching decisions that makes the army such a comfortable place for certain kinds of men. Civilian governments may come and go, and some may represent limited interests or limited parties and then, the very tradition by which armies are supposed to remain "outside of politics" makes it easy for the generals and the colonels to look upon themselves as loyal not to the particular government in power, but loyal instead to a higher if more mystical, abstraction: the state or the nation. All governments have domestic opponents, and all governments seek to weaken them, but if a government works too hard in this direction, army leaders who claim to be loyal to the "nation" rather than to the government, may refuse to co-operate. Generals have often refused to help a government stifle its domestic opposition. In this way, they have come to defy the government in the name of democracy and civil liberty, and their loyalty to the men in political office is thereby undermined.

Of course, many lesser motives impel army leaders to meddle in politics. Like all branches of government, the military services clamor for better treatment, more equipment, higher pay. No army, certainly not that of the United States, fails to lobby on its own behalf. When responsible civilian leaders feel their army's budget to be inflated, and try to reduce the army's share, they easily come into direct conflict with the vested interests of the army. Real or supposed grievances against civilian governments over pay, promotions, and equipment begin to look like a threat to the honor of the army. It is easy to begin to identify personal honor with national honor and to see politicians who simply want to cut the army's budget as undermining the nation's glory.

Army influence upon the government can assume many forms. All armies seek to influence policy and indeed we would feel that generals who failed to offer their advice and who failed to help the government formulate the best and most realistic policies of national defense were not carrying out their responsibilities. But only the finest line separates honest encouragement of appropriate policy from collusion with those who are most sympathetic to army interests. Necessary cooperation with suppliers of military hardware implies vested interests in a high military budget. Honorable

[3]The analysis in this and the following paragraphs depends heavily upon that of S. E. Finer's, *The Man on Horseback* (London: Pall Mall Press, 1962).

opposition to enemies of the state can lead to spying upon citizens who are imagined to be threats to the government and then to spying upon those whose are merely threats to vested army interests. By easy steps, the army may move to an ever more active cooperation with those politicians who offer return support. For a time, the generals may be content to work from behind the scenes. They may encourage, they may cajole, and then sometimes they may threaten. Finally, when there is no other way to make its influence felt, the army, or some part of the army, may resort to a coup d'etat.

The leaders of coups have occasionally had revolutionary goals, and a few coups have had revolutionary consequences, but in execution the coup is the very opposite of a revolution. The goal of the leaders is to capture a government, not to destroy it. They work from inside, subverting the government machinery to their own ends rather than mounting an open challenge from the outside. The leaders characteristically seek to win with a minimum of physical damage and a minimum of bloodshed. A revolution may last for years, but the tactics of a coup are those of careful planning and surprise, and if they fail to win within a few hours or days, they will almost surely fail.

All coups tend to have a good deal in common.[4] Conspiritors must first sound each other out. The inner circle must include men who are high in the government, and they must be in a position to lead others who can help seize control of crucial installations. Those most strategically placed to carry out a coup are, of course, the high military leaders, for they are given strength both by military hardware and by military habits of obedience, but a wider group must gradually be recruited. The leaders can play upon various motives among those they seek out—bitterness at the policies of the incumbant government, personal grievances, hopes for promotion or an increase in salary, ethnic or family loyalties. Some may see rebellion as the only way to curb corruption, and a good many men find it easy to persuade themselves that the nation needs their services. Of course, not all those who cooperate in a coup have high motives, but neither is it necessary to charge them all with simple self-seeking. Some assist a rebellion with nothing in mind but the good of the nation.

As the stage of preliminary discussion passes, the coup will develop a momentum of its own. More and more people must be drawn into the conspiracy, but as more are included, the danger of betrayal grows. Execution of the plot cannot be too long delayed. Even if the established rulers get hints of the plot, however, they may hesitate to act immediately to surpress it. In a political climate that is rife with rumor and counter rumor, they

---

[4]For detailed instructions on how to conduct a coup, see Edward Littwak's, *Coup d'etat: A Practical Handbook* (New York: Alfred A. Knopf, 1969).

may be uncertain of their information. They may prefer to wait until the leaders of the plot expose and incriminate themselves.

Execution of the plot must have an element of surprise. The regime may get hints that something is in the wind, but it must not be allowed to know the extent of the conspiracy or to learn its particular plans. Were it to learn too much too soon, it would surely have the power to surpress the conspiracy. The essence of a successful coup is sudden seizure of crucial people and installations. Victory must be achieved before one's opponents can gather enough information to take effective counter measures. Precise planning ahead of time and swift coordinated execution of the plans are absolutely essential.

Under conditions of modern technology, a few sympathetic technicians can disable the telephones and radio transmitters that the regime will need when it tries to summon loyal troups. A few trucks parked across airplane runways and a few snipers strategically placed to prevent their immediate removal can put an airport out of commission for the necessary hours. If advanced planning has been carefully done, the conspirators will have no need for these facilities, but they will be crucial for the defenders of the regime. Road blocks can slow the advance of loyalist troups and since those who set up the road blocks will wear the same uniforms as the commanders of the advancing columns, the rebels can appeal to the sense of comradeship and so persuade them not to fire. If those who defend the road blocks play their part with skill, they will themselves appear to be taking the defensive position. The onus of any attack will fall upon the loyalists. They would have to fire first should they insist upon passing the barricade. If communications have been properly disrupted, the loyalist commanders will each be ignorant of the true extend of the coup. None will know whom else to trust. It may take many hours to coordinate their defenses, and in these hours, the managers of a successful coup will have had ample time to arrest the previous leaders. They will have seized such symbolic centers of power as the royal or presidential palace, and such real centers of power as the military command post. By the time most of the nation has any clear idea of what has happened, the conspirators are able to go on the air themselves and assume the dignified role of the real rulers of the country. They can appeal for calm, and urge the citizens to go about their business in normal fashion. Now, wavering bureaucrats and military leaders will themselves appear to be in opposition should they still insist on defending the older regime. Many will prefer instead to accept the reality of the new situation. By offering their support to the apparent winners, they may hope to secure their position in the new regime. Before any opposition can crystallize, the new government will be in secure command.

Rulers must, of course, defend themselves against coups. Guards are posted at installations that coup leaders might try to seize, and all means must be used to gather information about potential conspiracies and then to infiltrate them and destroy them before they can succeed. These defensive measures are most successful against forces outside the government, but a coup, unfortunately, is an inside job or, at least, it depends upon the co-operation of some insiders. The very men upon whom the government relies for protection actively seek its overturn.

Against a coup, there are only two truly effective defenses: a widespread popular refusal to accept its verdict, and a political system too decentralized to be seized in a single blow. On both counts, the United States has been more fortunate than any Latin American republic, or than most of the newer nations of Asia and Africa. Typically these nations have both highly centralized power systems and relatively indifferent populations. In Latin America, it is generally quite sufficient to seize a few strategic spots in the capital city. Provincial centers are not accustomed to exercising independent power, and these can be counted upon to fall quickly into line. In the United States, power has become more and more centralized in Washington, but the 50 states and thousands of counties and municipalities still act far more independently than do the corresponding local governments of Latin American. A conspiracy that could simultaneously seize a significant portion of the state capitals, let alone city halls and county courthouses, is difficult to imagine.

At the same time, a coup cannot be successful without at least the passive acquiescence of the overwhelming majority of the people. Where citizens feel bound by strong political traditions, whether these traditions support older clan, ethnic, or family organization or where, as in the United States, there is widespread revulsion against nonorderly seizure of power, popular sentiments pose a powerful limitation on aspiring coup leaders. It is not so difficult to imagine a cabal of generals seizing several strategic locations in the United States. They might arrest the leading civilian politicians, and proclaim a government of national unity designed to clean up the mess. But it is certain that any cabal of generals that was tempted to try such an experiment would pause in the face of uncertainty about what might be expected to follow their coup. They might be so worried about the immediate and widespread opposition they would face, and indeed so worried about dissent in their own ranks by those who firmly disapproved, that they would be discouraged from even trying.

The power of popular sentiment was shown vividly in April, 1961 when four French generals seized power in Algiers and seemed, momentarily, on the brink of bringing down the government of France. Charles de Gaulle, however, appealed on the radio directly to the men and women of France, both to the civilians at home and to citizen soldiers in Algeria. He invited those at home to go to the airports and to plead with and reason with the troops, should they be flown in. He told the ordinary soldiers in Algeria, who could hear him on their transistor radios, that their generals were acting against their best interests, and against the best interests of France. Such was the upwelling of popular sentiment that the rebellious generals could no longer trust their own troops. In less than three days the coup had collapsed, and the generals were in ignominious flight.

Coups are more likely to succeed in relatively small and relatively poor nations where older traditions have decayed, but where no new traditions of electoral politics have taken root. When power is concentrated in a single capital city and when the new technology of radio, of airplanes, and of tanks are directed from this single center, then the conditions for a coup are ideal.

THE JUNTA

A coup d'etat can take many forms. The military may act alone—the classic barracks revolt—but when the economy of a nation is complex and the political and social problems intractable, the military leaders may realize their need for help. Then rebellion is more likely to involve a conspiracy of both military officers and civilian politicians. Some coups are dominated by a single general, but with increasing social, economic, and technical complexity, more Latin American coups are now the work of a committee—a junta—and in the initial act of overturning a relatively constitutional government, a junta has a considerable advantage over one-man leadership. A junta can be more persuasive in its claim to represent the whole nation and to constitute a government of national unity. Its members can call upon varied segments of the population and try to keep them all in line. Juntas must include some military men, but they sometimes include civilians as well. They may overturn an elected government, or they may replace another junta or a dictator. They may act primarily in their own self-interest, grasping at power for the sake of its manifest rewards, but they sometimes act in what they regard as the best interests of their country. Not infrequently have their moves been greeted with an outpouring of popular approval.

A junta may have substantial advantages over the government it replaces. If it follows a period of political confusion and economic chaos, it may be able to act with welcome dispatch. It can wield a cleansing broom into many corrupt corners of the government. Efficiently, if arrogantly, it may be able to correct the most blatant wrongs of its predecessors. Soon, however, a junta faces its own serious problems, and its first problem arises on the very day it seizes power: How are its actions to be legitimized?

No one is willing to justify a military coup as the ideal technique for changing the government. Not even those who have led the coup can justify their actions as entirely proper. Indeed, they would like to keep their actions from providing an inspiring example to others who might like to try a new coup, so they cannot possibly assert the general legitimacy of their methods. Some appearance of legitimacy can be given if a sufficiently broad range of civilian leaders is included in the junta, for they give it an air of solid purpose, continuity of policy, and respectability; but their only real claims, even to temporary support, are the emergency and their promise to correct problems that have resisted all alternate solutions. As a result, military regimes and military–civilian juntas usually come into office amidst self-righteous proclamations that the seizure of power is temporary. The junta will deal with the crisis and then turn power back to duly constituted authorities. It will hold elections. Such promises must be made if a new junta is to gain the broad support it would like. Only by such promises can it hope to gain the cooperation of either key figures or the general public. Of course, the declarations of democratic intentions may not be wholly honest. If the leaders learn to enjoy their power, they may come to regret the vigor with which they insisted upon the temporary and emergency nature of their regime. In their first days in power, they have little choice.

More practical problems than legitimacy also face a junta. First is its own lack of preparation. The military leaders may be excellently trained in military tactics, but very badly qualified for regulating an economy. In simpler days when a caudillo could lead his irregular cavalry to national dominance, the skills he used as he built his power were not so different from the skills he would need to run the country. He had to lead his men on the strength of his own personal ability and charisma. He had to reward his followers, and he had to forge alliances with other similar leaders. He needed military skills, but he could not rise without also possessing the essentially political skills of diplomacy, alliance, and power brokerage. Modern military skills and the skills needed for maintaining a nation's political and economic balance have diverged so far that men who rise through the army are no longer likely to make the most able ministers of state. Few generals are prepared to preside over the central banking system. The weak technical preparation of the generals gives them a strong additional motive for including civilian politicians within their junta. Civilians are needed not only to rally the population and provide an air of legitimacy, but to provide the skills that will keep the country functioning.

A junta may also have difficulty formulating a consistant long term policy. Military leaders may fully appreciate the seriousness of immediate problems. They are less likely to have the knowledge or the skill to see far ahead. A junta does not have to be in power for long before the first and most obvious reforms have been accomplished or before the first flush of enthusiasm for the new government wears off. Soon the junta will have to face the divergent interest groups within the country, with their various ideas about policy. With no clear plan of its own, a military government may satisfy no one completely. It soon runs the danger of losing the support that greeted its early triumphs. This may encourage a military government to do as promised and hold prompt elections. In the face of rapidly declining popularity, it may be the only graceful way out.

Civilians within the junta can help the generals with policy, just as they can provide technical skills and an aura of legitimacy. The civilian members of a junta, of course, are likely to be drawn from the opposition to the previous government, and their ideas are likely to be different from those who supported the former regime. They may have fairly clear ideas about policy, but the pursuit of any clear policy will alienate some sectors of the nation. Policies pursued too decisively can also undermine the stance of a junta that would like to present itself as a caretaker government preparing for renewed constitutionalism. Nevertheless, the crisis which gave it the excuse to seize power may demand vigor.

Clearly, a junta faces an insoluble dilemma. It is impossible to pose as a government of national unity and to pursue a vigorous set of policies at the same time. This dilemma offers ample scope for serious internal disagreements among members of the junta, both between military and civilian leaders, and among members of each group. No more than an oligarchy or any other committee government is a junta immune from internal divisions. However much the military leaders need the technical help of their civilian collaborators, they may still disagree on what actions are to be taken. The civilian leaders may regard themselves as more skilled in many matters and they will surely resent interference from the military, but the generals have the guns, and in the "crunch," they can have their way. Even when the military sponsors the most honest of elections and permits the winning civilians to form a government, the new leaders will always know that the generals are standing nearby, scrutinizing their moves. Such a government can no more ignore the military than the civilian members of a junta can ignore their military collaborators. Neither civilians nor generals can rule without the other's cooperation, but they are likely to resent and distrust one another. It is an uneasy alliance.

Rivalries are also likely to occur within both military and civilian groups. A junta usually comes to power as a rather loose team, united in opposition to the previous government, but united in little else. The period of conspiracy encourages the papering over of disagreements. So much careful planning must go into the conspiracy itself that plans for the time after the seizure of control are usually slighted. When faced with mundane problems of keeping the nation running, the members of the junta are likely quickly to disagree. Inevitably, personal rivalry will be added to policy disagreements, and this means that juntas tend to be distinctly unstable.

No more than an oligarchy or any other committee government is a junta immune from internal rivalry. A junta, by definition, has no single and dominant leader who can resolve these rivalries, and, as in assembly governments that have tried to rule without a statholder, king, or governor, the ensuing confusion may again encourage men to seek one-man leadership. If a junta does not act with dispatch to organize elections and step aside, and if it is not displaced by a new junta, it is likely that one man will eventually emerge as strongest. He will displace his former teammates, and assert himself as the top leader. Only in this way can the internal strains of a junta be resolved. A junta consists by definition of a committee whose members share power. There is no clear way to resolve the disputes that must divide this committee. Once a single man succeeds in settling enough disputes in his own favor, he will emerge on top, and in the process the junta will be destroyed. A military man has a better chance of climbing to the top than a civilian, for any civilian will have to deal with the firepower of the generals. If the man with the gun retains his veto, the man in office is not yet supreme.

ARMY GOVERNMENT IN ARGENTINA

We can return to Argentina for concrete examples of the difficulties faced by juntas and military governments, for the four decades following Uriburu's coup of 1930 have seen repeated military intervention. Reviewing these interventions is a disspiriting exercise, but it may be a valuable corrective to the remarkably widespread notion that an army has some special quality that places it above politics, or that allows it to clean up the mess made by others, act as a caretaker government, and work consistently toward the restoration of civilian rule. A review of the Argentine experience makes a mockery of the hope that the military is capable of constructing a government of national unity.

The coup of 1930 settled nothing. Its ostensible purpose was to oust the rascals and restore constitutional government, but President Uriburu, inspired in part by the European fascism of this day, ruled with dictatorial methods, and he quickly lost the wide approval which first greeted him. He failed to gain mass support and even a faction of the army, led by General Justo, came to oppose him. Justo planned to rebel but Uriburu, seeing the handwriting on the wall, conceded and allowed Justo to win the presidency by election in 1931. Without recounting the rather confused details of Argentine politics in the 1930s, it seems fair to characterize the period as a sort of a conservative restoration. Radicals were hounded out of office, and elections were again manipulated. The masses were neglected, and respect for democratic procedures was badly shaken. The opposition was muffled but not eliminated.

Argentine politicians had long conspired with military leaders. Before he had come to power, Irigoyen, the radical leader, had courted military support in the unsuccessful rebellions of 1890, 1893, and 1905, and the successful coup of 1930 could not help but increase the political role of the generals. Since the generals were never united among themselves, however, civilians out of power could always try to form alliances with dissatisfied military men. A number of officers joined radical conspiracies between 1932 and 1935, while others were attracted to Nazism, Falangism, or to the more traditional forms of Argentine authoritarianism.

Hopes for a regrowth of constitutionalism rose with the election of Roberto M. Ortiz in 1938, but illness soon forced him to turn his powers over to the vice-president, Ramón S. Castillo, an arch conservative. Castillo supported the Axis, censored the press, filled the Administration with patronage appointments, and manipulated or nullified provincial elections, while corruption permeated the government. The opposition parties tried to unite to form an opposition, but they did not trust the honesty of the elections, and they squandered their energy by squabbling among themselves. As in 1930, the country seemed pleased when, in June 1943, a sudden military coup removed Castillo from office.

The new government was a sprawling junta, and it had no visible program. Its members seemed badly divided, for the general first announced as provisional president was replaced by another general the very next day. The composition of the cabinet also fluctuated and its very lack of direction encouraged a certain amount of support, for such a leaderless government seemed to represent little authoritarian threat. The junta did embark on some spirited if poorly planned reforms. They fired supernumerary public employees, raised wages, and ordered price cuts, but Congress was dissolved, elections were called off, and it soon became clear that the new government had no respect for democratic processes. It acted instead as if the entire nation had to be placed under a sort of military discipline. A new and, to Argentinians, quite unaccustomed fear of government developed, but the junta did not really appear very strong, for it had no party behind it and no widespread political support. Jobs went to military officers and the government stayed in power simply by force of arms.

Inevitably, a struggle for power developed within the junta. Men of more moderate views were gradually forced out, and power came more and more to be monopolized by a group of ultra-nationalists. Finally, out of the competition, Juan Perón emerged as dominant. He imposed a personalistic rule, but by 1955, after a decade in power, he too had aroused so much opposition that another military rebellion succeeded in removing him. A new junta, led by another group of officers, came to power. It sought broad support by posing as a caretaker government and it permitted a largely civilian cabinet. Conciliatory policies were proclaimed and press freedom was restored, but once again quarrels within the junta ran deep.

Several viewpoints soon emerged in the armed forces. Some generals, including the first post-Perón president, General Eduardo Lonardi, took a moderate line toward the supporters of the exiled dictator. Others took a harder anti-Peronista line, and after 4 months this group succeeded in replacing Lonardi with General Pedro Aramburu. During the presidency of Aramburu, leftist officers were not permitted to argue openly for their policies, but some of them joined the secret Green Dragon Lodge which sought to acquaint younger army officers with the social problems of Argentina and with the social responsibility of the army. The leaders of this group of officers were eventually forced out by more conservative military men, but these conservatives were not united either. Some wanted to retain military rule indefinitely. These so-called *gorilas* had their chief strength in the infantry and engineering branches of the army. The more moderate *legalista* group was centered in the cavalry and tank units. The legalistas agreed upon suppression of the Peronistas, but they advocated a return to civilian government. The navy was more united than the army and always took a strong anti-Peronista position. The navy felt it had been shortchanged under Perón, but it later made a substantial comeback. Naval officers played a key role both in removing Perón, and then in the downfall 4 months later of the Lonardi government. The navy was rewarded with a new aircraft carrier and three new destroyers. The air force proved to be adroit in picking the winning side. It backed Aramburu against Lonardi, and it later helped purge both the leftist Green Dragon faction and rightist gorila faction of the army.

The government of General Aramburu sponsored elections in 1958 and allowed the civilian winner, Arturo Frondizi, to assume the presidency. Frondizi won, in part, by attracting Peronista votes, and he had to walk a narrow path between the suspicious generals on one side and, on the other, the Peronistas, whom he tried to conciliate and to reintegrate into political life. Frondizi managed to retain his office for 4 years, but in 1962 the various strongly anti-Peronista factions of the services united briefly and ousted the elected president who, they felt, had been too conciliatory toward the left.

As on so many other occasions, however, once in power the service factions fell to quarreling and it took a pitched battle in April, 1963 for the more moderate legalistas to put down the navy and the gorila faction of the

army. In that year the army, now under *legalista* control, once again permitted elections, but this time insisted upon sufficient safeguards to prevent the Peronistas from gaining too much influence. They believed they
had obtained the kind of civilian government they wanted with President
Arturo Illia, and the army retired once more to its barracks. It was clear,
however, that no civilian government would be able to rule without taking
the desires of the generals into account, and in 1966, the cycle repeated
itself when the army once again removed the elected president. Another
general, Juan Carlos Ongania, became president in a bloodless military
coup and for the next 4 years he gave Argentina an increasingly authoritarian military government. In 1970, Ongania, in his turn, was overthrown
and replaced by General Roberto M. Levingston who lasted less than a
year, and then in 1971, General Alejandro Lanusse, the army commander,
assumed the presidency, ostensibly because Levingston had not moved
rapidly enough toward the restoration of civilian government.

Military coups overthrew the Argentine government in 1930, 1943,
1955, 1962, 1966, 1970, and 1971, often with widespread popular approval, and usually amid promises to prepare rapidly for a return to
civilian rule, but what, in retrospect, has all this military intervention accomplished? Certainly not national unity. Certainly not stability. Certainly not purposeful efficient government. One can only conclude that
military intervention has achieved none of the goals by which it has so
often been justified. Anyone who imagines that the army of any country
is likely to do better than a stumbling civilian regime would do well to
ponder the lesson of Argentina. Among the economically most advanced
of the Latin American nations, its government has lurched from general
to general with no clear progression toward stability, unity, or civil freedoms. Once launched into politics, the army has found it almost impossible
to disengage.

THE DICTATOR

The instability shown by juntas is reminiscent of the instability of
civilian oligarchies, and like them, they seem pressed in two directions.
Lacking legitimacy, lacking expertise, and beset by internal rivalries, a
military government must move either toward the legitimacy and the broad-
ened government symbolized by elections and a return to civilian government, or else its own internal quarrels will degenerate into a rough and
tumble scramble for power until someone finally emerges as dominant and
narrows the government to one-man rule.

A one-man dictatorship has clear advantages over a junta. An able man
who somehow maneuvers his way to the top can act for more decisively than

any committee. He need not engage in the debilitating compromises that a committee demands. He may be able rapidly to consolidate his position, and he can take decisive measures against his enemies. An outward political stability may emerge. If he is bright enough or educated enough to understand practical economics, or if he is lucky enough to gather able economic advisors, he may be able to get his country started on a progressive economic path.

It is difficult, however, to justify the methods by which most dictators come into office. A few have been chosen in honest elections and only later sponsored the limitations on democratic freedom that accompany one-man rule. More often, they have come in by revolution or intrigue. It was by emerging as the strong man out of an army junta that Argentina's most dictatorial modern president, Juan Perón, arose. Perón was a regular army officer. He had been a captain in 1930 and had played an obscure role in the coup of that year. By 1943 he had risen to colonel. He was undoubtedly an abler man than most of his fellow officers, and he had the acumen to mobilize an alternative power base outside the army. He accepted the apparently thankless post of labor minister within the military government, and from this position was able to organize the laboring masses into a powerful force that could counterbalance that of the army. He was an important though not dominant figure in a clique of colonels who ousted the generals in early 1944 and by June, 1945 his moment for achieving supremacy had arrived. His fellow officers, fearing his growing power, arrested him, but the laboring masses, the so-called *descamisados,* or "shirtless ones" rose in protest. To avoid civil war, Perón's military colleagues had to call him back, and now that he was no longer subject to ready dismissal by his brother officers, he became the undisputed strong man.

In the Latin American context, Perón's sources of support were unusual, but in a broader view, he executed a familiar maneuver. Like any number of would-be autocrats before him, he appealed over the heads of his narrow circle of powerful associates and posed as a leader of more popular forces than the others represented. Here was the familiar alliance between the autocratic top and popular bottom against the oligarchical middle. In gaining and keeping power, he had to perform a rather delicate balancing act between his two major sources of support, the masses of labor and the army. No one else could bridge these two, and so long as neither gained predominant power, they blocked one another, and Perón could stay on top.

This particular combination of forces could only have emerged in a well-developed nation like Argentina where there was a large industrial proletariat. Few other nations of Latin America have offered quite the same opportunities, but in one way or another, strong men have emerged from many juntas. This would seem to be the logical outcome of the conflict of forces inherent in a committee form of government when the context gives firepower the final authority. Like Latin American juntas, dictators have felt called upon to proclaim their adherence to democratic principles, and to bolster their regimes by elections of some sort, even if they have to be fraudulent. Perón surrounded himself with elaborate pseudo-democratic forms. He had a constitution, managed elections, a packed supreme court, and a docile congress. Such devices may make it seem that the only sources of legitimacy available to a dictator are the same sorts of pseudo-democratic trappings used by self-perpetuating oligarchies and juntas but, paradoxically, the dictator may add to the advantages of decisiveness, an ideological advantage over a junta. He can more easily seize upon alternatives to democratic ideology and he can try to inspire the personal loyalty that Latin Americans call *personalismo*. Most often, dictators aim toward some combination of electoral and personalistic validation of their rule.

Perón proclaimed his adherence to democratic and constitutional principles, but assiduously promoted the cult of his own personality and he imported, with changes, a few ideas from fascist Europe. He and his wife Eva assumed a life of ostentatious if tasteless display with which the masses could vicariously identify, and he became a popular idol. He proclaimed the doctrine of *justicalismo* which served for a time to give some sort of ideological underpinnings to his regime, though it hardly stands scrutiny as a polished or logical political philosophy, and it was always more to Perón, the man, than to justicalismo, the philosophy, that the supporters of the regime gave their loyalty.

In other Latin American nations, other doctrines have been proclaimed from time to time in the hope of strengthening the regime. In Ecuador, when Velasco Ibarra was building up his own cult of personality, he liked to be known as "The National Personification," whatever that may mean, and any number of other dictators have tried to construct some sort of philosophical or ideological prop for their essentially personalistic rule. But it is the man, not the philosophy, that holds his countrymen's loyalty, and it is no wonder that the term "Peronism" is now more widely remembered than "justicalism."

Dictators may be less bound than either military juntas or self-perpetuating oligarchies by the restricting obligations of democratic forms or by the need to compromise, but they face their own problems. It really is not easy in the modern world to construct a satisfying political doctrine that will support a man in office without the sanction of some sort of elections. A Germany under a Hilter can construct a doctrine that for a time will be taken seriously enough to evoke the fanatical loyalty of great masses of people. It is not so easy to make any comparable doctrine seem plausible in as small and poor a nation as Ecuador. Even Argentina is only one among many Latin American nations, and after a time justicalismo begins to sound just a little silly.

Sooner or later, the craftiest, most popular, most personally appealing dictator is bound to arouse opposition, and the longer he stays in power, the more enemies he will make. Dictators have often been wildly corrupt. They have known very well that their rule might be ended abruptly through a new revolution and they have been eager to enrich themselves while they have had the chance. Corruption, failure to promote economic development, and an increasingly dissatisfied populace sooner or later combine to hasten the dictator's end. A new round of revolution can begin.

With the dictator, of course, we have come full circle, and are back to something very much like the caudillo, for the strengths and weakness of the 20th century military dictator are much like those of the 19th century caudillo. The difference between them is in the means by which they come to power. The man on horseback fought his way up as the leader of an armed band. His organization was rudimentary, his requirements satisfied by plunder. The man in a tank or jet plane can rise only as a member of a complex bureaucracy. He needs mechanics, bookkeepers, and space parts. The ambitious military leader today cannot start by simply assembling a few followers and a few guns, but must first rise through the ranks of the armed forces until a combination of military experience, skill at intrigue, and luck finally bring him out on top. Nevertheless, once in power, the difficulties faced by the caudillo and the modern dictator are not so different. Both must try to build personal loyalty, both have difficulty providing a successor to their own office, and both have often found opposition accumulating so fast that they have been forced out of office well before they are ready to leave.

THE RANGE OF POLITICAL PARTICIPATION

Many nations of Latin America seem trapped in an endless cycle of changing political forms, none of them capable of permanence. No search for a single cause for this instability can escape oversimplification, but one important factor has certainly been the difficulty of agreeing on the range of political participation. How large a group of people should participate in political decisions? Who can take part in choosing a president? Such questions have had ambiguous and widely varying answers in Latin America.

Latin America has certainly had its share of highly centralized regimes where decisions were monopolized by a single dictator, but even when dictators have stayed in office until death or until ready to retire, it has been impossible, as it is always impossible in a highly centralized regime, to find consistent techniques for their graceful replacement. The political system is eventually forced open. At the opposite extreme, a few nations, most notably Costa Rica, have had considerable periods of stable electoral government, but poverty and a lack of democratic traditions have often brought electoral regimes to grief. There was a time in European history when stable regimes could exist at an intermediate level of participation, but today no intermediate level seems capable of finding the necessary ideological support. Juntas and oligarchies may actually run the government for considerable periods, but they are always torn in two directions, both toward narrowing or toward broadening political participation.

Nowhere in Latin America has there been a political cycle as regular as some dynastic political cycles seem to have been. There seem to be too many directions in which a government can move. As in heredity regimes, the rules by which the top leader is chosen have not remained fixed for very long. Elections, coup d'etats, intrigue, and appointment compete for the chance to produce oligarchies, elected governments, juntas, and dictators. Every type of government seems to have such serious internal weaknesses that it sooner or later invites replacement.

Out of this welter of changing governments, modern observers sometimes see Mexico as offering a promise of a new stability and a uniquely Latin American solution to the political puzzle. The modern Mexican experiment is important enough to deserve special consideration.

REVOLUTIONARY MEXICO

After a century of political chaos, climaxed by one of Latin America's most violent civil wars, modern Mexico has emerged with one of the region's most stable governments, and in the past few decades, the country has achieved economic growth as consistent as any part of the hemisphere. Civilians control the government, the army is kept in its place, and presidents now follow each other in and out of office in peace. What is the secret? Has Mexico found an escape from the cycle of instability that has so long plagued her neighbors?[5]

For 7 years, from 1913 to 1919, Mexico tore herself to pieces in civil war. Finally out of an utterly chaotic rivalry, Venustiano Carranza, assisted by General Alvaro Obregón, emerged as the winner. Carranza's triumph over his various opponents was due in part to his more successful appeal for popular support. More than his rivals, he had advocated labor legislation, agrarian reform, and some satisfaction for the economic, social

---

[5]On the modern Mexican political system, I rely, in particular, upon the careful study of Frank Brandenburg, *The Making of Modern Mexico* (Englewood Cliffs, N. J.: Prentice-Hall, 1964).

and political needs of the country. He had sponsored a constitution and he had had himself elected under it, but he then disposed of his rivals so ruthlessly that he alienated a good deal of his support. By the time Carranza had won the war, many of his revolutionary followers had shifted their support to Alvaro Obregón, the general who had won many of the battles, but who was less tainted than Carranza with a reputation for political trickery. Carranza had made the fatal political mistake of permitting a single man to assume a clear second position, and once their common enemies had been eliminated, he and Obregón were almost fated to have a falling out. When Carranza tried to impose another man as his successor to the presidency, his military supporters were so completely alienated that Obregón had little difficulty rallying them to his side. Carranza was ousted, and in 1920 Obregón became president by right of military force. This was the last time a Mexican president would achieve office this way.

One of the rallying principles of the revolution had been that presidential terms were to be limited and that a man was not to be reelected. By the end of Obregón's term, the principle had been too often repeated and too widely accepted to be ignored, so Obregón had to be content with the next best thing to staying in office. He accomplished what Carranza had attempted: He made sure that his own hand-picked supporter would follow him. His choice was not immediately acceptable to everyone and there was an armed challenge, but this time the government forces put down the uprising and Obregón's man, Plutarco Elias Calles, served the 4-year term from 1924–1928, though Calles always shared real power with Obregón.

The Obregón–Calles team which was now dominant amended the constitution to provide for 6-year terms instead of 4, and to allow nonconsecutive reelection. They then engineered a new term for Obregón, but before taking formal office again, Obregón was assassinated. Calles was now left alone, but in the awkward position of being constitutionally unable to succeed himself. The army, more loyal to Obregón than to Calles, began to plot against the lame duck president, as did the surviving supporters of Carranza. Calles, however, skillfully salvaged his own position by finding an able and widely acceptable man, Portes Gil, to become provisional president. Calles had to take to the battlefield to put down the last of the dissatisfied generals, but this was the final open military challenge against the constitutional president. Calles now also organized a new national party that was to include within its broad embrace almost the whole spectrum of Mexican political forces. The Partido Naciónal Revolucionario (PNR) and its successors under other names was to serve as a channel for both military and civilian political ambitions, and it has become one of the main features of the present Mexican political system.

With the suppression of the military rebellion and a new party organization behind him, Calles was now able to concentrate on engineering the election of Pascual Ortiz Rubio, who then served out the term that was originally to have been Obergón's. The colorless Ortiz Rubio served as president until 1934, but he was never the real leader of Mexico. Calles continued to guide things from the background.

The Calles years saw the beginnings of real economic progress. Sound fiscal policies were established, roads were built, irrigation extended, and the power supply organized. Calles also managed to lead the army toward more professionalization and, it was hoped, away from a direct political role. As the years passed, Calles tended to become more conservative, but he bowed to the more radical members of his party by allowing Lázaro Cárdenas to become its official candidate for the presidency in 1934. Cárdenas came in with Calles's blessing, but once securely elected, he rather surprisingly and dramatically lived up to his campaign promises, and in the early months of his presidency, he pushed through a number of radical reforms. The reforms soon drew new mass support to Cárdenas, but they also antagonized the old leader, Calles. As a result Calles, like many other Latin American leaders, broke with his own chosen successor, but in this case the break came only after Cárdenas had already built up his position so successfully that he was able to out-maneuver Calles. Cárdenas had, in a sense, appealed over the head of his own boss for broad support. Calles was forced into retirement, but he was the first supreme leader of revolutionary Mexico to escape violent death. Cárdenas became not only official president of Mexico, but also the dominant leader.

Cárdenas reorganized the official party and his term saw considerable progress in social reforms and economic development. A real advance was made in the long promised land reforms. At the end of his own term, Cárdenas chose Ávila Camacho as his successor and since the two shared power during Camacho's term, the Cárdenas era can be said to have spanned 12 years. In 1940, Cárdenas and Camacho decided to step aside and allow their chosen successor, Miguel Alemán, to exercise his own initiative for his 6 years in office. Alemán's term represented a swing to the right, for he encouraged private and foreign investment, and downgraded the rights of labor, but solid strides were made toward industrial development. Alemán's term also was characterized by increasingly bountiful material rewards to the government leaders, and he chose as his successor a man who came from a wing of the party that many regarded as seriously corrupt.

At this point Cárdenas finally reasserted his still powerful influence. A good deal of haggling went on behind the scenes, but since all parties stood to benefit by avoiding an open break, they were eventually able to agree on a successor. Adolfo Ruíz Cortines became the party's candidate, and Alemán was allowed to serve out his term. At the end of the next term, the president was able to persuade the various components of the party and the government to accept Adolfo López Mateos as their candidate, and since then, at 6-year intervals, the party has chosen a new man and then united behind him to provide a smashing electoral victory at the polls.

What has made possible this increasingly placid succession to the Mexican presidency? Military support has not installed a president since 1920, and military rebellion in support of a loser has not had to be put down since 1928. A broad consensus has developed over the goals of revolutionary Mexico and remarkable economic and industrial progress has been achieved. Yet this has not been accompanied by the contested elections that Anglo-Americans expect, and ordinary Mexicans have little to say about the choice of their leaders.

The system rests upon several interrelated facets: a mass party which embraces most sectors of Mexican life, including agrarian, white collar, and labor; an inner group of leaders who guide the nation from behind the scenes and who effectively agree on power distribution among themselves and upon the selection of official candidates; a firmly accepted prohibition against reelection; and a commitment to economic development and the "continuing revolution" that is supposed to move toward constitutionalism and liberalism, even if effective suffrage and free political opposition must be postponed.

Crucial to the perpetuation of the system is the periodic selection of a new president. The single most important factor in this choice may be the preference of his predecessor, though this is not entirely decisive. The pattern that has emerged is approximately this: As each term draws to a close, the president consults the leading members of what has been called the "revolutionary family," and tries to find a consensus. This top group, perhaps about 20 in number, includes the incumbent president, a few national and regional political leaders, some outstanding members of the cabinet, a few labor leaders and weathy industrialists, and often the ex-presidents. The president himself is usually the most powerful member of this group, though a few ex-presidents have maintained their own paramount power into or clear through the administrations of their successors. This inner council sets long-term policy. It is consulted about the most important political matters, and, in particular, it considers the choice of each new president. The group has no official position and it does not meet formally, but its members maintain regular informal contact and they clearly stand to gain by unity. They would risk a great deal by an open split and they usually manage to agree.

Once they agree on a successor, the incumbent president announces his name and then the hundreds of men and organizations that are affiliated with the official party vie loudly with one another to see who can appear most eager to climb upon the band wagon. As soon as the successor is announced everyone wants to get as close as possible to the source of all future patronage. The candidate, really the president elect, generally goes on an extensive "campaign" which gives him broad national exposure, allows the leaders and citizens to tender their loyalty, and educates him in the intricacies of Mexican politics. After his tour of the nation, he should be able to make effective appointments and steer with skill among the various factions.

The election always brings a resounding victory to the official candidate, the ex-president steps into the background and the new man is able to use his massive patronage to move his own men into hundreds and thousands of bureaucratic positions. He can also generally choose the official party's nominees for the congress and the state legislatures and, since these nominees usually win, the president can very nearly be said to have the power to appoint his own congress. Opposition parties are officially permitted, but their accusations of electoral fraud are followed by every appearance of a meticulous checking of details and this serves only to validate in the public eye the overall justice of the elections.

The system works. Is it, however, something radically new? For all its revolutionary and left-wing rhetoric and for all its considerable economic accomplishments, the Mexican political system looks like nothing so much as the old 19th century oligarchies of some other parts of Latin America. To be sure, as the Mexican system has become stabilized, its leaders have managed to avoid quite such vigorous public debates as were engaged in by members of the older oligarchies. The Mexicans seem also to have learned not to appeal for military aid in the mutual competition that must go on behind the scenes, and they have pursued truly revolutionary goals in spreading mass education, and in encouraging major industrial development and agrarian reform. Most important, perhaps, the Mexican leaders have constructed a vast official party that embraces a far broader segment of the population than any organization of a 19th century oligarchy ever did. The Mexican party deserves scrutiny since it can be regarded as something of a prototype for the official parties of the many single-party states that have emerged in the post-colonial world. The Mexican party has played a vital political role, but it is not the same role that is played by parties that must compete to win. The Mexican party serves primarily as a device by which the leaders organize and control the masses. It is not a device through which the masses select their leaders.

The official party of Mexico has been developed in an attempt to counteract one of the traditional oligarchical weaknesses—the exclusion of the great majority of the population from any participation in the government. The organs of the Mexican party reach out to the masses and affiliate them with the government in a way that earlier oligarchies never did, but expressions of the popular will percolate only weakly and slowly upward through party channels. Labor unions, for instance, have been officially incorporated into the party, but the leaders of these unions have come to serve the party first and their own constituencies second. They deliver the labor vote and work to keep labor docile, rather than promoting the interests of the workers. Intermediate level officials are more dependent upon appointment from above than upon effective election from below. As a result, loyalty and responsiveness point upward to those who have the power to promote or dismiss, not downward to powerless constituents. Order might not have been brought to Mexico if some degree of centralization had not been imposed, but such a strongly centralized party serves only imperfectly as a channel through which the needs and desires of common men can be brought to bear upon those who formulate and execute policy.

The party gives the leaders a rather different means to control the nation than was available to the earlier oligarchies, but the parallels still run deep. Like the conservative oligarchies of the 19th century, the Mexican oligarchy is largely self-perpetuating. A small group continues to make the effective decisions and to impose its will upon the nation. As in the 19th century, the nominations of the new oligarchy are routinely ratified by elections, but the real decision is made earlier by an inner council working behind the scenes. It seems unlikely that the revolutionary family would permit an opposition candidate to use an election to overturn the official party. Furthermore, while the benefits of economic gains may be a bit more widely spread in Mexico than they were under 19th century oligarchies, the gains of the masses should not be exaggerated. The economic status of workers and peasants has not climbed nearly as rapidly as that of the industrial and governmental bureaucracies. Millions of very poor people still live in Mexico, and the contrast between rich and poor may be almost as extreme as in other parts of Latin America. At the top of the scale, high office in Mexico, as almost everywhere in Latin America, continues to be an opulent source of material gain.

Finally, insofar as they can be seen, the internal struggles within the ruling group also show parallels with those of earlier oligarchies. Appointment of one's own successor with the choice tempered by the sentiments of the ruling elite, an occasional attempt to choose a docile man who will allow an older leader to rule from behind the scenes, a few serious breaks between successive rulers when one president comes to assert his dominance at the expense of his predecessor—all these characteristics make the Mexican oligarchy seem rather familiar.

If the Mexican oligarchy resembles earlier ones, we must, of course, wonder whether it is not subject to the same kinds of internal strains. Can the Mexican system perpetuate itself more or less indefinitely, or will it be subject to the same drastic changes as its 19th century predecessors? Will those excluded from effective voice in the government not eventually work outside the system to bring its overthrow? Will there come a time when someone within or on the fringes of the oligarchy will again be tempted to appeal over the heads of his fellow oligarchs for popular or even military support? For how long can the inevitable divisions within the oligarchy be so successfully hidden that a united front can be presented to the world? For some decades, the Mexican system has been notably successful in productively channeling discontent within the party. Widespread student riots in 1968 served as a reminder that dissatisfied groups had rather meager means by which to express their discontent or to work peacefully but productively to modify the system from within.

In spite of its successes, moreover, a disinterested observer can find much to criticize about the government. Some 19th century oligarchies also brought great economic gains to their nations at the same time that a good many resources were diverted to the pockets of the leaders. Like its predecessors, the government of Mexico has been criticized for the degree to which its leaders have been able to enrich themselves, but, beyond charges of corruption, there is always room in an increasingly complex world for honest disagreement on policies. The most highly motivated Mexican critic who wants to urge his own policies, or who simply wants to restrict the self-enrichment of office holders, has few outlets by which to promote his program. To join an opposition party offers little real hope of success, but to work within the official party requires subjection to the very people to whom one may be opposed.

Some popular dissatisfaction is inevitable, but as long as the major elements of the party and government remain united, no opposition can become really effective. The most serious dangers to the Mexican system would seem to come from internal quarrels among the ruling elite. However much they stand to gain by keeping together, the potential for rivalry is ever present. If some members of the elite should feel so aggrieved that they are no longer willing to adhere to the consensus, they might then be tempted to go outside the usual channels and call upon the support of those who have otherwise had few means for expressing their wishes. Could student dissatisfaction, labor unrest, or popular revulsion against corruption find a champion who would use their support in building his own power in opposition to the rest of the oligarchy? Could such a man gain an ideological weapon, by demanding, for instance, more realistic electoral competition? Those favoring the status quo would face a dilemma in dealing with a strong movement of this sort. They might try to incorporate this new movement under the broad umbrella of the party, buying off the leaders perhaps, and seeking a quiet behind-the-scenes consensus that could be imposed upon the nation. But to the extent that dissident elements of this sort are admitted to the oligarchy, it will become difficult to compose the differences that divide them, and it will become more likely that some members will go outside the inner party and appeal to wide groups for support.

One cannot even be confident that the armed forces have been completely tamed. It has been many years since the army has intervened directly in a succession battle, but the hope that the army has forever been banned from politics may be a bit premature. Army officers continue to serve in important posts, including both cabinet and high party positions. The now aging revolutionary generals are committed to the revolution and can be counted upon to support the government, but below them are younger officers whose advancement has been slowed by those on top, and who may be waiting in the wings for the retirement of the older generals, hoping finally to take a more active political role. If sharp disagreements or irreconcilable personal rivalries occur within the ruling oligarchy, the temptation to call upon military support may arise, and younger ambitious officers may be tempted to cooperate. In the absence of other clearly defined rules or deeply ingrained traditions for settling disputes, one can hardly be confident that military force will not again be applied.

The Mexican economy has been expanding rapidly enough to satisfy the elite, but expansion must be fairly rapid just to keep up with the population, and any faltering in the economy, or even too long a postponement in spreading the new wealth among a broader range of the population could introduce the same kinds of intolerable strains that economic crises have brought to many earlier Latin American governments. An economic crisis would certainly make it more difficult for the ruling elite to maintain its unified monopoly of power. It is idle to speculate on the directions toward which such strains might impel the Mexican political system. It might be toward more open electoral competition for popular support, but it might also be toward a narrower, more personalistic and autocratic rule. The single prediction that a study of succession systems can suggest with any confidence is that a system is unlikely to persist for long without change. The equilibrium of the present system, though unquestionably impressive by Latin American standards, may in the end be subject to as many strains as the oligarchies of the last century, which were in some ways so similiar.

CONCLUSIONS

Great changes have come to Latin America in the century and a half of its independence. Economic development, population growth, and changing military technology have all had their impact, but it is hard to make a convincing case that Latin Americans have moved consistently closer to the kind of electoral democracy that North Americans so fondly imagine to be the hallmark of civilization. The caudillo may be gone, but the dictator is very much with us, and the chaotic parade of varied Latin American governments continues. Every type of government that Latin Americans have tried from the most liberal of democracies to the most oppressive of dictatorships seems to have had inherent internal difficulties. None has consistently provided real continuity and stability. Since most Latin Americans have lived under more than a single kind of government and since most have already lived through military regimes, further military intervention in government seems both more expectable and more acceptable than it does to Anglo-Americans. Having grown accustomed to the cycle of revolution, and having come to realize that a revolution does not, after all, bring the end of all civilized life, the Latin American may shrug his shoulders and proceed with his business.

The revolution that has had the greatest impact upon the Americas in recent years is certainly that of Fidel Castro's Cuba. To simplistic observers in both North and South America, Castro's government has been imagined to be a foreign implantation, a branch of international Communism planted just off our shores. However, it is worth considering Castro's actions in the light of earlier Latin American revolutions and other political philosophies, for it may turn out that Cuba's experience is not quite so unique as it is sometimes imagined to be.

Castro, to be sure, fought his way to power in an unconventional way. Most modern overturns of Latin American governments have come through disaffection within the regularly constituted parts of the government, whether by a barracks revolt of military leaders, or a more complex conspiracy of civilians and generals who are already within or at least close to the margins of the established government. Castro began with the far more romantic adventure of leading his bearded revolutionaries out of the mountains, and as a result he came to power with fewer obligations to surviving members of the old government than most conspirators have had. This left him far freer to carry out his program than the typical new president. Unquestionably, moreover, Castro and his colleagues seized their opportunity with more enthusiasm and efficiency than most new governments. With the help of the firing squad, they quickly cleansed Cuba of the remnants of the Batista regime, and their subsequent economic policies brought far deeper changes than the usual new Latin American government.

Nevertheless, recognition of these unique aspects of the Cuban revolution should not obscure its more familiar features. For one thing Castro, like other rebels, profited from the widespread popular disgust with an earlier tyrant. Almost automatically, he gained the initial support of all those who were fed up with Batista. At first, he seemed to offer hope for a more democratic and freer Cuba and in consolidating his position, he capitalized upon this hope. It was not long before the prospect for a government legitimized by open and contested elections gave way to a more personalistic rule, and here Castro has profited from the same kinds of claims upon personal loyalty that other Latin Americans have had from their followers. Castro's emergence from the mountains to win the revolution is the stuff of romance, and he and the other leaders of the Cuban revolution have capitalized upon their adventure. To be sure, the particular symbols of Castroism are different from those of, for instance, Peronism. Beards and fatigues replace the fur and the elegant military uniforms of Perón's Argentina, but as symbols, they are no less effective. Like Perón and a few other Latin American dicators also, Castro reached across the Atlantic for a political philosophy that might help to give credibility to his regime, and that might replace electoral validation with an alternative legitimizing principle. In the 1940s, Fascism seemed to provide a plausible political philosophy and with Latin American modifications, it was imported to bolster a few regimes. By the 1960s Marxism and Communism seemed more viable and they are invoked instead, but Cuban Communism, like the earlier Latin American Fascism, seems rather grafted onto the nation from the top. Cuba has never been the compliant satellite of the Soviet Union that the nations of Eastern Europe were in Stalin's day, and indeed Cuba has sometimes been as much of an embarrassment as a useful ally. One gets the impression that Castro has used Communism more than Communism has used Castro, and just as we can more easily use the term "Peronism" than the term "justicalism" for the Argentine regime and philosophy, so it seems more natural to speak of "Castroism" than of "Communism" to characterize the program of the Cuban government.

This is not to deny the social revolution that Castro has attempted to impose upon Cuba, but at the same time it is well to remember that Perón also tried to impose something of a social revolution upon Argentina, and the support of the two leaders has in some respects been similar. Perón built his power upon the descamisados, the urban proletariat of Argentina. He could inspire them to support him and so neutralize his opponents in the army. Perón inspired the workers to hope for a better life and he drew them into some sort of participation in the government. By relying upon labor, he drew a wider group into the political process than had ever participated before. Castro has promised similar rewards to the poor laborers of Cuba, and while these may work on rural sugar plantations instead of in the more developed urban enterprises of industralized Argentina, they both represent a proletariat that had formerly been relatively excluded from politics. Cuban sugar production and Argentine industry could both be accused of resting upon the exploitation of labor, and Perón and Castro both promised a revised social system that would bring dignity and eventually tangible economic benefits to the workers. The abstract differences between the modified Fascism of Perón and the modified Communism of Castro should not obscure these similarities.

In retrospect, it is easy to see that Perón failed dismally to fulfill his economic promises. Argentina slipped in relative economic position in Latin America. Agriculture declined and industry did no more than hold its own. Corruption was rampant and general economic dislocation was so serious that Argentina is still struggling to rid itself of the legacy of Peronist economic policies. Castroism is still relatively new and as long as it remains in power, we can hope that Cuba will escape Argentina's economic fate; but from what we know of Cuban economic trends, it takes rather deeply tinted rose-colored glasses to give one confidence that Cuba's economic development will show any spectacular successes. Sugar production has hardly been dramatic and the attempts to establish a more diversified industrial base have been disappointing. Castro's more or less Communist associates may be individually more honest than Perón's more or less Fascist associates, but whether their economic policies will in the long run be more successful must, for the present, remain in doubt.

One other similarity between Castro and Perón should be pointed out: their vitriolic attacks upon the United States. In both cases, the attacks seem to have grown partly out of some perfectly genuine grievances against the "Colossus of the North," but partly from a need to encourage a kind of nationalism that needed an enemy. In both cases, the United States has been a convenient whipping boy, and attacks upon it have helped to generate enthusiasm for the government. Finally, if we are to understand the relatively tolerant attitude of many Latin Americans toward the Cuban excesses that the United States has found so distasteful, we must recognize that Castro's methods can easily be matched by other supposedly more "democratic" regimes. Suppression of press freedom, restrictions on free assembly, suspension of civil liberties, and violent political death have all been found in many other nations than Cuba. Such political methods hardly distinguish the Cuban "Communist" regime from many others of Latin America.

The main question, however, must remain open: Has Cuba discovered some new and more satisfactory device for maintaining the continuity of the regime beyond the lifetime of its leader? Does Castro's government have greater staying power than the typical personalistic regime of Latin America? When Castro finally goes, what form of succession will provide the next president? It is difficult to see any institutional devices that have made Cuba different from any other Latin American nation in these re-spects. Surely Castro's policies, like those of every other autocratic ruler before him, have alienated large segments of the population. What if Castro should die? He is a young man, and may live for many decades, but he cannot live forever. It is hard to believe that his followers would not finally quarrel over the succession, just as followers of all other dictators in all other nations have always quarreled over succession. Castro's charisma is great, and for the present, he is no doubt capable of keeping his nation more or less united behind him. But his charisma can hardly be transferred intact to a successor, and to this extent it is difficult to see how Cuba's revolution has solved the political dilemma in which Latin Americans have so long been mired. As a personalistic regime, Castro's government is subject to the same weaknesses as other personalistic regimes. Whether the Marxism and Communism to which Castro's followers claim to adhere can provide new answers to the succession problem is a somewhat different question. For that it is more profitable to look to Eastern Europe and the Soviet Union where Communist parties have been in power longer, and where the regimes have already faced several successions.

CHAPTER 7

Eastern Europe
and the Soviet Union

IDEOLOGY

Of the many nonelectoral political systems that exist in the world today, only those that profess to be moving toward Communism hold any appreciable international attraction. The Soviet regime, moreover, has been in power for over half a century, a respectable life span for any governmental regime today, and on several occasions power has been passed successfully to a new man. Both its prestige and its longevity make the Soviet government important in any modern comparative political study, and this importance seems to justify a rather detailed treatment of the actual successions that have occurred. We can examine the varied strategies that have been used or that might be used by men who compete within the Soviet government or within those governments that have been modelled upon it. We must ask, specifically, whether Communism has provided any new or different solutions that have escaped the nonelectoral regimes of other parts of the world.

One unique feature of the Soviet style of government is its possession of a complex and prestigious ideology, a century old doctrine that can be invoked to justify every action. This ideology, with its claim to universal applicability, has helped to make of Communism a far more formidable political challenge than the many more nationalistic doctrines, such as Nasserism or Peronism, that have recently found temporary acceptance in one or another corner of the world. Men and parties invoking Communist ideology have now been in power long enough to let us ask how, in the absence of either heredity or of openly contested elections, their governments have coped with the problem of succession and whether they have coped with the problem more successfully than the world's other nonelectoral regimes.

Since it is so important in distinguishing "Communist" regimes from other modern nonelectoral systems, we must turn first to the ideology, but one who examines the teachings of Marx and Engels for illumination on succession practices is doomed to disappointment.[1] Marx had little to say about the problem, and, indeed, the very nature of his social theories must have led him to minimize its importance. Marx was concerned with broad social forces, with the clash of economic interests and their resolution, not with power struggles among individuals. He had much to say about the transfer of power from one class to another but little to say about its transfer from individual to individual. Where revolutionary direction was needed, he seems to have expected leaders to emerge by some sort of spontaneous but ill-defined process. Presumably, the unity of interests within the working class would facilitate agreement on leadership, but the expectation that Communism, once achieved, would permit the state to wither away did little to encourage much serious thought about how the state should operate.

---

[1]No problem arises in using such expressions as "Communist ideology," or "Communist party," or even "Communist leader," but one faces a real terminological dilemma when decidng how to refer to the governments that these parties and leaders direct. In the West, these governments (like the party and the leaders), are often called "Communist," but since the participants in these governments do not yet consider themselves to have achieved "Communism," this is hardly a felicitous terminological choice. The term they themselves use to describe their governments is "Socialist," but for the Western reader, unfortunately, this term raises other, and quite different, connotations. My compromise in the following pages is to place the word "Communist" in quotation marks whenever I can find no other simple manner of referring to those governments whose leaders profess to be working toward Communism.

Nevertheless, while Marxism provides no recipe that could be followed in deciding issues of succession, the ideology has been used to help define and justify the distribution and use of power, and these in turn have influenced the manner in which succession to office has occurred.

Communist ideology has looked forward to a better world to come and has encouraged revolutionary violence to bring about the necessary changes. An apocalyptic vision of the coming world is used to justify everyday political tactics, and if strength and even violence are needed to provide necessary conditions for social advance, then strength and violence are desirable. Paradoxically, therefore, an ideology that promises great ultimate benefits for all mankind can be used to justify today's tyranny. The assurance of working toward a better future has freed leaders from traditional restraints upon their own exercise of power. The common ideology and the conviction of working with a disciplined group and progressing in a scientific manner toward an inevitably better future has provided powerful motivation for rank and file party members, and this has meant that no Communist leader is ever able to disregard ideological considerations. Were he to do so, he would undermine his own claim to support.

To insure unity in the movement, the ideology has had to be absolutistic. Where party members are supposed to be able to act under the certainty that they are conforming with the historical truth, pragmatic compromise with opponents becomes difficult. The world comes to be perceived as split into two implacably hostile camps, those who believe in and act in conformity with this truth, and those who do not. The ideology makes it possible to recognize the true Communist, and it encourages the conversion or destruction of everyone else.

Schisms, to be sure, have occurred repeatedly within the Marxist movement ever since the Bolsheviks and Mensheviks split before the First World War, and since the ideology offers no possibility for compromise among different versions of the truth, Communist schisms have been marked by a special bitterness. Schisms give rise to competing claims to the truth and these undermine a system that demands a unified ideology. Where the world is seen in blacks and white, any compromise becomes an admission of weakness. Debates turn into stark polemics. Communist leaders have often vilified their opponents at home with no more room for compromise than when they attack the capitalist villains abroad. No one is so reviled as a defeated Communist. He risks being accused of deviating from the pure "scientific" Marxist–Leninist position. At times this rigid ideology has served Communism well. At best, ideological dogmatism has supported a rigorously united and centrally directed movement of enormous strength. At other times, however, ideology has inhibited reforms and cornered the leadership into inflexible and unresponsive policies.

An observer can easily come to imagine that in the cutthroat rivalry so characteristic of high "Communist" politics, ideology has become nothing but a means by which one rationalizes his actions. Men may seem to act in their own best interests, and only then to justify their actions by reference to the ideology. But men who have spent their entire lives climbing through a system where ideology is constantly invoked can never quite free themselves of its influence. At the very least, they must always act as if they believe their ideological pronouncements, and perhaps there are times when the best actors are those who act from conviction.

The ideology, moreover, has given its adherents some valuable insights into the world they face and into the potentialities for changing it. By non-Communist standards, the ideology may not be "scientifically" correct but it is by no means simply wrong; it led, for instance, to an early appreciation of the strategic importance of the world's colonial areas. But the ideology has also led Communist leaders into some notable blunders. Lenin and his collaborators were willing to sign the sacrificial treaty of Brest-Litovsk which pulled Russia out of the First World War because they were convinced that Germany would shortly be overturned by a Communist revolution. After the Second World War, the Soviets counted too long and too hard on an American economic depression because Marxism persuaded them it was inevitable. Khrushchev placed too much faith on Communist ideology as a binder that would hold the Soviet Union and its allies together, even in the absence of Stalinist controls, at the same time that Communist leaders were exaggerating the likelihood of bitter divisions among the Western powers. Thus, the ideology has cut both ways: It has provided strength and brought dissention; it has provided astute insights and led to serious blunders.

LENIN

No realistic appraisal of power in the "Communist" world can fail to take account of Marxist ideology, but the teachings of Marx were certainly inadequate on the specifics of state organization. It was left to Lenin to fill in many of the details. On the specific question of succession to top office, Lenin was not a great deal more explicit than Marx had been, but the political system that Lenin constructed provided the context within which his successors, and later the successors of Stalin and of Khrushchev, would struggle for power; and much of the Leninist system came to be duplicated in Eastern Europe as well. It is necessary, therefore, to outline some aspects of the Soviet governmental system, a system for which Lenin, more than any other man, was responsible.

Lenin firmly believed in central control and in central decision making.

Fortified by an unquestioning faith in his own personal Marxist infallibility, Lenin visualized the party as a tightly disciplined body whose members would unswervingly follow him, their inspired leader. Indeed, no one who was unwilling to submit to such discipline would be admitted to the party. Thus, Lenin sought to create and to lead a tightly disciplined group of professional revolutionaries, and from the beginning, he made a distinction between the full-time party professionals and those other party members who worked in factories, in agriculture, or in the professions. Lenin, guided by Marxism, would lead the party professionals, and these people would lead the rest of the party. The party, as vanguard of the proletariat, would lead the workers, and the workers would lead the nation. Tight centralization was dictated in part by a realistic appraisal of the prospects for revolutionary activity that had to be conducted under the constraints imposed by Tsarist Russia, in part by Lenin's study of earlier revolutionary movements, and in part by Lenin's personal preferences. Centralization meant, in particular, that lower leaders would always be appointed from above rather than elected from below.

Centralization was by no means inherent in Marxist doctrine, but it was incorporated at an early date into the Communist movement and it has been perpetuated into all later "Communist" regimes. The principle came to be known and justified by the term "democratic centralism." The principle allowed open discussion until a decision was made, but once made, that decision would be binding upon all. The minority would have to conform actively to the majority and, most important, decisions made at the central point of the system would always be binding upon the wider circles. The assertion of democratic centralism can be seen as an open proclamation of a principle that has been covertly accepted in many other one-party states. In Mexico too, appointments are made from the center, and the rank and file tend to follow central decisions. But in the Soviet Union, the principle has been openly asserted to be desirable in a way that is unusual in other one-party regimes today. The principle became a cornerstone of political control, and it operated both at the time of Lenin's first seizure of power and later as the more permanent organs of the new Soviet government were established.

Lenin's opportunity for seizing power came during the turmoil of wartime Russia. By 1917, government control was faltering, and the troops proved unwilling to put down demonstrations by workers who opposed the war. In army units and in factories, representative bodies known as "soviets" sprang up, and Lenin led his Bolsheviks to mobilize the soviets. The first soviets tended to reflect the genuine desires of their constitutents, but their membership was politically inexperienced, and they proved to be far more amenable to manipulation than any parliament of experienced politicians would have been. The Bolsheviks were the only disciplined group operating within the soviets, and they alone had a consistent program. Lenin was able to capture the soviets and from this base he could then reach out for even broader support. He organized an army and undermined the national parliament by his tight control of the minority Communist representation. His opponents were disunited and such democratic elements as existed lacked firepower. Democrats were finally left with a choice between Lenin's Bolsheviks and the White Russian armies, and on the whole the Bolsheviks probably appeared to be the lesser evil.

Lenin proclaimed the superiority of the soviets over more traditional parliaments, and he justified his preference by lauding the soviets as the instruments of the proletariat while parliaments were derided as the instruments of the bourgeoisie. Lenin proclaimed the slogan "all power to the soviets," but as the soviets became subjected to the central control of the Bolshevik party, it became abundantly clear that the soviets had lost their independence. They come to constitute, instead, the next circle of control beyond the party. As he consolidated power, Lenin was forced to make economic concessions and tactical alliances, but he never compromised on the political doctrine of democratic centralism, for it was this that secured all strands of authority in the hands of the top party leaders.

The system that emerged from the Bolshevik victory was an extraordinarily complex one. It has been continuously tinkered with in detail, but from the beginning, it has consisted of a set of concentric circles of control, each outer circle being subjected to the control of the circles within. The outer circle is formed of the soviets, now given authority by the constitution. The supreme soviet at the top replaces the older parliament, and lesser soviets exist in every city, district, and constituent republic of the union. Membership in the soviets is gained in elections that are attended by vigorous campaigning and widespread discussion. These elections are expected to rally the soviet people, demonstrate their unity, and to involve them in the system.

The soviets, however, have never become genuinely democratic or representative institutions, for they are closely controlled by the Communist Party. Nominations to the soviets are in party hands, and since there is usually no choice of candidates, the voter has no alternatives other than acceptance and rejection. Rejection requires the voter to cross out the nominee's name, and since this must be done in public, secrecy, allowed in principle by the constitution, is entirely subverted. Such elections mean that, in fact, if not quite in principle, the party appoints the members of the soviets.

The soviets continue, as in Lenin's day, to be rather amateur bodies. They meet for only a few days each year, and they do not take the primary responsibility even for the legislation with which they are charged. Distinguished or reliable citizens and workers are nominated to take a few days off from their regular jobs. They attend the soviets as a reward for their past services, not for the purpose of exercising legislative initiative. Meetings of the Supreme Soviet, the highest governmental body of all, have become massive conventions of loyal appointees who dutifully ratify decrees of the smaller and more permanent governing groups. About three quarters of the members of the Supreme Soviet are party members, and never in the history of the Soviet Union have these legislative bodies had any tendency to escape close party control. The committee work of the Supreme Soviet does provide a final scrutiny for a good deal of legislation, and elections provide an opportunity for mass involvement. The soviets legitimize the decisions of the party, but they never act independently.

The party amounts very nearly to a parallel government, for it also has organs in every republic, district, and locality. Membership in the party is supposed to be limited to those willing to take active leadership, and its members are expected to lead the nonparty members of their unions, their cooperatives, their schools, and their soviets. Party members should persuade the others to move closer to the ideas of the party. This privileged role in leadership is explicitly recognized in the Soviet constitution, and of course no other party is allowed to compete with it. Since the party is the custodian of the "true" and "scientific" doctrine of Marxism and Leninism, and the only body capable of interpreting and applying this doctrine to modern conditions, the monopoly of the party is seen as serving the ends of justice.

In principle, the members of each local party unit elect delegates to the City or District Conferences. These in turn elect delegates to Provincial and Regional Conferences and finally these elect delegates to the national Congress of the Communist Party of the Soviet Union. The national Party Congresses take place every few years, and they have gradually grown larger until today they have become the occasion for several thousand stalwart party members to gather for a few days in Moscow. Like the Supreme Soviet, the Party Congress is far too large and meets too briefly and infrequently to take continual direction over party affairs, and so it elects a smaller Central Committee to maintain the continuity of party policy between congresses. Like most party organs, the Central Committee has shown a pronounced tendency to expand over the years, for it has proven easier to add new members than to drop old ones. Lenin's Central Committee had 27 members and he proposed expanding it to 50 or 100; but by the time of the 22nd Party Congress in 1961, the Central Committee had grown to 300 members, 175 of whom were designated as "full members," the other 125 as "alternate members." The Central Committee meets for a few days two to four times a year but like its parent, the Party Congress, it has become too large and meets too intermittently to take continuous responsibility. It too, delegates major responsibilities to its leading organs, the Presidium and the Party Secretariat.

On paper, then, party democracy, though indirect, proceeds in several stages from the lowest level to the highest, but the principle of democratic centralism has always allowed the higher organs to guide, lead, and direct those below them. The lower bodies have been obliged to accept the advice of those above them, including even recommendations about whom to elect as delegates. The Presidium, therefore, has always been able to control the membership of the Central Committee by submitting nominees to the Party Congress. These bodies in turn could control who would be sent as delegates to the Party Congress. Local initiative over whom to send as representative to the City or District Party Conferences has been entirely out of the question. Party members have simply been expected to ratify the choice of the higher party organs.

Two parallel hierarchies exist, that of the government (the soviets) and that of the party. At every level the party sets the policies and is expected to control the government, and the higher bodies control those below. Curiously, however, at the very top there is ambiguity. Neither in the constitution nor in practice has a single supreme office been unambiguously dominant. Several offices and several councils have shared topmost responsibility.

One of these is the Council of Ministers of the Supreme Soviet, known in Lenin's day as the Council of People's Commissars. In theory, this is the top organ of the government, the closest parallel to a western cabinet. Its members lead the various ministries and they take charge of the day-to-day administration of the many branches of government. The Council of Ministers holds governmental authority between sessions of the Supreme Soviet, but since its membership is chosen by the party rather than by any real initiative of the Supreme Soviet, the Council of Ministers is, in practice, responsible to the party rather than to either the Supreme Soviet or to the general electorate. The Council of Ministers is in turn guided by an inner council that consists of the prime minister and a few of his chief deputies.

The second leading organ is the Party Presidium (known during some periods as the Politburo). Though fluctuating in size, the Presidium has tended in recent years to include about a dozen full members, and it acts as something of a policy-making committee for the party and in turn for the government. Generally including the party's leading figures, the Presidium has tended to be at the focus of major soviet power struggles, but even within the party, the power of the Presidium is in some degree balanced by a third organ of control, the Party Secretariat. The Secretariat is directed by its first secretary (sometimes known as the general secretary), and it is responsible for the day-to-day administration of the vast party bureaucracy. Both Stalin and Khrushchev used the post of first secretary, with its control over appointments and its vast network of influence, information, and patronage, as the base from which they manuvered to the dominant position of leadership.

This high potential of the first secretary's office has emerged only from the struggles among the top leaders, however, for the post is nowhere even mentioned in the Soviet constitution, and even in the party rules, it is not designated as supreme. Moreover, the division of responsibilities among the Council of Ministers, the Presidium, and the Secretariat has never been as clear as a neat organizational chart might seem to imply. There has always been a good deal of overlapping membership on these three bodies, some men sitting on two or even all three of them simultaneously. Simply by changing hats, the same men are able to make policy, guide the administration, and determine the destinies of both party and government. As long as everyone knows who is in charge, it makes relatively little difference which office or offices he fills. If he has the power to appoint whom he pleases to the other offices, he will be supreme, whichever office he chooses to take for himself. Since the supremacy of the office of first secretary has not gone unchallenged, the struggle for leadership in the soviet system involves not simply the struggle for a particular office, but a struggle among offices as well.

In Stalin's day, centralization was carried to its logical conclusion. Stalin, sitting at the apex of the party and the government, could designate the membership of all the highest bodies in the land. The Party Presidium, the Secretariat, and the Council of Ministers of the Supreme Soviet were filled by those whom Stalin designated and, from there, the principle of democratic centralism insured that control would spread through the wider and wider organs of both party and state. But the principle of democratic centralism has to break down at one crucial point, for it can provide no mechanism for choosing the highest leader. A Lenin or a Stalin who is unambiguously acknowledged as supreme can fill all secondary and lesser posts, but there is no one who can designate the man on top. How is this man to be chosen? This is the riddle of succession, and to answer it we must look at the specific historical cases.

STALIN

Lenin's own power was always more personal than institutional, for it derived from the loyalty of his lieutenants rather than from any formal office. He held the office of Chairman of the Council of People's Commissars, (the earlier name for the Council of Ministers), and his chief aides were included in the seven-man Party Politiburo. Besides Lenin, these seven included: Trotsky, who as War Commissar led the army and was second only to Lenin in brilliance and fame; Zinoviev, who commanded the Leningrad branch of the party and led its international wing, the Comintern; Kamenev, who had a strong base in the Moscow party machine; Rykov, who was Lenin's deputy chairman in the Council of Ministers; Tomsky who was head of the trade unions; and, finally, Stalin. Stalin was made general secretary of the party's Central Committee. This office would come to the strongest in the nation, but it was first conceived as largely a bookkeeping operation. His colleagues accepted Stalin in this post since he seemed to be an able and efficient administrator, and he was willing to do the routine paper work which more colorful leaders like Trotsky were happy to avoid. Stalin was not as well known to the public as several of his Politburo colleagues, but his office gave him a strategic bureaucratic niche, and he slowly, but doggedly, built up his power by skillful appointments of his own loyal followers. He wielded patronage with skill, and created a master filing system that included all party members. So long as Lenin ruled, however, neither Stalin nor his office could have been confidently predicted as destined for dominance.

Lenin was crippled by a stroke in May, 1922, less than 5 years after the October Revolution and only 2 years after the end of the civil war. He lived until March, 1924, and he tried to participate in the leadership but he was never again able to assume full command. Stalin used the intervening period to consolidate his direction of the party bureaucracy.

Lenin had constructed an elaborate party and governmental machine, but he failed to provide any clear provision by which his own successor should be designated, and it may be that he intended his power to be wielded collectively by his followers. The collegial nature of the Presidium would suggest that this may have been his intention, but if so, he underestimated the difficulties such a system would encounter in a time when there was desperate need for a single focus of final decision making. Had Lenin been unambiguous in his preference, his choice might have been honored by enough leaders to make it effective. Lenin might have been able to appoint his own successor had he wanted to. Between the time of his first stroke and his death, however, he never abandoned the hope of recovery or the hope of resuming command, and he hesitated to make any choice completely clear, lest his own authority be undermined. He did make some suggestions, and as is now well known, he cautioned his colleagues against Stalin. Since his remarks were not made fully public, Stalin was able to ignore them, and the succession could be resolved only by maneuver and intrigue.

Lenin's best known surviver was certainly Trotsky, but Trotsky's very prominence led him to be distrusted by others. The Soviet leaders were fond of looking to the French Revolution for parallels with their own revolution and they feared the emergence of a Russian Bonaparte. As war commissar and as a popular leader, Trotsky was the most likely candidate for such a role, but he was himself unwilling to assume a Bonaparte-like stance, and others certainly did not encourage him. To prevent Trotsky from making any moves toward becoming dominant, Stalin, Zinoviev, and Kamenev, probably the three next most powerful figures, formed an alliance against him and, like all subsequent disputes within the top Soviet leadership, the dispute between this *Troika* and Trotsky had both ideological and personal sides. Trotsky stood for more ideological vigor and for a more forceful pursuit of revolutionary goals, but he was defeated by the superior political in-fighting of his opponents. Trotsky disdained petty bureaucratic maneuver and preferred instead to make a vigorous frontal attack upon all his enemies at once. Stalin, the competent though less flamboyant administrator, appealed implicitly to the yearnings of many of the rank and file party members for some stability and calm, and for an end to the more radical program of international revolution. Step by step, Trotsky was isolated and eased out of power.

For some time, the Politburo remained stable in composition except that Lenin's six survivers co-opted Bukharin to replace Lenin. The Troika of Stalin, Zinoviev, and Kamenev became dominant, however. The Central Committee grew from 27 to 53 members between 1922 and 1926 and its independence was correspondingly reduced. The Secretariat, dominated by Stalin, came more and more to exercise the real power.

Once Trotsky's decline was assured, a falling out between Stalin on the one hand, and Zinoviev and Kamanev on the other was inevitable, and relations between them deteriorated in 1925. This, even more than the dispute with Trotsky, was a personal rivalry, but it also took on ideological overtones. Stalin's opponents argued for more forceful industrialization at home and more forceful support for revolution abroad. Stalin posed as the champion of "socialism in one country" and of the more relaxed program of the New Economic Policy, but the key factor in Stalin's victory over Zinoviev and Kamenev was his control of the central apparatus of the Communist Party. Stalin placed so many of his own loyal followers into strategic positions that his rivals were isolated. Stalin packed the Central Committee, and by 1927 he was able to remove his opponents from the Politburo.

Stalin had disposed of what is remembered as his "left opposition," but Bukharin, Tomski, and Rykov remained on the Politburo and they became known as the "right opposition." Their major strength was in the government apparatus rather than the party, and they might have found support among the less doctrinaire bureaucrats, but the government did not have the prestige and leading position of the party. Bukharin, Tomski, and Rykov tried, too late, to unite with the remnants of the left opposition, but these opposite wings of the party had nothing in common except their opposition to Stalin, and both distrusted each other more than they distrusted him. The rightists now advocated the more lenient economic policies which Stalin had earlier seemed to support; but by the end of the 1920s, with the left out of the way, Stalin usurped some aspects of its earlier position, and he embarked on a forceful policy of collectivization.

In the end, Stalin had relatively little difficulty disposing of his right opposition, for they had failed to build a strong faction within the party. By 1930, Stalin controlled the Central Committee and its Secretariat, and he was able to form a new Politburo in which he was the only survivor from Lenin's time. Stalin was now the undisputed leader, and until the end of his reign, he would crush any one who came at all close to a position of rivalry. By the end of the decade, the purges were in full swing. To political maneuver, Stalin added police terror as a technique of control. He was completely unassailable.

The elements of a thousand succession struggles in a hundred nations and empires were reproduced in Stalin's climb to complete power: the expression of will by the previous ruler; rivalry among the former chief lieutenants; intertwining of personal rivalry with ideological or policy arguments; appeal, even if covert, to popular yearnings; the skillful use of patronage. But an orderly set of rules was certainly lacking. Nothing in Marxist doctrine defined the terms of the struggle, and Lenin added only a few largely ignored suggestions about particular people. Stalin did little to improve the method of selection, and the doctrine of democratic centralism, from which Stalin never deviated, made an orderly system almost impossible. As a result, the next succession crisis showed a number of parallels to the one in which Stalin triumphed.

KHRUSHCHEV

Many men rose and fell during Stalin's reign, but none was ever allowed to gain an unambiguous second place. Stalin kept his subordinates in too close a balance to let any one challenge him, as someone in clear second place might have done. One of Stalin's leading deputies, Zhdanov, died in 1948, and Malenkov, who was sent by Stalin to conduct a purge of Zhdanov's followers, became the only figure, other than Stalin himself, to have posts in all three top councils of the regime. Stalin then brought in Khrushchev to balance Malenkov on both the Politburo and the Secretariat, and Khrushchev was also given the leadership of the Moscow provincial party organization. He was in a position to block any effort Malenkov might have made to reach for more power than Stalin cared to confer. No one knew better than Stalin the importance of keeping his subordinates in rivalry.

Shortly before his death in 1953, Stalin seemed to be moving toward a renewed purge. The 10-member Politburo was expanded to a 25-member Presidium, presumably to dilute the influence of the older members and to insure Stalin's own control. The Secretariat was also expanded, and then the doctors' "plot" was unveiled. This was to provide an excuse for ridding the party and government of those whom Stalin felt he no longer needed, but he died before the purge could be carried out, and it was then immediately abandoned. The Presidium was again reduced in number as the older leadership drew together and attempted to give their succession arrangements the greatest possible appearance of legitimacy. In some manner well obscured from public view, the successors agreed generally that each would continue his former duties. Malenkov became the head of government and very briefly also assumed first position in the Secretariat, since during the final period of Stalin's rule he had held second place in both. Molotov took charge of foreign affairs. Beria took the police. These three men seemed to be forming a troika in which Khrushchev was not included, but Khrushchev followed Malenkov in the Secretariat. He now assumed second place where he had been third under Stalin.

In these early days after Stalin's death, the men in power had to put on the best possible appearance of unity, but the rivalry among them could not long be contained. Almost immediately, Malenkov seems to have overreached himself, and he must have aroused the suspicions of his colleagues. Within a few days of Stalin's death, he withdrew from his position in the Secretariat, and Khrushchev was allowed to take charge of this leading party organ. At this point, the mutual suspicions of the leaders must have made them all unwilling to let any single person monopolize the levers of power. They preferred to see the two top positions, that of the government and that of the party, held by separate men. In his last years, Stalin had let the party organization suffer by comparison with the government, and it may be that Malenkov calculated that as prime minister he would be in a stronger position than he would as first secretary of the party. If so, he calculated incorrectly, but in the short run, he still seemed to have the leading position.

The next rearrangement came in July 1953, 4 months after Stalin's death, when Beria was abruptly removed from office. Beria seems to have been conducting his own power play, using the police system which he controlled and also appealing for support from the minorities and nationalities. All the other leaders had much to fear from the man who controlled the secret police, and they united to destroy him. The precipitating factor in his fall was the outbreak of riots in East Germany which the security police had failed to prevent, but at the same time, the leaders were coming to realize that many economic enterprises that the police had been running with the aid of political prisoners were far from efficient. Manpower was now in short supply and it could be utilized more effectively outside of forced labor camps than inside them. Most important, perhaps, the very fact that Beria had led the hated secret police made him a perfect scapegoat. The remaining leaders could blame him for all past difficulties. They united long enough to dismiss Beria and they curtailed the police. Henceforth, the police ceased to be a direct threat to those at the top of the hierarchy. Struggles had to be conducted by other means than police terror.

The remaining leaders assumed varying strategies. Malenkov tried to dominate the Presidium and he used his office of Chairman of the Council of Ministers (Premier) as a forum from which he could address the entire nation as the top man in the government. He appealed for collective leadership and thereby tried to limit the power of the Party Secretariat where Khrushchev was in command. Economically, Malenkov advocated the "New Course" in which heavy industry was to be down-graded, and a new importance was placed upon consumer goods. Attempts were made to rationalize the top-heavy and often bungling methods of state planning, and Malenkov posed as the most liberal member of the leadership. Some elements of the party still nursed a grudge against Malenkov for his part in conducting the Leningrad purge against the supporters of Zhdanov a few years earlier, but he played for the support of the economic bureaucracy and his policies implied a diminished role for the party.

Khrushchev, as first party secretary, had a smaller but, as it turned out, more strategic power base. During Stalin's last years the party had suffered to some extent, but the enormous party bureaucracy remained ready to respond to the man who would champion its cause. The party apparatus included thousands of full-time professional members who had come to regard themselves, in good Leninist fashion, as the vanguard of the proletariat and as the leaders of the revolution. By 1953, however, this bureaucracy was no longer genuinely revolutionary, but had built up a solid vested interested in the existing system. Malenkov's emphasis upon the governmental hierarchy, his attempts at economic rationalization, and even his emphasis on light industry threatened the party's position. Khrushchev made himself champion of the party apparatus. From his office of first secretary, he was able, like Stalin before him, to move his own supporters into strong positions and he built up the role of the Secretariat and of its parent body, the Central Committee. Khrushchev became master of the party machine and he blocked Malenkov's attempts to centralize economic administration within the government.

Khrushchev also seized and used with great success an issue which must have looked unpromising to his competitors. Agriculture had always been slighted in soviet economic planning, but Khrushchev loudly proclaimed its importance. Nobody could openly attack the desirability of improving agriculture, and Khrushchev launched into his scheme for opening the virgin lands. Here, Khrushchev had a considerable advantage over his colleagues. He really knew a good deal about agriculture and he could speak with an authority his rivals lacked. He could argue for his plans with impressive detail. Several years later, it became apparent that most of his vast schemes were failing, but by then Khrushchev had consolidated his leading position. Agricultural failure could then no longer threaten him.

Khrushchev also showed skill in his choice of other issues. He conciliated the advocates of heavy industry (the "steel eaters" as he would later call them) who felt threatened by Malenkov's support for consumer industries. To the steel eaters, to their allies in the army, and to the old line Stalinists like Molotov, Kaganovich, and Voroshilov, all of whom were still members of the Presidium, Khrushchev looked like a lesser threat than the economically innovating Malenkov. Malenkov became increasingly isolated from his colleagues until, in February, 1955, he was forced to resign the premiership. Khrushchev now looked like the strongest single member of the Presidium, but he did not yet dare assume the post of premier. Bulganin was installed as an amiable and harmless neutral.

Malenkov was no sooner demoted than Khrushchev began to have trouble with his erstwhile Stalinist allies. Khrushchev now, in effect, appealed over the heads of his fellow Presidium members by launching his destalinization campaign. In his battle against Malenkov, he had played the role of a Stalinist, but he now shifted ground and by February, 1956, when the 20th Party Congress met, Khrushchev was ready to launch his unprecedented attack upon Stalin. His secret speech at that Congress would have far-reaching consequences in shaking up the entire international Communist movement, but initially it must be seen as an audacious play for support among the broader ranges of the party and the nation. Khrushchev now identified himself dramatically with those who desired a break with the past. He reassured the party that he was not another Stalin, and he managed by clever historical selectivity to subtly implicate his Presidium rivals in the errors of Stalin. Clearly, Khrushchev and such old line Stalinists as Molotov and Kaganovich were heading for a crisis.

It came in June, 1957, when a majority of the Presidium abruptly demanded Khrushchev's resignation. Only two Presidium member gave him support: Mikoyan who had been encouraging destalinization; and Kirichenko who was always a close ally. Even such relatively neutral men as Bulganin and Shepilov seem to have calculated that Khrushchev was finished and that their best interests would be with the Stalinists.

Khrushchev, however, proceeded to do an absolutely unheard of thing. He appealed over the heads of his fellow Presidium members to the larger Central Committee. He argued that since the Central Committee had elected him first secretary, the Presidium had no power to remove him. This was, in fact, the letter of the law, but in the past the rule of democratic centralism had always prevailed, and the Central Committee had always ratified the decisions of the Presidium. Now, however, the Presidium was divided and this presented the Central Committee with a choice. As in so many other political systems, a struggle at the top was opening the soviet system to a wider participation.

Khrushchev had an ally in Marshal Zhukov. Army planes were sent to round up friendly members of the Central Committee, and strategic troop maneuvers near Moscow showed where army preferences lay. The generals had ample grievances against Stalin and many were happy to support a candidate who promised an end to Stalinist controls. At this point, it seems, a few of Khrushchev's opponents on the Presidium began to waver.

Khrushchev won his gamble. His duties as first party secretary had allowed him to secure a strong following in the Central Committee. This now gave him sufficient support so that instead of being evicted himself, he forced out his enemies. Malenkov, Molotov, and Kaganovitch left both the Presidium and the Central Committee, and their ally Shepilov left the Secretariat. Others were demoted. Khrushchev would henceforth call these men the "anti-party" group. In reward for his help, Marshal Zhukov was made a member of the Presidium, the first time in soviet history that a professional military man reached the top circle of power.

Khrushchev had scrambled into undisputed first place and to consolidate his triumph, he had only to rid himself of those who had been too reluctant in their support and of those who had shown too much power as they gave their support. Khrushchev could hardly afford to let the army grow too strong, and in November, 1957, Marshal Zhukov was stripped of his offices. In March, 1958, Bulganin, who had waivered in his support of Khrushchev, was removed as prime minister, and Khrushchev now assumed this office, adding it to his earlier post of first secretary. The two main offices were finally reunited in the same man. Khrushchev now belonged to all three of the most powerful groups, the Council of Ministers, the Secretariat, and the Presidium. All other leaders paid him their allegiance, and Khrushchev's cult of personality began to blossom.

To all outward appearances, Khrushchev seemed to have repeated Stalin's earlier triumph, and his techniques had not been so different. He had attended to the details of party administration. He effectively appealed to party interests, and he exploited the divisions among his opponents. He had even, like Stalin, successfully usurped some of the policies of his defeated rivals. Just as Stalin came to occupy a good deal of the ideological ground formerly occupied by his defeated "left opposition," so Khrushchev came to champion the light industry and economic reform that Malenkov had once advocated. But despite outward appearances. Khrushchev never came close to the uncontested supremacy of Stalin. Khrushchev was never able to dispose of his rivals with Stalin's efficiency, and he always had to maneuver with the greatest care. Within a very few years of his triumph over the anti-party faction, other members of the ruling group were resisting one or another of his policies. Khrushchev stayed in office until October, 1964, but in retrospect, one can see that his power was being checked at least as early as 1960. Khrushchev could never exert police terror against his close associates, he never succeeded in filling the majority of top positions with obedient sycophants, and he never rid himself entirely of those with whom he disagreed or of those who threatened him.

THE FALL OF KHRUSHCHEV

Several factors restrained Khrushchev from building an autocracy like Stalin's.[2] We should not discount the possibility that Khrushchev saw his own role as that of a liberalizer. Perhaps he wanted to be remembered in history as a man who ended tyranny. Whatever his personal motives, however, his own penchant for dramatic crash programs, for rushing off full tilt in support of one favorite scheme after another, must have made his more stolid associates jittery. The most important single restraint upon Khrushchev, however, was probably the memory of Stalin held by his associates. Everyone around Khrushchev would have been endangered by the emergence of another Stalin and everyone had the best of motives to resist that. Here, as in so many other political systems, was a point at which the characteristics of one reign imposed conditions that made the next reign different. The very nature of Stalin's rule made it impossible for his successor to duplicate it. Those around Khrushchev had good reason to restrain him from pushing his destalinization program too far.

Khrushchev was never able to control the Presidium in the way that Stalin once had. New appointments had something of an appearance of a compromise between factions that did not entirely trust each other. Khrushchev never ceased his restless innovation, but he would have had to dispose of his rivals in high places before having anything like the power that Stalin had once had.

---

[2]The details of political maneuver in the final Khrushchev years and in the early post-Khrushchev period are given most fully by Michel Tatu, *Power in the Kremlin* (New York: The Viking Press, 1969).

His technique, once again, was an appeal to a broader group. This appeal came most dramatically at the 22nd Congress of the Communist Party of the Soviet Union when he launched the most bitter attack yet upon the men of the anti-party group. Since these men had now been safely out of office for 4 years, the attack can hardly have been aimed primarily at them. It was certainly intended as an indirect attack against some of his remaining rivals who were still in power and who were still checking his moves. As on earlier occasions, Khrushchev was using the superficially democratic, though in reality quite demagogic, technique of appealing to a wider group than that which had traditionally made decisions. The massive Party Congress, assembled for only a few brief days, might be led by a dramatic appeal and so be used to apply pressure on higher officials. It could neither make a sober appraisal of the situation nor reach a democratic decision about policy. Nevertheless, here in the Soviet Union in the 1960s the same forces were at work that so often before had served to broaden the range of political initiative. Divisions within the ruling circle have always tempted some men to appeal to broader constituencies. These broader constituencies, such as the Party Congress, have often supported a dominant figure, such as Khrushchev, as their champion. Together, they might hope to cut down the oligarchical middle, which here consisted of top leaders, but has elsewhere been composed of aristocrats, wealthy burghers, or oligarchs.

Khrushchev had a symbolic victory when the congress agreed to remove Stalin's body from the Lenin mausoleum, but otherwise his attacks served only to consolidate his Presidium opposition. They could hardly agree among themselves on all issues, but they could at least agree not to let Khrushchev use destalinization as the banner under which to institute a new purge of his own. They let Khrushchev have his symbolic but empty victory at the mausoleum, but they dragged their feet on all the real issues. They could unite in refusing to allow another Stalin to emerge.

Membership in the Presidium remained stable. It was in every member's interest to prevent a shake-up of any sort. Any reorganization would have been risky and so each member was willing to leave everyone else in his place, so long as his own position was secure. It became increasingly difficult to pry a man loose once he had gained a seat in the Presidium. Security of office allowed a slightly more open expression of differences, and divisions in top circles gave room for maneuver to all the wide-ranging circles of the bureaucracy. Each divergent interest might now hope to find its own champions safely ensconced on the Presidium.

Khrushchev never ceased a restless experimentation. He reorganized the bureaucracy; he moved people about. No doubt he hoped to move his own loyal men into strong positions, but at the same time he could not help threatening the security of others. On some issues he was forced to backtrack. He had allowed a golden interlude for writers and the intellectual avant-garde, for he foresaw that publications such as Solzhenitsyn's *A Day in the Life of Ivan Denisovitch* and Yevtushenko's *Stalin's Heirs* could serve as potent weapons against his enemies, but when the writings of the intellectuals began to move beyond simple anti-Stalinism to a more general attack upon the entire political system, Khrushchev had no choice but to clamp down upon the writers. He also suffered from the outcome of the Cuban missile crisis, for which he would surely have claimed personal credit had the venture been successful.

At one period Frol Kozlov became a challenger to Khrushchev's position. Koslov suffered a severe heart attack which temporarily set the opposition back, but Khrushchev continued to face opposition from many sides. The harvest of 1963 was disastrous, he could not control the Presidium, and the Chinese were berating him. He had antagonized many branches of the administration by his radical and sometimes chaotic attempts at reorganization. By his penchant for constant meddling in all areas of government and for dispensing advice to all sides, he aroused enmity among the diplomats, the planners, the agronomists, the steel eaters, and the military.

Still, a coup would be dangerous and it might not have been attempted so soon, had Khrushchev not threatened yet another organizational upheaval. He seems to have proposed to give his Presidium colleagues detailed administrative responsibility for supervision of agriculture, and to have desired still another major bureaucratic reshuffle. Khrushchev's colleagues again felt threatened, and a plot took final form on the weekend of October 10th and 11th, 1964, though the leaders must have had preliminary discussions earlier. Khrushchev was away from Moscow at the Black Sea and Mikoyan joined him there, probably to keep him off guard. Suslov may have been the main plotter, but Brezhnev, who was second in the party apparatus, and Kosygin, who was second in the government hierarchy, were the main formal beneficiaries of the reshuffle, and they must have worked closely with Suslov in making the arrangements. By Monday there was rapid mobilization. The Central Committee of the party was rather selectively summoned to Moscow. Members known to be critical of Khrushchev were carefully tracked down while some of his more vigorous supporters who happened to be out of town or abroad were overlooked. As late as Tuesday morning, Khrushchev still had no foreboding of his imminent downfall, but he was then called back to Moscow to face a Presidium united in opposition. Brezhnev had already been selected as the heir to the position of first secretary, and Kosygin was ready to direct the government and economic apparatus. If Khrushchev still had any allies, they moved quickly to disassociate themselves from him and to join the side they could see would win. Indeed, Podgorny, who had always been one of Khrushchev's most reliable supporters, emerged from the coup with dramatically enhanced prestige. Perhaps he was being rewarded for siding with the plotters, but since he stood to inherit the loyalty of Khrushchev's closest followers, it was in the interest of the others to consolidate this bloc on their side by embracing its new leader. Otherwise they might have been thrown into immediate opposition.

This was the second time that Khrushchev had faced a Presidium intent on getting rid of him. The previous time, he had upset the plans of the anti-party group by appealing to the Central Committee, and no doubt he would have liked to repeat his performance now, but this time he was out-maneuvered. The plotters had already called the Central Committee and had assured themselves of its support. On Wednesday morning, the Central Committee ratified the action of the Presidium majority, and the Khrushchev era came to an end. Ironically, Khrushchev's own earlier appeal to the Central Committee had helped to build its stature to the point where it could now assist in his efficient dismissal.

Unlike the typical Latin American coup, the dismissal of Khrushchev was not directed by military men, but it still deserves to be called a coup, for it amounted to a conspiracy of high officials against the top man. As in the case of many other successful coups, moreover, the new leadership had no well-defined or vigorous policy of its own to pursue. The coup had been taken to defend offices, rather than to push a particular plan. The leaders did want to call a halt to radical destalinization, but they never threatened to launch any corresponding dekhrushchevization. All the survivors were, to some extent, Khrushchev's men, just as they were all Stalin's men, and the less the past was dredged up, the safer all would feel. Any renewed attack upon Stalin or any vigorous attack upon Khrushchev could only have been a sign of a power play among the surviving leaders in which the real target would remain hidden under the camouflage of an attack upon an old leader.

COLLECTIVE LEADERSHIP

Like any Latin American junta, the new leaders were united by their need to justify and legitimize their action and to consolidate their own position. They moved quickly to gain broad support among the masses who had not been consulted earlier, by declaring an extra New Year's holiday, by distributing flour, by making concessions to the peasants in agricultural policy, and by edging cautiously toward an international detente. However, no more than any junta, could they please everyone for long, and soon all the old policy dilemmas rose again. The new leaders were no more united than the old and no more able to resolve the issues that faced them.

In fact, they were even less able to resolve them now, for they lacked the leadership that Khrushchev had once provided.

Khrushchev's removal altered the conditions of rivalry and new alliances were suddenly possible. Resolution of disputes was slow, however, for each leader was inclined to grant security to his rivals in return for his own security. Membership in the Presidium was extremely stable. The Secretariat underwent more changes, but the Presidium quickly asserted its own primacy, though it assumed an anonymous collective style and hid internal differences behind a veil of secrecy. Kosygin seems to have had little ambition to compete with Brezhnev for political leadership, but he had advocated economic reforms and was given a relatively free hand to direct the economy without party interference. Brezhnev had the top party office, but he was kept from complete dominance by Podgorny who was just behind him and who could count upon the support of many of Khrushchev's more loyal followers. Rivalry between the two was inevitable, but it took Brezhnev 9 months to get Podgorny moved from the Secretariat into the ceremonial office of head of state, and even then, Podgorny remained on the Presidium. Since Brezhnev himself had already recovered from a similar term as head of state, Podgorny could not be regarded as decisively eliminated. Suslov continued his preference for operating cautiously behind the scenes. He seems to have been close to Brezhnev, but probably acted to stabilize and regularize procedures. Other leaders maneuvered just behind these four.

Soon the flaws of collective leadership began to appear. The old issues did not go away, and it became more difficult to settle them decisively. There was ample scope for differences of opinion among the top leaders: the line to take toward China; the degree of detente desirable with the West; the priorities for agriculture, heavy industry, and light industry; the relation of the party to the state; the degree of liberalization to be allowed in the arts. Every issue came to be subject to haggling, and the divided leadership became responsive to lobbying by interest groups. The army and the steel eaters pushed for more vigorous support. The economic reformers and managers argued for more managerial responsibility and less party interference. The vast party apparatus had grown into a conservative and aging bureaucracy with deep vested interests, and it dragged its feet on economic rationalization. The party resisted any liberalization in the arts, but in the absence of a single decisive voice at the top, liberal writers dared to speak up, and attempts to supress them were no more consistent than were other policies.

The weakness of the collective leadership was shown in the slow and incomplete moves toward economic rationalization that the Soviet Union so desperately needed, and it was displayed dramatically both in the June War of 1967 and in the Czechoslovakian crisis of 1968. Moscow drifted into the Middle Eastern crisis of 1967, arming the Arab nations, and encouraging their belligerence, but never realistically appraising the military situation, nor providing restraints that would keep the Arabs from acting rashly and letting the situation explode. In the end, Kremlin prestige suffered almost as much from the June War as it had in the Cuban missile crisis. The next year, the Soviet reaction to developments in Czechoslovakia can only be described as vacillating and clumsy. Czechoslovakia was kept within the Soviet orbit, but its government turned out to be far less submissive than the Soviet leaders expected, and the Soviet invasion drove much of the international Communist movement into direct opposition to the Kremlin.

The years following the invasion of Czechoslovakia brought few dramatic changes in Soviet leadership. Brezhnev slowly consolidated his position, and to a very modest degree, he seemed to be duplicating the path taken both by Stalin and Khrushchev. Like them, Brezhnev was building power from his base as first party secretary. He could hardly think of removing his fellow Presidium members, however, and this meant that he had far less power than his predecessors had once had. He seems never to have contemplated the kind of dramatic gestures by which Khrushchev bypassed the Presidium, and he was certainly restrained by his colleagues from any temptation to use Stalinist techniques of police terror. If Brezhnev was top man, he stood only slightly above the others. A few feeble beginnings of a cult of personality appeared on Brezhnev's behalf, but his colleagues were ready to resist any tendency for him to outshine them by too much, and the cult of personality was countered by renewed insistence upon the virtues of collective leadership. Perhaps in reaction against Khrushchev's flamboyance, Brezhnev hoped to convey the image of conservative reliability. He was presented as a man unlikely to promote rash policies, even as a man who had few policies of any sort. Such an image was useful in its context but it was far less susceptible to building into a cult of personality than was Khrushchev's. By the early 1970s Brezhnev was clearly in first place, but reports of struggles in the Kremlin never stopped filtering out of Moscow. It was obvious that nobody had yet come close to building a position like that of Khrushchev, let alone that of Stalin.

Divided leadership seems to have interfered with Kremlin decisiveness, and perhaps only the reemergence of a single dominant individual can bring dynamism back to the government. In the years following Khrushchev's overthrow, however, the fear of renewed tyranny has made the leaders too suspicious of one another's ambitions to let anyone become dominant. We can see here the same dilemma between the need for leadership and the fear of tyranny that has faced so many other leaders of so many other political systems.

It is interesting to speculate on ways in which this dilemma might be overcome, and there are two rather obvious innovations that would seem to offer some appeal to the men in the Kremlin. One would be to clarify which office is dominant, and the other would be to introduce a fixed term for that office. If the post of first secretary of the party could at least be made dominant in principle and not simply by expediency, that would clarify the ground rules of the struggle and make it possible to work toward more orderly procedures. Beyond this, one would suppose that the leaders would have much to gain by introducing a fixed term of office. If, like the Mexican leaders, they would loudly and repeatedly proclaim that the man in office would step out after 4 or 6 or 8 years, they might be less reluctant to grant him temporary authority. One would even suppose that some men would be happy to accept honorable retirement after a fixed term.

Clarification of which office is dominant, and the establishment of a fixed term for that office might yield something rather similar to the Mexican political system. Every few years, a small group of men might then agree among themselves upon a leader for the next term. The others might step temporarily to one side to give freedom to their nominee. Of course, such a system would entail its own problems, the same problems as the Mexican system faces, but from the point of view of many men now in power, it would seem to represent an improvement over the present ill-defined practices. So far, however, no one has publicly suggested even these modest devices toward regularization. No way for a leader to retire gracefully has yet been evolved, and as long as it is difficult to get rid of the top leader, the Presidium members are likely to be unwilling to yield too much power to the first secretary, lest he grow powerful enough to dismiss them. The result is a Presidium where no man is dominant, a strange island of democracy in a sea of democratic centralism.

For Americans who tend to think of the Soviet Union as the ultimate autocracy, it is worth pointing out that if Brezhnev was, in 1973, the most powerful man in the Soviet Union, he still had fewer prerogatives than the American president or a West European prime minister. The president or prime minister can select his own cabinet, but the Soviet leader cannot even choose his immediate subordinates. He cannot resolve policy disputes. Worst of all, since he can never forget Khrushchev's fate, even the top Kremlin official must be constantly aware that his colleagues may, without warning, evict him from office. It is an ironic fate for the successor to Stalin.

PATTERNS OF SOVIET SUCCESSION

To some degree, Soviet experience suggests an oscillation between two quite different systems of political leadership—the autocratic rule of a single man, and the oligarchy that the Soviets call collective leadership.[3] The death or removal of each autocrat has brought a period of cautious maneuver when several men of approximately equal stature have competed. Only gradually has one man finally been able to emerge triumphant and impose a new period of autocracy. The interregna have each lasted for several years, and they have been characterized by greater stability in the top leadership than the periods of one-man rule. The consolidations of both Stalin and Khrushchev were marked by rapid promotions and demotions, and Stalin continued to move his lieutenants up and down as long as he lived. By contrast, the leadership remained quite stable in the years following the deaths of both Lenin and Stalin, and the leadership was notably stable after the coup that evicted Khrushchev. If past experience is any guide, we might conclude that the collective leadership of the post-Khrushchev period is fated once again to give way when one person emerges with decisive authority.

But the past is not destined inevitably to be repeated, and there are times when past experience offers such clear warnings that men are careful to prevent any repetition. From Baganda to China, the succession practices of hereditary monarchies changed over the generations because men learned from the errors of their predecessors and sought to avoid their mistakes. In the same way, the heirs of Stalin and the heirs of Khrushchev have worked to prevent the emergence of new autocrats. It is presumably for this reason that each consolidation of power in the Soviet Union has taken longer than the ones before. Within 4 years of Lenin's first stroke, Stalin had disposed of Trotsky and the remaining members of the "left opposition," and he was ready to complete his consolidation by crushing the "right opposition." Four years and three months after Stalin's death, Khrushchev evicted the anti-party group, having previously helped to destroy Beria and demote Malenkov, but even then he still had Zhukov and such reluctant supporters as Bulganin to deal with. Eight years after Khrushchev's dismissal, no one had yet destroyed anyone. It was proving far more difficult for a strong leader to emerge than had been the case in the past. We might imagine that future consolidations will proceed even more slowly.

But prediction of the Soviet future by extrapolation from past trends is as risky a business as prediction of the Bemba or Chinese dynastic future by reference to apparent dynastic cycles. The same uncertainty is inherent in both trends and cycles. We have every reason to conclude that succession practices are unlikely to be perpetuated unchanged across the decades, but just as several alternative and even contradictory cycles are always avail-

---

[3]The view that Soviet power tends to oscillate between autocratic and oligarchical phases, is expressed most forcefully by Myron Rush, *Political Succession in the USSR* (New York: Columbia University Press, 1965).

able when we try to interpret a string of events, so are several alternative and mutually contradictory trends. Different predictions result when we emphasize different trends, and there seems to be no way to decide which trend is dominant, except to wait and see. One who extrapolates from the trends since Khrushchev's ouster in 1964 might conclude that Brezhnev is destined to continue slowly but doggedly to make his way to dominance. If one extrapolates, instead, from all Soviet history, he might conclude that Brezhnev is likely to consolidate his rule more slowly and less completely than Khrushchev, just as Khrushchev's consolidation was slower and less complete than Stalin's. By this reckoning, the next man might be expected to consolidate his rule even more slowly than Brezhnev. But if one looks even further back into Russian history, he might conclude that periods of autocracy have come in cycles, and that Stalin's period can be seen as only the latest of several examples. Another autocratic cycle may be in store.

Placed side by side, these varied extrapolations allow us to predict almost anything we like, and the safest conclusion may be that predictions are quite impossible. The trends or cycles of Soviet and Russian history are like the dynastic cycles of hereditary monarchies. Both offer useful schemes by which we can interpret the sequence of past events. Neither can help us to predict the future. Nevertheless, if we limit ourselves to the Soviet period, we can at least see the techniques and strategies which rising leaders have used in the past and which seem to be promising for those aspiring to future power. Power has been sought in various steps.

1. Finding a Patron

The path to power in the Soviet system begins with a climb through the bureaucracy, usually through the bureaucracy of the party, less often through that of the government or the army. What an ambitious young man needs, above all else, is a patron, a man with influence in high places who can help his clients to rise. The history of Soviet politics is the history of maneuver among powerful men, each of whom strives to place his own clients in strategic positions. Of course, the more skillful the client and the more useful he is to his patron, the better will be his chance to move up.

2. Picking the Winner

In attaching himself to a patron, the young man wants a winner. Nothing but disaster is in store for the unfortunate client who becomes irrevocably associated with a losing patron. Of course, by keeping his channels of communication open, a client may be able to desert a faltering patron and transfer his allegiance to another and more successful man. With adroit footwork, he may avoid the fate of his fallen patron. Thus, the system encourages rapid consolidation behind apparent winners and constant attempts to jump upon successful bandwagons. Nothing illustrates this more clearly than the speed with which Khrushchev's support evaporated once his fate had been clearly sealed. Only a very few of his closest clients were even dismissed from office. The others nimbly shifted their allegiance to the surviving leaders. As a man rises in the system, he will want to make himself useful to one or, preferably, to several of his superiors and best of all to the top man. Only by satisfying those at the top can he hope to be invited to join them, and if he can be useful enough to the man at the very top, he may find himself advancing rapidly.

3. Mobilizing Clients

In pleasing his superiors and then competing with his rivals, a man needs supporters, people scattered throughout the government and the party apparatus who will assist him in pursuing his objectives. This is the other side of the patron–client relationship for just as a client needs his patron's pull, so the patron needs his client's push. The patron must do all he can to support his clients, so as to encourage their loyalty and mobilize their assistance on his behalf. Patron–client relationships may be concentrated within a single branch of the bureaucratic system so that one man may have his chief base of power in the party or in one of its branches while another has his base in the government or in a particular ministry, but alliances that reach across ministries, geographical areas, or even into the army can prove useful and occasionally they may be crucial.

Soviet leaders have shown the same mistrust of factions that was so characteristic of the imperial government in China. Lenin forbade factions as early as the 10th Party Congress in 1921 when he was trying to minimize arguments in high party circles and get the first major purge of dissidents under way. But the same pressures that caused factions to rise repeatedly in China have also made them a permanent feature of Soviet life. Every ambitious man needs friends, high and low, whom he can call upon for help and whom he must help in return. Webs of criss-crossing influence develop, which parallel the formal administration only in part.

4. Being in the Right Place at the Right Time

Good luck is needed at every turn, but perhaps never more critically than at the death or departure of a top leader. When a Stalin or a Khrushchev goes, the survivors must dig into their positions and consolidate their inheritance. At first, each man tends to take command of the administrative branch where he had been working before. A man may be second in command of the Party Secretariat only on sufferance of the first secretary. It is good luck to be there when the first secretary dies and good sense to hang on tight to one's winnings.

5. Dividing Opponents

If one has reached the top ranks but desires to strike out for the pinnacle, it is essential to exploit the divisions among one's rivals and to build successive winning coalitions against erstwhile equals. Stalin and Khrushchev played this game with consummate skill. Both men sided with some of their colleagues to dispose of others and both brought their own men in to fill the resulting vacancies. In all his purges, Stalin used some of his subordinates to dispose of others. This was the Stalinist version of the general principle that the top man must always keep his subordinates in rivalry so that they will check one another's power. Khrushchev's decline began as soon as he could no longer exploit the internal divisions among his lieutenants and no longer use them to destroy one another. Fifty years of Soviet history finally taught the leaders how dangerous it could be to support a dominant figure in a purge of one's associates. The usual fate of those who help with a purge is to become the victims of the next purge. The men in Moscow seem to know this now, and it has become more difficult than it once was to exploit the divisions among one's rivals or subordinates.

6. Policy and Ideology

Personal rivalries become inextricably intertwined with questions of policy, and in the Soviet system, policy must always be justified by invoking ideology. Thus, leaders constantly strive to demonstrate the sound ideological foundation of their position and to show up the ideological weakness of their opponents. Ideology justifies Communism as a world movement, it allows men to label their programs as "scientific," and it holds out the hope that one is on the side of the inevitable trends of history. As such, ideology can never be ignored. In working one's way up, it is helpful to show skill in the dialectic and once on top, it is desirable to get a reputation for being able to set a sound ideological line.

7. Appealing to Interest Groups

As rivals maneuver, an appeal to interest groups may be essential. After Stalin's death, each major contender for power made some such appeal: Beria to the nationalities; Malenkov to the consumer; Khrushchev to the party apparatus. Where interests clash, unfortunately, the appeal to one group may antagonize others. Malenkov's appeal to the consumers, for instance, seems to have aroused the enmity of the vested interests of heavy industry. Communist ideology tends to deny the possibility of conflicts of interests within "Communist" society, or at least to suggest that there can only be one "correct" solution to such conflicts. This makes it extremely difficult to mediate or compromise between conflicting interests, but no dogmatic denial of their existence can make them disappear or prevent leaders from becoming identified with particular interests.

8. Applying Force

Carefully applied, a little force or a little terror can do wonders for consolidating a man's position, though as long as there is a near balance at the top, it is risky for any one to apply force against his rivals—they may retaliate in kind. Nevertheless, if one can control the army, troops can be maneuvered at suitable moments, and if one can control the police, enemies can be arrested.

The army is the more visible of the two major agencies of force, and by and large, the Soviet leadership has been careful to keep it tightly subservient to party control, even at the risk of undermining military morale. Stalin, however used the police freely, even against high party officials, and in the end, the police were answerable to no one but Stalin himself. Since Stalin's fall, both the police and the army have given occasional signs of increased autonomy. Beria's power rested to a considerable extent upon the police, and Marshal Zhukov's rise suggested that army leaders might be able to take more initiative. Beria and Zhukov were both disposed of efficiently, since the other leaders realized how dangerous it would be to let either the police or army get out of hand, but as long as the government feels it must maintain an army and a police force, the danger will exist that these agencies of force will come to be directed against the leadership instead of being mobilized by it.

9. Building a Cult of Personality

If one is finally to rise above one's rivals, it helps to assume an aura of special virtue, and the entire system fosters sycophancy. A leader hardly has to encourage others to build his cult, though men with personalities like Stalin's or Khrushchev's are hardly likely to discourage it. Even Brezhnev, certainly a drab figure when placed beside his predecessors, turned out to have had heretofore unsuspected moments of heroism, which writers began to exploit once he seemed to be next in line. Latin Americans are not alone in their susceptibility to "personalismo."

Americans who criticize the Soviet system would do well to remember that most of techniques by which men rise to power in the Soviet Union are equally characteristic of the United States. In America too, a man who would climb to high office must cultivate the friendship of influential men as much or more than he must seek enlightened policy. He must be clever enough to join the ranks of those who can win and nimble enough to jump onto winning bandwagons. He must distribute patronage with skill, and he must opportunistically seize whatever good fortune comes his way. He must sow dissention among his rivals and opponents, even while mouthing the democratic platitudes that the voters seem to expect. He must try to place himself at the leadership of some interest groups while doing his best not to alienate others. If he would rise to the presidency, he must pretend to the nearly superhuman qualities that voters seem to demand at the same time that he engages in backroom haggling and compromises with unscrupulous and self-seeking men.

To be sure, there are differences in emphasis between the systems. Americans are less inhibited than the Soviets about appealing to interest groups, and ideology does not have quite the same place in the American system as in the Soviet system. More importantly, when competing for top office, Americans have usually avoided the direct appeals to force that the Soviets have indulged in, and Americans have rather consistently insisted upon electoral ratification of their politician's choices. In other ways, politics in America follows many of the same rules as politics in the Soviet Union.

EAST EUROPE

The three transitions of power that have taken place in the Soviet Union form too small a sample to allow confident generalizations, but as late as 1973, they were the only ones to have occurred in an independent "Communist" nation. The independent regimes of China, Yugoslavia, and Albania had yet to experience a succession in top leadership, though one aspect of the cultural revolution in China was certainly a sort of anticipatory succession struggle. Moscow has always had a hand, usually the predominant hand, in selecting the top leaders in its East European dependencies, and of course, this makes the problem of succession quite different than in an independent political system.

On three occasions, however, developments in Eastern Europe have escaped Soviet control. In each case, the Soviet government finally took measures to reassert its authority, but even the brief periods when the Soviets stood back and let developments follow their own course illustrate some political potentialities that are rather different from those that have so far occurred in the Soviet Union. In particular, these examples illustrate the several alternative strategies that are available to men who seek leadership within a "Communist" system. It seems worthwhile to consider Hungary and Poland in 1956 when, against the Kremlin's will, Nagy and Gomulka came back into power, and Czechoslovakia in 1968 when Dubcek, who had first assumed office with Soviet acquiescence, if not with wholehearted approval, proceeded to consolidate his leadership by truly revolutionary means.

The first post-World War II regimes of Eastern Europe can only be described as extensions of the Soviet government. The details by which they were established were varied, and showed differing styles of compromise with the shattered remains of prewar institutions, but the essential elements in setting up the new governments were the Red Army, the Soviet police, and the fact that, of all the competitors for leadership, only the Communists had a consistent well-developed plan of action. Prewar politicians had been badly discredited during the Nazi period, and the Soviets were often welcomed as liberators. Communist leadership backed by the Soviet government gained immediate sympathy by vigorous support for popular programs such as industrialization, land reform, and the punishment of Nazis and their collaborators. Most of the new Communist leaders had been trained in Moscow, and they were wholly loyal to Stalin, but any tendency to deviate in their loyalty was checked by concrete institutional devices. A Soviet ambassador always stood close by. He reported local developments to Moscow, and he issued instructions to the satellite leaders. There was frequent direct consultation between East European leaders and Moscow, and close contact between the various party organs and those of the Soviet Union. Each nation was tied directly to the Soviet Union by economic, political, and party bonds, but multilateral cooperation among the satellite nations was discouraged. Finally, there were Soviet guns. Only in Yugloslavia did a leader arise without direct Soviet help, and although Tito first played the role of a model ally and disciple of the Soviet Union, his own independent ambitions soon brought him into such conflict with the Stalinist system that he could no longer submit to Moscow.

As long as Stalin lived, Soviet domination over Eastern Europe tightened. Soviet officers served in the national armies. Soviet secret police controlled the local police and on their own initiative arrested local citizens. The region was exploited economically and, except in Yugoslavia, Stalin's word became law as firmly as in the Soviet Union itself.

Stalin's death, like the death of many other autocratic rulers in other areas, brought a prompt loosening of control over the dependent territories. Perhaps the East European leaders saw themselves as relatively equal in stature to the new men in the Kremlin. They may have been less willing to submit themselves to the new men than they had been to Stalin. The most important cause of looser control, however, was rivalry in the Kremlin. At the center, leadership was no longer unified, and this gave the East European leaders more freedom to maneuver. Like Maratha chiefs after the death of a peshwa, the East European chief could now hope to make his influence felt in the capital. As on countless other occasions in the most diverse types of political systems, rivalry at the top tended to open the Soviet system to slightly wider participation, and rivalry could break forth only with the death of the old leader.

The destruction of Beria and the resulting weakening of the Soviet secret police brought some immediate loosening of control over the East European regimes, and Malenkov's economic New Course brought some economic concessions and allowed some economic experimentation. The preoccupation of the men in the Kremlin with internal matters left East European leaders somewhat more on their own. It was, however, Khrushchev's de-stalinization campaign and above all, his attempts at reconciliation with Yugoslavia that had the most shattering implications for the East European regimes. Khrushchev's policies undermined the doctrinal assumptions under which the East European leaders had been operating. Good Stalinists that they were, they now resisted destalinization, and they objected strenuously when Khrushchev tried to make peace with a regime that Stalin had taught them to villify. Ironically, even these Stalinist objections demonstrated a degree of independence from Kremlin control that would hardly have been tolerated by Stalin. By seeming to forgive Tito for his very much more vigorous independence, Khrushchev appeared to countenance far more local initiative than East European leaders had ever before thought possible.

In Poland and Hungary, events moved dramatically away from the Stalinist past until they temporarily escaped Kremlin control. The two cases had many parallels but differed in a few crucial details, and their outcomes were dramatically different.

HUNGARY

Matjas Rakosi led the Communists of his country from the time the Soviet Army first drove the Germans out of Hungary until a few months before the revolution of 1956. Rakosi belonged to the so-called "Moscovite" wing of the party, for he had lived and been trained in Moscow and had returned to Hungary only after its liberation at the close of the war. Other Moscovites returned with Rakosi, but the party also came to include both old time members who had stayed in Hungary through the war, and new recruits who joined in the first post-war years and whose indoctrination was relatively shallow. Men who had always lived in Hungary were suspected by Moscow of less devotion than the Moscovites, but Rakosi was put in charge, and during the Stalinist period he was able to impose unity over the diverse elements of the party. Rakosi was slavish in his devotion to Stalin, merciless with his enemies. Solidly backed by Soviet guns, he had no difficulty staying in power as long as Stalin lived, but his autocratic methods earned him nearly universal enmity outside the party, and even among a large segment of the party itself.

Imre Nagy, who would later play such a dramatic and tragic role in the revolution, was eased out of the government in 1949. He had occupied a high, though by no means commanding, position in the leadership. In spite of some independent views, he had been a loyal party member, and since he had gathered no personal following and created no power base of his own, he posed no threat to the higher leadership. Dismissal did not bring arrest or trial to Nagy, as it did to so many others in Stalin's day, but he was permitted a respectable if obscure year of teaching. Rather accidentally, this year of exile from high office gave him the chance to become better acquainted with the realities of local agricultural problems than most other leaders, and in 1950, he came back to the government. He was readmitted to the Politburo in 1951 and received one of the five deputy premierships in 1952, but he was still below the top ranks.

In the vacuum of power left by the death of Stalin, orders from Moscow were no longer unambiguous. This encouraged local leaders to take more initiative, and disagreements among them were less consistently suppressed. Advocates of legal and economic reforms began to find their voices and, in the absence of a clear line from Moscow, policy disputes broke out which eventually touched upon the techniques of political control. The Hungarian party went through a protracted struggle between reform-minded members and the entrenched Stalinists. In the course of this struggle, the effectiveness of government control declined, and many intellectuals became alienated from any allegiance to the ruling group. Massive social unrest and economic disorganization could no longer be controlled by heavy-handed Stalinism.

In June, 1953, several Hungarian leaders, including both Rakosi and Nagy, were summoned to Moscow. This was during Malenkov's ascendancy and the Hungarians were ordered to introduce changes that reflected the new Soviet prime minister's policy of economic reform. This was also the period of collective leadership in Moscow, and in imitation of the new style in government there, Rakosi had to resign one of his posts so as to allow others to join in collective responsibility. Nagy, slightly more moderate than Rakosi and probably more pragmatic and realistic in economic matters, must have seemed in close agreement with the new course advocated by Malenkov. Moscow, therefore, selected Nagy as prime minister, while Rakosi remained party secretary. To Moscow, it may have seemed desirable to split the offices and responsibilities since the two men would then be forced into some degree of competition. They might have had to complete for Moscow's support, struggling to outdo one another in their expressions of loyalty. With divided leadership, no single man would be strong enough to defy Moscow by himself. Perhaps the corresponding dangers of divided leadership were not fully realized by Moscow, or perhaps the divided leadership in the Kremlin could not agree to back a single man. In any case, the dangers for Moscow were real. It could happen that the rivals might compete for local support instead of for support from Moscow, and thus come to rely upon their popularity among their constituents instead of upon help from the Kremlin. This would imply a sudden reversal in the direction of responsibility of the satellite leaders and a serious decline in central authority, hardly a desirable goal to anyone in Moscow. There was also the danger that competing provincial leaders might come to be associated with different factions at the center. As Maratha chiefs and monarchs knew so well, intrigue is a two-way process. Provincial politics could come to influence the power struggle in the capital.

Whatever Kremlin intentions may have been, Nagy managed, in a somewhat inconsistent and perhaps unplanned way, to capture the imagination of a good part of his nation. Soon after his appointment, he made an electrifying speech to parliament, in which he condemned earlier policies and promised sweeping changes. Quite unexpectedly, he praised the moribund Hungarian parliament, and the legality and orderliness that it represented. He permitted the collective farm system to collapse, and he pushed for the rehabilitation of political prisoners. These policies brought Nagy support from hitherto suppressed public opinion, but they alarmed the older party leadership which was still controlled by Rakosi. Since he lacked a personal faction within the party apparatus, Nagy had to rely upon more popular sources of support if the conservatives of the party were not to overwhelm him. Opinion became polarized between the intransigent Stalinist minority and the poorly organized majority that desired reforms. Nagy achieved some rehabilitation of prisoners and brought a reduction in police terror, but he was blocked by party conservatives from accomplishing much in the economic sphere.

Rakosi hung on. He succeeded in isolating Nagy from the remaining Communist leadership and he waited for the situation in Moscow to settle down. Rakosi also kept his relations with Malenkov's rivals in Moscow in good order, and a few days after Malenkov's resignation from the premiership in 1955, Rakosi informed the Hungarians that Nagy was ill and needed to be relieved of office. Nagy then left the government. During his time as prime minister, he had not yet generated massive popular support, but he left a memory of a relatively mild regime. No one could now forget that even under a "Communist" regime, an alternative to Rakosi's autocracy was possible, and though Nagy had never hinted at any disloyalty to the

Communist movement, and though his practical achievements had been modest, he came gradually to symbolize opposition to all that was brutal in the earlier regime. A plausible second man had appeared behind whom all opponents of the leader could rally. Rakosi's intransigent opposition made it all the easier to attribute virtue to Nagy. Back in full command, Rakosi tried to undo the damage. He tried to reverse the economic New Course, to return to earlier police methods, and to end the rehabilitation of political prisoners. He goaded the supporters of Nagy and tried to silence the intellectuals. Rakosi, however, lacked the tactical plasticity of Khrushchev, and he badly misinterpreted Khrushchev's triumph, assuming it to represent a return to old-fashioned Stalinist rule. The reconciliation with Tito, therefore, came as a terrible rebuff for a faithful Stalinist like Rakosi. It turned out that he did not have full support from Moscow after all. At a time when he no longer had any effective means to destroy his opponents, his attempt to use Stalinist methods simply alienated more and more of his countrymen. He faced a slow but seemingly irresistible growth in intellectual opposition. It grew, during the period when Khrushchev was promoting the thaw, and it blossomed after Khrushchev's destalinization speech at the 20th Party Congress in 1956. Even segments of the Hungarian party were affected by the new atmosphere and, in the absence of firm leadership from above, some elements of the party began to court the public for support. At the same time, continued pressure for economic rationalization threatened some vested interests within the party and brought a slump in party morale. Since it had always claimed credit for every success, it was now natural to blame the Rakosi regime for every difficulty.

Intellectual opposition became more and more strident in the period following the 20th Party Congress. Though lacking any formal organization, the opposition had the ideological initiative and it attracted increasing popular support, not only from intellectuals and students, but also among workers and even within the army. The more stubborn Rakosi and his associates became, the more they drove everyone else into opposition.

Finally, the situation became so turbulent that Moscow had to step in. Rakosi was simply losing control, and Khrushchev was unwilling to give this intransigent Stalinist the police and army support that he would have needed to stay in power. In July, 1956, Mikoyan arrived unexpectedly in Budapest for a meeting of the Hungarian Central Committee and he informed Rakosi that he was dismissed. The incredulous Rakosi could only be convinced by a telephone call to Khrushchev, but he finally had to bow to Moscow's superior wisdom, as he had always done in the past.

Moscow named Erno Gero as Rakosi's successor. This proved to be an unfortunate choice, for the psychological advantage that might have been gained by Rakosi's ouster was soon dissipated when Gero's government proved to be as unwilling as Rakosi's to compromise with the ever more clamorous demands for reform. Had Moscow been astute enough to appoint Nagy as party secretary, the course of Hungarian history might have been more like that of Poland under Gomulka, but in the crisis, Gero must have seemed to be about the only trustworthy man upon whom Moscow could rely.

The switch did little to pacify the Hungarians. The few concessions that were offered were too modest and came too late. Nagy was readmitted to the party but given little active role. He was, however, mentioned more and more widely as the man who should be brought back to power. He became the symbol of the opposition even for many party members who saw him as the only man capable of saving it. The response of the leaders was consistently too weak to suppress the growing disaffection, but never so conciliatory as to undercut it.

Then came the news of Poland's resistance to Soviet domination, and large numbers of Hungarians, especially the youth, became intoxicated with hope. On October 23, mass demonstrations turned into armed revolt and the government panicked. It appealed for help from the Soviet Army, but at the same time the Central Committee of the Hungarian Party, apparently acting without Soviet advice, yielded to popular pressure and appointed Nagy as prime minister. Gero clung to the first secretaryship, and in doing so simply insulted the people. Once again, Nagy found himself cast into a position of rivalry with the party leadership, but this time the central apparatus of the party had been catastrophically weakened, and in the provinces, the party structure had simply evaporated. With no party supporting him, Nagy was impelled into leadership of those who were now taking the initiative both behind the scenes and on the streets and who were doing everything possible to destroy what remained of the party apparatus. At first Nagy continued to act as a rather orthodox Communist. He still seemed to want to work within the party, but the remaining party leaders would only grudgingly compromise with him. Finally, on October 25, Gero left his post and Kadar became first secretary. Kadar and Nagy now stood as the two public spokesmen for the regime: Kadar for what was left of the party; Nagy for the government.

And then, for a few glorious days, Nagy and the revolution embraced one another. Nagy physically transferred his base of operations from the party headquarters to the parliament buildings, and he agreed to demands for a multi-party system, open elections, and all democratic freedoms. Workers' councils blossomed in the factories and ejected party hacks from management. Cardinal Mindszenty was freed from house arrest and other political prisoners released. Nagy announced Hungary's intention of withdrawing from the Warsaw Pact, and he began to negotiate for the withdrawal of Soviet troops.

The end was decisive. Soviet troops using Kadar as their front man simply imposed a new government. Nagy's government faded as quickly as had the party machinery. There was scattered armed resistance, but it never had a chance against the Soviet juggernaut. Once Moscow determined to impose its will, it could not be stopped.

The rise of Nagy to his short and tragic term was made possible by a curious interplay between discontent at home and fumbling Soviet policy. Nagy himself has to be understood more as an instrument of the revolution than its leader. He joined the revolution only in its final stages and only at the very end did he accede to all the popular demands. Only reluctantly, it seems, did he break away from his party colleagues at home or from the leadership in Moscow, but when he finally gave up all hope of securing their cooperation, he was left with little choice but to look elsewhere for his support. The other party leaders could never bring themselves to compromise with the revolutionary yearnings of their countrymen or with the one man who finally did compromise. It was the other leaders who forced Nagy into the embrace of the revolution.

One can only conclude that the revolution was the result of Soviet blunders. For understandable reasons but with disastrous results, opposition sentiments were permitted expression and were allowed to build up to a revolutionary pitch. The Soviet leadership neither compromised effectively nor, until its final military intervention, exercised sufficient force to contain the opposition. The unforeseen power of the revolution and the degree of national unity it evoked would long stand both as a temptation and as a warning—a temptation to a leader who might hope to channel that power to his own support, as Nagy had only reluctantly done; but even more, as a warning to those in power of the terrible dangers that might arise if strict controls were ever allowed to lapse.

POLAND

Poland underwent many of the same experiences as Hungary. Both countries had endured the same occupation by the Red Army, the same imposition of a Soviet sponsored government, the same purges, and the same tightening of controls in the last years of Stalin's rule. Gomulka had been secretary general of the Polish Communist Party in the immediate post-war years, and behind the facade of a government headed by non-Communist premiers, he was the effective ruler of the country. Gomulka had not lived in the Soviet Union, but had remained in Poland throughout the war, and he gained considerable popularity among his countrymen by his modestly nationalistic stance. Just after the war, he is even reported to have ordered Polish troops to fire upon Russian soldiers who were caught looting. Initially he gave a favorable reaction to the Marshall Plan proposals, and had favorable things to say about Tito. In a period of tightening Soviet controls, he could not last, and in 1948, Stalin replaced him with Boleslaw Bierut, a Moscovite, who, like Hungary's Rakosi, had spent the war years in Moscow and who was more malleable to Stalin's will than Gomulka.

The death of Stalin, the denuciation of the cult of personality, and the economic New Course had repercussions in Poland just as they had in Hungary. The economy had developed the usual dislocations and anomalies of the Stalinist era, and Malenkov's New Course at least permitted criticism of past practices, though it brought no dramatic cure. Cultural controls also loosened, and writers began to express themselves more openly, but until 1956, Bierut and the Stalinists remained very much in command.

Bierut died suddenly in Moscow on March 12, 1956, while attending the 20th Congress of the Communist Party of the Soviet Union. This was the Congress at which Khrushchev read his secret speech denouncing Stalin, and Bierut's death at that moment was rather providential for Poland, since it removed, without a struggle, the major symbol of Polish Stalinism. Poland did not have to undergo as embittering an experience as that of Hungary before disposing of its leading Stalinist. Khrushchev flew to Warsaw to take personal supervision over Bierut's replacement. He vetoed the Stalinist party man, Roman Zambrowski, on the grounds that, being a Jew, he would alienate the Poles, but he sponsored another supposed Stalinist, Edward Ochab. Like Gero in Hungary, Ochab gained office by appointment from Moscow, but Ochab proved more flexible and more willing to bow to local desires than Gero. Berman, another Stalinist party member, was eased out of office. It was announced that Gomulka had been freed from prison, and other rehabilitations were made. A growing press freedom and much freer economic discussion were allowed. In these ways, the Polish Communist Party responded far more flexibly than the Hungarian party to the desires of reformers. It was able to incorporate within the party much of the reformist sentiment. By contrast, the inflexible attitude of the Hungarian party drove everyone, eventually even Nagy, into opposition.

From the summer of 1956, Gomulka was in consultation with members of the Polish Politburo, but as in Hungary, the party included many conservative Stalinists who could not think of compromise. These came to be known as the Natolin group, and like the Rakosi-Gero group in Hungary, they had a vested interest in the Stalinist system and feared its dismantling. The difference was that in Poland they were not in charge, and the Polish leadership permitted a more liberal wing of the party to express itself and to maintain links with Gomulka and with the still more liberal voices in the background. There was rivalry between the Stalinist Natolin group and the slightly more liberal leadership, but some of the latter, including Ochab, the first secretary, made trips to China and to Yugoslavia at this time, and apparently they were encouraged in their more liberal line.

By October, the Stalinist opposition was becoming alarmed, and they planned a coup for the 15th. They were stopped when a list of 700 people whom they had intended to arrest was prematurely disclosed and the victims warned, but a crisis was now inevitable. The liberals both in and out of the party had increasingly looked to Gomulka as the man to represent them, just as their Hungarian equivalents had looked to Nagy. The situation grew more tense as power tended to polarize between the Stalinist Natolin group and the ever more strident popular voices for reform, but enough members of the party, either from personal conviction or through realistic appraisal of events, were ready to adjust to popular demands. Ochab seems finally to have been persuaded to yield to Gomulka. The decision to allow Gomulka to become first secretary came as a result of intraparty negotiation, not by Moscow's choice. Khrushchev had, in effect, appointed Ochab; Gomulka came to office against his will. That is how far events in Poland moved between March and October, 1956. The Polish leaders prepared a list of names, including Gomulka's, which was to be submitted on the morning of October 19th to the Central Committee of the Polish Communist Party. It was to constitute the new Polish Politburo.

At this point, a high-ranking delegation from Moscow descended unexpectedly upon Warsaw. Khrushchev, Molotov, Mikoyan, and Kaganovich, accompanied by an array of high military men, demanded a conference with the Polish leaders. The Polish delegation included Gomulka (now proposed as the new party secretary), and one of the most dramatic confrontations of East European politics ensued. The Soviet leaders were alarmed, and they were determined to put an end to the liberal Polish tide. Khrushchev is said to have ignored Gomulka, called Ochab a traitor, and to have shown cordiality only for Marshal Rokossovsky, a Soviet citizen who had been Polish Minister of Defense and Commander of the Polish Army. Rokossovsky was Moscow's man in Poland, but he had come to symbolize foreign oppression to most Poles. Rokossovsky had to inform his Kremlin superiors that the Polish troops under his command could not be counted upon to obey his orders, and both sides at the negotiating table seem to have been in telephone communication with military commanders in the field. Russian troops stationed in Poland moved toward Warsaw, but other Russian troops were delayed by Polish border guards from crossing from East Germany. Polish security forces, now loyal to Gomulka and the liberal wing of the Polish Party, moved to protect key buildings in

Warsaw. The truth was that the overwhelming majority of the Polish people, and even the majority of the Communist Party, were ready to support Gomulka against the visiting Russians.

Gomulka apparently threatened to take his case away from the negotiating table and appeal by radio to the Polish people. Khrushchev, with memories of Tito's schism and fearful of a rebellion that could easily have spread to Hungary, had also to recognize that Ochab and Gomulka were, after all, sincere Communists. Khrushchev finally backed down, and the Russian delegation flew back to Moscow. On October 21, the Polish Central Committee voted on the proposed new Politburo. In conformity with the principle of democratic centralism, the nominations had been agreed to ahead of time by the leadership, but in a desire to legitimize and consolidate their position, nominations from the floor and a secret ballot were allowed. Ochab received every vote of a possible 75, and Gomulka 74. Rokossovsky, who was nominated from the floor, received only 23 votes and he was removed from the Politburo. The final vote confirmed the official nominees, and the new government was officially installed. It received the grudging acceptance of the Soviet leaders.

Gomulka had a terrifyingly narrow path to walk between the very suspicious Kremlin leadership and the vociferous popular demands for ever more liberal reforms. He was helped immeasurably by the Soviet suppression of the Hungarian rebellion, for it served as a horrifying object lesson to all Poles who wished to push too fast. He was also helped by the drama of his selection. It served to emphasize the break with the past, and having faced down the Soviet leadership once, the Polish people could hope he would do it again. Gomulka allowed great press freedom and so conciliated the liberals who were, in any case, less likely to push too fast after the Hungarian suppression. He reached a compromise with the church and allowed the collectivization of agriculture to be dismantled. At the same time, he placated the Russians by resisting all temptations to export his ideas to other countries, and by supporting the Soviet Union in its international policies. The Polish liberalization was to be strictly confined to internal affairs. Slowly, but with increasing confidence, Gomulka consolidated his position as he came to be recognized by both the Soviet leaders and the liberals at home as the only man who could possibly represent them in dealing with the opposite group.

In a sense, the Polish revolution succeeded, while the Hungarian revolution failed. For a few years, Poland achieved an independence second only to Yugoslavia within the eastern bloc, while Hungary was forced securely under the Soviet yoke. Ironically, a decade later, Moscow's own man in Hungary, Janos Kadar, led as liberal a regime as was found anywhere within Moscow's orbit. The Polish government, by contrast, had become

more and more authoritarian, and Gomulka appeared to be the most willing of Moscow's dependents. In a final irony, Gomulka himself was expelled
from office in 1970 after riots in several cities of Northern Poland. He was
pushed aside by forces not unlike those that had once brought him to power.
It seemed that the change came as a result of internal pressures, rather than
at the dictation of Moscow. Fourteen years of increasingly close ties between
Gomulka and Moscow had not yet brought Poland back to the same degree
of dependence it had once had. Kremlin leaders had appointed both Bierut
and Ochab. They did not appoint Gomulka and they do not seem to have
appointed Gierek. Democratic centralism, Moscow style, which under Stalin
allowed the Soviet Union to appoint the leaders of its satellites, seems to
have not yet been fully reconstituted.

CZECHOSLOVAKIA

Czechoslovakia escaped the wave of revolution that nearly upset Moscow's hegemony in Hungary and Poland, and for the next decade, it was
known as the most docile of satellites. Antonin Novotny, the general secretary of the Czechoslovakian Communist Party, was unswervingly loyal
to his masters in the Kremlin, but by 1967 signs of internal disaffection
were appearing—not unlike the signs of strain that appeared in Poland and
Hungary in the year preceding the outbreaks of 1956. Years of blundering
leadership had brought deteriorating economic conditions. Solutions were
desperately needed, and rumors circulated of an impending shakeup in the
administration. Novotny had been in charge for 15 years, and he seemed
incapable of responding to the most patent needs for economic reform.
He had been in office so long that it was impossible not to blame him for
all that was wrong in the country. For the Czechs, he became the symbol
of stagnation. In June, 1967, a group of writers issued a manifesto in which
they appealed for the support of world opinion in their struggles against
censorship. In October and November, students demonstrated, at first
simply for improvements in their living conditions, but when they felt their
actions had been unfairly reported in the press, their demonstrations took
on an increasingly political flavor.

Brezhnev visited Prague unexpectedly in early December, 1967, apparently summoned by Novotny, who probably felt the need for Moscow's
help in shoring up his regime. Novotny's call may have done him more
harm than good, however, for a fierce struggle took place during the Central Committee meeting of December 19–21, and Novotny was sharply
criticized by some of his colleagues even for having sent for Brezhnev. This
was seen as opening up Czechoslovakian politics to Soviet interference.
The December meeting ended in a stalemate, but the Central Committee

met again from January 3–5, and its members conducted their business with unprecedented democratic procedures. After a generation of democratic centralism, the Central Committee suddenly acted as a true deliberative body, and after vigorous debate, its 110 members elected several new members of the Presidium. Novotny relinquished his post as secretary general and was replaced by Alexander Dubcek. In defiance of customary East European practice, Dubcek gained office, not as a result of Soviet appointment, but by election by the Central Committee. Soviet support may have helped Novotny to retain the presidency, but real power resided in the Presidium, and its newly elected members assured Dubcek a safe majority.

Dubcek's selection came as a surprise to Czechoslovakia, but the Soviet government acquiesced, and indeed it must have seemed a rather fortunate choice to the Kremlin. Dubcek was young enough and new enough to symbolize a break with the old unpopular leadership, and he was even young enough not to be tainted by involvement in the earlier Stalinist trials or purges. At the same time, Dubcek had a long and honorable Communist background. He had lived in the Soviet Union with his parents during the 1930s, had been a member of the party since 1939, and had worked his way up through the party apparatus. For 3 years, between 1955 and 1958, he had been fortified ideologically by attendance at Moscow's Party School for Advanced Politics, and since then, he had faithfully served in responsible party and government posts in Czechoslovakia. As a member of the Slovak section of the party, he was identified with a vigorous application of economic reforms, now referred to as the New Economic Model and made respectable by Kosygin's occupancy of the Soviet Prime Ministry. If the men in the Kremlin had doubts about Dubcek, they might have found comfort in recalling 1956 when concession to Gomulka and to the reformist pressures in Poland had proved to be a far more successful policy than the backing of intransigent Stalinists like Rakosi in Hungary.

Dubcek faced many of the same problems that Gomulka and Nagy had once struggled with. The deteriorating state of the once advanced Czech economy demanded vigorous measures, but Novotny remained as president, and his friends, like Rakosi's friends in Hungary or the Natolin group in Poland, could be counted upon to resist too rapid reforms. Reforms might have been supported by those outside the party, but Dubcek had to be careful not to be so caught up by nonparty pressures as to be isolated from his party, as Nagy had once been. Dubcek came in with the great advantage of Central Committee support, however, and his problem was to strengthen the support he already had without giving Novotny and his group the means to upset him. One strategy available to Dubcek was to appeal to a wider public than other leaders had done, and quite early, he expressed a cautious willingness to invite wider participation. The very method by which he had gained the post of secretary general—the free vote of the Central Committee—augured well for future free debate.

In February, a month after taking office, Dubcek promised economic reforms. He called for a thoroughly democratic system of collective farm management, and he permitted increasing press freedom. By March, the press was bursting forth with free expression, extensive political amnesties were under consideration, proposals to strengthen the National Assembly were being actively considered, and Dubcek was given widespread credit for these popular programs. A few of the hard line supporters of Novotny began to be removed from office, but instead of simply firing them, as had been traditional in the East European regimes, the new leaders insisted upon adhering closely to formal legality. They carefully refrained from the kind of personal attacks that had characterized earlier purges, and by the disarmingly simple expedient of letting public opinion express itself through constitutionally regular procedures, they rid themselves of many of their most bitter rivals and gained for themselves an ever broadening base of popular support. As the newly responsive apparatus began to adjust to the desires of the majority, it became clear that the old guard would have to go. Novotony tried to appeal to the workers, among whom he expected his support would be strongest, and he argued that the economic reforms of the new regime would hurt them; but in the open competition now possible, Novotny's support withered even among the workers. In April, he resigned the presidency and was replaced by General Svoboda, a Communist military hero of the Second World War who had been imprisoned during Stalin's era, but who emerged with broad popular respect. There was an almost clean sweep of the Novotny forces from both the party and the government.

The liberalization program developed its own momentum. Popular euphoria greeted the abolition of censorship and the assertion of the constitutional guarantees of free speech, association, assembly, and travel. Dubcek rejected a multi-party system, but he seemed to welcome almost unlimited intraparty democracy. The National Assembly was even permitted an unprecedented divided vote of 188 to 68 as it elected Josef Smrkovsky as its chairman. There was talk of a new electoral law, guarantees of inviolability of the mails, and rehabilitation of political prisoners. Czechoslovakia had suddenly shifted from the most conservative and reliable of Moscow's satellites to the most revolutionary. Czechoslovakia was an exciting place to live in the Spring of 1968, but it posed a horrible dilemma for the nervous old men of the Kremlin.

As the reforms gathered momentum, Moscow had every reason to panic. Had the Czechoslovakian movement become contagious, Gomulka and the East German leaders would have unquestionably followed their friend Novotny into oblivion and the Rumanians were finding the indecisiveness of the Soviet regime an ideal time for pursuing their own independent, though hardly liberal, course. Nothing less than the fragmentation of Moscow's empire was threatened. The Czechoslovakian reforms challenged the entire East European political system.

Czechoslovakia's most fundamental threat to her neighbors was its challenge to the doctrine of democratic centralism. The doctrine came under explicit criticism in Czechoslovakia, and every move toward inner party democracy suggested that the leadership was fully prepared to submit itself to control by the membership. Dubcek and his allies showed every sign of allowing lower bodies to exercise genuine initiative in their elections of representatives to the higher levels. This upset the hitherto universal practice of letting the higher authorities appoint the lower, and it reversed completely the direction of responsibility of the party and government apparatus. Instead of being responsible upward to the Czech leaders and beyond them to Moscow, they became increasingly responsible downward to the voters. The challenge to democratic centralism, the respect for constitutional procedures, and the new willingness to allow popular opinions to be expressed were all, of course, profound sources of strength to the new leadership. Whether or not they believed ideologically and abstractly in the value of honest and contested elections, or in the popular control that elections imply (and there is every reason to believe that many of them did so believe), allowing free expression and free choice brought Dubcek and his associates undreamed of support. Always in the past, when a man was needed for one of the multitude of party or government committees that form the vast and complex web of control in these countries, he had been nominated from above and his election served merely to ratify the nomination. Now, real elections were permitted, and every winner of every election could thank the leadership for having allowed him this means of gaining office. The elections themselves ensured loyalty at the same time that they brought more popular leaders into a host of junior offices. These orderly procedures, it turned out, disposed of opponents even more successful than the more familiar techniques of polemics and purge had done, for there was a satisfying legitimacy about voting a man quietly but decisively out of office. An election might leave the loser disappointed and frustrated, but a purge would leave him nursing an additional grievance at the unjust procedures by which he had been victimized.

Of course complex policy questions would ultimately have to have been faced by the new leadership and these would have introduced divisions within the nation, but on the two most pressing issues—the liberalization itself and resistance to Moscow's domination, Dubcek and his associates had the very nearly universal approval of the nation. A party congress was called for September, and there was hope that it would confirm the new party democracy and reject forever the doctrine of democratic centralism. Of the many motives that finally provoked Soviet intervention, fear of the results of the Party Congress may have been most decisive.

The end we know. No Czechoslovakian protestations of loyalty to Communism and no degree of careful adherence to all its international agreements with members of the Soviet bloc could prevent the final intervention of the USSR and her allies. That the Soviet Union failed dismally in its search for a quisling who would invite Moscow's help in establishing a new regime demonstrates how completely Dubcek and his associates had gained the confidence of the nation, and how wretched was the understanding of the Soviet leadership about events in their empire. Their only recourse was to the brute force of their army.

To Western sympathizers, it seemed particularly tragic that four East European satellites supported the Soviet Union with troops, but the motives of the satellite leaders are not mysterious. Of the four, the Bulgarians and East Germans had never shown any appreciable independence from Moscow, but their fear of sharing the fate of Novotny gave them an independent motivation for supporting the intervention. Gomulka had long ago forfeited his claim to liberal backing, but by 1968 his chief opposition came from a regrouped set of hard liners and Natolinists, now led by S. Moczar. Moczar took a nationalist, anti-Semitic, and hardly democratic line, but while he was in no sense a liberal, Moczar's independent nationalism did threaten Moscow's hegemony, just as Czech liberalism did. Gomulka may have needed Moscow's support badly enough to make him happy to help in Czechoslovakia in return for Moscow's help against Moczar. Hungary was the least enthusiastic of the four satellites that finally sent troops, but in the last months before the invasion, the three most independent East European nations, Yugoslavia, Rumania, and Czechoslovakia were drawing together and tending to support each other in their varying but always independent policies. These three would have very nearly surrounded Hungary in a sort of little entente, which may have seemed threatening to the Hungarian leaders. In the final showdown, Kadar probably had little choice but to obey Moscow's orders.

PREDICTABILITY

Predicting events in the Eastern bloc has been a hazardous undertaking. Few of the dramatic events of its history—the Polish and Hungarian revolutions, the Czechoslovakian reform, the overthrow of Khrushchev, the Soviet break with China, the cultural revolution—were foreseen by outside observers, and it is easy to find confident predictions by well informed authorities that have been belied by events. It may seem that the difficulty of prediction is the result of our faulty knowledge, the hazy perceptions through which we must follow events. It would be wrong to suppose, however, that even the most intimate knowledge could ever allow us to predict the outcome of the next succession struggle. Indeed, it is in the very nature of such struggles that prediction is impossible. We might even speak of a sort of uncertainty principle which rules out predictability.

The study of succession, certainly of succession in the Eastern bloc, seems always to resolve itself into the study of power struggles. No power struggle would ever take place if its outcome could be known ahead of time by the contestants, but if the contestants themselves are unable to predict the results, outside observers are even less qualified. Not even Khrushchev had premonitions of his impending doom. How could an outside observer have foreseen it? Once a struggle has been resolved, it may be possible to interpret the motives and strategies of the actors and to judge their varying successes and failures. We may then understand how the winner managed to win. It is, in principle, quite impossible to do this ahead of time. To the extent that anyone can make a confident prediction, to that very extent the struggle is already over.

STRATEGY

While we cannot hope to make successful predictions, an understanding of the structure of power in the Soviet regime and in the regimes of Eastern Europe can give us insight into the range of possibilities open to those who struggle. We can outline the kinds of strategies that are available, even if we cannot tell which strategy will be successful, let alone predict who will use which strategy on which occasion.

The man who would reach for or consolidate paramount power would seem to have two very general alternative strategies at his disposal. These strategies correspond to the opposing pressures that we have seen in all oligarchies, those pressures which push toward a broadening or toward a narrowing of participation. The first strategy is to try to narrow and finally to monopolize power by the application of force or terror—the strategy of a new Stalin. The other is to appeal for more popular support, thereby implying a broadening, rather than a narrowing, of participation.

The balance of power among the top Soviet leaders has provided a temporary protection against the strategy of force, but the men of the Presidium and the Central Committee cannot live forever, and the inertia that may be inherent in divided leadership may eventually encourage the re-emergence of another strong man. Certainly it would be rash to imagine that the precarious balance of the post-Khrushchev era forecloses all possibility of renewed one-man rule. The caution of the present leadership might make it easier for someone from the periphery of the system to gain control than somebody at its heart. A new strong man might even be a general or someone who directs the police apparatus rather than a more traditional party man. The party leadership has usually been careful to keep the generals in their place, but even Zhukov's brief period of power shows that the leadership is not immune to military influence.

A man who relies upon guns and terror to consolidate his position would not necessarily bring radical changes to the government, and even a military strong man might introduce fewer changes than is sometimes imagined. It is interesting to speculate on the program that might be instituted should a general become powerful enough to take over. His tanks might help him to destroy his opponents with efficiency, and so he might resolve the dilemmas of divided leadership. At the same time, he would have the same desperate need as any other military strong man to justify his actions, to appeal for popular support, and to make his government appear to offer continuity, legitimacy, and stability. A military strong man in the Soviet Union would certainly be tempted to claim that his government provided a return to the true path toward Communism, that he had intervened only to dispose of the deviationists who had been in charge. A military government would not necessarily be more aggressive toward other nations than the previous civilian government. The new leadership would face the same strategic realities as a civilian leadership, and the history of military governments in other parts of the world, whether in Argentina, Greece, Pakistan, or Thailand, does not suggest that they are inevitably tempted to aggression. Like any other powerful figure, a general might find the fruits of running the system at home a good deal more satisfying than the risks of adventures abroad. He could be expected to defend his interests vigorously, both domestically and among his nation's allies, but his political stance would not necessarily be very different from that of his civilian predecessors. The suggestion of dramatic change that the threat of a military government seems to imply may be rather exaggerated.

What military leadership might accomplish is what might also be accomplished by a single strong civilian leader. Tighter controls might be reimposed, and a return to the internal autocracy of Stalin's era might allow other high officials to be readily dismissed or transferred. If the new leader were astute enough to force a rationalization upon the economic system, he might bring the country new economic strength. If he could act consistently in foreign relations, he might rebuild and unify at least a part of the Soviet empire.

What a general could not do is what a civilian dictator could not do: Solve the succession problem. Old soldiers do die, and eventually the Soviet Union would be faced with the same old dilemmas. Perhaps the nation is fated to go on oscillating between dictatorial and oligarchical regimes, and to the extent that a strong man, whether military or civilian, resolves the dilemmas of collective leadership, he will again create the reciprocal dilemmas of autocracy. A strong man need not think beyond his own reign. Surely there must be men in the Soviet Union who dream of imposing their own dominant rule, and it is difficult to find any developing institutional devices that can give us any confidence that strong-arm methods will not again be used to re-establish supreme power.

But what about the alternative strategy to the use of force and terror—the appeal for wider support with its implication for broadening, rather than narrowing, the power base? Khrushchev appealed beyond the usual narrow limits of the leadership when he sought the support of the Central Committee. He did the same, far more dramatically in the destalinization campaign. Even more radically, Dubcek appealed beyond the narrow group in command of Czechoslovakia—both to the rank and file of the party and then even further to national public opinion. Somewhat against their will, Gomulka and Nagy became the beneficiaries of popular movements. The rise of all four leaders demonstrates the power that public approval can give, once it is let loose to find its voice. It is interesting to compare the events surrounding the rise of these four men, and to speculate on the future potentialities of similar strategies, for just as there must be men in the Soviet Union who dream of imposing their own autocratic rule, so must there also be men who dream of putting themselves at the head of a popular movement.

Dubcek and Khrushchev made rather deliberate appeals for broad support; Gomulka and Nagy stumbled into popular leadership. Of the two who gained their popularity more accidentally, Nagy finally embraced his supporters closely and rather recklessly, Gomulka with more circumspection. In the end, Gomulka can only be said to have deserted them. Of the two who made more deliberate appeals, Khrushchev acted more as the demagogue, Dubcek more as the constitutionalist. Khrushchev finally fell when he lost the confidence of his immediate subordinates; Dubcek was stopped only by massive outside intervention. During his few months of independence, Dubcek succeeded magnificiently. It seems likely that no other Communist leader has ever evoked the same degree of genuine popular enthusiasm. Dubcek threatened nothing less than to turn upside down the traditional methods of control, to replace democratic centralism with democracy, central control with popular choice of leaders, the closed society with the open. It was a challenge that most Communist leaders have every reason to fear, for if broadly applied, it would mean the end of their own careers. Perhaps only a new man in office, untainted by too many past mistakes, can attempt this strategy with much hope of success.

It is misleading to contrast the strategy of popular appeal too starkly with the strategy of force. As the countless tyrants of human history have known so well, an appeal for popular support can be a device by which to cut down one's immediate rivals and so gain a greater monopoly of power. Perhaps any successful man will have to combine the two strategies to some extent. A leader may use judicious police terror as he climbs to dominance, and then go on to consolidate his position by making popular appeals. Or, he may begin with what looks like a popular program but then, when he fears a loss of popularity, cling to his job by force. He may appeal to some groups, suppress others. The Eastern bloc has provided examples of many mixtures of these strategies: Gomulka moving from popular backing to increasing autocracy; Tito starting with strongly centralized control but shifting increasingy toward more liberal methods; Khrushchev experimenting restlessly with both.

Nevertheless, the two strategies are, in some degree, mutually contradictory, and the contradiction appears most starkly in the differing manner by which subordinate officials are selected. Political power consists, above all else, of the ability to appoint and dismiss others from office. The logical limit of autocracy is a Stalinism in which one man can snap his fingers and thereby promote or dismiss whomever he chooses. The logical flaw in this system is the difficulty of replacing the Stalin. To let the next circle of powerful men choose the new leader limits that leader's autocracy and in some degree, sovereignty is thereby shifted to this larger group. When the Soviet Union has lacked a single dictator, the Presidium has tended to gain a sort of collective sovereignty, but the problem then arises of how to select Presidium members. To let a single man make the appointments would be to revert to autocracy, but the only alternative is to move in the opposite direction and let a larger group, presumably the Central Committee, make the choice—as indeed the party statutes say it should. But this would simply decentralize power even further and the same question will just arise again: Who is to name the members of the Central Committee? And if the answer to this is to let the Party Congress choose them, then we will have to ask how the Party Congress members are to be selected. The strategies for gaining power imply either a centralization or dispersion of appointment, and to this extent the two strategies are at least analytically distinct, and there must be contradictions involved in any attempt to combine them, as there surely were in Khrushchev's maneuvers.

In the years that followed the fall of Khrushchev, the leaders in Moscow successfully restrained one another either from making popular appeals or from moving toward a personal and autocratic power; but the conditions that made Dubcek's strategy possible in Czechoslovakia are present in the Soviet Union too. The Soviet Union lacks the democratic history that must have helped to inspire Czechoslovakia, but the Czech and Slovak leaders of 1968 were not mysteriously resurrected democrats. They were stolid Communists, rationally responding to urgent social forces. To be sure, the Soviet Union cannot have one vital unifying factor that was present in Czechoslovakia—it has no great towering neighbor against which popular sentiments can be suddenly if covertly mobilized. Every possibility for mobilizing sentiments against the United States and China must already have been exhaustively exploited. Nothing any Soviet leader could do could compare in dramatic popular appeal to the magnificence of the Czechoslovakian leaders who stood up to the Soviet Union.

Nevertheless, the structures of the government, party, and economy of the two countries are so much alike that many of the same social forces are surely at work. Haunted on the one side by the ghost of Stalin, the Soviet leaders must be equally haunted by the ghost of Dubcek on the other. Dubcek showed them how precarious their own positions would be if popular forces were to be let loose in their own country. So terrifying was his program that the Soviet leaders had to attempt its suppression by ruthless military intervention. But the ghost of Dubcek will not be so easily exorcised. For a few men the temptation to duplicate his achievement must be strong, just as for others, the temptation to become the next Stalin must be equally strong. Like the oligarchies of other continents and of other centuries, the men of the Kremlin lead a government that is subject to opposing pressures of centralization and dispersal of power, and there are men who will attempt to profit by one or the other of these pressures. It seems unlikely that the Soviet Union will quickly resolve the contradictions that are inherent in these opposing pressures.

CONCLUSION

One final question remains: To what extent has the Soviet or "Communist" system found new solutions to the dilemmas of succession? On the whole, the answer must be that its solutions are neither very new, nor very promising.

The parallels between Stalinist centralism and other centralized systems, even those as remote in time and ideology as that of Imperial China, run remarkably deep. The rule of Stalin, like that of the strongest Chinese emperors, constituted a kind of ultimate centralism, a political system in which all power was concentrated in the hands of a single man. This man could appoint and dismiss his subordinates at will, and this meant that the entire apparatus had to be entirely subservient to him. Under both Stalin and the emperors, a huge bureaucracy developed with complex internal checks and balances that kept it subservient to the top leadership. In neither of these bureaucracies, however, could prohibitions from the top ever stop the formation of factions or of relationships of patronage and clientship by which men sought to protect and to help one another.

Both systems also faced the dilemmas that any centralized system must face when a successor must be found, though the dilemmas have been more severe for the Soviets than for the Chinese. By allowing each emperor to appoint his own successor, the Chinese carried appointment to its logical extreme, and this delayed for a few generations the final weakening of top leadership that finally accompanied the decline of the dynasty. It is hardly likely that appointment of one's own successor could be institutionalized under the modern conditions of the Soviet Union. Appointment would face at least as many difficulties as the appointment of one's own successor has always faced in Latin America. As a result, whenever a strong leader goes, the Soviet system risks a convulsive power struggle. This tends to undermine the principle of democratic centralism, and to allow more freedom of maneuver at all levels of the hierarchy.

Segments of the empire, moreover, have their best chance to maneuver toward independence during succession struggles when the top Soviet leaders are divided. At that time, the entire logic of the political system is called into question. The more extreme the centralization of a political system, the more starkly will its internal contradictions stand out when the top man finally goes, and nowhere are the contradictions more serious than in the Soviet Union.

Collective leadership amounts to a partial resolution of the dilemma, but it raises a host of new problems of its own. As with other governments, the solution to one set of dilemmas simply presents a new set, so that the system may be driven ever further from its origins. Collective leadership represents a kind of oligarchy, and oligarchies everywhere have been riven by internal disputes. Oligarchies represent an incomplete centralization, but in the modern world it seems difficult to stabilize political participation at any point between an extreme centralization and a broad democracy. The internal rivalries of oligarchies always give outsiders the hope of making their desires felt. Thus, as long as the Soviets avoid complete centralization, they will face the danger that their rivalries will open the system even wider. Both satellite leaders and second-level leaders within the Soviet Union itself can always act more independently when the leaders above them are divided.

The instability of much of the underdeveloped world can be seen, in part, as a failure to settle down at a single, well accepted level of political participation. To the extent that the "Communist" world has been more stable, it has endured less violent swings in participation. As we have seen, however, no highly centralized system can be maintained indefinitely, and any intermediate level of participation seems destined to instability. For those who would like to see the Soviet system modified, these considerations might provide a note of cautious optimism. Neither of its two modes, the centralization of a Stalin or the oligarchy of collective leadership, seems to have indefinite staying power. At the same time, it is well to remember just how impossible it is to predict the directions in which a political system will move. One resolution to the kind of rivalries inherent in a collective leadership is renewed centralization, and one can hardly rule out a new Stalinism as one possible direction in which the Soviet Union might move. In the long run, this too would face its own internal contradictions, but the long run could be very long indeed.

CHAPTER 8

Conclusions:
Both Theoretical and Applied

A THEORY OF SUCCESSION

The examples set forth in the six central chapters of this book have been diverse and complex, but my intention has not been to overwhelm the reader with a mountain of facts. Rather, I have wanted to search for the general principles that govern succession everywhere and to investigate the implications of succession practices for the other aspects of government and society. To that end, I have tried, from time to time, to make comparative statements and to draw general conclusions, but it may be difficult to sort out these conclusions from the wealth of detail in the examples. Now, at the end, it seems appropriate to summarize, in a single place, the principles that seem to me finally to emerge from a comparative study of the long and tortured experience of dozens of succession struggles.

I take the principles listed here to be theoretical claims. Collectively these principles should help to bring order and clarity to the data that have been presented. I feel the principles are made plausible by the cases I have examined, but like any theoretical claims, they will always be subject to further testing and I do not want to pretend that they have been or could be "proved." Data drawn from additional societies might well force a revision or modification of some of these claims. In the meantime, these statements point to areas that could be fruitfully examined when considering succession in other societies. Page references in the paragraphs to follow refer to more extensive discussions of these points found in earlier chapters and to examples where they are illustrated in particular societies.

1. The Need for Succession

In most human societies, leadership culminates at a single and supreme center of power. To say this is, in some degree, to do no more than to state a definition, for we tend to *define* a society as any segment of mankind that acknowledges the authority of the same center. When we find a group of people who acknowledge a single center of leadership, we call that group a society. Where we find two power centers, we usually feel that there are two societies (Bemba: pp. 26, 46). At a very primitive level, however, there are people with diffusely distributed leadership rather than a single dominant center, and we may still want to regard them as forming a single society (Siuai: p. 14ff.).

Most centers of power, in turn, have been headed by a single office and single man—a chief, a king, a president, a prime minister, or a party secretary. Here, the major exceptions are at the opposite extreme from primitive, for it is only a few modern experiments, notably the government of Switzerland and that of the Soviet Union during its periods of "collective leadership" (p. 222 ff.) that suggest that a committee can offer a viable alternative to a single man executive (pp. 47–48).

Societies without a single dominant office—both those with the diffuse primitive variety of leadership and those with the modern committee variety—have often been weakened by internal disputes. Co-equal leaders find it difficult to agree on policy or to coordinate their activities. Teams, triumvirates, juntas, committees, and many sorts of legislatures and assemblies have tried to lead governments, but these have often been wracked by internal quarrels. In times of crisis, such governments frequently prove so ineffectual that men turn once again to a single strong leader (Europe and the United States, pp. 130–133; Latin America, p. 168 ff., p. 181 ff.). As a result, both the diffuse leadership found among some primitive peoples and the committee executives attempted in a few modern nations have tended to lose out in competition with societies that are led by a single office and a single man. The overwhelming bulk of human experience suggests that a single man tends to rise to the top. If a society is defined as embracing those men who acknowledge the leadership of a single center of power, and if this society is to outlive the man who leads it at any particular moment, then this man will sooner or later have to be replaced. The succession problem is concerned with the techniques by which the replacement can be achieved.

2. The Inevitability of Succession Struggles

If one man could occupy an unambiguous second position in his society, then he might be able to step up to the top office as soon as it became vacant. A man or an office with an unambiguous second position, however, is as rare as an unambiguous first position is usual. This is because anyone who gains a clear second position poses an immediate threat to the man on top (Swazi: p. 23; Marathas: pp. 61, 64). If a man occupies a clear second place, every opponent of the top man will tend to rally around him, and he will then become a serious rival to the man on top. As a result, the top man always has strong motives for cutting down anyone else who threatens to emerge as his second. The most effective technique by which the top man can forestall such challenges to his own position is to grant his closest lieutenants more or less equal power and even to keep them in rivalry. In this way, as soon as one man begins to look like a threat, the leader can turn to others who will help to block their rival and to undermine his power (China: p. 94 ff., p. 115; USSR: p. 214; many others).

In the absence of a clear second-in-command, it is difficult to designate a successor until the old leader prepares to step down, and the choice must often await his death (most hereditary and most non-electoral systems). Then, with their old leader gone, his closest collaborators and lieutenants may try to agree upon a successor. Often, however, these lieutenants are more immediately concerned with protecting their own positions than with ensuring the strength and continuity of the regime. They may prefer a weak man who will leave them alone over a stronger man who will provide effective leadership (Marathas: p. 71; Holy Roman Empire: p. 134). The internal rivalry that almost always characterizes the relationships among the lieutenants of a top leader, however, is generally fated to continue after the old leader's departure, and this makes it difficult for the survivors to agree even on a weak man.

These factors, the need for a single dominant leader combined with the rivalry and near equality of his immediate subordinates, mean that the automatic transfer of power from one top leader to a successor is impossible.

Periodic succession struggles, therefore, are an inevitable feature of all political systems. These struggles, however, assume widely varying forms.

3. Succession at the Top and Its Relation to Other Offices

The patterns by which struggles over the top office are resolved often reflect quite closely the patterns by which lower offices are filled. Particular patterns of inheritance, choice within a small circle of associates, and the details of electoral practice, for instance, may all be found at both the top and lower levels of a society (Swazi: p. 23; Nupe: p. 34; Marathas: pp. 58–67 passim; many others). Perhaps the choice of the top man is made easier when that choice follows principles that the people have grown accustomed to with lower level offices. One means by which lower offices can be filled, however, is not available at the top: Only the lower offices can be filled by appointment. Even when lower officers are not appointive in principle, moreover, higher leaders often exercise some influence over them. At a minimum, the higher man may be able to arbitrate disputes among those contending for a lower office (Marathas: pp. 74–75). Since (by definition) there can be no "higher" authority to make or to influence the "highest" appointment, succession to that office always has unique elements that are found nowhere else in the system.

With the top office, arbitration from above is impossible, but the stakes in that struggle are particularly high. Competitors for the top office, therefore, tend to mobilize all possible forms of support. Every person and every institution in the society may be periodically called upon to assist one or another of the contenders. Techniques for carrying on a succession struggle include intrigue, appeals to various sorts of electorates, and armed battle, but when the sides are evenly matched, none of these may be sufficient to resolve the issue. The outcome may be the collapse of the old order and the shattering of the political realm into smaller parts. Even when events do not proceed so far, succession struggles may result in a loosening of the bonds that hold the component parts of the society together. Central control is often weakened (Africa: pp. 24–39; Marathas: pp. 70–74; Eastern Europe: p. 232). Successions, therefore, are critical periods in a society's history with far-reaching implications for every aspect of its political and social system. Successions are also times that an observer should find particularly revealing, for ties of political strength and the fissures of political weakness that at other times may be more or less hidden from view then become obvious.

4. Change

From generation to generation and from century to century, the rules of succession have a characteristic tendency to change. One reason for this is that the circumstances of one succession often leave the survivors with vivid memories of specific problems. To avoid these problems, they often try to arrange matters so that the results will be different the next time around.

For one thing, men may hope to avoid violence. To this end, they may try to minimize rivalry and to provide circumstances so clear and unambiguous that one man will be able to step into office without a struggle (China: pp. 101–102; Argentina: p. 165). Such efforts, however, frequently lead to weak leadership. A man who gains office without a struggle misses an important chance to prove himself in competition. Then, with no personal triumph to his credit, he may have a relatively weak claim upon the loyalty of others. Moreover, when no struggle is involved, incompetent men cannot be so reliably eliminated (China: pp. 118–119; Latin America: pp. 163, 167).

For instance, a well defined hereditary system seems to offer one way to avoid a scramble for office, but the hereditary definition of an heir runs twin risks. If it is too well defined, it may bring a child or an imbecile to an office that is supposed to be powerful. Alternatively, it may designate an able man, but do so too soon. An able heir apparent poses all the threats to the top leader that any clear second poses. So great are these threats that the ruler may feel obliged to restrict the movements and the contacts of his heir. Only in this way can he be kept away from men who would try to plot with him to undermine the man in office. Only in this way can the heir be prevented from fomenting trouble. Such restrictions may deprive the heir of the kinds of education and experience he will need if, when his turn finally comes, he is to be an effective ruler (Marathas: p. 68; China: p. 101).

Attempts to avoid succession struggles, therefore, tend to result in weak leadership, and this, in turn, encourages further change. When the occupant of the legitimate office is weak, others may have to assume de facto power. The result may be a regency, a caretaker government, or a usurpation (Baganda: p. 44; Marathas: p. 63 ff.). A successful usurper will strive to give his rule legitimacy, and to the extent that he succeeds, later succession struggles will center on his office rather than upon the office of the former ruler. If the new office is acquired by the same rules as the old one, little will have changed. If, however, the new office is acquired by new means (e.g., when an elected prime minister begins to take over duties formerly left to an hereditary monarch), the result may be a profound mutation in the political system (Holland and England: pp. 139–141).

For all these reasons, the rules of succession tend to change. Changing succession patterns have been characteristic of political systems as different as those of tribal Africa and the Soviet Union. If succession patterns are so likely to change, then we are unjustified in our frequent assumption that social organization has some sort of inherent stability or continuity. Here is one aspect of social organization that does not, and perhaps cannot, remain unchanged. Social organization, in other words, is not an inertial system that continues unchanged unless acted upon by external forces. Rather, it is a dynamic system that carries within itself the tendency to change (Baganda: p. 39).

5. Cycles, Trends, and Predictability

If a system has an inherent tendency to change, then the only way to maintain a faith in some sort of long-term continuity is to suppose that succession practices tend to keep changing until they complete a cycle, at which point the social patterns return to their starting point. In many parts of the world—in Africa (pp. 45–46), India (p. 84), China (pp. 119–122), and even in Latin America (p. 157)—it is tempting to recognize cycles. Societies that seem always to be changing seem finally to get nowhere.

Once we see cycles, it is also tempting to try to make predictions. A cycle that has held in the past might be expected to continue into the future. Unfortunately for soothsayers, however, the past can usually be interpreted in several different ways. Several different cycles may all seem to work together, and at any given point in history, it is quite impossible to know which of these cycles will move on toward completion. It is not even possible, except in retrospect, to know what point in a cycle has been reached at a particular moment (Bemba: pp. 45–46; China: pp. 119–122).

Much the same thing can be said for the attempt to extrapolate past trends into the future, even when the trends are regarded as linear rather than cyclical. Several trends always develop concurrently, and it is impossible to know which trend is destined to continue (USSR: pp. 226–227). Trends that reverse themselves, of course, can be regarded as cycles, and this means that most historical processes can be interpreted either by trends or by cycles. No interpretation that is so universally applicable can offer much help in predicting the future.

It is also quite useless to try to predict the outcome of a particular succession struggle. Rivalry for the top position implies an uncertainty about the results. Men stop struggling once they know who the winner is to be. If those most deeply and intimately involved in succession struggles—the rivals themselves—do not and cannot predict the outcome with confidence, no outside observer stands much chance of doing better. We can recognize and describe patterns by which decisions are characteristically made, but predicting the outcome of a particular succession struggle is, in principle, an unpromising enterprise (USSR and Eastern Europe: pp. 246–247).

6. Heredity and Its Alternatives: A Typology

When the successor is too clearly designated, weak leadership is often the result. When he is not designated clearly enough, the result may be a destructive succession struggle (see Section 3). Throughout most of human history, the most frequent compromise between these unattractive alternatives has been an hereditary system that designates a range of suitable heirs, but does not unambiguously specify a single heir.

Hereditary systems can assume many forms, and they may rely upon many alternative genealogical rules. Inheritance through the male line tends to be more common than inheritance through the female line, however, and succession by sons is more common than succession by brothers. Sons, therefore, are the most strategically placed of all kinsmen, but the specification of which particular son is to succeed (e.g., strict primogeniture, or strict ultimogentiure) is unusual (pp. 49–52).

Once we have noticed how widespread hereditary succession once was, we must also be struck by its rapid collapse as a legitimizing principle in the 19th and 20th centuries (pp. 141–143). With the disappearance of heredity, several alternative techniques for achieving top office have come into use, sometimes in relatively pure form, often in varying combinations. Four techniques, each tending to lead to a characteristic type of government, can be distinguished.

a. The Strong Man. Under sufficiently unsettled conditions, a man may simply gather henchmen and shoot his way to the top. In the early years of Latin American independence many leaders gained office in this way, and this was the origin of many dynasties. A dynasty that is to be perpetuated, however, must rely upon other techniques in subsequent generations.

b. Self-Perpetuation. The top man may designate his own successor, or the succession may be arranged by a private agreement among some sort of self-perpetuating oligarchy of important men. Conservative oligarchies of wealthy families often approximate this system, but so do some single party governments that claim to be revolutionary in character (Argentina: pp. 163–168; Mexico: p. 196).

c. The Coup d'etat and Subsequent Intrigue. A coup d'etat often brings some sort of committee or junta to power, but then intrigue within the junta often leads to the re-emergence of a single leader (Latin America: pp. 176–184).

d. Contested Elections. Elections have been regularly used as a means of selecting leaders in a few areas of Europe and America, but in many parts of the world, they have had little of the stabilizing effect which is sometimes claimed for them.

If the manifest deficiencies of heredity have finally led to its decline, it must nevertheless be acknowledged that none of the alternative methods that have now taken its place can be credited with consistent success either in providing able leaders, or in accomplishing their peaceful selection. Still less, of course, do the methods now in use regularly provide leaders who give their nations what they want or need. We are led to the depressing conclusion that no method is capable of really working in the way that men would like it to.

7. Range of Participation

Political systems have varied widely in the proportion of their population that has been able to participate effectively in government. In particular, they have shown broad variation in the number of those able to make their influence felt in the selection of their great or lesser leaders. The term "political participation" can be used to refer to the range of men who are able to make their desires and interests felt, particularly in the choice of leaders. One extreme of political participation is that of the ideal democracy of the town meeting where every adult debates, votes, and has an equal share in choosing his leaders. The other extreme is that of the highly centralized autocracy, where appointments are monopolized by the man on top and where no decision is safe from his veto (China: pp. 94–98; the Soviet Union: pp. 207, 211).

Most real political systems lie between these extremes: oligarchies, aristocracies, a regime of the "richest families," the dictatorship of an elite party, and more or less democratic systems in which varying proportions of the population are actually able to participate. All real systems are also subject to competing pressures. In some ways, they are pushed toward more centralization of decision and of appointment, but in other ways, they are pushed toward a broader participation (Europe: pp. 133–136; Latin America: pp. 190–191; USSR: p. 247).

A man who emerges as the top leader usually works to centralize his government and to narrow participation. He usually has strong motives for concentrating as much power as possible into his own hands, for doing whatever he can to weaken all competing clusters of power, and for depriving others of the ability to participate in decisions that would threaten his own freedom of action. Even leaders who are originally selected by their constituents often come later to dominate their own electors (Italian cities: p. 131; Holland: pp. 131–132; Latin America: pp. 153–154).

Broadening of participation is particularly likely during periods of succession. Succession struggles force the competitors to seek allies and supporters wherever they can be found. Among other things, the competitors are constantly tempted to recruit support from those segments of the society that had formerly been excluded from politics. They must offer rewards to those they would recruit, and this opens the way to broader participation. Competitive efforts of this sort, made when each man seeks to improve his own position vis-à-vis his rivals, are the most important mechanisms by which political systems are opened (Greece: pp 123–124; Rome: p. 125; Florence: pp. 134–136; Holland: pp. 136–138; the United States: pp. 143–144).

Even a man who has reached the pinnacle may seek to consolidate or strengthen his position by appealing over the heads of his closest lieutenants (who are often his most dangerous potential rivals) in the hope of broadening his own base of support. Superficially, this appears as a rather different process than the more balanced competition of rivals who seek supporters when competing for office. Both processes, however, grow out of rivalry at the top and both result in a broadening of participation. When the man on top seeks to broaden his support, a characteristic alliance is often formed between the top man and the more or less democratic or popular base. These extremes then unite against the oligarchical or aristocratic middle (Florence: pp. 135–136; Holland: p. 137; Latin America: pp. 170, 188; the USSR under Khrushchev: pp. 218, 220).

These considerations imply that two alternative strategies are available to aspirants for power. They may seek to undermine everyone else's position so as to concentrate all stands of power into their own hands, but alternatively they may try to gain the support of others by promising them a fuller participation in the political process (East European leaders: pp. 247–251).

8. Stability

Because of the continual pressure both toward expanding and toward restricting the range of participation, the definition of who is and who is not able to take part in selecting leaders is often unclear. The absence of a clear definition is an important source of political instability. Thousands of bitter struggles have pitted those advocating a broadening of participation against those seeking to hold the line or to restrict participation. Stable regimes can exist at all levels of participation, however, for stability depends less upon the actual range of participation than upon a clear and general consensus about what that range shall be. Stability is possible both in highly centralized regimes with a single all-powerful head and in regimes with the widespread participation implied by broad and effective suffrage (China under the Manchus as contrasted with Western electoral regimes). At an intermediate level, the Venetian Republic once earned a famous and enduring stability by drawing a sharp and absolutely unbridgeable boundary between the several hundred members of the "noble" families who participated freely and continuously in politics, and all other residents who were severely excluded from voting or holding office (pp. 138–139). The least stable regimes today are those which oscillate violently between experiments with universal suffrage and tight authoritarian dictatorships (Latin America: pp. 190–191).

9. Centralization

To characterize a regime as "centralized" implies that participation is severely limited and, in particular, that the powers of appointment and dismissal are concentrated at the top. Highly centralized regimes, such as China under its strongest emperors or the Soviet Union under Stalin, have approached the centralized extreme. Stalin, like the Chinese emperors, was able to appoint and dismiss his subordinates virtually at will.

To anyone who occupies a secondary position of power, the difference between centralization and decentralization lies in the direction of his responsibility. When a man has been chosen by and is responsible to those beneath him, he can act in relative independence of those above. With high centralization, he will have to obey those above him, but he will be able to act in relative independence of those below (Mexico: p. 196; Democratic Centralism: p. 207 ff.). Real political systems, of course, show various compromises between these extremes. Men must always show some degree of responsiveness both upward and downward. Nevertheless, political systems do vary widely in the division of responsibility that men must show in the two directions. Rapid change is possible when those accustomed to directing responsibility upward suddenly find that they can or must respond instead to those below (Hungary: p. 234 ff.; Czechoslovakia: p. 245).

When subordinate officials are responsible only to those above them, and when they have no legitimate power base of their own, they will be tempted to seek informal alliances with one another. They will form many sorts of cliques, factions, and parties, and they will enter into all sorts of relationships of patronage and clientship in which the participants hope to give one another mutual assistance. In particular, they will seek to protect each other from the arbitrary authority of those above them. These cliques will thus look threatening to the man on top, and he will always be tempted to denounce them as subversive (China: p. 98; the USSR: p. 228).

10. Appointment of One's Own Successor

At the logical extreme, all offices except the highest may be filled by appointment, and finally men may even try to make the top position appointive. Such ultimate centralization is approached most closely when each ruler is allowed to appoint his own successor (China: p. 118; Latin America: p.156, pp. 167–168). If the appointment is made before the older leader is ready to leave office, however, he will immediately face the dangers posed by any clear second (see Section 2). Power will slip prematurely to the appointee. In anticipation of the future, men will begin to respond to the new man, rather than to the old. In order to minimize the danger posed by an heir apparent, the appointment is often postponed until the last possible moment, but a testament made only on the deathbed may deprive the heir of sufficient time and opportunity to consolidate his own power, and so it may not prevent a succession struggle (Marathas: p. 61; China: p. 99).

Once he has appointed his successor, the old ruler may attempt to step into the background, but it is difficult for him to retire completely. The old leader will have acquired the habit of ruling, and many of his loyal followers will be jealous of the new man. If the appointee defers to the old man too consistently, he will be nothing but a figurehead and will not really have assumed full power. If he is to assume command, he cannot avoid going, to some degree, against the wishes of the appointer. Thus, a characteristic conflict often develops between an appointer and his own appointed successor. The new man struggles to free himself from the shackles imposed by the old man, while the old man resists his final deposition (China under Ch'ien-lung: p. 105; Argentina: p. 164; Mexico: pp. 192, 193). Even if the old man provides for a peaceful transfer of power and then retires unconditionally, the new man will still face problems. The very ease with which he steps into office deprives him of the chance to demonstrate his own ability, and with no personal triumph to his credit, he will always remain in the shadow of his predecessor.

All these difficulties suggest that the easier an office is acquired, the weaker will be the man who gains it (China: pp. 118–119; Latin America: pp. 167–168). Appointment by the predecessor cannot work indefinitely. Sooner or later, men will again have to struggle for the top position.

11. Centralization Weakness

The more centralized the political system, the greater is the danger that the leader will be trapped into a dangerous ignorance by those around him. Where the position of the subordinates is entirely dependent upon the will of the man above, they must work very hard to please him. This encourages sycophancy and it encourages them to hide unpleasant truths. Thus, the leader can become increasingly isolated from realities that he must understand if he is to make intelligent decisions (China: pp. 103–104).

A highly centralized system also poses special problems when a succession struggle finally takes place, as sooner or later it must. Centralization trains men to be responsive to those above them. When men must finally struggle for the top post, however, they must compete for the support of those lower down. This reverses the usual direction of initiative and it seriously undermines the familiar patterns of power. The greater the centralization, the more likely it will be that succession struggles will raise ambiguities about the precise range of political participation. The monopoly of power by the center will be destroyed.

Even the most autocratic system, therefore, always undergoes periodic phases when wider groups can make their influence felt. No government, in other words, can remain permanently centralized. This must be counted as an inherent weakness of any highly centralized political system (China: pp. 117–119; the USSR and Eastern Europe: p. 252).

APPLICATIONS

The eleven points offered in the last section are intended to be theoretical statements and, in presenting them, I have tried to remain ethically and morally neutral. But the issues arising from succession bear so heavy upon our lives that I cannot retain my neutrality indefinitely. This is particularly the case since, as stated in the Introduction, it was more in my role as citizen than in my role as anthropologist that I was originally drawn to the study of succession. I now feel pressed to draw conclusions that are not so much theoretical as applied and personal. I was concerned, and I remain concerned, with leadership selection in the modern world, and so, in concluding this book, I must consider the implications that I see the comparative study of succession holding for our practical political lives.

For an anthropologist who has imagined himself to be committed to the ideas of cultural relativism, it is a bit unsettling to finish a comparative study by gaining a sharply increased appreciation of the practices of his own society. Nevertheless, that is what I have gained from an intensive look at succession practices elsewhere. I have achieved no admiration for the self-perpetuating techniques of oligarchies, the appointments by dictators of their own successors, or the behind-the-scenes manipulations of one-party regimes, and certainly none for the military coup. Yet these seem to be the only alternatives to some sort of election. Every alternative that I have investigated seems far worse than our own.

Even while proclaiming my general admiration for electoral succession, to be sure, I must insist that I mean no sweeping endorsement of every detail of the American political system. Indeed, I find much to be wrong with my government, and it might even be argued that the advantages of our system are balanced by disadvantages that I have not considered. Simply to point with pride to stability, for instance, does not get us very far, for stability is hardly valuable in itself. There are times when the instability of revolution offers far more hope for human well-being than does the stablest of tyrannies, though one must also concede that a good many unpleasant events can come along with unstable politics, and many of the things we prize most highly can only be achieved in a climate of some degree of order and regularity. But stability aside, there are many detailed features of our electoral system that deserve close scrutiny: our electoral college, our nominating conventions, the role of the vice-presidency, the line of succession following the vice-president. No degree of admiration for electoral succession in general should imply support for these particular details.

Nevertheless, a look at alternative systems suggests that they suffer from serious problems, many of them far more severe than our own. Anyone who prizes the traditions of liberty and of orderly political life that electoral succession has helped to make possible in a few nations of western Europe and America, must be concerned about the preservation of these traditions and about the mechanisms that make them possible.

In this light, Americans are right to be disturbed at the increasing centralization of power in their country. I share the concern of an increasing number of my contemporaries with the seemingly inexorable growth of the presidency. If any single conclusion emerges with clarity from the examples I have given in this book, it is that no system of succession seems capable of indefinite perpetuation. All have internal pressures that promote change. In the American case, the presidency has been accumulating power over the course of almost two centuries, and one wonders how long this trend can continue before a president will finally be able to use his massive power to subvert the very system that put him into office. The Watergate revelations suggested to many Americans that this danger was more immediate than they had supposed.

Most of the proposals we have heard for reform, however, strike me as remarkably unimaginative. At one extreme, we once heard mindless shouts that by tearing down what we have we will permit something better to emerge, though just what was to emerge and how we could have confidence that it would be better, remain a mystery. More rationally and more modestly, we have had proposals for tinkering with a few technical details of our system—to abolish the electoral college, for instance, or to make nominating conventions more responsive to grass roots opinion—but I do not see how such modest changes would reverse the trend toward the centralization of power in the presidency. They might well speed up the process instead.

In considering our presidency today, we may well wonder whether it has not simply grown too big for a single man to handle. Conceivably the Russians, in the collective phases of their political cycle, have been right to assert the advantages of collective leadership. It does no good to point out, as I did earlier, that the accumulated experience of human history demonstrates that single-man executives tend to win out over collegial executives. I also pointed out the advantages that heredity has over other types of succession, but in the last 200 years, we have learned to live without hereditary succession and we are, I believe, the better for it. It may be that in the next 200 years we will learn to live with collegial executives. The fact that it has been the Soviet Union that has been loudest in praise of such executives does not, of course, mean that they are limited to nonelectoral systems. Perhaps we should look more closely at the collegial executive of the Swiss.

FOREIGN AFFAIRS

Even so radical a proposal as a collegial executive falls far short of what many Americans have been willing to accept for other nations. Doubting our older methods and recognizing the urgency and complexity of the problems that face mankind, worldly Americans, knowledgeable about practical problems and seeking pragmatic solutions, have been disturbingly ready to believe "realistically" that a new nation's need for stability is greater than its need for democracy. I would even charge the doctrine of cultural relativism with having rationalized, for some Americans, their acceptance of forms of government for others that they would never accept for themselves. We have repeatedly imagined that strong men are needed to bring order out of a country's chaos. We have supposed that some nations were not ready for electoral governments and we have so overlearned the lesson of cultural relativism that we have believed some peoples to be more amenable to tyrannical leadership than ourselves, more likely to achieve economic development if pushed from above than if freed from below, too ignorant to choose their own leaders.

Americans have not all agreed on which tyrannies to admire or to tolerate. A few once saw Stalin as a benevolent father figure who could be counted upon to coax his reluctant people into the 20th century. Many more now imagine that they see in Mao or in Castro some magic answer to humanity's problems. Americans of other persuasions have been more inclined to find hope in a Chiang Kai-shek or a Franco, or at least they have been willing to support, with money and arms, dozens of contemptible Latin American and Greek dictators. Americans are not alone, of course, in their romantic hope that a strong leader will unify his people and promote their welfare, but I believe one of mankind's great illusions to be the idea that unity is to be desired, either for a people or for their leaders. Many in the United States now look back with nostalgia to a time when they suppose we had a firmer sense of national unity, and countless dictatorships and juntas in other parts of the world have justified themselves by the promise to build some sort of government of national unity behind which all citizens could unite.

But liberties never flourish, except where leaders are divided, and it is fortunate for liberty that divisions have such a wonderful way of reappearing even after the most heavy-handed periods of tyranny. Only when leaders disagree does the common man have any hope of participating in political decisions; only then can he add his own small voice on one side or the other of a dispute; only then will leaders have any need to adopt popular policies. In most of human history, the little man has made his desires felt only in times of violence. Then he might choose which army to join, or, at least, he could decide whether or not to fight with enthusiasm. There comes a time in any political system when even very humble men can decide which way to point their arrows or their guns. It is then that the popular will is felt.

Of course when arrows or bullets fly too thickly, little men lose far more in blood than they gain in influence. With no contest at all, humble men have no way to make their desires count, but with too violent a contest, they may lose everything. What they need is a contest without blood, and I count it as an advance in civilization when humble men can make their power felt by casting a ballot instead of by casting a stone. But ballots are no more useful than guns when the leadership is united or when its members hide their divisions so as to exclude others from their debates. Americans who should know better have argued that people fighting desperate economic conditions and struggling to build new nations cannot afford the luxury of electoral politics, but must submit instead to the discipline of a single party and leader. To me, it seems more sound to argue that struggling and "developing" countries cannot afford the luxury of that false unity which a single party or a single dictator imposes. There can never be a guarantee that such a party or leader will really give the people what they want or need. Rather, when the people have no way of making their desires felt, one can be very nearly certain that the leaders will ignore them.

Those who prize their freedoms ought to find it heartwarming to observe the regularity with which the fall of the world's Peróns, Nkrumahs, and Diems, and even of its Stalins and Novotnys have been accompanied not only by suddenly released popular fury, but also by the revelation, surprising only to an outsider, that their tyranny did more to hide inefficiency than to encourge development. The enlightened despot of one decade has a curious way of looking like a plain ordinary despot from the vantage point of the following decade. One suspects that such a fate lies in store for the Francos and the Castros, the Chiangs, and the Maos who remain in power in 1973. At least such must be the hope of those who would prefer to live under a less autocratic government than these men represent.

To me, the most tragic aspect of American international policy has been our all too frequent preference for the short run and superficial stability imposed by a strong but autocratic ruler for the public chaos of electoral competition. Centralized and autocratic rule is stable only in the short run. In the long run, electoral processes have the advantage. It may be mere ethnocentrism on my part, but I have found a peculiar beauty in the sight of a high caste Indian politician venturing into his district, shaking the hands and even sharing the food of his low caste constituents while seeking their approval and their votes. There may be a large measure of cynicism in this politician's actions, but the ballot does confer power on the little man as nothing else does quite so well, and I would have liked my government to have been less culturally relativistic and, even at the cost of some modest ethnocentrism, to have done more to encourage other nations to hold elections.

Here, perhaps, I can find a partial escape from the discomfort that an anthropologist must feel when admitting to a special fondness for an aspect of his own culture. With good anthropological conscience, at least, I can castigate my own government for its short-sighted and even immoral foreign policy. But here I am criticizing it for its failure to be true to its own ideals, and such criticism comes from a different angle than is conventional for anthropologists, for we more often deplore our tendency to impose our culture upon the rest of the world than bemoan our unwillingness to do so. But I cannot help asking how much more honorable the American position might have been after the Indo–Pakistan war of late 1971 had our government properly appreciated the electoral democracy of India and refused to support the military dictatorship of Pakistan. How much ghastly agony might have been saved both for ourselves and for the Vietnamese had the United States government only withdrawn all support from the Diem government of South Vietnam once it had become clear that the government had no intention of submitting itself to the elections for which the Geneva convention had provided. I do not mean to suggest that we can or should impose our own type of government upon others. We might at least be less eager to encourage other types of government.

Of course, I must rush to balance my criticism of American support for right wing and military dictatorships with an equal criticism of those other and more "liberal" Americans who have been willing to accept and even admire dictatorships that claim to be "revolutionary" or of the "left." I wish Americans would be less eager to be "realistic," less ready to condone tyranny of either the right or the left. I wish they would be less willing to conclude that our type of government is not suitable for other people. I would even charge the anthropological doctrine of cultural relativism with rationalizing and justifying, in some eyes, the existence of tyranny.

Events of the 1960s led a few Americans to question the basic justice of our "system." Some have lost faith in its ability to survive at home, and our government has done little to encourage electoral succession in the areas of the world under our influence. At the same time, most Americans, whether of the left or right, have probably exaggerated the strength, stability, and staying power of the governments of Eastern Europe and the Soviet Union. Communism once appeared as a monolithic monster, ready to engulf any chunk of territory with weak defenses, ready to subvert any nation that relaxed its vigilance. Then, it was easy to see Communism as an implacable foe that could be defeated only by head-on opposition. But Stalin died and the terror of his days diminished. The nations of Eastern Europe began to shake themselves loose from Soviet domination, and China was convulsed by the internal struggle of the cultural revolution. Perhaps, after all, Soviet practices have a few weaknesses of their own. What we need may be more patience and fewer pyrotechnics. To be sure, it is still difficult to find convincing evidence that political structures are evolving in the Soviet Union or in Eastern Europe that could be counted upon to withstand a new growth of Stalin-like terror. We have yet to see whether these nations can evolve any regular and orderly system of succession. Perhaps we can take a wry satisfaction in the thought that if they do evolve more orderly succession rules, these will probably help to reduce both the internal and external fury of their tyranny, while if they do not, then they are quite likely to be periodically convulsed with succession struggles that will weaken them internally and that will encourage the further fragmentation of their empire. Democratic centralism is more likely to change in response to its own internal contradictions than by pressures from the outside. It has within itself those famous seeds of its own destruction.

Electoral succession is far from a perfect system. Injustice, inequality, and slavery have all flourished in America under a system of popular elections. Electoral succession is a fragile system, one that has been overturned many times in human history; and it is a system that cannot survive without a large measure of faith or without wide consensus on the part of the people in the procedures for resolving conflicts. It also seems doubtful whether electoral succession can survive in the face of grinding economic hardship. Electoral succession is neither a perfect nor a foolproof system. The most one can say for it is that it works better than any other system that men have yet tried.

Inheritance of Bemba Titles

Bemba chiefs passed through a sequence of ever higher titles in their climb toward the highest title of all, citimukulu. The complexities of the process begin with a number of formal genealogical rules by which men pressed their claims and justified their actions. In outline, these rules were as follows.

Male titles were first passed on to one's next youngest brother and failing a brother, they would go to a sister's son or even to a sister's daughter's son. If more than a single sister had sons, all those cousins would be equally eligible, and so even within a single generation a title might pass, not only among true brothers, (the children of the same mother), but among a larger set of "classificatory" brothers (the sons of a set of sisters). Conflicts could arise between the competing claims of cousins and nephews. Cousins would have generational seniority and very likely chronological seniority, but the nephew would be the closer kinsman. The rules for resolving the ambiguity between the rights of nephews and cousins were not entirely clear, but one consideration was the actual age of potential claimants for the office. A man had to be old enough to assume the responsibilities of a title without resorting to a regency. Bemba children did not assume titles.

The rules for succession to women's titles were different. Younger sisters had first priority, but in the absence of a younger sister, a granddaughter rather than a daughter was supposed to succeed. The Bemba rationalized this peculiar rule in a rather complex way, arguing that if a woman assumed her own mother's title she would then act as the sociological equivalent of her own father's wife. To become the sociological equivalent of one's grandfather's wife by assuming one's grandmother's title did not seem to cause concern, but even the rule against taking a mother's title was sometimes ignored, and some Bemba women did obtain titles that their mothers had held.

Beyond these basic rules were the expectations that the mwamba stood next in line to the citimukulu and that the citimukulu's mother should once have held the title of candamukulu, but the real intricacies of these rules can only be grasped by following the history of a number of titles. The details are tortured, but if the reader will refer continuously to Figure A-1 and follow these notes with care, he should be able to get an idea of how the various factors worked out in practice over a period of several generations. In Figure A-1 the titles each man or woman held are listed (in small capital letters) under his name (written in upper and lower case letters). In all cases, the titles were held serially, the one written above being abandoned when the next below was assumed. Since the personal names are difficult to remember, I will refer to the men and women on the chart by the letters and numbers found on the diagram, the letters standing for the generation and the numbers for seniority within the generation. This diagram traces the royal family back to A-2 (whose name was Cileshe Cepela) who seized the throne from his kinsman, A-7. After A-2's time, all the important titles were held by his branch of the royal clan.

First we can trace the title of mwamba. A-2, the first citimukulu of this line appointed his younger brother, A-3, to this title. When A-3 died, their surviving brother, A-6, should have been next, but he was passed over. The explanation for this is simple: A-6 was mentally deficient. The title of mwamba was given instead to the senior nephew, B-3, who stood next in line. For reasons to be explained later, B-3 was passed by for the citimukuluship, and by the time of his death, most if not all of the men of his generation were either dead or already holding a higher title. The title of mwamba then passed to C-2, the senior man of the next generation. What

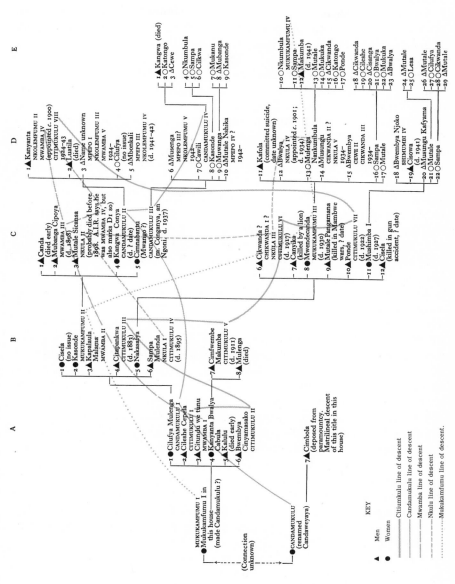

Figure A–1. Descent of Bemba titles. [Reprinted with permission of Macmillan Publishing Co., Inc. and Routledge & Kegan Paul Ltd. from *Order and Rebellion in Tribal Africa* by Max Gluckman. © Max Gluckman 1963.]

273

happened at the death of C-2, the third mwamba, is not certain. The title may have gone either to his younger brother, C-3, or directly to his nephew, D-1. Since C-3 seems to have died before or soon after C-2, he may have been out of the running. At any event, the more pressing question is why both C-6 and C-10 were bypassed in favor of D-1.

By the time of C-2's death, C-6 held the title of nkula, (see below), but the title of mwamba was supposed to rank higher, and as a member of generation C, he should have taken precedence over D-1. C-6, however, declined the title of mwamba, saying he preferred to keep the title of nkula which he would have had to relinquish had he assumed the mwambaship. C-10 should then have been next in line, and in fact C-10 did try to move into the mwamba's territory and claim the title. At this point, however, C-10 was accused of having killed the previous mwamba by witchcraft, and on this basis his claim was contested. By this time British power was making itself felt, and the British exercised their influence against C-10, so the mwambaship was dropped to the next generation. Had the British not been on the scene, C-10 and his supporters might very well have fought out their dispute with D-1 and his supporters. The final step in the inheritance of the mwambaship was entirely normal. When D-1 became citimukulu, his next surviving younger brother, D-3, became mwamba.

The title of nkula was regarded as nearly the equivalent of mwamba. It was created by B-4, the third in this line of citimukulus, and given to his younger brother, B-6. When B-6 moved up to become the fourth citimukulu, the title of nkula passed to his nephew C-3. C-3's elder brother, C-2, was passed over perhaps because he had already attained the higher title of mwamba, although we have an unexplained problem here which hinges upon whether B-3 or B-6 died first. If B-6 died before B-3, then the title of nkulu would have been the first to pass to the next generation, and C-2 should have had seniority instead of C-3 who actually inherited the title. On the other hand, if B-3 died before his younger brother, B-6, it is not clear why B-3's title of mwamba did not pass on to B-6 instead of going immediately to the next generation. Perhaps the simplest explanation for the events is that the two titles were close enough in rank and power to discourage the shift in residence that a new title would require. One's vested interest in a nominally lower rank might discourage a man from accepting an only slightly higher rank. This certainly seems to have been a consideration in some later decisions.

Another apparent deviation from strict application of the rules must be noted. Neither of the two titles, mwamba nor nkula, was given to B-7, a cousin of B-3 and B-6. B-7 certainly outlived B-6, but he was passed over for the ukulaship. The reasons are obscure, but it may be that even more than for the citimukuluship, the claims of real nephews to these secondary titles could compete successfully with the claims of classificatory brothers.

In the next generation, however, the claim of a cousin did take precedence over that of several nephews. When C-3 died, his cousin C-6 became the nkula. This can be regarded as the proper succession, though it required the title to switch from one diverging branch of the royal family to another, and after that time it stayed permanently in this branch. For personal reasons, C-6 seems to have preferred his older residence and his former title of cikwanda to that of nkula, and he soon resigned his new title. At this point, the nkula passed to his own nephew, D-12, instead of moving back up to D-1, D-6, or one of their brothers who should have been senior. The nkulaship seems to have been retained in the junior line through the influence of C-10, who by all the rules should have been next in line himself. At that time C-10 had great influence with B-7, who was then the citimukulu. C-10 declined the nkulaship, presumably because he enjoyed wielding de facto power at the capital more than the prospect of de jure power in the provinces. By having his nephew named nkula, C-10 may have gained great influence over the territory anyway. The final transfer of the nkulaship was normal—to D-14, the next younger brother of D-12.

The real importance of the tortured history of these titles is to note that as the generations passed, the two major subordinate titles of the kingdom drifted apart into separate branches of the royal lineage. Indeed, this was bound to happen sooner or later. The occasional tendency of men to decline new titles in favor of those already held, combined with the ability of nephews to claim precedence over distant classificatory brothers, meant that sooner or later the titles would begin to drift apart into separate branches of the family, and the men who held the various titles would come to be less and less closely related. The two chief women's titles drifted apart in a similar way.

A-2, who founded this royal line, bestowed the title of mukukamfumu upon his mother, and the title of candamukulu upon his older sister, A-1. When his mother died, her title dropped, according to the proper rule, to her senior living granddaughter, B-2. B-2 seems to have died later than her younger sister, B-5, since the latter did not have a chance at the title, but it is not clear why it passed to a niece, C-8, since, in the absence of sisters or cousins, normal succession should have been to a granddaughter. Since C-11 died before C-8, the title next went by normal rule to E-10, the eldest granddaughter of C-8 and the title of mukukamfumu seems by that time to have become rather securely attached to the same branch of the royal family as the title of nkula.

When A-1, the first candamukulu died, she was properly succeeded by her senior granddaughter, C-4, who in turn was normally followed by C-5, her younger sister. Then when C-5 died, her own daughter was allowed to succeed on the grounds that the only granddaughter who was yet old enough to assume a title was mad. Apparently, the title of candamukulu had now become securely attached to the same branch of the family as the mwambaship.

The inexorable tendency for titles to draw apart and become lodged in separate branches of the royal family would be slowest to affect the highest title, the citimukulu. Men would be reluctant to let that title slip irrevocably to another branch of the family and of all the offices, that of citimukulu shows the strongest tendency to shift back and forth between the diverging family lines.

Once again we can pass by the usurpation of A-2 and start with his death. His younger brother, A-3, had died earlier and the next man in line, A-6, was, it will be recalled, not very bright. He had already been passed over the title of mwamba, but when A-2, the first citimukulu died, this gentleman was invested with the office of citimukulu, as required by the most strict provisions of the genealogical rules. Possibly the council of officials exercised a legalistic influence, which encouraged literal adherence to a rule in spite of its manifest unsuitability in this case. It was not a stable situation, however, and before long A-6's nephew, B-4, rose in revolt, seized the citimu-kuluship for himself, and deposed his defective uncle. It was because of B-4's initiative that B-3, who was then the mwamba, never attained the citimukuluship. Once B-4 had seized the throne, his older brother seems to have been out of the running.

Following this seizure, the citimukuluship passed several times in completely normal fashion, first to a younger brother, B-6, then to a younger cousin, B-7. C-2, a nephew, may have had a chance to attain the citimukulu-ship instead of the cousin, B-7, for C-2 is said to have turned it down on the grounds that he was already mwamba, which he regarded as equally important. Possibly C-2 was rationalizing his own weak position, but at any rate, the cousin B-7 did assume the title. B-7 had no sisters and all of B-2's sons died before B-7, so when he died, the title reverted to the children of B-5. The title then passed properly to C-6, the man who had earlier declined the mwmambaship and abdicated the title of nkula. When C-6 died, the title passed normally to his next living younger brother, C-10.

When C-10 died, however, a dispute broke out. D-12 claimed that by this time, his branch of the royal family (that which had descended from B-5) had the right to claim the title, while D-1 claimed that as the senior brother in the senior branch he took precedence. Had this dispute not been settled by the British, it might well have resulted in armed battle. By this time, the royal family had grown so large that only a forceful reconcentration of titles within a smaller group of kinsmen might have been capable of preserving the unity of the nation.

Perhaps the Bemba needed a coup every few generations to reconcentrate the titles, but it is worth noting that some force was brought to bear upon succession even more often than that. B-4 seized the throne in his generation as A-2 had done in his, and had the British not been present, violence between D-1 and D-2 would have been likely. The citimukuluship seems to have passed into and through generation C in peace, though even in that generation, there was a show of force over the mwambaship when C-10 tried unsuccessfully to assert his claim to the title. A-2's usurpation was more thoroughgoing than the others, since he alone redistributed other titles, and thus reorganized the distribution of power rather fully; but in no generation did Bemba succession rules succeed in completely checking violence.

The Maratha Rulers

The examples of Maratha power struggles given in Chapter 3 are drawn from the entire century and a half of Maratha rule. Here, I offer a more chronological account of each reign and of each succession to the throne.

1. Shivaji (1627–1680). Although first to rule, Shivaji built his empire on the basis of his inheritance. His father, Shahji had risen to some prominence in the service of the Nizamshahi sultanate, one of several sultanates that then ruled in south India. By Shahji's time, however, the Nizamshahi sultanate was collapsing under the pressure of the expanding Mughal empire and in the resulting chaos, Shahji emerged briefly as the power behind the throne of a young Nizamshahi prince. He was soon defeated by the Mughals, and he then moved to south India, where he served as general in the army of the ruler of Bijapur, another sultanate which would also shortly acquiesce to Mughal hegemony. When Shahji moved south, his own son,

Shivaji, then only a boy, stayed behind with his mother on his father's jagir at Poona, and this patrimonial estate formed the base of power from which Shivaji was to expand.

Shahji acquired possessions in south India to add to those around Poona, but when he died, his son Ekoji, Shivaji's half brother, fell heir to most of these southern possessions. Shivaji committed armed aggression against his half brother in order to make good his claim to a share of what he regarded as their joint patrimony. Here he had to consolidate his claims on the basis of tradition and heredity, and in doing so he confirmed Ekoji in some of their patrimonial territory, and he even conferred "complete hereditary succession" over one territory to a lieutenant of Ekoji.

His main power base was further north, however, and here he could override inherited tradition more freely. He expanded from his jagir at Poona, incorporating neighboring territories until his realm assumed a significant place in Indian politics. He even grew strong enough to challenge Mughal forces. Shivaji created a more centralized regime than most contemporary Indian states, but it depended crucially on the personal authority of the monarch, and no successor could hope to fill Shivaji's role. Moreover, in spite of many successes, Shivaji failed badly in providing for clear succession.

2. *Sambhaji (1658–1689)*. Shivaji had two sons, Sambhaji, who was 22 at the time of his father's death, and Rajaram who was only 10. There had been discussion about the disposition of the kingdom before Shivaji died, and Shivaji may have suggested that his younger son Rajaram inherit the central and more settled part of the kingdom, leaving the southern and more unruly section to his older and more experienced half brother. Perhaps Sambhaji felt cheated at the prospect of such a division, and very likely, interested parties tried to build up the role of one or the other brother. At any rate, Sambhaji's partisans accused Rajaram's mother, Soyara Bai, of actively promoting her son's cause. As a result of such unpleasant rivalry, Shivaji and Sambhaji came into open conflict, and for a time, Shivaji placed his older son in confinement in order to keep him out of mischief. The bitterness between them was so great that Sambhaji even defected temporarily to a Mughal general who was then fighting Shivaji. Sambhaji eventually returned to his father's side, but the seeds of later dissention had been planted. After Shivaji's death in 1680, his ministers could not agree upon the succession. Some backed Soyara Bai, the ambitious mother of the younger brother, but others rallied to the older brother. Sambhaji was temporarily victorious, and he placed his half brother Rajaram and his stepmother Soyara Bai in close confinement. Sabhaji never ceased to be embroiled in conflict with his own kinsmen, however, and he mistrusted many of his father's most able helpers. Some of these were arrested

and, after an unsuccessful attempt upon Sambhaji's life, he had several suspected opponents executed, including his stepmother Soyara Bai, the mother of Rajaram. Fortunately for the Marathas, the Mughals, with whom they were contending, were also weakened by internal dissention at this time, so Sambhaji was able to hold out for a number of years. But in 1689 Mughal forces, acting upon intelligence supplied by Sambhaji's Maratha opponents, succeeded in capturing him. Sambhaji was tortured and killed, and his heroic death is recalled as finally inspiring Maratha loyalty as no action he had taken in life had been able to do.

3. *Rajaram (1670–1700)*. When Sambhaji died, his younger brother, Rajaram, was 19. Fearing him as a potential rallying point for his opponents, Sambhaji had kept him in confinement, but upon his brother's death, Rajaram was released by one of the military commanders and proclaimed chhatrapati. Sambhaji had left a son, however, the 7-year-old Shahu, and some commanders offered their allegiance to him instead of to Rajaram. Before any serious clashes occurred between the supporters of the uncle and of the nephew, Shahu and his mother followed Sambhaji into Mughal captivity. The Mughal emperor, Aurangzeb, was then waging a relentless war against the Marathas, and for many years, he kept Shahu in reasonably comfortable confinement, hoping to be able to use him as a pawn in Maratha politics. The immediate result of Shahu's capture, however, was to leave Rajaram in uncontested first position. Some of Shivaji's most able lieutenants were now released from Sambhaji's imprisonment, and they undertook to prosecute the never-ending war with Aurangzeb's Mughals. It was at this time that the jagirdari system decisively re-emerged as the basic organizing principle of Maratha provincial government.

4. *Tara Bai (1675–1761)*. Rajaram died in 1700 at the age of 30, only 11 years after his brother's capture and death. Rajaram's death left three possible claimants to the throne. His nephew Shahu was still alive, and although he was still in Mughal captivity, some Maratha commanders acknowledged his moral claim to the throne as the son of Shivaji's eldest son. At home, however, were two young sons of Rajaram. One was the 4-year-old son of Rajaram's senior wife, Tara Bai, and the other was the son of Rajas Bai, his junior wife. These two children were too young to act in their own right, but they were not in captivity, and they could be used as royal symbols by those seeking their own advancement. Out of a period of feverish intrigue, the widow Tara Bai emerged triumphant and came to be acknowledged as the de facto leader of the Marathas, though she could rule only in the name of her 4-year-old son, who was now formally installed as the Chhatrapati Shivaji III.

Tara Bai inevitably made enemies. The other widow, Rajas Bai, and her son, known as Sambhaji II, had their own supporters who set them up as rival claimants to the office of chhatrapati. They captured less real power than Tara Bai, but their moral claim could never be entirely discounted. At the same time, other Marathas continued to look to Shahu as their rightful leader, and some of them maintained correspondence with him, waiting for the time when he might return. A serious blow to Tara Bai's position came as her young son, Shivaji III, proved to be utterly incompetent, apparently being mentally deficient. Nevertheless, for the time being, Tara Bai herself proved to be a resourceful and effective leader, and between the time of her husband's death in 1700, and Shahu's release in 1707, she was the most powerful single Maratha. She has been credited with saving the state from being crushed by the Mughals.

5. *Shahu (1682–1749).* For 17 years after his capture as a child, Shahu and his mother, together with a number of followers and retainers, remained as captives in the camp of Aurangzeb, the Mughal emperor. Though restricted in their freedom, this was not a rigorous captivity. Shahu associated with high Mughal leaders. He received some education, and since he was being built up as an alternative Maratha leader, he was allowed to keep in contact with potential supporters. Neither Aurangzeb's hope that Shahu might be used as his own pawn in Maratha politics, nor Shahu's complementary hope of cooperating with Aurangzeb to gain his freedom were in any way implausible. Shahu's father had once defected to the Mughals, and it was not difficult for Shahu and his mother to see themselves as opponents of Rajaram and then of Tara Bai, who might be charged with having usurped Shahu's rightful throne. Shahu could legitimately hope to use Mughal power to regain his position, for it was still common practice for Maratha leaders to cooperate with the Mughals just as they and other Hindu chiefs had done for generations. In the political system of his time, there was nothing contradictory in Shahu's acknowledging the overriding authority of the Mughal emperor while simultaneously aspiring to the leadership of the Marathas.

Aurangzeb died in 1707, and in the confusion that followed, Shahu gained his freedom. He worked his way back to the Maratha country and presented himself as an alternative to the claims of his aunt Tara Bai and her imbecile son. The details of the ensuing diplomatic maneuvers and military engagements can be passed over, but the crucial factor was whether Tara Bai or Shahu could more effectively command the loyalty of the numerous Maratha chiefs and commanders. Shahu could claim to some precedence on the basis of being the son of Sambhaji, who had been the older brother of Rajaram, but Rajaram had been the more recent monarch. Tara Bai had the advantage of being on the ground before Shahu, but her mentally deficient son did not provide a strong figure for inspiring Maratha loyalty. In the end, Shahu may have been the more skillful politician and in any event, he finally emerged successful. More than anyone since his grandmother, Shahu was able to gather able lieutenants and to keep their loyalty, but he won by diplomacy where he could, rather than by brute military force. Many followers of Tara Bai were gradually weaned away by promises to support their position, so the kingdom that Shahu came to lead was far less centralized than the one his grandfather had created. Shahu's power rested upon the support of men who had an independent interest in their own territories. They were feudal potentates, powerful in their own right. With decentralization, heredity came to be an ever more important means of gaining office. Not only feudal chiefs, but even official positions of the central government soon came to be regarded as belonging by right to particular families.

Shahu never even completely displaced his cousins, the sons of Rajaram, though he came to surpass them substantially in strength. In 1714, a palace revolution, quite possibly abetted by Shahu's agents, overturned Tara Bai and her son in favor of Rajas Bai and her son, Sambhaji II. Tara Bai was imprisoned, but Sambhaji II, the first cousin of Shahu, reigned for many years in reasonable independence. No one in the party of Sambhaji II was as ambitious as Tara Bai, however, and as the years went by, the bitterness went out of the quarrel with Shahu, and in some degree the two chhatrapatis, Shahu and Sambhaji II, managed to divide the areas of their interests, Sambhaji II ruling in the south from his capital at Kolhapur, while Shahu was dominant in the north. In the long run, Shahu was much the more powerful, and it was his government that provided the link with all the later Maratha governments.

From his escape from the Mughals in 1707 until his death in 1749, Shahu had a longer reign than any other Maratha ruler. This was a time of almost incessant warfare in which Maratha power inexorably, though with interruptions, expanded northward at the expense of the Mughals and of other lesser states. Except for his relatively quiescent cousin, Sambhaji II of Kolhapur, who claimed to be at the head of an independent and equal Maratha domain, Shahu was generally accepted as the supreme head of the Marathas, although local chiefs attained great power in their own areas.

In the south, the earlier chiefs were largely confirmed in their position in return for their expressions of loyalty. In the north, where the major military expansion took place, Maratha commanders were rewarded with huge jagirs, and the powerful jagirdari families which rose upon these northern conquests came to play an important part in all later Maratha politics. Shahu managed to stabilize his external position to some extent by negotiating an agreement with the Mughal regime in Delhi. The Mughals recognized him as the rightful Maratha ruler, and Shahu in turn acknowledged the supreme overlordship of the Mughal emperor, though this agreement never really interfered with the substance of Shahu's own power and, in fact, the Maratha kingdom continued to expand at the expense of the Mughals.

6. *Nana Saheb, The First Ruling Peshwa (1721–1761)*. Shahu had two sons, but their mothers were secondary wives and they were never even considered as possible candidates for the throne. The sons were provided with modest jagirs, but Shahu searched among his distant collateral kinsmen for an heir. He searched as far as the descendants of Shivaji's brother Ekoji, and even among the descendants of Shivaji's uncles. These second and third cousins had played no significant role in the affairs of the kingdom, but they were still regarded as more plausible successors than Shahu's own but not fully legitimate offspring. Shahu finally settled upon the so-called grandson of Tara Bai, but after Shahu's death, real power fell to the peshwas.

Nana Saheb, the son of Bajirao, and the grandson of Balaji Vishvanath, was the third in the line of Shahu's peshwas, and after Shahu's death, he assumed the chief power (see Chapter 3), but the peshwas's rise to dominance did not pass uncontested. Leaders who had quarreled with the peshwas could ally themselves with Tara Bai, who once again tried to take power. Although Tara Bai and her allies were finally defeated again, this rivalry loosened still further the increasingly tenuous ties that kept the component parts of the kingdom together. Some of the chiefs, particularly those who ruled in the newly conquered territories of the north, owed their position to the peshwas, and they became the major support of the new regime. Others continued to nourish resentment, and while they could not challenge the peshwa's power individually and openly, they could drag their feet on financial contributions to the central treasury, respond slowly to his calls for military support, and on occasion, they could even join his enemies and bring considerable dissension to the kingdom. When the peshwas had to expend their energies trying to coerce dissident southern chiefs into loyalty, even their more loyal northern dependents were left to their own initiative, and they could consolidate their local power. While willing to recognize the supreme authority of the peshwa, the northern chiefs came into increasing rivalry with one another. In particular, the two most powerful northern houses, the Holkars and the Sindias, which had both begun as military chieftaincies under the early peshwas, became ever more antagonistic, and their rivalry would ultimately help to break up the kingdom.

In spite of these internal difficulties, Maratha military power continued to expand. The power of the chiefs reached so far north that they began to intervene directly in the politics of the now crumbling Mughal dynasty. Their northern advance was halted only when they came into conflict with the Afghans, who were moving southward into the same power vacuum that the Marathas were filling from the south. The Marathas suffered a disastrous defeat at the hands of the Afghans at the famous third battle of Panipat in 1761; but since the Afghans soon retired to their home, the Marathas were able to recoup most of their losses. More serious for Maratha hegemony than the thousands of deaths suffered at Panipat was the death a few months later of Nana Saheb, the third peshwa.

7. *Madhavrao I (1755–1773).* By the time of Nana Saheb's death, the inheritability of his office had become as unquestioned as the inheritability of the office of chhatrapati. Nana Saheb had three sons. He had designated the eldest son, Vishvasrao, as his heir, but Vishvasrao was killed at the battle of Panipat and the second son, Madhavrao was next in line. His father seems to have agreed to Madhavrao's claim before his death, and this probably encouraged most of the Maratha leaders to go along, but Madhavrao was only 16 when his father died, and his mother's assistance was crucial in securing his claim. Through Madhavrao's short but success-ful reign, he maintained close ties with his mother, seeking her counsel in all matters and writing her detailed letters about his activities when they were separated.

Madhavrao I achieved the throne with rather less immediate dissension than existed at the deaths of some earlier and later monarchs, but at the age of 16, he could not immediately take complete charge or assume full powers. His mother was expected to counsel him, and his uncle Raghuna-thrao, the brother of his father, acted as regent. Raghunathrao, however, nursed ambitions to rule himself, and he was able to gather considerable backing from some Maratha chiefs. He was finally put down only by the military force of Madhavrao I and those loyal to him. Raghunathrao was imprisoned by his nephew, but even from confinement, he continued his conspiratorial efforts throughout Madhavrao's reign. After being seriously ill, Madhavrao I died in 1772 when only 27 years old. In his short reign of 11 years, he had managed to unite the dissident parts of his kingdom with considerable success, and he is remembered as both an efficient military commander and as a skillful and impartial civil ruler.

8. *Narayanrao (1755–1773).* Madhavrao I died without sons. Rag-hunathrao was still in prison and still raising trouble, but there seems to have been general agreement among the still united followers of Madhavrao I that the peshwaship should be bestowed upon his younger brother, Narayanrao, who had been nominated by his elder brother before his death. A good deal of the real power now passed to a council of ministers who had served Madhavrao I. Inevitably differences began to arise among these ministers, and the inexperienced Narayanrao was by no means successful in keeping them united. He began to attract opposition, and once again Raghunathrao was able to profit by the disagreements. After only 9

months in office, a plot for Narayanrao's overthrow developed, and in a brief palace struggle Narayanrao was murdered.

Raghunathrao was now the only surviving male member of the peshwa's family. He began to administer as peshwa and, in the absence of any alternative, many people acquiesced in his leadership. Nevertheless, Raghunathrao was widely blamed for setting off the chain of events that led to his nephew's murder, and while he had not personally committed the act, some suspected that he had ordered it. Revulsion against him was widespread. Enemies threatened to rise in all parts of the far flung empire, and Raghunathrao's control at the center was extremely shakey.

9. *Madhavrao II (1774–1795).* An alternative to Raghunathrao presented itself when one of Narayanrao's widows, a girl named Ganga Bai, turned out to have been pregnant at the time of his death. A number of high officials quickly formed themselves into a council, first to protect Ganga Bai, whose life may have been in some danger from the followers of Raghunathrao, but also to oppose Raghunathrao and reach out for effective rule themselves. Most of the important men who had served Madhavrao were members of this council, the *barabhai,* and to their great rejoicing, Ganga Bai's child was a son, providing a symbol behind which to rally resistance to Raghunathrao. The baby became known as Madhavrao II, and in his name the council of officials was able to take charge. Raghunathrao's supporters began to desert him, and after a number of military skirmishes, he was defeated, though he retained enough covert support to allow him to elude capture and flee to British protection. At that time the British were beginning to play for real power in India, and here as elsewhere, they were able to insinuate themselves effectively into the succession battles that were so characteristic of all Indian kingdoms. For a time, they supported Raghunathrao against his new nephew, but British pressure was not yet strong enough to be decisive and it could not displace the supporters of Madhavrao II.

Out of this period of confusion, two men finally rose to preeminent power. Nana Phadnis became the dominant member of the council or barbhai at Poona, while Mahadji Sindia, the head of an important northern family, became the most powerful military leader; but both acted only in the name of the infant peshwa. Nana Phadnis stayed at the capital and took charge of the central records and of the revenue gathering apparatus, but he never had a military command. Mahadji Sindia, by contrast, was only a provincial leader, but his military skills allowed him to achieve a dominant position. As long as each kept within his own sphere, the two men managed to cooperate as often as they quarreled, but they never really trusted each other. Nana Phadnis continually suspected Mahadji of conspiring with his enemies, but Mahadji's power grew to cover a great part of north central

India, until finally he could even impose his will upon the Mughal court at Delhi. Sitting at the Maratha capital in Poona, Nana Phadnis had control of the young peshwa, their symbol of authority, and he kept close watch over the boy as he grew to manhood. The divided rule of these two men formed the final period of reasonable stability in Maratha history.

In 1792, after a 12-year absence from the capital, Mahadji Sindia finally visited Poona. Much to the consternation of Nana Phadnis and of his many adherents, Mahadji brought a large retinue and a strong military force. The young Peshwa Madhavrao II was now 18 years old, and a period of intrigue and dispute between Nana Phadnis and Mahadji Sindia began, with the peshwa standing in the background. Mahadji had the decisive military power under his command, and he seemed on the point of displacing Nana Phadnis and gaining control in Poona, but before the situation was really clarified Mahadji Sindia died. He was 67 and the year was 1794. His death left a serious power vacuum that was only partially filled by his adopted son Daulatrao, who had been designated as his heir. The next year Peshwa Madhavrao II also died, following a fall from a balcony. He may well have taken his own life. He had been raised in the most sheltered and protected circumstances, but he was then thrust into a world of high intrigue and mutual suspicion and he seems to have found himself incapable of finding his way in a world for which he was utterly unprepared.

10. Bajirao II (1775–1851). Once again the search for a successor began. By this time, old Ragunathrao had finally died, but the only remaining males in the peshwa's family were Raghunathrao's sons. At a time when he had despaired of having legitimate sons of his own. Raghunathrao had adopted Amritarao, but he had subsequently had two natural sons, Bajirao the elder and Chimnaji, the younger. His natural sons were widely regarded as less capable than the adopted Amritarao.

Madhavrao II's death unleashed an unruly general scramble for power and position. Nana Phadnis was at first the most powerful figure, and for a time it might have seemed that he would be able to repeat the performance of the peshwas, who in an earlier generation had displaced the ruling family and secured all power to themselves. Nana Phadnis even had some hereditary claim to his office, since an ancestor had held the same office as early as the first part of Shahu's reign. Certainly Nana Phadnis tried to maintain his powerful position, but he had made many enemies during his career, particularly during his final conflict with Mahadji Sindia. Having no military skills, he did not feel able to rule by his own might. He needed a figurehead peshwa. He first tried to use Chimnaji, Raghunathrao's younger son. When this did not work to his satisfaction, he finally supported Bajirao the elder brother, although he had formerly been bitterly opposed to him.

Bajirao had spent much of his childhood sharing the restrictions which

Nana Phadnis imposed upon the family of Raghunathrao and even after Raghunathrao's death, Bajirao had remained in confinement along with his mother. This upbringing had hardly provided him with a suitable training for political leadership, but it had unquestionably left him with every reason to hate Nana Phadnis. Nana Phadnis was finally displaced and circumstances did not allow him to secure his office for his descendants.

To fully appreciate the turmoil of the years that followed, it must be understood that the same forces which were bringing divisions among those who ruled at the center of the kingdom, were also bringing divisions to several of the chiefly families. In particular, two great northern families, the Holkars and the Sindias, were becoming divided in ways that paralleled those of the central government. Both the Holkars and the Sindias had risen to prominence under the early peshwas. During Shahu's reign, the peshwa had guided Ranoji Sindia, Malharrao Holkar, and some other chiefs, to an agreement to divide up the northeastern Maratha conquests into various spheres of influence. The Sindias came to lead a rather independent domain based upon Gwalior, far to the north of the main center of Maratha power, and the Holkars led a domain based upon Indore (see Figure 3-1, p. 56). Unfortunately for Maratha unity, the Sindias and Holkars came into increasingly bitter competition during their unceasing but fluctuating military adventures.

When Ranoji Sindia died in 1745, he left four sons, all said to be valiant and capable (see Figure A-2). Jayappa, the eldest, became head of the

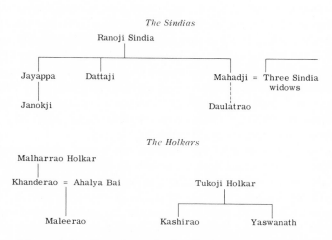

Figure A–2. Genealogy of subordinate Maratha families.

family, and he soon had a serious dispute with Malharrao Holkar over a succession in a Rajput family in which they both had an interest. Jayappa was murdered by Rajputs, and feelings against the Holkars rose even higher as the Sindias, rightly or wrongly, suspected them of having had a hand in Jayappa's murder. Jayappa, however, left instructions to his brother Dattaji to carry on in the name of his (Jayappa's) son Jankoji. A few years later, the fatal battle of Panipat very nearly wiped out the house of Sindia and only the youngest of Ranoji's four sons, Mahadji, was left alive. This had the compensation of clarifying the succession, though even then it was not completely uncontested, since Raghunathrao demanded a large *nazarana* (succession fee) which Mahadji was unable to pay. Raghunathrao tried to put some rather distant cousins in charge of the Sindia domains, but Mahadji was an exceptionally able soldier and he managed to fight his way to survival until he finally triumphed as the strongest Maratha chieftain of all the northern territories, and for a time he was the most powerful Maratha anywhere.

When Mahadji died in 1794, however, he left no natural sons, and his place was taken by his adopted son Daulatrao, the son of a cousin. Daulatrao sustained himself by an alliance with Bajirao II, the last of the peshwas, but he made no notable contributions to Maratha unity or welfare, and he quarreled with his adopted father's widows. These remarkable women took control of some of the forces of their dead husband and caused the war of the Sindia widows to break out. They tended to ally themselves with Yaswanath Holkar who controlled part of the old Holkar domains, and who at the time was supporting Amritarao for peshwa, in opposition to Bajirao II.

The Holkar domains had become established at the same time as those of the Sindias. Malharrao Holkar participated in the northward expansion of the Marathas, but his only legitimate son, Khanderao, died before him, and Khanderao's only son, Maleerao, died soon after. The Holkar family was then left with no male heir. A dispute about the appropriate succession was resolved by allowing Ahalya Bai, who was Malharrao's daughter-in-law, and the widow of Kanderao, to administer the family property and take charge of finances, but entrusting command over the family armies to a man named Tukoji.

Tukoji was no kinsman of the Holkars, but he was an experienced subordinate chief, and he had been a favorite of Malharrao. For a number of years, leadership over Holkar affairs was split between the widow Ahalya Bai and Tukoji Holkar as he came to be known. He became powerful enough to assert himself as the Holkar leader in struggles over succession to the office of peshwa. After Tukoji and Ahalya Bai had died, no possible heirs to the Holkar domain remained except for the several sons of Tukoji.

By this time they could claim inheritance themselves, and they became the effective heirs of the Holkar land and power. Here, as in the case of the peshwas, rulership was transferred from one family to another; but in both cases, the transfer needed enough time to allow the new family slowly to accumulate the legitimacy that could only come with heredity.

No sooner had control over the Holkar domains been firmly secured by Tukoji's family than this family too began to split. The oldest son of Tukoji received some backing, and he became a supporter of Peshwa Bajirao II, and thus an ally of Daulatrao Sindia. But a younger son, Yaswanath, seems to have been more able, and he became the more powerful. He, of course, allied himself with the enemies of his older brother's allies, and the result was that Yasawanath helped the three Sindia widows, and for a time, he and the widows tried to support Amritarao, the adopted brother of Bajirao II, as an alternative peshwa. Thus, each of the three families, the Holkars, the Sindias, and the Peshwas, were split into opposing factions which fought on opposite sides.

In the face of such turmoil, Bajirao II could wield no more than the most precarious kind of authority. He did manage to rid himself of Nana Phadnis, but by this time the pieces of the kingdom were flying apart and no single leader could any longer hope to weld them together under a single command. European pressure was also increasing, and the British succeeded in amputating various parts of the kingdom and placing them under their own protection. Bajirao II was left with a much reduced realm. Finally, after a last desperate effort to assert his own independence, Bajirao II was removed in 1818 by the British, who were now allied with some of his Maratha enemies. Maratha independence had come to an end.

The Ming Dynasty

It is unfair to imagine that the experience of a single dynasty must necessarily reflect eternal Chinese practices, and in particular, the foreign origin of the Manchus must make us wonder whether earlier Chinese practices might not have been quite different from theirs. A full exploration of succession in earlier dynasties can only be undertaken by a sinologist, but even a brief glimpse of the preceding Ming dynasty can offer some confidence that Manchu experience was not totally out of line with that of their predecessors.

The Ming dynasty lasted for almost three centuries, from 1368 to 1644, just a bit longer than the Manchu dynasty. Sixteen emperors reigned during this time, six more than during the Manchu period. This gave the Ming shorter average reigns than the Manchu, though the difference would be less if the two exceptionally long Manchu reigns of K'ang-hsi and Ch'ien-lung were not included. T'ai-tsu, who founded the Ming dynasty, rose to power more quickly than did the later Manchu emperors, for he started from the humblest of backgrounds but climbed to the throne himself. The Manchus took three generations to build up the power that could collect the pieces of the shattered Ming empire.

T'ai-tsu did not share the Manchu's background of steppe feudalism, but his early government showed some of the same organizational principles as did the early Manchu government. T'ai-tsu willed the throne to his grandson, Chien-wên (the latter's father, I-wên, the eldest son of T'ai-tsu, having died), but he set up 9 of his 24 sons as princes over 9 separate geographic divisions of the empire. These principalities combined the leadership of a royal prince (reminiscent of the later Manchu banners), with a geographic base (reminiscent of the Chinese feudatories of the earliest Manchu period). Such a realm could serve as power bases for a rebellious prince, and Yung-lo, the fourth son of T'ai-tsu, did indeed rebel (see Figure A-3). He waged a successful war against his nephew Chien-wên, and he seized the throne in 1402, only 4 years after T'ai-tsu had died.

Yung-lo's reign was followed by a very brief reign of his first son Hung-hsi, who in his turn was followed in 1425 by his first son Hsüan-tê, the fifth emperor and great-grandson of the founder. Hsüan-tê's uncle, Kao-hsu, brother of the briefly reigning Hung-hsi, and second son of Yung-lo, now tried to repeat his father's performance by rebelling against his nephew. This time, however, the reigning emperor won, and feudal insubordination by dissident male kinsmen of the emperors did not again become a problem for the Ming.

Following this second and unsuccessful revolt, the succession to the throne was able to proceed for some time in an orderly fashion. The

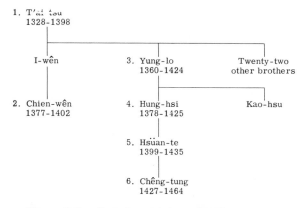

Figure A–3. Genealogy of the early Ming emperors.

throne generally passed to the eldest son of the previous emperor, but even more quickly than among the Manchus, the real power of the emperor was soon captured by members of the emperor's household. From as early as the sixth reign, that of Chêng-t'ung, which began in 1435, 63 years after the founding of the dynasty, a series of eunuchs came to dominate the administration. Occasionally eunuchs became the rulers of the nation in all but name. The later history of the dynasty is a rather sordid tale of eunuch power, allied from time to time with various empresses, and only occasionally interrupted by the influence of reform-minded ministers.

A full review of the complex details of the transmission of Ming power would require many tedious pages, but in broad outlines, the development of the Ming shows remarkable parallels to that of the Manchus: an early period of rivalry and insubordination among male kinsmen of the emperor and among men with a geographical base in a more or less "feudal" domain; a second period of more regular succession and the apparent acquiescence in regular procedures by other family members; finally, the capture of real power by the "inner court" or household of the emperors. This final period was characterized by a succession of ineffectual titular emperors, but complete failure on the part of those who held real power to legitimize their position. The Manchu emperors held on to real power for longer than the Ming. They were able to do so partly by their good luck in having two very long reigns. Once the Manchus began to weaken, however, their decisive end came more quickly, in considerable part, no doubt because of the insistent pressures of Western intervention. Still, the sequence of events in the two dynasties shows striking similarities, and in all probability, earlier dynasties would show some of the same features.

Bibliographic Notes

GENERAL

No one can possibly read the thousands of books that bear upon the problem of succession, to say nothing of the periodical literature or the manuscript sources. Any general account of the kind I have attempted must, inevitably, rely upon secondary and tertiary sources, and these notes are intended to acknowledge, in a feeble way, my impossibly heavy debt to the historians, anthropologists, sociologists, political scientists, and journalists who have written on the various areas I have surveyed.

Succession has been seen as a general problem for as long as there have been political theorists, and statements that pose the problem in very much the same way that I do go back a very long time. Typologies of political systems, which go right back to Aristotle, have always been based in considerable measure upon the method by which political leaders gain office. In Chapter 19 of the *Leviathan*, Hobbes outlined the problems of succession, and Max Weber dealt with succession as part of his interest in charismatic leadership. More recently, Frederick Mundell Watkins gave an astute analysis of the problem in an article entitled "Succession, Political" in the *Encyclopedia of the Social Science* (1934). In a brief, but penetrating fashion, Watkins raised many of the same questions that I raise in this book, and he pointed to the dilemmas posed by the need to find a successor. He emphasized the crucial importance of succession for every aspect of the political process.

In view of the clarity with which the problem has so long been seen, it is strange to find that modern political scientists have largely ignored it. Carl J. Friedrich is exceptional among American writers of textbooks on government for including succession as an important topic of a chapter in his *Man and His Government* (Chapter 28, "Succession and the Uses of Party," New York: McGraw-Hill, 1963). Most modern textbooks of political science pass by the problem in silence. Myron Rush does devote a few incisive pages to a general statement of the problem in his *Political Succession in the USSR* (New York: Columbia Univ. Press, 1965) and Paul Kecskemeti points out some of the difficulties that totalitarian regimes face at times of succession ("Totalitarianism and the Future," Carl J. Friedrich, ed., *Totalitarianism,* New York: Grosset & Dunlap, 1964). These are unusual in modern political science writing, however, and recent interest in the comparative aspects of succession seems to have been nearly nonexistent. An issue of *The Journal of International Affairs* was entitled "Statesmen and Succession" (Vol. XVIII, No. 1, 1964), but its contents were limited to discussions of the current situation in a number of countries and to speculations about who might succeed to power in subsequent years. A search of the footnotes of this issue disclosed not a single reference to any general discussion of the succession problem, and none of the authors seemed interested in placing his examples in any theoretical or comparative perspective.

Some political scientists today use the rubric, "elite recruitment," a phrase that might appear to be the modern equivalent for the older term "succession." Those concerned with elite recruitment, however, have actually looked at a very different set of problems than have been classically covered by "succession." "Succession" has referred to the mechanics by which particular men gain particular offices, especially the highest office, while "elite recruitment" refers to such matters as an analysis of the social class background of those who enter politics. See, for instance, Dwaine Marvick (ed.), *Political Decision Makers* (New York: The Free Press of Glencoe, 1961), and Harold Lasswell and Daniel Lerner (eds.), *World Revolutionary Elites* (Cambridge, Mass.: MIT Press, 1965). Elite recruitment theory is concerned with large scale phenomena, often with phenomena that are susceptible to statistical analysis; succession theory is more often concerned with the detailed rules of interpersonal relations within small groups. It is the latter, not the former, with which I am concerned.

Perhaps it is less surprising than it first appears that anthropologists have given more detailed and explicit attention to succession than have recent political scientists. Anthropologists, after all, with their interest in a more diverse range of societies, have been able to take less for granted, and they also have a tradition of studying the interpersonal relations among small groups—as in their studies of kinship, for example. Thus, anthropologists have written fairly detailed accounts of succession practices in a number of primitive tribes, and the fullest general treatment I know of that poses questions about succession in a way I find congenial is the work of anthropologist Jack Goody (ed.), *Succession to High Office* (Cambridge Papers in Social Anthropology, No. 4, Cambridge: The University Press, 1966). Goody's book includes an excellent general and theoretical analysis of succession by the editor, and sound case studies of succession in several African societies.

I have profited from a reading of many other anthropological works on government and politics, and although these do not deal specifically with succession, they have certainly helped to mold my general outlook upon the comparative study of government: Michael Banton (ed.), *Political Systems and the Distribution of Power* (A.S.A. Monographs 2, London: Tavistock Publications, 1965); Max Gluckman, *Order and Rebellion in Tribal Africa* (London: Cohen and West, 1963); I. Schapera, *Government and Politics in Tribal Societies* (London: C. A. Watt's, 1956); and Marc J. Swartz, Victor W. Turner, and Arthur Tuden (eds.), *Political Anthropology* (Chicago: Aldine, 1966).

However, it is neither to political scientists nor to anthropologists, but to historians that I feel most heavily indebted. Historians have provided the data upon which I base most of my case histories, and their works form the largest fraction of those mentioned in the notes on succeeding pages. To an anthropologist, like myself, historians must occasionally seem rather strangely unaware of, or unconcerned with, the broader comparative aspects of the events they study, but this anthropologist, at least, can only look with awe and admiration upon the meticulous scholarship, subtle analysis and graceful prose of many historians. They have provided hundreds of detailed descriptions of the forces acting upon particular succession struggles, and if they have not tried to offer comparative analyses of the problem it is, no doubt, because they know better than to attempt the impossible.

CHAPTER 2: OUR TRIBAL HERITAGE

The cases described in this chapter, unlike those of the remaining chapters of the book, are based upon the work of anthropologists, and they reflect both the close attention that anthropologists have given to social structure and their relatively feeble historical knowledge. Melanesian big men have been described by a number of anthropologists, the most detailed treatment being that of Douglas L. Oliver's *A Solomon Island Society* (Cambridge, Mass.: Harvard Univ. Press, 1955) from which I draw my example of the Siuai. The term *big man* has become current among anthropologists since the analysis of Marshall Sahlins in "Poor Man, Rich Man, Big Man, Chief: Political Types in Melanesia and Polynesia," *Comparative Studies in History and Society* (Vol. V. 1963), pp. 285–303.

British anthropologists have devoted extensive and penetrating attention to African political systems, and my account of African societies is based largely upon their work. *African Political Systems,* edited by Meyer Fortes and E. E. Evans–Pritchard (London: Oxford Univ. Press, 1940), was a landmark in comparative studies of these systems, but since the appearance of that volume, our knowledge of African political organization has been expanded by many new field reports and synthesizing comparisons.

The background of Bantu culture, the growth of the Zulu state out of its Bantu antecedents, and the repercussions of the Zulu explosion upon its neighbors have all received extensive attention. I found John D. Omer–Cooper's *The Zulu Aftermath: A Nineteenth Century Revolution in Bantu Africa* (Evanston, Ill.: Northwestern Univ. Press, 1966) to be a superb historical synthesis of these events, and one which helped to place the Swazi in a broader perspective. The Swazi political system itself is described in more detail in Hilda Kuper's deservedly famous work, *An African Aristocracy* (London: Oxford Univ. Press, 1947).

Audrey I. Richards' many works on the Bemba are rightly regarded as forming one of the great contributions to African ethnology. Her book, *Land, Labour, and Diet in Northern Rhodesia* (London: Oxford Univ. Press, 1939), contains her fullest account of the Bemba, but several of her articles address themselves more directly to questions of social and political organization, particularly her article "The Political System of the Bemba Tribe—Northeastern Rhodesia," in Fortes and Evans–Pritchard (eds.), *African Political Systems* (London: Oxford Univ. Press, 1939), but also other and later articles which use Bemba materials to exemplify general political principles: "Social Mechanisms for the Transfer of Political Rights in Some African Tribes," *Journal of the Royal Anthropological Institute* (Vol. 90, 1960), pp. 175–90; "African Kings and Their Royal Relatives," *Journal of the Royal Anthropological Institute* (Vol. 91, 1961), pp. 135–50. Some idea of place of the Bemba in the context of neighboring tribes and of their similarities and differences from these neighbors can be found in Wilfred Whiteley, *The Bemba and Related Peoples of Northern Rhodesia (Ethnographic Survey of Africa. East Central Africa,* Pt. 2. London: International African Institute, 1950).

Max Gluckman has also written an intriguing paper concerned specifically with Bemba succession and with the drifting apart of titles: "Succession and Civil War Among the Bemba: An Exercise in Anthropological Theory," *Human Problems in Central Africa* (Vol. 16, 1954), pp. 6–27, reprinted in Gluckman's book *Order and Rebellion in Tribal Africa.* Gluckman based his analysis in large part upon W. V. Brelsford, *The Succession of Bemba Chiefs: A Guide for District Officers* (Lusaka: Government Printer, 1948), which, however, I have not seen. The special characteristics of matrilineal descent have been widely discussed, most incisively in my opinion by David M. Schneider in his "Introduction" to *Matrilineal Kinship,* Schneider and Kathleen Gough (eds.) (Berkeley: Univ. of California Press, 1961).

My summary of Nupe is based entirely upon S. F. Nadel's great work, *A Black Byzantium* (London: Oxford Univ. Press, 1942), which describes the workings of the Nupe state in extensive detail. The general nature of circulating succession is dealt with by Jack Goody in his article "Circulating Succession Among the Gonja in his *Succession to High Office,* pp. 142–176. The standard reference on the Baganda is an old work by John Roscoe, *The Baganda* (London: Macmillan, 1911), but much of his description has been superceded by the more recent and far more penetrating analysis of Martin Southwold, *Bureaucracy and Chieftainship in Baganda* (East African Studies, No. 14, London: Kegan Paul, Trubner, 1961); "Succession to the Throne in Baganda" in Goody (ed.) *Succession to High Office,* pp. 82–126; "The History of a History: Royal Succession in Baganda" in I. M. Lewis (ed.) *History and Social Anthropology* (A.S.A. Monographs 7, London: Tavistock Publications, 1968), pp. 127–151. The problems raised by fraternal succession are incisively dealt with in Goody's introduction to *Succession to High Office.*

CHAPTER 3: THE MARATHAS OF INDIA

Having lived in relatively recent times, the Marathas left a far larger corpus of historical documents than did their Indian predecessors, larger, no doubt, than that of any other Hindu kingdom. Europeans were moving into India in ever greater numbers during the time of Maratha rule and they left extensive records which bear upon Maratha history, but the Marathas themselves produced masses of administrative reports, letters, leases, contracts, and treaties. The kingdom, moreover, has inspired a good deal of work by Indian historians, so that ample secondary sources are also available. An early general history of the kingdom was written by James Grant Duff, *History of the Marathas* (3 vols., London: Longman, Rees, Orme, Brown, and Green, 1826 and later editions).

In this chapter, I rely most heavily upon a much more recent and much fuller synthesis, G. S. Sardesai's *New History of the Marathas* (Bombay: Phoenix Publications, 1946–48), which incorporates the mass of scholarly work that has been done since Duff's day. Sardesai is an unabashed Maratha partisan, and his work occasionally has a slightly one-sided slant. He castigates enemies for pillaging Maratha territories, but does little more than regret the reciprocal pillaging that made the Marathas feared and hated over much of India in their later years. The death of a Maratha may be attributed to the barbaric treachery of an enemy, while an enemy death may be seen as a sad but inevitable step in the consolidation of Maratha hegemony. Nevertheless, Sardesai's facts seem reliable, and I have depended heavily upon his work.

Several more specialized volumes deal with various Maratha personalities or with limited periods, and I have used some of these for their insights into particular incidents. Among these, the works of Jadunath Sarkar, *House of Shivaji* (Calcutta: M. C. Sarkar, 1955) and *Shivaji and His Times,* (London: Longmans, Green & Co., 1920) strike me as better balanced than most, but I have also consulted Brij Kishore, *Tara Bai and Her Times* (Bombay, New York: Asia Publishing House, 1963), Surendra Nath Sen, *Administrative System of the Marathas* (Calcutta: University of Calcutta, 1925), and *The Military System of the Marathas* (Bombay: Orient Longmans, 1928). To try and gain some idea of Indian political theory that may have helped to form Maratha ideas, I have consulted a chapter by A. L. Basham, "Some Fundamental Political Ideas of Ancient India" in his *Studies in Indian History and Culture* (Calcutta: Sambodhi Publications, 1964), John W. Spellman's *Political Theory of Ancient India* (Oxford: Clarenden Press, 1964) and U. N. Ghoshal's much fuller *History of Indian Political Idea* (Bombay: Oxford Univ. Press, 1959), and I have used R. Shamasastry's translation of Kautilya's *Arthasastra* (Mysore: Sri Raghuveer Print Press, 1951).

Several general histories of India have been written. For general background and as close an approach to social history as I have seen, I would refer the reader to Thapar's and Spear's *A History of India,* Vol. I by Romila Thapar (Baltimore, Md.: Penguin Books, 1966), Vol. II by Percival Spear, (Baltimore, Md.: Penguin Books, 1965). A much duller book, but one with more facts about battles, dynasties, and dates is *Advanced History of India,* by R. C. Majumdar, H. C. Raychaudhuri, and Kalikinkar Datta (London: Macmillan, 1946).

A sober assessment of Indian "feudalism" will be found in Daniel Thorner, "Feudalism of India" in Rushton Coulbourn (ed.), *Feudalism in History* (Princeton, N.J.: Univ. Press, 1956), pp. 133–150. Thapar (*op. cit.*) devotes a chapter, the 11th, to the rise of Indian feudalism. My own feeling for the nature of Indian "feudalism" has been enriched by a reading of

James Tod, *Annals and Antiquities of Rajastan,* William Crooke, (ed.) (London: Oxford Univ. Press, 1920), which gives a lively personal 19th century account of an area adjacent to that of the Marathas.

CHAPTER 4: CHINA OF THE MANCHUS

Trying to gain a fairly thorough knowledge about a limited aspect of Chinese history can be a frustrating experience for one not brought up as a sinologist. When historians of China write for each other, they credit their readers with a massive and detailed knowledge, and without this knowledge an outsider may be left quite helpless. On the other hand, when they write for a wider public, they must cover too much territory to permit an intensive look at any single part. Thus a masterful and modestly massive survey of Chinese history, such as *East Asia: The Great Tradition,* by Edwin O. Reischauer and John K. Fairbank (Boston: Houghton-Mifflin, 1960) does not even give the names of most of the emperors, let alone describe the circumstances by which they attained power. One even suspects that sinologists have reacted so strongly against old-fashioned political history that they have shunned the details of court intrigue in favor of what, for many purposes, are the more important social and economic developments. There turns out to be no detailed and modern political history in a Western language of even the most recent dynasty of China.

By piecing together information from various sources, however, even a nonsinologist can build up a tolerably complete picture of what happened. I found Franz Michael's *The Origin of Manchu Rule in China* (Baltimore: John Hopkins Univ. Press, 1942) to be an excellent account of the forces at work in the early part of the dynasty, and Li Chien-nung's *The Political History of China, 1840–1928,* (Princeton, N.J.: D. Van Nostrand, 1956) gives rather full information on its later stages. For the period between, as well as for a supplement to the information from these two books, I have relied heavily upon a truly monumental work of scholarship: Arthur W. Hummel (ed.), *Eminent Chinese of the Ch'ing Period (1644–1912),* (2 vols. Washington, D.C.: Government Printing Office, 1943–44). In 1,100 large double-columned pages, this work gives biographies, ranging from a paragraph to a few pages in length, of hundreds of eminent Chinese. While hardly the most convenient source to use, it is magnificiently indexed and cross-referenced, and one can leaf back and forth among its pages and learn a great deal about the people who were making decisions during the Manchu dynasty and about the social constraints within which they worked. Sinologists regard Hummel's work as reliable, and I have depended more upon it than upon any other source for a factual outline of Manchu history and for the details of many incidents. For dates and certain minimal genealogical information, I have relied upon the chronological tables provided in Arthur C. Moule's *The Rulers of China, 221 B.C.–A.D. 1949* (New York: Praeger, 1957).

The organization of the Manchu government and of its various components has been rather well described by Hsieh Pao-chao in *The Government of China (1644–1922)* (Baltimore: Johns Hopkins Press, 1925), though Hsieh is better on organizational structure than on the dynamics of its operation. He gives little chronology, and his references to the changes that took place in the course of the dynasty are not full. Edmund Backhouse and J. O. P. Bland, in their *Annals and Memoirs of the Court of Peking* (Boston: Houghton-Mifflin, 1914) give many colorful descriptions of incidents in late Ming and Manchu history, and they help to convey some feeling for life at the capital and elsewhere, but it is difficult for a nonsinologist to judge the detailed reliability of their work.

A number of more recent works deal intensively with one aspect or one period of Manchu China: Ping-ti Ho, *The Ladder of Success in Imperial China,* (New York: Columbia Univ. Press, 1962); Chung-li Chang, *The Chinese Gentry,* (Seattle, Wash.: Univ. of Washington Press, 1955); Jonathan D. Spence, *Ts'ao Yin and the K'ang-hsi Emperor: Bondservant and Master* (New Haven, Conn.: Yale Univ. Press, 1966); and Franz H. Michael, *The Taiping Rebellion* (Seattle, Wash.: Univ. of Washington Press, 1966).

For subtle insights into a number of aspects of Chinese civilization, I have found some of the articles in a series of volumes published under the auspices of the Committee on Chinese Thought of the Association for Asian Studies to be very valuable. These include *Studies in Chinese Thought,* Arthur F. Wright, (ed.), (Chicago: Univ. of Chicago Press, 1953); *Chinese Thought and Institutions,* John K. Fairbank, (ed.) (Chicago: Univ. of Chicago Press, 1957); *Confucianism in Action,* David S. Nivison and Arthur F. Wright, (eds.) (Stanford, Calif.: Stanford Univ. Press, 1959); and *The Confucian Persuasion,* Arthur F. Wright, (ed.) (Stanford, Calif.: Stanford Univ. Press, 1960). Among the many articles in these volumes, I found a few to be particularly helpful: James T. C. Liu's "An Early Sung Reformer: Fan Chung-yen," and Charles O. Hucker's "The Tung-lin Movement of the Late Ming Period" in the volume edited by Fairbank, and a masterful analysis by David S. Nivison, "Ho-shên and His Accusers; Ideology and Political Behavior in the Eighteenth Century," in the volume edited by Nivison and Wright. Three valuable articles were published as a symposium on "New Views of Ch'ing History" in the *Journal of Asian Studies* (Vol. XXVI, Feb. 1967): "The Significance of the Ch'ing Period of Chinese History" by Ping-Ti Ho, pp. 189–195; "The Politics of Filiality" by Harold L. Kahn, pp. 197–203; and "The Seven Ages of K'ang-hsi" by Jonathan Spence, pp. 205–211. I was also impressed by Harold Kahn's "Some Mid-

Ch'ing Views of the Monarchy," *Journal of Asian Stuides* (Vol. XXIV, 1965), pp. 229–243.

Historical sources on the Ming are more difficult to find. A presumably reliable but very superficial outline of genealogy and chronology can be ferreted out of the biographies in Herbert A. Giles, *A Chinese Biographical Dictionary* (Shanghai: Kelly and Walsh, 1898). The organization of the Ming government is skillfully but very briefly described in Charles O. Hucker's *The Traditional Chinese State in Ming Times, 1368–1644* (Tucson, Arizona: Univ. of Arizona Press, 1961), and one notable part of this government is given much fuller treatment by the same author in *The Censorial System of Ming China* (Stanford, Calif.: Stanford Univ. Press, 1966).

Discussions which deal directly either with the abstract principles of succession or with the details of particular cases of imperial succession at any time in China's history are either incredibly rare or hidden away in thoroughly obscure places. One important exception is Harold L. Kahn's *Monarchy in the Emperor's Eyes: Image and Reality in the Ch'ien-lung Reign* (Cambridge, Mass.: Harvard Univ. Press, 1971), pp. 231 ff., which not only gives a detailed view of the Chinese monarchy, but includes much the fullest and most explicit account of Manchu succession practices that I know of. I obtained this excellent book only after I had drafted my chapter on the Manchus, but I was gratified to find that Kahn's more knowledgeable interpretation varies in no serious way from mine.

The changes in succession practices which take place in the course of a dynasty are, of course, one aspect of the much larger problem of the dynastic cycle. A number of interesting discussions of the dynastic cycle have been assembled by John Meskill (ed.), *The Pattern of Chinese History: Cycles, Development, or Stagnation?* (Boston: D. C. Heath, 1965).

CHAPTER 5: THE DECLINE OF HEREDITY

No anthropologist can remain undaunted in the face of the vast libraries of books that bear, in one way or another, upon the acquisition of high office in the Western world. The outpouring of historical and political writing from Europe and America means that my sketch of aspects of a few European and American experiments can be nothing but superficial. I have, of course, been tempted to take the easy course which would be to declare myself an anthropologist who is concerned only with the more remote and exotic areas of the world. In that way, I could omit the West entirely. European and North American practices have had so much impact upon the rest of the world, however, that to omit them would have left a serious gap in the story, but here, even more than in the other sections of the book, I am forced to rely upon secondary, tertiary, and quartanary sources. In this chapter, I intend nothing more than to suggest a few points that I feel are important to my story while I try not to get bogged down in the infinite detail that would keep the book from ever ending.

Much can be still learned about the sequence of political forms in the ancient world from the classical work of Fustel de Coulanges, *The Ancient City* (Garden City, N.Y.: Doubleday & Co., 1956), first published as *La Cité Antique* in 1864. More recent and more specialized studies include Gustave Glotz, *The Greek City and Its Institutions* (London: K. Paul, Trench, Trubner, 1929), which gives an outline of the development of Greek political institutions, and J. A. O. Larsen's rather specialized *Representative Government in Greek and Roman History* (Berkeley, Calif.: Univ. of California Press, 1955), which argues at length for the representative character of some ancient institutions, particularly those of Athens. A few hours with Aristotle's *Constitution of Athens* and with his *Politics* can disabuse one of any notion that these problems are new, or only recently perceived. On Rome, I have consulted Frank C. Bourne's general book *A History of the Romans* (Boston: Heath, 1966); Martin P. Nilsson's *Imperial Rome* (London: G. Bell, 1926); Frank Frost Abbot's *A History and Description of Roman Political Institutions* (Boston: Ginn & Co., 1901 and later editions); and George H. Stevenson's *Roman Provincial Administration* (Oxford: Blackwell, 1939).

For a background into the post-Roman period, nothing can replace Marc Bloch's masterful *Feudal Society* (Chicago: Univ. of Chicago Press, 1961). For specific data on the remarkable institution known as the Holy Roman Empire, I have relied upon James Bryce's old but still impressive book *The Holy Roman Empire* (New York: Macmillan, 1887, reprinted by Schocken Books, 1961). E. A. Thompson's *The Early Germans* (Oxford: Clarendon Press, 1965), describes the political organization of the Germanic areas north of the boundaries of the Roman Empire. Maude V. Clarke's *The Medieval City-State* (London: Methuen, 1926) served as an introduction to city life of the middle ages and on Florence, I relied largely upon the massive *History of Florence* by Ferdinand Schevill (New York: Harcourt, 1936). Certain aspects of Venetian political organization are covered in *The Decline of the Venetian Nobility as a Ruling Class* by James C. Davis (Baltimore, Md.: Johns Hopkins University Press, 1962). On Holland, I have relied very largely on a graceful general history by G. J. Renier, *The Dutch Nation* (London: George Allen and Unwin, 1944).

R. R. Palmer's *The Age of the Democratic Revolution* (Princeton, N.J.: Princeton Univ. Press, Vol. I, 1959; Vol. II, 1964) threw shafts of light for me in many directions. Palmer deals primarily with Europe and America in the final decades of the 18th century, but among other things, he describes the constituted bodies of the preceding era as part of the background to his subject, and he also describes the expansion of the franchise in the new American states and their experiments with constitution writing at the time of the revolution. Jack Richen Pole's *Political Representation in England and Origin of the American Republic* (London: Macmillan, 1966), was also helpful on developments on both sides of the Atlantic. More exclusively devoted to American affairs in the period surrounding the revolution are: J. P. Selsam, *The Pennsylvania Constitution of 1776: A Study in Revolutionary Democracy* (Philadelphia, Pa.: Univ. of Pennsylvania Press, 1936); Allan Nevins, *The American States During and After the Revolution, 1775–1789* (New York: Macmillan, 1924); W. N. Chambers, *Political Parties in A New Nation: The American Experience, 1776–1809* (New York: Oxford Univ. Press, 1963); and Richard Hofstadter's elegant book *The Idea of a Party System; The Rise of Legitimate Opposition in the United States, 1780–1840,* (Berkeley, Calif.: Univ. of California Press, 1969). I looked up a few constitutional points in Francis Newton Thorpe, *Federal and State Constitutions,* (Washington, D.C.: Government Printing Office, 7 vols., 1909). Two books dealing more specifically with the later development of the presidency are Clinton L. Rossiter's *The American Presidency* (New York: Harcourt, 1956), and Rexford G. Tugwell's *How They Become President: Thirty-Five Ways to the White House* (New York: Simon and Schuster, 1964). The latter deals specifically with the techniques by which men have sought and gained the presidency.

CHAPTER 6: LATIN AMERICA

It is unquestionably presumptuous for one who does not read Spanish to attempt any analysis of Latin American politics, but a vast literature exists even in English. The colonial period is given the most graceful of treatments in Charles Gibson's brief but masterful book, *Spain in America* (New York: Harper, 1966). A somewhat longer account, also limited largely to the colonial period, is given by John A. Crow's *The Epic of Latin America* (Garden City, N.Y.: Doubleday, 1946). For a fuller treatment of the post-colonial period, one can turn to Hubert Herring's bulky *A History of Latin America* (New York: Alfred A. Knopf, 2nd rev. ed., 1961), which is probably the best general history of the area in English.

Many books have appeared recently that offer analyses of the political, economic, and social systems of Latin America. Of these, I found Jacques Lambert's *Latin America: Social Structure and Political Institutions* (Berkeley and Los Angeles, Calif.: Univ. of California Press, 1967) to be particularly useful, though I have also consulted Joseph Maier and Richard W. Weatherhead (eds.), *Politics of Change in Latin America* (New York and London: Frederick A. Praeger, 1964); Seymour Martin Lipset and Aldo

Solari (eds.), *Elites in Latin America* (New York: Oxford Univ. Press, 1967); James Petras and Maurice Zeitlin (eds.), *Latin America: Reform or Revolution?* (Greenwich, Conn.: Fawcett, 1968); Kalman H. Silvert, *The Conflict Society: Reaction and Revolution in Latin America* (New York: American Universities Field Staff, 1961) which among other things offers an interesting typology of revolutions. Tad Szulc, *The Winds of Revolution* (New York: Praeger, rev. ed., 1965), gives a somewhat more temporally oriented account of political developments in the later 1950s and early 1960s, and Edwin Lieuwen's *Generals vs. Presidents: Neomilitarism in Latin America* (New York: Praeger, 1964), reviews the military coups of 1962–64 and poses the dilemmas which face both North and South Americans in responding to these coups.

A useful if depressing collection of histories of earlier dictators and their governments is found in Alva C. Wilgus (ed.), *South American Dictators* (New York: Russel and Russel, 1937). Two articles by Richard M. Morse, "Latin American Cities: Aspects of Function and Structure," *Comparative Studies in Society and History* (Vol. IV 1962), and "Some Characteristics of Latin American Urban History," *American Historical Review* LXVII, 1962) have clarified the role of urban development for me, and an astute analysis of the role of the caudillo is found in Eric R. Wolf and Edward C. Hansen, "Caudillo Politics: A Structural Analysis," *Comparative Studies in Society and History* (Vol. IX, 1967), pp. 168–179.

A number of general and analytical works that do not restrict themselves to Latin American examples have been written on the patterns of military government and on the mechanism of the coup d'etat. I would call particular attention to Edward Littwak's *Coup d'etat: A Practical Handbook* (New York: Alfred A. Knopf, 1969), which gives a wonderfully detailed set of instructions on how to organize a coup and put it into effect, and S. E. Finer's *The Man on Horseback* (London: Pall Mall Press, 1962), which provides a careful analysis of the strengths and weaknesses of military governments and of the way in which military influence is brought to bear in various types of political systems.

A useful though very brief introduction to the history of Argentina is provided by Arthur P. Whitaker's *Argentina* (Englewood Cliffs, N.J.: Prentice-Hall, 1964). The same author's *Argentine Upheaval; Perón's Fall and the New Regime* (New York, Praeger, 19456), gives an excellent account of the circumstances surrounding the end of Perón's rule. For more detailed history of the earlier periods of the nation, I relied upon Ysabel F. Rennie, *The Argentine Republic* (New York: Macmillan, 1945), and F. A. Kirkpatrick, *A History of the Argentine Republic* (Cambridge: The University Press, 1931) which is somewhat more thorough than Rennie's book for the earliest periods of independence. Robert A. Potash, *The Army and Politics in Argentina* (Stanford, Calif.: Stanford Univ. Press, 1969) is an intensive study of the political role of the army and of army factions from the period that led up to the 1930 coup until the rise of Perón. For Ecuador, I have consulted George I. Blanksten's *Ecuador: Constitution and Caudillos,* (Berkeley, Calif.: Univ. of California Press, 1951), and Albert B. Franklin's rather more interpretative *Ecuador: Portrait of a People* (New York: Doubleday, 1943).

For Mexico, I have relied heavily upon Frank Brandenburg's *The Making of Modern Mexico* (Englewood Cliffs, N. J.: Prentice-Hall, 1964), which strikes me as an unusually penetrating description and interpretation. Brandenburg gives a careful summary of political developments since the revolution and a knowledgeable analysis of the modern political system. I have also consulted the rather more superficial work of L. Vincent Padgett, *The Mexican Political System* (Boston: Houghton-Mifflin, 1966), and William Weber Johnson's exciting account of the revolution, *Heroic Mexico* (Garden City, N. Y.: Doubleday, 1968).

CHAPTER 7: EASTERN EUROPE AND THE SOVIET UNION

A vast store of historical, political, factual, and interpretive works are available on the history and structure of Communist politics, and this seems to be the only part of the world where political scientists have given recent attention to the specific question of succession. Perhaps the best general introduction to the overall history of the world Communist movement is Hugh Seton–Watson's *From Lenin to Khrushchev* (New York: Praeger, 1960), which traces the movement from before the First World War through the 1950s both within and outside of the Soviet Union. Several good accounts of the organization of the Soviet government are available, and I found L. G. Churchward's *Contemporary Soviet Government* (London: Routledge and K. Paul, 1968) particularly helpful. *Political Power: USA/USSR* (New York: Viking Press, 1963), by Zbigniew K. Brzezinski and Samuel P. Huntington is a penetrating and often fascinating comparison of the structure of power of the two countries, and it is excellent for helping an American to gain some understanding of the Soviet system. Brzezinski's *Ideology and Power in Soviet Politics* (New York: Praeger, 1962) consists of several interesting essays exploring the nature and implications of Soviet ideology.

Several excellent studies have addressed themselves specifically to the problem of the transfer of power. The work coming closest to the topic of this chapter is by Myron Rush, *Political Succession in the USSR* (New York: Columbia Univ. Press, 1965), which, however, except for a few last minute revisions, was written before the fall of Khrushchev. Rush gives a good account of the successions following the deaths of Lenin and Stalin, and he suggests that the USSR is fated to oscillate between oligarchical and one-man rule, and he describes the differences between the two alternating types of government.

The more recent period of Soviet history, including the decline of Khrushchev and the first period of the post-Khrushchev government is described in astounding detail and with awe-inspiring authority by Michel Tatu in *Power in the Kremlin* (New York: Viking Press, 1969; French edition, *Le Pouvoir en USSR,* Paris: Bernard Grasset, 1967). Tatu's book, therefore, conveniently supplements that of Rush. Robert Conquest's *Power and Policy in the U.S.S.R.* (London: Macmillan, 1962) was written a few years earlier even than Rush's book, and while I found it a bit discursive, it provides a useful additional account. *The Fall of Khrushchev* by William Hyland and Richard Wallace Shryrock (New York: Funk & Wagnalls, 1968), largely duplicates the considerably more detailed work of Tatu, though it is comforting to find that it reaches very similar conclusions. I drafted this chapter before the appearance of the Khrushchev memoirs, *Khrushchev Remembers* (Boston, Toronto: Little, Brown & Company, 1970), but, unfortunately, except for a few anecdotes about the fall of Beria that are difficult to confirm, this fascinating document adds little to our knowledge about the struggle for power within the Kremlin.

Communist Eastern Europe has also been the subject of extensive scholarly scrutiny. I found Zbigniew K. Brzezinski's *The Soviet Bloc, Unity and Conflict* (Cambridge, Mass.: Harvard Univ. Press, rev. ed., 1967) to be an extraordinarily penetrating account of relationships among the East European nations during the Communist period. Brzezinski subtly relates the internal politics of the various states to their international relationships. Hugh Seton–Watson's *The East European Revolution* (New York: Praeger, 3rd ed., 1956), gives excellent historical background, but it was completed before the Hungarian and Polish revolutions of 1956 that shook up the Communist bloc. Several more introductory works on the politics of Eastern Europe are available. Among them are H. Gordon Skilling's *The Governments of Communist East Europe* (New York: Crowell, 1966) and *The Politics of the European Communist States,* by Ghita Ionescu (London: Weidenfeld & Nicolson, 1967).

Polish history leading up to and briefly following the Polish October of 1956 is described by Richard Hiscocks in *Poland: Bridge for the Abyss?* (London: Oxford Univ. Press, 1963). Hiscocks is something of an apologist for Gomulka and, as his title implies, he was a bit more optimistic than proved to be justified by subsequent events. Paul E. Zinner's *Revolution in Hungary* (New York: Columbia Univ. Press, 1962) is a sympathetic account based in considerable degree on interview materials from refugees.

Zinner conveys a sense of the motivations and the excitement of the people involved in the Hungarian revolution. For my summary of events in Czechoslovakia, I relied largely upon the continuing reports published in the magazine *East Europe*.

Events as recent, as shrouded in secrecy, and as open to varying interpretation as those described in this chapter, demand cautious critical judgment, and it is difficult for a nonexpert to have confidence that he has not become hopelessly captured by the biases of his sources. It is some comfort, therefore, to note that the authors I have relied upon have satisfyingly diverse backgrounds. Rush is a Rand Corporation researcher. Brzezinski, Huntington, and Zinner are American academics. Seton–Watson is British; Churchward, Australian, and Hiscocks, Canadian. Tatu was for many years the Moscow correspondent for the Paris newspaper *Le Monde*. The observations and conclusions of these assorted authors strike me as supporting each other in all essentials. It must be admitted, however, that from the Communist viewpoint, all are equally subject to the misinterpretations and biases of the capitalist West.

Index

Figure and Table are designated by F and T respectively throughout.